THE
EARLY RECORDS
of
LANCASTER
MASSACHUSETTS
1643–1725

Edited by

Henry S. Nourse, A.M.

The Comisioners apoynted by the genrall Court to order and setle the afaires of Lancaster being asembled at John Prescots' house September ye eight 1657... doe Judge meet to order and Conclud as followeth.......Alsoe that the Select men tak spesiall care for the preseruing and safe keeping the townes Records. And If they se it need full, that they procure the same to be writen out fairly into a new booke, to be keept for the good of posterity. —*Lancaster Records.*

HERITAGE BOOKS
2012

HERITAGE BOOKS
AN IMPRINT OF HERITAGE BOOKS, INC.

Books, CDs, and more—Worldwide

For our listing of thousands of titles see our website
at
www.HeritageBooks.com

A Facsimile Reprint
Published 2012 by
HERITAGE BOOKS, INC.
Publishing Division
100 Railroad Ave. #104
Westminster, Maryland 21157

Clinton:
Printed by W. J. Coulter, Courant Office
1884

Maps drawn by Harold Parker.

— Publisher's Notice —
In reprints such as this, it is often not possible to remove blemishes from the original. We feel the contents of this book warrant its reissue despite these blemishes and hope you will agree and read it with pleasure.

International Standard Book Numbers
Paperbound: 978-1-55613-757-0
Clothbound: 978-0-7884-9227-3

NOTE BY THE COMMITTEE OF PUBLICATION.

AT the adjourned March meeting of the town of Lancaster, 1883, it was voted "to appropriate five hundred dollars for publishing some of our earliest town records under the direction of the Library Committee; to be prepared by Henry S. Nourse."

The committee thus authorized to oversee the publication now presented to the town, must not omit to testify here to their conviction of the eminent ability and fidelity with which their associate has completed his task, and of the greatness of the debt under which the town has been brought to him by this, as well as by other labors in the same field. They have found that their duty, as aside from his, has devolved upon them little more than a careful reading of his manuscript; while the toil, the care, and the zeal which the matter in hand demanded, and that have been spent upon it, have been expended by him:

"And all for love, and nothing for reward."

It may not be useless for them to remind the town of some of the reasons that gave rise to the resolution under which they were appointed. Among these were the risk of destruction by fire; the wasting material of the originals; the desirableness of supplying imperfections, as far as possible, from other sources; clearing up obscurities by intelligent annotation; and such a multiplication of copies as it may reasonably be hoped and expected will be called for.

They have understood, however, that the work was to be undertaken primarily, not in the interest of the historiographer, but for the use of the town; for its more familiar acquaintance with, and its surer preservation of, its own annals. It is from this consideration that the editor has added some notes which he would otherwise have withheld. Nevertheless they are well aware that these "Early Records" are not confined for edification to their own townsmen; and that any intelligent person of New England birth may not only behold, as with "ancestral eyes," therein "the doings" that are described, but, more or less, the causes also which, from without or within, gave the current of events this or that direction; and see, as in a mirror, the operation of the forces that in this country "developed local self government, and furnish the basis of our political history."

It gives the committee pleasure, as well for the name as the convenience of so doing, to consign the printing of this book to a local press.

LANCASTER, March, 1884.

LIBRARY COMMITTEE.

GEORGE M. BARTOL.   WILLIAM H. MCNEIL.
CHARLES T. FLETCHER.   NATHANIEL THAYER.
ANNA H. WHITNEY.   HERBERT PARKER.
            HENRY S. NOURSE.

INTRODUCTION.

FROM the year 1726 the records of Lancaster become continuous, are complete, and in good condition. All before that date is fragmentary. The earliest existing volume opens with A. D. 1653, in which year the Nashaway Plantation was formally given the classic name it now bears. The earlier pages of that book, however, are a copy, made about 1657, of the first records. Of "the old book," often referred to therein, no leaf remains, and many pages of the transcript have disappeared, while others are badly worn and almost illegible. During the first seventy-five years of the town's life, the inhabitants nearly all held proprietary rights in the common lands; and we find the clerks recording indiscriminately, often upon the same pages, action of the freemen as electors, of the proprietors dividing their landed estate, and of the people directing local improvement and church administration. After the settlement of Rev. John Prentice in 1708, special church records begin, and a register of births, marriages and deaths dates from about 1718, in which a few earlier dates have been casually inserted. This register is exceedingly imperfect. The earliest recorded meeting of the proprietors, as distinct from the town-meeting proper, was Feb. 4, 1716, statute provision having been made for such meetings March 25, 1713. The doings of regular town-meetings continued, however, to be recorded with proprietary action until 1726, when a new book was opened for the former. The proprietors used the old volume until 1810, about which time the proprietors' clerk made a careless copy of the whole, by which we know that the records were then in the same imperfect condition as at present. The common land was all divided before 1836, and their last recorded meeting was held April 6, 1846.

The Book of Lands, dated probably from the days of the commission in 1657. The original volume has been long missing, but a transcript of it was made in 1763, by Caleb Wilder, then proprietors' clerk. This is the only town book that contains records made between the massacre of 1676 and 1716. Three large volumes continue the registry of lands therein begun. The Book of Roads dates from 1729, and the Book of Estrays was begun in 1755.

Not only are the earliest notes of the town's action, as set down by the clerks, always curt, and many of them not to be found, but during a long and eventful period of our colonial history, all town records entirely fail us. A woful gap of forty-six years yawns between the last entry of Ralph Houghton and the first of Joseph Wilder; from the sixth of February, 1671, to the fourth of February, 1717. How or by whom the records of the town-meetings were kept during this period we have no *direct* information, and the time and manner of their loss is unknown. Of the years since 1708 we glean a few meagre facts from Rev. John Prentice's records of baptisms and church membership; but for the nine years previous to 1653, and the forty-six succeeding 1670, we must seek the town's annals in documents scattered here and there through the Massachusetts Archives and the records of the Middlesex County Courts. With such of these documents as have, by diligent search, been discovered, throwing light upon the history of Lancaster, our imperfect records are herein supplemented. Many of these have never been before in print, and others are now for the first time copied verbatim. To preserve so far as is possible the savor of the olden time, the spelling, punctuation and capitalization of all original manuscripts have been faithfully retained. To those who will charge — and justly — that the editor has magnified his office by multiplying comments of his own, he would state that, in what he has intruded, he is honestly striving only to bring into light something heretofore obscured, or to adduce evidence respecting matters in doubt, or to combat those false impressions about men, localities, and events which his experience has found unwarrantably rampant among us.

Even though considered — as by too many it will be — merely a list of the Nashaway pioneers, and a schedule of their landed possessions, this transcript of our forefathers' records is of especial value; but it has a deeper import. It is Lancaster's modest contribution to the story of the growth of human freedom. The planters of Massachusetts brought with them dogmas of spiritual tyranny, and old world political formulas, which proved too inelastic when framed into social and civic institutions, for the government of a restless community facing the deprivation, toil, and dangers of the colonist. Struggles with savage men and savage nature compelled self dependence, and soil and climate favored liberty of thought and conscience. As novel external conditions modified daily life and individual character, political life progressed, and ever towards freedom. The process of this progression — so painful and slow that the actors were perhaps unconscious of advance — is nowhere more plainly depicted, and nowhere offers more of interest to the student of history, than in the records of our older towns. In the "orderly agitations" of the New England town-meeting was cradled the germ of our nation's constitutional life.

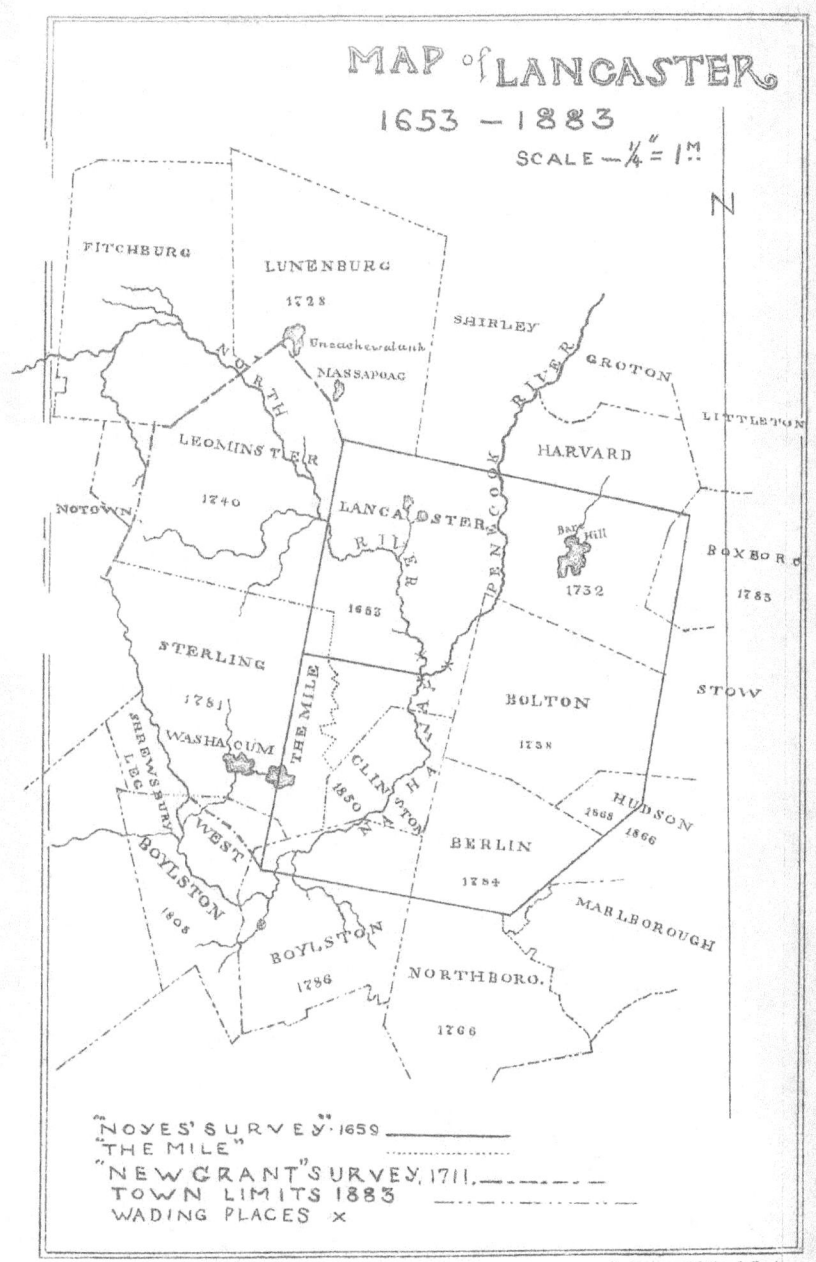

ANNALS

OF THE

NASHAWAY PLANTATION.

1643–1653.

NASHAWAY, or Nashawog, in the Indian tongue, means *the place between*, or *land in the angle made by two rivers*, and is descriptive of the locality. The pioneers soon attached the name exclusively to the south branch of the river, the other branch being known as the North River, and the main stream being called the Penecook.

THE SYMONDS AND KING TRUCKING HOUSE.

Like many another American town, Lancaster finds its origin in an Indian trading post. Although no contemporary mention appears of this, the first mercantile enterprise on Lancaster soil, it must have been founded before the autumn of 1643. Whether it preceded, or was subsequent to, the purchase of eighty square miles of land from Sholan, cannot be told. Both Symonds and King so soon disappear from the scene that they have been commonly treated in our history as mere real estate dealers, who sold their bargain at the first advantageous offer. Is there not in the scanty facts which follow, heretofore ignored, something that suggests rather trouble, sickness and disappointment, than the harvesting of profit?

Henry Symonds, the senior partner and capitalist of the

Nashaway trading house, planted on the southeast slope of George hill, was an energetic citizen of Boston, and a freeman. His name heads the list of the associates who in 1643 contracted to convert the useless marshes of the cove into a valuable tidal mill power. Before any of his well laid plans bore fruit, Symonds died. This was in September, 1643. His widow, Susannah, in 1644 married Isaac Walker, which perhaps explains the presence of Walker's name among the Nashaway proprietors for a few years thereafter. The junior partner, Thomas King, outlived Symonds little more than a year, dying December 3, 1644. He was a young man, probably under thirty years of age, with a wife Mary and two young children, Mary and Thomas, and lived in Watertown. His inventory, found in the Suffolk Registry, sums but 158^l. 3^s. including a dwelling-house, barn, and four acres of land in Watertown, and 74^l. 7^s. of debts due him. He was therefore a poor man at his decease, and nothing in the brief list of his assets gives evidence of commercial gain at Nashaway, save the item among the debts due, "18^l. of the Indyans." Reverend Timothy Harrington asserts that King sold all his interest here to the company. John Cowdall was soon after in possession of the trucking house lot, which he sold to John Prescott, October 5, 1647. King's widow, if we may trust the record, on March 9, 1645, married James Cutler, whose name the same year appeared among the Nashaway proprietors.

1643. Others of the same town [Watertown] began also a plantation at Nashaway some fifteen miles N. W. from Sudbury. . . .
[John Winthrop's History of New England, II, 152.]

7th of 1st month 1643/4 . . . . At this Court Cutshamequin and Squaw Sachem, Mascononoco, Nashacowam and Wassamagoin two sachems near the great hill to the west called Warehasset, came into the court and according to their former tender to the Governour desired to be received under our protection and government upon the same terms that Pumham and Saconosoc were : So we causing them to understand the articles, and all the ten Commandments of God, and they freely assenting to all,

they were solemnly received and then presented the court 26 fathom more of wampom, and the Court gave each of them a coat of two yards of cloth, and their dinner, and to them and their men every of them a cup of sack at their departure. So they took leave and went away very joyful.
[John Winthrop's History of New England, II, 189.]

1644 Wassamequin, Nashoonon, Kutchamaquin, Massaconomet and Squaw Sachem did voluntarily submit themselves to us: as appears by their covenant subscribed with their own hands. . . . . . .
[Daniel Gookin's History of the Christian Indians.]

Nashacowam and Nashoonon are aliases of the Nashaway sachem usually called Sholan or Showanon. Wasamegin was sachem at Quaboag [Brookfield]. Warehasset is John Winthrop's orthography of Wachusett, which in the Indian tongue was Wad-chu-sett, "the great hill."

May 1644. Many of Watertown and other towns joined in the plantation at Nashaway, and having called a young man, an university scholar, one Mr Norcross to be their Minister, seven of them who were no members of any churches were desirous to gather into a church estate: but the magistrates and elders advised them first to go and build them habitations &c (for there was yet no house there) and then to take some that were members of other churches, with the consent of such churches, as formerly had been done and so proceed orderly. But the persons interested in the plantation being most of them poor men, and some of them corrupt in judgment. and others profane, it went on very slowly, so that in two years they had not three houses built there and he whom they had called to be their minister left them for their delays.
[John Winthrop's History of New England, II, 161.]

29th May 1644 The petition of Mr. Natha: Norcrosse, Rob'rt Childe, Stephen Day, John Fisher &c. for a plantation at Nashawake, is granted: pvided that there shall not be more land allotted to the towne or pticular men (notw'thstanding their purchase of land of the Indians) then the Gen'rall Co'rt shall alowe.
[Massachusetts Records.]

Robert Child's prominence in the company was perhaps Nashaway's first misfortune. He was of Watertown, coming thither from Northfleet, Kent County, England. He had received the degree of A. M., in 1635, at Corpus Christi College, Cambridge, and the degree of M. D. at Padua. Gifted with great mental force, he held ideas of man and nature in advance of the age, and was ambitious to become a leader among the people. We shall probably not be far wrong in ascribing the inspiration of this westward movement from Watertown, not alone to the proverbial Saxon greed of land, but partly to Doctor Child's sanguine expectation of mineral wealth to be discovered in the western hills, and the acceptance of his liberal theories by congenial spirits. It is noteworthy that of the chief men in the enterprise more than half, namely: Prescott, Day, Garret, Hill and Jenkes, were workers in iron. Little aid or sympathy could be hoped for by the company from magistrates or ecclesiastics, while it remained under the influence of one who was esteemed by them a factious schismatic. A few months later Doctor Child's petition for the enlargement of political and religious privilege, just and moderate as it now seems, so roused the ire of the Massachusetts theocracy that he was compelled to seek safety from his intolerant persecutors by flight across the seas.

Nathaniel Norcross received the degree of A. B. at Catherine Hall College, Cambridge, 1636–7. He very soon abandoned the company of which he was only the available clerical figurehead. The cause assigned for his defection by John Winthrop, quoted on the preceding page, differs radically from that set down by Reverend Timothy Harrington one hundred years later. The former may record the excuse of the deserter; the latter, the tradition of a belief that had justified itself to the deserted. Mr. Norcross neither here, nor afterwards in England apparently, gave sign that he had in him the stuff of which apostles or martyrs are made, and even vexatious delays were not an unalloyed misfortune that put Joseph Rowlandson in his place.

1645. The humble petitō of the Company Intended to plāt at Nashaway 12 June 1645.

To the right Worp[ll] Tho. Dudley Esq[r] Gou[r]nour and the rest of the Magistrates and deputyes now Assembled in the Generall Court at Boston. Yo[r] petitioners, whose names are Vnderwritten Humbly Sheweth vnto yo[r]

Worp^s y^t wheras wee haue formerly received favour from this Court in haueing Liberty granted vs to plant att a place called Nashaway some 16 myles beyond Sudbery. Wee the sayd petitioners doe find itt an vtter Impossibilitye to proceede forwards to plante at the place aboue sayd except wee haue a conuenient way made for the transportation of our Cattell and goods ouer Sudbery River and Marsh. Now although Sudbery men haue begun to sett vpp a Bridge ouer the Riuer yett the worke is now decisted, And the bridge left altogether vnusefull, and the marsh now way mended, soe that wee caunot passe to the plautation abouesd without exposing our persons to perill and our cattell and goods to losse and spoyle: as yor petitioners are able to make prooffe of by sad experience of what wee suffered there within these few dayes. Yo^r petitioners haue beene & are much damnifyed by the badnesse of the way at this place: for many of vs haue beene dependant on this worke aboue these two yeares past, much tyme and meanes haue beene spent in discouering the plantation and prouiding for our setlinge there. And now the Lord by his prouidence hath gone on thus farre with the worke that diuers of us have covenanted to sitt downe together And to Improue ourselues there this summer that wee may liue there the wynter next Insueing if God permitt. But vnlesse some speedy course bee taken yt wee haue a way made for the transplanting ourselues, cattell and goods we may perish there for want of Reliefe, not being able to prouide for our subsistance there this wynter. Vnlesse wee expose ourselues and goods to the perill and spoyle as abouesayd. Yo^r petitioners doe therefore humbly Beseech yor Worships that as you haue beene pleased to Countenance our beginnings, soe you would please to order that a conueniant way bee made at the place aforsd for transportinge our persones cattell & goods, that the worke of God there begun may further proceede and wee haue Incouragement to carry on the worke else our tyme, meanes and labour hitherto expended will be lost. But if yor worp^s please to further our proceedings herein yor petitioners shall euer pray &c.

NATHANIEL NORCROSSE
JOHN PRESCOT
STEPHEN DAYE
HARMAN GARRETT
THOMAS SCIDMORE
JOHN HILL
ISAACK WAKER
JOHN COWDALL
JOSEPH JENKES

The above petition is in Massachusetts Archives CXXI, 5. The names were signed by the same hand that wrote the rest of the document, probably that of the minister, Nathaniel Norcross. Endorsed upon it is this action of General Court:

> The magistratˢ think fitt that 20ˡᵇ should be allowed to the towne of Sudburye towarde the finishing of their bridge & waye at the ende of it to be payd them when they shall haue made the way passable for loaden horse —, & desire the concurrence of the deputyes herein.
>
> Jo. Winthrop D : Go :
>
> The house of Deptyes doe concurr with oʳ honnored magistˢ herein so it be doune wᵗʰin a twelue monthe.
>
> Edward Rawson

The mention of "sad experience" in the petition, is explained by the following "special providence" narrated by Winthrop in his "History of New England," II, 306:

> Prescott another favourer of the petitioners lost a horse & his lading in Sudbury River, and a week after his wife and children being upon another horse were hardly saved from drowning.

That the dangers and difficulties of this crossing were not overrated by these pioneers, is proven not only by the above stated facts, but because one hundred years later the bridge and causeway —" half a mile long "— were complained of as *dangerous*, and in floods *impassable*. Travellers were obliged to make long detours to avoid it, and in 1759 and 1761, lotteries were granted for its improvement, the proceeds of which, amounting to 1227ˡ, were expended upon it. It is not surprising that the twenty pounds allowed in 1645 proved an insufficient inducement to the Sudbury men for the completion of the bridge. The deputy governor and magistrates had no sympathy to expend upon the troubles of a company wherein Robert Child, or any of his favorers, had an interest. Therefore they permitted the Sudbury marsh to remain a lion in the path to the Nashaway Plantation, and this was one cause of the delays which not only, as John Winthrop records in the passage quoted, drove the first minister from the enterprise, but also disheartened every member of the copartnership, save their stalwart leader, John Prescott, whom neither Sudbury marsh nor deputy governor could daunt.

The 3^d of 8th month 45. To the honored Gou^{r}no^r wth the Rest of the Magistrates and Deputes now Asembled at Boston — the Humble petition of the undertakers for the plantation of Nashawaye:

Whereas wee perceive there is some of the men excepted Agaynst y^t weere presented to this honoured Court in our petition yesterday: we humbly desire to present these men whose names are underwritten for the worke mentioned in that petition, in they^r Roomes that are Excepted Against, humbly Intreating this honored Court that you will please to depute all or p^t of these men for the worke there mentioned: and the whole company shall ever pray.

     John Hill   Isaac Waker Samuel Bitfield
     Sernt John Davis James Cutler Mathew Barnes
     John Chandler Thomas Skidmore

The petition of the day before, above referred to, has not been found. As John Prescott's and Stephen Day's names are omitted in this list, they were probably "excepted agaynst." This petition is from Massachusetts Archives, CXII, 16, and is endorsed thus:

The magistrates are willing that Jo: Hill, Serient Jo: Davis Jo: Chandler Isaake Walker, Sam^{ll} Bitfield, and Mathew Barnes or any 3 of them shall haue power to sett out Lotts to all the Planters belonging to the sd Plantation — Prouided they sett not their houses too far asunder & the greater Lotts to be proportionable to mens estate & charges, and that no man shall haue his Lott confirmed to him before he hath taken the Oath of Fidelity before some magistrate — and desire the consent of the Deputies herein. Jo: WITHROP D: Go:

 Consented to by ye deputies EDW. RAWSON.

Capt. Pellam, Left Willard & Segnt. Wheeler are appointed Commissioners for this Courte to lay out ye planters of Nashaway such proportions of land as they shall judge fitting for their present occasions & not prejudiciall to them y^t hereafter may desire to sitt downe there. Ye Deputys desire ye magist^s consent hereto. EDWARD RAWSON

"Samll Bitfield" is crossed out — also the paragraph added by the deputies appointing three commissioners — also this clause, which had been inserted at first after the word provided: "They shall not lay out aboue six acres to any first Lott."

11th Nov. 1647. Whereas ye Corte hath form^{r}ly granted a plantation at Nashaway vnto Jno. Chanl^r, Isa.· Walk^r, Jno. Davies, Jno Hill, & Math:

Barnes & yt Jno. Hill is dead, Jno. Chanl^r. Isaac Walk^r & Jno. Davies have signified unto ye Corte yt since ye said graunt they have acted nothing as und^rtak^rs y^r nor lajd out any lands, & furth^r, have made request to ye Corte to take in ye said graunt, manifesting their utt^r unwillingness to be engaged y^rin, ye Co^rte doth not thinke fit to destroy ye said plantation, but rath^r to incurage it. onely in regard ye psons now upon it are so few & unmeete for such a worke care to be taken to pcure oth^rs, & in ye meane time to remaine in ye Co^rts pow^r to dispose of ye planting & ord^ring of it.

[Massachusetts Records.]

11th Nov. 1647. Towne Marks agreed by ye General Co^rte for horses &c . . . . ordered to be set upon one of ye nere q^rrs. ✕ Nashaway

[Massachusetts Records.]

1648. Showanon the great sachym of Nashaway doth embrace the Gospel & pray unto God, I have been foure times there this Summer, and there be more people by far then be amongst us, and sundry of them do gladly hear the word of God, but it is neer 40 miles off and I can but seldom goe to them: whereat they are troubled and desire I should come oftener, and stay longer when I come.

[John Eliot's letter in Edward Winslow's "The Glorious Progress of the Gospel amongst the Indians in New England."]

1648. This year a new way was found out to Connecticut by Nashua which avoided much of the hill way.

[John Winthrop's History of New England, II, 325.]

1649. I had, and still have a great desire to go to a great fishing place Namaske upon Merimak; and because the Indian way lyeth beyond the great River which we cannot passe with our horses, nor can we well go to it on this side the river unless we go by Nashaway which is about and bad way unbeaten, the Indians not using that way: I therefore hired a hardy man of Nashaway to beat out a way and to mark trees so that he may Pilot me thither in the spring, and he hired Indians with him and did it, and in the way passed through a great people called Sowahagen Indians, some of which had heard me at Pautucket and at Nashaway . . . . . . There is another aged Sachem at Quabogud three score miles Westward, and he doth greatly desire that I would come thither and teach them and live there, and I made a journey thither this summer, and I went by Nashaway; but it so fell out that there were some stirres betwixt the Nazagansit and Monahegan Indians, some murder committed &c, which made our church doubtful at first of my going, which when the Nashaway Sachem heard, he commanded twenty armed men (after their manner) to be ready, and himself with these twenty men; besides sundry of our neer Indians went along with me to guard me, but I took some English along with me also. So that hereby their good affection is manifested to me and to the work I have in hand.

[John Eliot's letter in "A further Discovery of the present state of the Indians."]

Namaske is now Amoskeag — The "hardy man of Nashaway" it is quite certain was John Prescott, who also was the discoverer of the new way to the Connecticut previously noted. *Quabogud*, i. e. Quoboag, now Brookfield.

June 19 1650. Whereas John Prescot & others, the inhabitants of Nashaway pfered a petition to this Courte desireinge power to recouer all common charges of all such as had land there, not residinge wth them, for answer whereunto this Court, understandinge that the place before mentioned is not fit to make a plantation, (so a ministry to be erected & mayntayned there,) which if the petitioners, before the end of the next session of this Court, shall not sufficiently make the sajd place appear to be capable to answer the ends above mentioned doth order that the pties inhabitinge there shalbe called there hence, & suffred to live without the meanes no longer p. curia.

[Massachusetts Records.]

1650 . . . That whereas at my first preaching at Nashaway sundry did imbrace the word, and called upon God, and Pauwauing was wholly silenced among them all: yet now partly being forty miles of, and principally by the slow progresse of this work, Sathan hath so emboldened the Pauwauees that this winter (as I learn to my grief) there hath been Pauwauing again with some of them.

[John Eliot in "A further Discovery of the present state of the Indians."]

1651. Declaration of Elizabeth the wife of John Hall of Nashaway against George Whaley of Cambridge. [*MS. torn*] Sheweth vnto this honored Court that about foure moneths since George [Whaley] Steuen Day & Samuell Rayner of Cambridge were at Nashaway and [*MS. torn*] the house of John Prescott there fell out a discourse betweene John Prescott & Steuen Day in wch discourse John Prescott did speake against John & his wife Steuen Day did vindicate the cause of Goodwife Hall in her absence against John Prescott till at length George Whaley bade Steuen Day that he should not goe about to justify the woman for Whaley [*MS. torn*] that when Sr Phillips came from Nashaway he came into the buttery at the College in Cambridge where the said George Whaley demanded of Sr. Phillips how all their friends at Nashaway did, to wch Sr Phillips answered they were all well. Mr Whaley further demanded how he liked the place, he answered uery well. It is a desirable place as any was in the country as he conceaved. Mr Whaley further asked how he liked the people, he answered he liked them uery well only there were some that held this opinion, that all things were common & said he came one morninge to goodwife halls house & as soon as he was come goodwife hall demanded of him whether all things were not common now as in the apostles tyme, & before that Sr. Phillips could give answer she did further say that this is my judgment, that all things are common, mens wiues alsoe, at wch speech Steuen Day was much troubled and grieued & had not one word more to say, & in the morning after, the said Day & Reynor [went] to goodwife halls house & being sad at the report he there expressed his greife in these words. I feare there is an [*word illegible*] amongst you, I wish he may be found out, to wch goodwyfe hall answered if any of them gave any thinge against me if they will tell mee of it I will give them satisfaction, Steuen Day said he was glad to heare it for out of thy owne mouthe they will judge thee. for thus Mr Whaley [says] that Sr. Phillips hath reported of thee as is before expressed goodwife hall denyed that euer she spake any such thinge, nor did she hold any such opinion. herevpon Steuen Day demanded of Samuel Rayner whether Mr Whaley did not speake as he had then related, to wch Samuel Rayner answered yt was soe & he would take his oath of it, This relation of Steuen Day in goodwife halls house & Samuell Rayners [relation] of it was in goodwife halls house Richard Smith present. Goodwife hall much greived at it that such a scandall should be raysed against her, knowinge herself free & cleare, desired to speake with Mr Whaley & on the next day after, in the morninge did take Richard Smith and Lawrence Waters with her wch sd Smith & Waters cominge to Mr Whaley desiringe to speake wth him he bade them take heed how they did speake anything for the woman, yet promised to speake wth her after breakfast at wch tyme Steuen Day, Richard Smith & Lawrence Waters & goodwife hall came to Mr Whaley; goodwife hall demanded of Mr Whaley what he had against her   Whaley answered that Sr Phillips in the buttery at the College had spoken as before expressed, only he did then leaue out _ mens wiues. this testified Richard Smith Lawrence Waters & Steuen Day

 To Steuen Day & Samuel Reyner of Cambridge. You are hereby required to appear at the next Court held at Cambridge the 7th day of ye eight moneth next to wittnes for the wife of John Hall of Nashaway in a case in difference betweene her & George Whaley of Cambridge — & hereof you are not to fayle at your prill.
  dated the 12th day of the 7th mo 1651. By the Court
            HUGH GRIFFYN C.

 The testimony of Goodman Prescot & his wife

After that Mr Phillips came from Goodwife Halls hee told mee and my wife that goodwife Hall did aske him what he thought by ye judgment of those that hold that all things are comon. Mr Phillips asked her how shee [meant] all things comon whether as it was in ye Apostles tjme, her answer was all things without any exception, and Mr Phillips said it was a

damnable opinion; yea indeed (shee said) I have knowne sad effects come of it, and in further discourse hee said shee said shee kept one in her house which was of that opinion.   JOHN PRESCOTT
Attested uppon oath by John Prescot in Court   The mark ✕ of
        TH. DANFORTH Record^r MARY PRESCOT

    The Testimony of Richard Smith & Lawrence Waters concerning the speeches of George Whaley against hall.

    Cominge to Mr Whaley in the next morninge after the relation of Steuen day at goodwife halls the said Smith & Waters desired to speake with Mr Whaley, he bade them take heed how they did speake any thing for the woman, yet promised to speake with her after breakefast at wch time, Steuen day beinge allsoe present goodwife hall demanded of Mr Whaley what he had against her, to wch Mr Whaley made this answer that Sr Phillips in the buttery at the College in Cambridge cominge into the buttery answered to him as followeth. Mr Whaley demanded first how did all freinds at Nashaway. S^r. Phillips answered they are well. Whaley further demanded how he liked the place, he answered very well, it was a desirable place as any was in the country, as he conceived. Mr Whaley further demanded how he liked the people, he answered he liked them well only there was some that held this opinion that all thinges were common, Mr Whaley demanded who they were, he answered John Hall's wife.

    The Testimony of Samuel Raner is that he heard Lieft. George Whaley say y^t Sr Phillips told him y^t Goodwife Hall asked whether all things were comon.   Attested uppon oath in Court.
                                        THO DANFORTH Rec.

    The Testimony of Stephen Day is that he heard Lieft George Whaley say y^t he received by report of Sr Phillips that Goodwife Hall had proposed a question of this import whether all things w^r common. Attested . . . . . .

The foregoing documents in the case of Elizabeth, wife of John Hall, vs. Lieut. George Whaley, for slander, are in the Court files of Middlesex County. Lawrence Waters had sold his first house-lot of about seventeen acres, and the house upon it, to John Hall. Elizabeth Hall was living there, while her husband at this time was in England. He soon sent for her to come to him, and the estate was sold to Richard Smith. The suit against Whaley never came to judgment.

5th 8th mo 1652. Hermon Garret vs John Hall for takeing away part of their night pasture fence which fencing cost 11£., 13ˢ., 4ᵈ. The Court refuseth to take cognizance of this case bec. the Damage cannot be made appeare to be aboue forty shillings and do graunt the Defft costs one pound eight shillings.

[Middlesex Court Records.]

A bill of Charges given in to the Court by the Auturny of Jno Hall of Nashaway defendant in the case of Harmon Garret & John Shawe. Aturney & Witnesses

John Tinker 2 days from Boston	4ˢ
Richard Smith & Lawrence Waters from Nashaway foure dayes 1£. 0 apeece at 2ˢ 6ᵈ p daye	1 4
Goodman Lenton 4 daies from Nashaway at 2ˢ 6ᵈ per day	0,,10ˢ
Totall is	£1 14ˢ

The Court allow for Costs 2ˢ pr diem which is one pound 8ˢ & 2 another witness 2ˢ to be taken off, in all one pound 2ˢ

[Middlesex Court Files.]

The above document affords the only evidence we have of John Shaw's connection with the Nashaway Company. Therein also is the earliest mention of *the night pasture*. This common field, often referred to in the records, is the subject of a strange error. Under the mistaken idea that it had some connection with a transient proprietor, Philip Knight — who built his house next to Prescott's on the southeast slope of George Hill — it has been called "the Knight pasture," and this in spite of the fact that it is never spelled with a *K* in any original record. All that area of land bounded by the rivers on the east and south, and northerly by the present highway from the Sprague bridge to the site of the Penecook wading place near the corner southeast of Charles L. Wilder's house — except Lawrence Waters' seventeen acres at the west end — was, in the infancy of the settlement, set apart and fenced as a common pasture, wherein the kine, horses, goats, sheep and swine of the settlers could be assembled and cared for at night. When several years later an appropriate allotment of land was sought for the Reverend Joseph Rowlandson, it was finally laid out to him "*in the night pasture, within that fence that was formerly sett up by the copartners.*" A night pasture was the public institution preceding nearly all others, in the planting of a New England town. That of Boston was established in 1634 by the following order: "Item : That there shalbe a little house built, and a sufficiently payled yard to lodge the Cattell in of nights att Pullen poynt necke." We find the name in Boston records even as late as 1699, attaching to a field at Rumney Marsh. The "night pasture" of Roxbury has frequent mention in the land records, while Concord, Groton, and other towns of early origin, afford in their annals abundant proof that the custom was universally observed, of driving the common herd afield daily during the season of forage, under the care of children and keepers. Strict rules were formally adopted by the towns for the guidance of proprietors and herdsmen. In Watertown the enclosure was called the " cow pen " or " wolf pen," and this latter name is suggestive of a reason other than convenience, for the ancient usage. In 1634, Nathaniel Ward, in "New England's Prospect," says "a few posts and rayles . . . . . keepes out the Wolves & keepes in the cattle." Wolves were to the pioneer of New England the most troublesome of all wild beasts, being too cunning to be trapped, too cowardly to come within reach of the gun, and fearfully destructive in their midnight forays upon the unhoused stock. It was soon found out, it would seem, that to the wolfish sagacity a fence was an impenetrable mystery.

1652. Reverend Timothy Harrington, in "A Century Sermon," states that the petition of the nine families of the Nashaway settlement for township rights was dated May 18, 1653. We now know that it was the year previous, and although that petition can be nowhere discovered, the action of the General Court upon it in 1652 is duly recorded, with subsequent amendments.

The Courtes answer to a petition psented from the inhabitants of Nashaway, año 52 concerning the settleing of the plant. in seuerall pticulers.

1 First, it is detirmined that the orderinge & disposinge of the plantation of Nashaway is wholey in this Courts power, as appeares by an order of the Generall Court in año 1647.

2^{ly} Consideringe that there is already at Nashaway about 9 familyes, & that seuerall, both freemen & others intend to goe & settle there, some whereof are named in theire petition, this Court doth hereby giue & graunt them libertyes of a townshipp, &, at the request of the inhabitants, doe order it to be called PRESCOTT.

3^{ly} That theire lymitts shalbe set out accordinge to a deede of the Indian sagamore, vizt Nashaway Riuer, at the passing ouer to be center, & fiue miles north, fiue miles south, fiue miles east & three miles west: & y^t this Court appoynt some commissiono^{r}s to se these lynes extended & theire bounds lymitted.

4^{ly} That Edward Brecke, Nathaniel Hadlocke Wm Carley, Thomas Sawyer, John Prescott & Ralph Houghton, or any fower of them whereof the majo^r part to be freemen, to be for psent the prudentiall men of the sd towne, both to se all allottments lajd out to the planters in due pportion to theire estates & also to order the prudentiall affayres vntill it shall appeare to this Court that the place be so farre settled with able men as the Court may thinke it capable of giueing them full libtie of a townshipp accordinge to law.

5^{ly}. That all such psons who haue possessed & contynued inhabitants at Nashaway shall haue theire lotts formerly lajd out confirmed to them, pvided they take the oath of fidelity.

6^{ly}. That Sudbury should make cartwayes within theire bounds to pass to & from sd plantation.

7^{ly}. That the sd inhabitants be rated for publicke charge within the county of Midlesex & to that end the towne may choose a constable.

8^{ly}. That they take care that a godly ministery may be mayntayned amongst them, & y^t no euill psons, enemies to this Comonwealth in judgment or practise, be admitted as inhabitants amongst them, & none to haue lotts confirmed but such as take the oath of fidelity.

9^{ly}. It is hereby declared, that although the first vndertakers & copartners in the plantation of Nashaway are wholey evacuated of theire clayme in lotts there, by order of this Court, yet that such psons of them who haue expended either charge or labour for the benefitt of the place, & haue helped on the worke there from time to time, either in contributinge to ye ministery, or in the purchase from the Indians or in any other publicke worke that such psons are to be considered by the towne, either in

pportion of land or some other way of satisfaction, as may be just &
meete, pvided such psons doe make such theire expences clearly appeare
in six monehts.

Here the action of the Court naturally closed, and the
usual sequence of the concurrence of magistrates and executive
would be expected. But no! Some one, whether
magistrate or one higher in authority is beyond our finding,
seems to have bethought himself that not even a Governor
of the Colony had been so much honored as to have a town
named for him, and objected to thus dignifying the busy
blacksmith of Nashaway, who was not only no freeman,
but had once seemed to sympathize with Dr. Child's criticisms
of the colonial system of taxation without representation.
Amendment was carried as follows, ignoring the
inhabitants' request :

> This Court, takeing the condition of Nashaway into further consideration
> doe order, that it shalbe called henceforth WEST TOWNE, & doe
> further confirme there graunt of 8 miles square which was formerly
> graunted them, which will encourage many to plant there.

This meaningless substitute for a name was doubtless
not kindly received by those who had expected one euphonious,
significant, and of their own choosing. Another
petition met the next general court, of which we know
only the answer, dated May 18, 1653.

> In answer to another petition from the inhabitants of Nashaway for
> settling of theire graunt, this Court doth order the plantation at Nashaway
> to center, as in the Court order of *May* 52 (which is the foregoing
> order,) and to be layd out in pportion to eyght miles sqare, & that the
> seueral pticulers being in number nyne, be confirmed to them, save in the
> close of the 2^d article about the name of the towne, that the name of it
> be henceforth called LANCASTER, & in the sixth article that Sudbury &
> Lancaster lay out high wayes according to ye Court order, for the Countryes
> vse & them repayre as need shalbe, & that instead of six monehts expressed
> in the close of the 9th article, such psons to haue twelue monehts
> from the end of this session for such demaundes : and that the intrest of
> Harmon Garrett & such others as were first vndertakers or haue ben at
> great charges there, shalbe made good to him, them or his or theire heirs

in all theire allottments as to other theire inhabitants in pportion to charges expended by him and such others aforesd, pvided they make improuements of such allottments, by buildinge & plantinge, within three yeares after they are or shalbe layd out to them, otherwise theire intrests hereby pvided for to be voyd, & all such lands so hereby reserued to be at the towns dispose.

1653. At a county court held at Cambridge the 5. 2 mo 1653. This Court doth order that the Inhabitants of Nashaway Plantation at or before the 20[th] of this p[r]nt month do send downe one able man to be sworne before some magistrate, for the constable of there plantaĉon.

[Middlesex Court Records.]

John Prescott

Steven Day Ralph Houghton

William Kerley

Thomas Rowlandson
Jonas Fairbank   Richard Smith
Lawrence Waters
John Prescott Junior Jonath Prescott

Joseph Rowlandson
Alice Whiting   Mary Gardner
John Moore   John Rugg
Sam: Carter   John Moore Ensigne
Jacob Farrer   John Wpohcom
Cyprian Stevens
Daniel gains   Roger Sumner
John Lewis   John Prentice
          William Kerley Junr
                   Henery Kerley
Thomas Wilder Josiah Whitney
Simon Willard
John Houghton Towne Clerk

EARLY RECORDS

OF

LANCASTER, MASSACHUSETTS.

THE so called act of incorporation of Lancaster, dated May 18, 1653, as copied by Master John Tinker, forms the first page of the town's records. The leaf is badly torn, and many words have crumbled away. It has slight verbal differences from the original in the records of the general court, and from an official copy by Secretary Edward Rawson, in Massachusetts Archives, cxii, 54–55.

COPPIE OF THE COURT'S GRANT.

At a Gen^{rll} Court of Election held at Boston the 18th of May 1653.

1. In answer to the Peticon of the Inhabitants of Nashaway the Court finds according to a former order of the Gen^{rll} Court in Anno 1647 no 6: 95: That the ordering and disposeing of the Plantation at Nashaway is wholly in the Courts power

2. Considering that there is allredy at Nashaway about nine ffamilies and that severall both freemen and others intend to goe and setle there some whereof are named in this Petition the Court doth Grant them the libertie of a Toneshipp and orders that hensforth it shall be called Lancaster

3. That the Bounds thereof shall be sett out according to a deede of the Indian Sagamore, viz. Nashaway Riuer at the passing ouer to be the Center, fiue miles North fiue miles south fiue miles east and three miles west by such Comissioners as the Courte shall appoint to see theis Lines extended and their bounds limitted

4. That Edward Breck, Nathaniell Hadlocke, William Kerley, Thomas Sayer, John Prescot and Ralph Houghton, or any foure of them, whereof the maior Parte to be freemen to be for present the prudentiall men of the said Towne both to see all allottments to be laid out to the Planters in

due proportion to theire estates and allso to order other Prudentiall afaires vntill it shall Appeare to this Court that the Place be so farr seated with able men as the Court may Judg meet, to give them full liberties of a Townshipp according to Lawe.

 5. That all such Persons whoe haue possessed and Continued Inhabitants of Nashaway shall haue their Lotts formerly Laid out confirmed to them provided they take the oath of fidellitie

 6. That Sudbery and Lancaster Lay out highwaies betwixt Towne and Towne according to order of Court for the Countries vse and then repaire them as neede shalbe

 7. The Court Orders That Lancaster shall be rated wthin the County of Midlesex and the Towne hath Liberty to choose a Constable.

 8. That the Inhabitants of Lancaster doe take care that a godly minester may be maintained amongst them and that no evill persons Enemies to the Lawes of this Comonwealth in Judgment or Practize be Admitted as Inhabitants amongst them and none to haue Lotts Confirmed but such as take the oathe of fidellitie

 9. That allthough the first Undertakers and partners in the Plantacon of Nashaway are wholy Evacuated of theire Claimes in Lotts there by order of this Courte yet that such persons of them whoe haue Expended either Charge or Labor for the Benefitt of the place and haue helpped on the Publike workes there from time to time either in Contributing to the minestrie or in the Purchase from the Indians or any other Publike worke, that such persons are to be Considered by the Towne either in proportion of Land or some other way of satisfaction as may be Just and meete. Provided such Persons do make such theire expences Cleerly Appeare within Twelue monethes after the end of this Sessions for such demandes and that the Interest of Harmon Garrett and such others as were first vndertakers or haue bin at Great Charges there shalbe made good to him them his or theire heires in all Allottments as to other the Inhabitants in proportion to the Charges expended by him and such others aforesaid. Provided they make Improuem^t of such Allotmt^s by building and Planting wthin three yeares after they are or shalbe Laid out to them, otherwise theire Interest hereby Provided for to bee voyde, And all such Lands soe hereby Reserved to be thencforth at the Townes Dispose: In further Answer to this Peticon the Court Judgeth it meete to Confirm the aboue mentioned Nine perticulers to the Inhabitants of Lancaster, and order that the bounds thereof be Laid out in proportion to eight miles square.

Following this, by the same hand, were nineteen numbered pages, of which only the last twelve are now extant. It will be noticed that in dates the name of the month is sometimes found. After Governor John Winthrop's time this new method began to be observed by some, but usually the heathen names of months and days were carefully avoided, and the ordinals used, March being the first month.

OF THE COVEN^T; CHURCH LAND; MEETING HOUSE, LOTTS 10^s: &C:

1653 18 : 8 m⁰. *The bond to binde all comers.* Memorandum, That wee whose Names are subscribed, vppon the Receiueing and acceptanc of our severall Lands, and Allottments wth all Appurtinances thereof, from those men who are Chosen by the Generall Court to Lay out and dispose of the Lands within the Towne of Lanchaster heertofore Called by the name of Nashaway doe hereby Covenant & binde ourselues our heires Execut^{rs} & Assignes to the observing and keepeing of these orders and Agreements hereafter mentioned and Expressed.

Church Lands. ffirst ffor the maintainanc of the minestree of Gods holy word wee doe Allowe Covenant and Agree that there be laid out Stated and established, and we doe hereby estate and establish as Church Land with all the priuilledges and Appurtinances therevnto belonging for ever, thirty acors of vppland and fortie acors of Entervale Land and twelue acors of meddowe with free Libertie of Commons for Pasture and fire wood, The said Lands to be improved by the Plantation or otherwise in such order as shalbe best Advised and Concluded by the Plantation without Rent paying for the same, vntill the Labours of the Planters or those that doe improue the same, be ffully sattisfied. And wee doe agree that the Plantation or Sellect men shall determine the time, how Longe every man shall hold and Improue the said Lands for the proffit thereof. And then to be Rented according to the yearly vallue thereof and paid in to such persons as the Plantation or Sellectmen shall Appoynt to and for the vse of and towards the maintainanc of the minester Pastor or Teacher for the time being, or whomesoever may bee stated to preach the word of God among vs : or it may be in the Choyce of the minester to Improue the said Lands himselfe.

Meeting house. And ffurther wee doe Covenant and Agree to build a Convenient meeting house for the Publique Assembling of the Church and People of God, to worshipp God according to his holy ordinances in the most eaquall and Convenient place that may be Advized and Concluded by the Plantation.

Ministers house. And to Build a house for the Minester vppon the said Church Land.

house lotts to pay 10ˢ *p ann to the minester.* And ffurther we doe Engage and Covenant every one for himselfe his heires Executors & Assignes to pay to and for the vse of the minestree abouesaid the sume of ten shillings a yeare as for and in Consideracon of oʳ home Lotts yearly for ever, our home Lotts to stand Engaged for the payment thereof, and what all this shall fall short of a Competent maintinance we Covenant to make vpp by an equall Rate vppon oʳ Goods, and other improved Lands (not home lots) in such way and order as the Country rate is Raised. And in case of vacansy of a minester the maintainanc Ariseing from the Church Land and home Lotts abouementioned, shalbe paid to such as shalbe Appoynted. for the use of a scoole to be as a stock: or as stock towards the maintainanc of the minester, as the Plantation or Sellect men shall think meetest.

To build Inhabit &c in a year or loose all and pay 5: ˡᵇ And for the better Promoteing and seting forward of the Plantation wee Covenant and Agree, That such person or persons of vs who haue not inhabited this Plantation heretofore and are yett to come to build Improue and Inhabitt That we will (by the will of God) come vpp to build to Plant land and Inhabit at or before one whole yeare be passed next after oʳ acceptance of oʳ Allottments, or elc to Loose all our Charges about it, and our Lotts to Return to the Plantation, and to pay fiue pounds for the vse of the Plantation.

What Inhabitants not to be Admited. And for the Better preserveing of the puritie of Religion and ourselues from infection of Error we Covenant not to distribute Allottments and to Receiue into the Plantation as Inhabitants any excominicat or otherwise prophane and scandalus (known so to bee) nor any notoriously erring against the Docktrin and Discipline of the Churches and the state and Governmᵗ of this Comonweale.

to end all difrenc by Arbitracon. And for the better preserveing of peace and love, and yet to keepe the Rules of Justice and Equitie amonge ourselues, we Covenant not to goe to Lawe one with an other in Actions of Debt or Damages one towards an other either in name or state but to end all such Controversies among ourselues by arbitration or otherwise except in cases Cappitall or Criminall that sinn may not goe vnpunished or that the mater be aboue our abillities to Judge of, and that it bee with the Consent of the Plantation or Sellect men thereof.

To pay 10ˢ *p Lott.* And for the Laying out measureing and bounding of our Allottments of this first Diuision and for and towards the Satisfieing of our Engagemᵗˢ to the Generall Court, to make payment for purchase of the Indians we Covenant to pay ten shillings every one of vs for our severall Allottmᵗˢ, to the Sellect men or whome they may Appoynt to Receive it.

Equall Lotts first Diuition, in 2nd Diuitions acord to Estates: And, whereas Lotts are Now Laid out for the most part Equally to Rich and poore, Partly to keepe the Towne from Scatering to farr. and partly out of Charitie and Respect to men of meaner estate, yet that Equallitie (which is the Rule of God) may be observed, we Covenant and Agree, That in a second Devision and so through all other Devitions of Land the mater shall be drawne as neere to equallitie according to mens estates as wee are able to doe, That he which hath now more then his estate Deserveth in home Lotts and entervale Lotts shall haue so much Less: and he that hath now Less then his estate Deserveth shall haue so much more. And that wee may the better keepe due proportion we Covenant and agree thus to account of mens estates (viz) ten pounds a head for every person and all other goods by due vallue, and to proportion to every ten pounds three acors of Land two of vpland and one of Entervale and we giue a years Libertie to Euery man to bringe in his estate.

Gifts free. Yet Nevertheless it is to be vnderstood That we doe not heereby preiudice or Barr the Plantation from Accomodateing any man by Gifft of Land (which proply are not Allottm^{ts}:) but wee doe reserve that in the free Power of the Plantation as occation may hereafter be offered: And in Case The Planters estate be Lowe that he can claime Nothing in other diuitions yet it is to be vnderstood that he shall enioy all the Land of the first Devision.

in 2nd Deuition. And further we Covenant That if any Planters do desire to haue his proportion in the second devition it shalbe Granted.

Rules for Proporcon of Meddows. And ffurther wee Covenant to lay out Meddow Lands according to the preasent estates of the Planters, with respect to be had to Remoteness or Neereness, of that which is remote to giue the more and of that wch is neere to giue the Less.

And Concerning the 30 acors of vppland and 40 acors of Entervale aboue Granted as Church Land It is agreed and concluded to Lye bounded by John Prescotts Ditch vppon the South and the North Riuer over an ends [*anenst*] Lawrenc Waters vppon the North and so Rangeing allong westward.

And for the Preventing of Inconveniences and the more peaceable Isuing of the business about building of a meeting house it is Considered and Concluded as the most equall place that the meeting house be builded as neere to the Church Land and to the Neck of Land as It can bee without any notable inconveniencie.

And it is allso agreed That in all partes and Quarters of the Towne where Sundry Lotts do Lie together they shalbe ffenced by a Common ffenc according to proportion of acors by every planter, And yett not to barr any man from perticuler and priuat Inclosure at his pleasure.

This is a true Coppie of the Lawes and orders ffirst Enacted and made by those Appoynted and Impowered by the Genrall Court as it is found in the old book.

THOSE NAMES Y^T HAUE SUBSCRIBED TO THESE ORDERS:

EDWARD BREK
ROB^{RT} BREK: } I subscribe to this for my selfe and for my sonn Robert saue that it is agreed that we are not bound to come vpp to inhabit wthin a years time in our owne persons: This is a true Coppie:

J^{NO} PRESCOTT.
WILLIAM KERLY
THOMAS SAYER
RALPH HAUGHTON } These subscribed together the first

J^{NO} WHITCOMB Seni^r:
J^{NO} WHITCOMB Juni^r: } Subscribed 20: day: 9 m^o: 1652

RICHARD LINTON.
J^{NO} JOHNSON.
JEREMIAH ROGERS } Subscribed: 4th: 9 m^o: 1654

J^{NO} MOORE: Subscribed: 11th: first m^o: 1653
WILLIAM LEWES:
J^{NO} LEWES. } Subscribed: 13th: 1 m^o: 1653

TH^O: JAMES: mark 21th: 3 m^o: 1653

EDMUND PARKER.
BENIAMINE TWITCHELL
ANTHONY NEWTON. } Subscribed: 1th: 8 m^o: 1652

STEEPHEN DAY
JAMES ADERTON } Subscribed: 15th: 1 m^o: 1653 both of y^m.

HENRY KERLY:
RICHARD SMITH.
WILLIAM KERLY Junr.
J^{NO}. SMITH. } Subscribed 15: 1 m^o: 1653

LAWRENC WATERS
J^{NO}. WHITE: Subscribed: 1th May 1653
J^{NO} FFARRER: Subscribed: 24: Septemb^r 1653
JACOB FFARRER: Same date
JOHN HAUGHTON
SAMUEL DEANE } Sub^d: same 24: 7 m^o: 1653

JAMES DRAPER.
STEEPHEN GATES: Senr: } Subscribed: Aprill 3: 1654

JAMES WHITING or WITTON: Subscri: Ap^{rll} 7th: 1654

J^{NO}. MOORE and
EDWARD KIBBIE } 13: 2 m^o: 1654 Subscribed

This name has always been erroneously printed "Rigbe." Kibbie was of Roxbury, a sawyer by trade, and did not long remain here. Lydia Kibbie, perhaps his daughter, became wife of George Bennett of Lancaster.

JNº MANSFIELD: 13: 2 mº: 1654
JNº TOWERS:
RICHARD DWELLY } Subscribed 18: 2 mº: 1654
HENRY WARD.
JNº PEIRCE.
WILLIAM BILLING } Subscribed 4th: 7 mº: 1654.
RICHARD SUTTON: ap^rll 1653
THOMAS JOSLIN. } Subscribed the 12th: 9 mo: 1654. and there is granted
NATHANIELL JOSLIN } to them both 50 acres of vpland & Swamp together for theire home lotts and allso forty acors of Entervale.
JOHN RUGG: Subscribed, 12th: 12 mº: 1654
JOSEPH ROWLANDSON: } Subscribed 12th: 12 mº: 1654: and it is agreed by the Town that he shall haue 20 accors of vpland & 40 acors of Entervale in the Night Pasture:
JNº RIGGBY: Subscribed 12th: 12th mº: 1654 and he is to haue 20 acors of vpland & ten acors of Entervale
JNº ROPER: Subscribed 22: 1th mº: 1656

All these before mentioned are subscribed & theire names Entered according to theire Severall Dates in the old Book & Coppied per JNº TINKER *Clerk*

JNº TINKER Subscribed yᵉ first of ffebb^r: 1657
MORDICA MACLODE his ✕ mark set 1 march $\frac{1657}{1658}$
Jonas ffairbanks: Subscribed the 7th: 2 mº: $\frac{1658}{59}$
  JONAS FFAIRBANKS
Roger Sumner subscribed the: 11th of Aprill: 1659
  ROGER SUMNER
Gamaliell Bemand Subscribed: the 31th: of may 1659
  GAMALIELL ⊔ BEMAND
   his marke
Thomas Wyelder: Subscribed the 1th of July 1659
  THOMAS WYELLDER
Daniell Gaines Subscribed the tenth day of march $\frac{1659}{1660}$
  DANIELL GAIENS

 1653. The arrival of Prescott's millstone in Lancaster must have been an event of matchless interest to every man, woman and child in the settlement. Until that began its tireless turning, the grain for their every loaf of bread had to be carried to Watertown mill, or ground laboriously in a hand quern, or parched and brayed in a mortar Indian fashion, or hulled and softened with lye and crushed, as is the practice to this day in some regions of North America. The Nashaway planters might well wish to honor their beneficent neighbor by naming the township for him. To his capacity and business energy they owed nearly all they had thus far attained, and no sooner had township organization been secured, than we see John Prescott turning his attention to this new enterprise, which found shape November 20th, in the following agreement:

> Know all men by these presents that I John Prescott blackesmith, hath Covenanted and bargained with Jno. ffounell of Charlestowne for the building of a Corne mill, within the said Towne of Lanchaster. This witnesseth that wee the Inhabitants of Lanchaster for his encouragement in so good a worke for the behoofe of our Towne, vpon condition that the said intended worke by him or his assignes be finished, do freely and fully giue grant, enfeoffe, & confirme vnto the said John Prescott, thirty acres of intervale Land lying on the north riuer, lying north west of Henry Kerly and ten acres of Land adjoyneing to the mill : and forty acres of Land on the South east of the mill brooke, lying between the mill brooke and Nashaway Riuer in such place as the said John Prescott shall choose with all the priuiledges and appurtenances thereto apperteyneing. To haue and to hold the said land and eurie parcell thereof to the said John Prescott his heyeres and assignes for euer, to his and their only propper vse and behoofe. Also wee do couenant & promise to lend the said John Prescott fiue pound, in current money one yeare for the buying of Irons for the mill. And also wee do couenant and grant to and with the said John Prescott his heyres and assignes that the said mill, with all the aboue named Land thereto apperteyneing shall be freed from all comon charges for seauen yeares next ensueing. after the first finishing and setting the said mill to worke. In witnes whereof wee haue herevnto put our hands this 20th day of the 9mo In the yeare of our Lord God one thousand six hundred fifty and three.
>
> Subscribed names
>
> | | | |
> |---|---|---|
> | WILL_M KERLY SEN^R. | LAWRENCE WATERS, | THOMAS JAMES, |
> | JNO PRESCOTT, | EDMUND PARKER, | JNO LEWIS, |
> | JNO WHITE, | RICHARD LINTON, | JAMES ATHERTON, |
> | RALPH HOUGHTON, | RICHARD SMITH, | JACOB FFARRER. |
> | | WILL^{M.} KERLY JUN^R. | |

Memorandum, that Jno Prescott finished his mill, & began to grind corne the 23th day of the 3mo, 1654.

At a meeting of the Comissioners for the genrall Court, the 9th of September 1657 at Jno. Prescott's house, the Towne consented that the immunityes of Jno. Prescott prouided for in the covenant should continue and remayne to him the said Jno Prescott his heyres and assignes vntill

the 23 of May in the yeare of our Lord sixteen hundred sixty & two, 1662.
SIMON WILLARD
EDW. JOHNSON
THOMAS DANFORTH

The above contract is not found in any records of the town, but was duly recorded in the Middlesex County Registry.

FIRST GRANT OF LOTTS:

1653 : 30th : 9m^o : Mem^{r}nd^m, That we Edward Brek Jno Prescott William Kerly Ralph Haughton and Thomas Sayer, being Chosen by the Gene^{rll} Court, To lay out Allottments and to order the prudentiall affaires of this Plantation at Nashaway now Named Lancaster do Lay out and Appoynt Lands and severall Lotts with all the priuilledges and Appurtinances thereof vnto these severall persons whose Names and Allottments are hereafter mentioned and discribed To haue and to hold to them their heires Executors and Assignes for ever

The Lotts of this Plantation are Laid out partly on the west side of the Riuers of Nashaway and the North Riuer, and partly on a parcell of Land Called the Neck Lying betweene the North Riuer and that which hath bin Named and Hereby is named Penecuck Riuer which Taketh his name and begineth at the meeting of Nashaway and the North Riuers

Penacook is said to be an Algonquin word, meaning "a crooked place," from *penaqui*, "crooked," and *auke*, "place," and the New Hampshire name is supposed to be thus derived. Here the word in early days was spelled Penecook or Penicook, and may have had a differerent origin. Again, *pen*, plural *penak*, means "ground nut" or "wild potato," a favorite food of the aborigines; while used as a prefix penak denoted "a fall in the land." Hence, other meanings are suggested as possible. The name was soon dropped.

The Lotts on the west side of Nashaway and the North Riuers are formed duble, a highway Runing through as a street, on either side whereof Lotts are Laid to butt vppon the said highway:

LOTTS OF JNO PRESCOT

The ffirst Lott as the Scenter from which other Lotts may take theire boundings and discriptions North and South, is the Lott of John Prescot who is one of the first Inhabitants, he hath his Lott on the west side of Nashaway and the North Riuers Containing 20 Acors in place where sometimes one Mr Symons and Thomas King built a trukeing house, Butting Easterly vppon the highway and westerly towards the Comons, His Entervale Lott containeth 50 accors, Butteth vppon the North and Nashaway Riuers Easterly and tendeth Westerly as it is now ffenced and one part Lying Northerly of the Highway and another part Southerly from the Lott of Thomas Sayer:

OF JNO JOHNSON

The Lott of Jno. Johnson Contayning 20 Acors is the second Lott Northerly from John Prescots   Butted and bounded as the former.

HENRY KERLEY

The Lott of Henry Kerley Containing 20 acors is the 5th Lott from John Prescotts Butted and bounded as the fformer.

W^M KERLY SEN^R

The Lott of William Kerly Containing 20 acors is the 6th Lott ffrom Jno. Prescot,

ditto Kerly The Lott of William Kerly which he purchased of Richard Smith is the 7th Lott, both buting & bounding as the former.

JNO SMITH

The Lott of John Smith is 8th Lott Containing 20 acors butted & bounded as the other

W^M KERLY JUN^R:

The Lott of William Kerly Junior Containing 20 acors is the 9th Lott buting & bounding as the former

JNO. PRESCOT

That Lott of John Prescott Containing 20 acors which Lyeth on the east side of the High way over against his former Lott Described butteth vppon the high way westerly and the Comons Easterly

JNO. MOORE

The Lott of Jno Moore, Containing 20 acors is the first Lott from the Lott of Jno Prescot, on the North butted & bounded as the other

THOMAS SAYER

The Lott of Thomas Sayer is the first Lott Containing 20 acors on the South side of this Lott of Jn° Prescot butting & bounding as the former. *his Entervale.* The Entervale Lott of Thomas Sayer Containing 20 acors Lyeth betweene two pcells of Jno Prescots Entervale Lott butting vppon Nashaway Riuer

ENTERVALE LOTTS ON THE WEST SIDE OF THE NORTH RIUER:

The first Lott begineth at a litle brooke which Cometh from the west & Runeth into the North Riuer:

WILLIAM KERLY SEN[R]

The 2[d] Lott is the Lott of William Kerly Senior Containing 20 acors butteth Esterly vppon the west side of the North Riuer.

his purchas. The Lot of William Kerly which he purchased of Richard Smith is the 3[d] Lott Joyning to his owne pp [pioper] Containing 20 acors Lyeth on the south side is Butted & bounded as the former.

WM. KERLY JUN[R]

The Lott of William Kerly Jun[r] Containing 20 acors is the 4th Lott butted and bounded as the fformer

JNO MOORE

The Lott of Jno Moore Containing 20 acors is the 5th Lott Butted & bounded as the other

The Lott of Henry Kerly Containing 20 acors is the Last Lott Lying to a brook w[ch] is on the south side and Runeth into the North Riuer:

Neck side. The Lotts vppon the Neck Lyeth betweene the North Riuer and Penecuck Riuer a highway Runing between them:

LOTTS OF EDWARD BREK

The Lott of Edward Brek is the first Lott Containing 20 acors which Lyeth butting vppon the highway vppon the west and Penecuck Riuer vppon the east and Runeth to the Riuer (which somtimes was intended for Mr Bowman) [Probably Francis of Watertown.] His Entervale Lott Lyeth on the East side of Penecuck Riuer Containing 20 acors bee it more or Less, it Runs East and west and boundeth westerly vppon Penecuck and vppon the South is bounded by a new ditch: & ffrom this Lott Northerly & Southerly are other Lotts Numbered & bounded and is the first Lott.

RI: LENTON

The Lott of Richard Lenton, Containing 20 accors is the 2[d] Lott and Lyeth on the North side of the Lott of Edward Brek butteth on the High way westerly & Penecuck Riuer on the East, Ralph Haughton vppon an exchange made, is planted vppon the East end thereof

RA: HAUGHTON

The pp [proper] Lott of Ralph Houghton is Next vnto Richard Lenton Containing 20 acors butted and Bounded as the other being the 3[d] Lott Northerly.

his purchas. The Lott of Ralph Haughton wch he purchased of John Prescot Adioyning to his owne pp on the North side Containing 20 acors is the 4th Lott. His Entervale Lotts Lye on the other side Penecuck Eastward Containing 70 acors being the 3^d and 4th Lotts from the Lott of Edward Brek Northerly

Rob'rt Breck

The Lott of Robert Breck Containing 20 acors Lyeth on the west side of the Neck begineth at the south side Neere to the house of Richard Lenton, vppon a Line Ruñe 9 of 1mo 1654 from the highway to the Riuer 95 rods in Length butting on the highway on the East & the North Riuer on the west and tendeth Northerly. His Entervale Lott Containing 20 acors Lyeth next to the Entervale Lott of his father Edward Brek and is the second Lott from his Northerly butted and bounded as is his fathers.

James Atherton

The Lott of James Atherton Lyeth next vnto the Lotts of Ralph Haughton on the North and is the fiffth Lott Containing 20 acors butted & bounded as the other. The Entervale Lott of James Atherton Containing 20 acors is the 5th Lott Northerly from the Lott of Ralph Haughton butting & bounding as the former

Jno White

The Lott of John White Containing 20 acors is next to the Lott of James Aderton on the North and is the sixt Lott butting & bounding as the other. His Entervale Lott containing 20 acors is next to the Entervale Lott of James Atherton on the North & is the sixth Lott.

William Lewes

The Lott of William Lewes Containing 20 acors is the seauenth Lott & is next to the Lott of John White on the North butting & bounding as the other. His Entervale Lott allso Lyeth next to John Whites & is the 7th Lott norward Containing 20 acors butting & bounding as the other.

Jn^c Lewes

The Lott of John Lewes Containing 20 acors is the eight Lott & Lyeth next to the Lott of his father William Lewes on the North, butting & bounding as the other. His entervale Lott is the eight Containing 20 acors is butted & bounded as the other.

Tho. James

The Lott of Thomas James Containing 20 acors is the Ninth Lott & Lyeth next to the Lott of John Lewes on the North butting & bounding as the other. His Entervale Lott is the Ninth lott, Northerly of John Lewes butted & bounded as the other.

The Lott of Edmund Parker Containing 20 acors is the tenth Lott and Lyeth Next to the Lott of Thomas James on the North butted & bounded as the other. His Entervale Lott Containing 20 acors is the tenth Lott Lying on the North side of the Lott of Thomas James butted & bounded as the other.

The Lott of Richard Smith Containing 20 acors Lyeth alone and is a tryangle, bounded by a fenc on one side towards the entervale and on an other bounded by the North Riuer and by a parcell of Comon on the 3^d side through which a highway is to pass :

Thus far the records, copied from the old book, are in the quaintly neat hand-writing of Master John Tinker, who at his coming hither was at once largely entrusted with the management of public affairs.

COPPIE OF PETITION FOR TOWNSHIP: & ANSWER:

To the hono^{ed} Go^{u}no^r the Dept Go^{u}no^r and the Rest of this hono^{ed} Court both magistrates & deputies.

The humble petition of the Inhabitants of Lancaster humbly sheweth that whereas it pleased this honoured Court to giue power to six men formerly to dispose of Lands, and to giue out Lotts vnto such men as did desire to sitt downe att Lancaster, they hauing Hitherto acted accordingly, and wee being now about twentie familyes, and one of the six men being dead, and an other liuing remote from vs, and sum others of them being desirous to Leaue of that power giuen to them by the Court; Conceiuing it to be agreeable to Law and profitable to the towne, in the further Carieing on and ordring of the planting and prudenciall affaires of the towne, and alsoe in the further disposing and raising maintainance for the minestrie amongst vs, wee with the Comisioners who haue sett their hands Hervnto with ourselues, doe humbly intreat this Honoured Court that the power which was formerly granted to those six men, may be granted to the towne, and inhabitanc in genrall that therein they may act togather as in other townes, and as wee Conceiue vnder fauor the Law doth allow. And alsoe that this Court would be plesed to apoynt sum man or men who in wisdome you think meet, to Lay out our towne bounds according to this Courts grant, which if it shall pleas this Honoured Court to grant vnto vs, we shall remaine further obliged and as wee ar in dutie bound Continue to pray for you.

William Kerley Sen	Edmund Parker
William Leweis	Thomas James
William Kerly Jun	John Whitcombe 2
Richard Smith	Lawrenc Waters
Henry Kerley	Richard Linton
John Leweis	

The desir of your peticioners is that they desired the full power and priuilledges of the plantacion and for the present they desire and shall be well satisfied if the Court doe grant seauen men out of tenn hervnder writen to order the prudenciall afaires for this year ensuing And that afterwards it shalbe Lawfull for the plantacion to make their Elecions, and to order their prudenciall businesses in full state of a plantacion according to Law.

Edward Brecke	John Whetcomb
John Prescott	John White
William Kerley	William Leweis
Ralph Houghton	Richard Smith
Thomas Sawyer	Edward Kibie

Of theis ar freemen

Edward Breck	William Leweis
William Kerley	John Whetcombe
Thomas Sawyer	

Answer to the petition:

The Comitie thinke meet that the inhabitance of Lancaster haue those Liberties of a towne shipp that the Lawes alow, vntill the genrall Court take further order theirin, And that Leiftenant goodenough and Thomas dainforth Lay out the bounds of the said towne according to the Courts grant at the townes Charg and mak returne theirof vnto the next Court of Election.

The deputies aproue of the returne of this Comitie And desire our Honoured magestrats Consent Hervnto.

10th : May, 1654. WILLIAM TORIE *Clarke.*

The Comitie :   HUMPHREY ATHERTON
                THOMAS CLARKE
Consented to by the magistrats   ELEAZER LUSHER
                JOSEPH HILL

The above, from town records, differs in slight particulars from the original in Massachusetts Records.

November 1, 1654. Whereas Shawanon, Saggamore of Nashaway, is lately dead, and another is now suddainly to be chosen in his roome, they being a great people, that haue submitted to this jurisdiccon, theire eyes being vppon two or three of the blood, one whereof is very deboist & a drunken fellow, and no freind of ye English another is very hopfull to learne the things of Christ, this court doth therefore order, that Mr Increase Nowell and Mr John Elliott shall and heereby are desired to repaire to the Indians, and labor by theire best counsell and perswasion to pvayle wth them for the choosing of such a one as may be most fitt to be theire sagamore, which would be a good service to ye countrje.

[Massachusetts Records.]

Their counsel prevailed, and Matthew, nephew of Sholan, was chosen; but "deboist" Sam bided his time. The tribal government was an elective monarchy, sons of a deceased sachem being ineligible if nephews and brothers were available.

MENS ESTATS TO DRAW MEDDOW & 2^D DEUISION

1654. These seurall Estats of the planters who by Couenant and according to the rules theirof haue engaged that theirby it may be knowne what shall be ther pporcion of Land which by Couenant eurie planter may make Claime vnto in a second third or other deuisions of Land and alsoe of medow within this towne of Lancaster.

	lb s d		lb s d
John Prescott	366 = 15 = 00	John ffarer	107 = 00 = 00
William Kerley Sen.	270 = 00 = 00	Richard Smith	313 = 13 = 10
Edward Brecke	202 = 11 = 00	John Leweis	018 = 10 = 00
Ralph Houghton	264 = 04 = 00	Thomas Josllin	210 = 00 = 00
Edmund Parker	098 = 00 = 00	Steeuen Gats Sen.	314 = 00 = 00
Thomas James	036 = 00 = 00	John Whetcomb	241 = 00 = 05
John Johnson	030 = 00 = 00	Jo: Whetcomb Jr.	029 = 00 = 00
John Smith	058 = 19 = 00	Nathaniell Josllin	155 = 00 = 00
James Atherton	069 = 05 = 00	Lawrenc Waters	277 = 00 = 00
Thomas Sawyer	110 = 00 = 00	Jacob ffarer	107 = 10 = 00
Robert Breck	010 = 00 = 00	John Whit	380 = 06 = 02
William Kerley Jun.	186 = 00 = 00	Henry Kerley	078 = 04 = 00
John Rugg	083 = 10 = 00	Richard Linton	090 = 00 = 00
John More	110 = 00 = 00	Phillip Knight	100 = 00 = 00
William Leweis	285 = 09 = 00	John Roper	100 = 00 = 00

The Estats of seurall entred sinc the 9 day 1655

Roger Sumner his Estat giuen in is	232 = 00 = 00
Jonas ffairbanke his Estat is	172 = 00 = 00
Jacob farer aded when his wif came	168 = 07 = 00

DEUISION OF MEDOWES ALLREDIE DEUIDED.

Medowes allowed to eurie hundred pound estat is fower accors to which proporcion it followeth

Numbr of lots.

	John Prescott hath of medowes in all	24 accors
27	William Kerley sen hath	10 accors & $\frac{4}{5}$ ptes
11	Edward Brecke	8 accors & $\frac{1}{10}$ pte
9	Ralph Houghton	10 accors & $\frac{1}{2}$ & $\frac{1}{16}$
2	Edmund Parker	4 accors
17	Thomas James	$1\frac{1}{2}$ accor
26	John Johnson	1 accor & $\frac{1}{5}$ pte
24	John Smith	2 accors & $\frac{2}{5}$ ptes
25	James Atherton	2 accors & $\frac{3}{4}$ ptes
5	Thomas Sawyer	4 accors & $\frac{3}{5}$ ptes
	Robert Brecke not sufred to haue a lot.	o
14	William Kerley Ju.	2 accors & $\frac{1}{2}$
18	John More	4 accors & $\frac{2}{5}$ ptes
15	John Rug	3 accors & $\frac{1}{3}$ pte
7	William Leweis	11 accors & $\frac{2}{5}$ ptes
16	Richard Smith should be 12 . $\frac{1}{2}$ · $\frac{1}{25}$ is but 9·$\frac{3}{4}$	(12$\frac{1}{2}$ accors & $\frac{1}{25}$
3	John Leweis	o$\frac{3}{4}$ ptes
28	Thomas Josllin	8 accors & $\frac{2}{5}$ ptes
13	Steeuen Gates sen.	12 accors $\frac{1}{2}$ & $\frac{1}{20}$ pte
21	John Whetcomb sen.	9 accors $\frac{1}{2}$ & $\frac{1}{8}$ pte
22	John Whetcomb Ju.	1 accor & $\frac{1}{5}$ pte
10	Nathaniell Josllin	6 accors & $\frac{1}{5}$ pte
4	Lawrenc Waters	11 accors & $\frac{1}{11}$ pte
29	Jacob ffarer	4 accors & $\frac{3}{10}$ ptes
20	John Whit	15 accors and $\frac{1}{4}$ pte
23	Henry Kerley	3 accors & $\frac{1}{8}$ pte
12	Richard Linton	3 accors & $\frac{1}{2}$ - $\frac{1}{10}$ ptes
19	John Tinker for 100 good^n Knight	4 accors
1	John Roper	4 accors
6	Master Rowlandson	6 accors
8	John Tinker hath 6 acc. $\frac{1}{2}$ was goodman Rowlandsons & and 2 to draw	8 accors for his owne estat
	Roger Sumner	9 accors $\frac{1}{4}$ pte
	Jonas fairbanke hath 6 accors, is to draw $\frac{7}{8}$ ptes, which makes	6 accors & $\frac{7}{8}$ ptes
	Jacob ffarer by his estat & by his wife	6 accors & $\frac{3}{4}$ ptes
	Jacob ffarer for John farers estat	4 accors & $\frac{1}{4}$ pte

SUM GRANTS OF LAND AND ORDERS BY THE FIRST SIX MEN APOYNTED.

The 9th of the first mon. 1654 It is ordred and agreed by the selectmen of the plantacion the Land which Lyeth betweene the lott of Edward

Brecke and that of Richard Smith shall Ly in Comon for the plantacion

Itt is ordred by the greater voat of the selectmen that noe second deuisions of Land shall be Laid out to any planter within the Compass of two miles of the house of Richard Linton

It is ordred and granted by the greater voat of the select men that a Certain pte of Entervaile Land which Lyeth betweene the lottes of Robert Brecke and Ralph Houghton shall be and remaine vnto the said Robert and Ralph, their heirs and asignes for euer and that vpon resonable and good Considracion

Upon resonable and good Considracion it is ordred and granted by the greater voat of the select men that Thomas Sawyer shall haue fiue accors of Land Lying on the south sid of the dich of John Prescott and on the north sid of the High way buting vpon the Entervaile East and the Comons on the west to him his heirs and asignes for euer to plant a hous vpon — vpon Condicion that he returne to the towne fiue accors of his home lott in Lew theirof at the east end of his lott.

At a towne meeting it was voted and agreed by the plantacion upon a legall warning asembled that the acts of the selectmen who were Chosen by the Court to dispose of lotts and to act the prudenciall afairs of this plantacion contained in this book by them or the greater voat of them acted, shall hencforth be accounted Legall and is herby established and confirmed

Att a towne meeting asembled vpon Legall warning it is agreed by the towne that their should not be taken into the towne aboue the number of thirtie fiue familyes and the subscribed names ar to be vnderstood that hencforth they ar to be accounted townsmen

Edward Brecke	John Johnson	William Kerley Jun
Master Joseph Rowlandson	John More	John Smith
John Prescott	William Leweis	Lawrence Waters
William Kerley sen.	John Leweis	John White
Ralph Houghton	Thomas James	John farer
Thomas Sawyer	Edmund Parker	Jacob ffarer
John Whetcomb Sen	James Atherton	John Rugg
John Whetcomb Ju^r	Henry Kerley	
Richard Linton	Richard Smith	

ORDERS ABOUT THE FIRST DEUISION OF MEDOW.

25 : 4th : mon 1655   The towne meet about a first deuision of medow and ordred and agreed as followeth.

Itt is this day ordred that a deuision of medow shall bee Laid out, with all Convenient Speed, of fower accors to a hundred pound estate : As it is entered into the towne booke, to be deuided by Lott, And it is agreed to begin at the south medow, and soe to the medow by Gibsons hill, and to quasaponikin medow, and all medowes knowne on the neck, and soe com to the vpmostt medow on Nashaway riuer, and the Still riuer, and soe follow them downwards to the plum trees, And soe Round to the ponds, and wataquadock and such medowes as are knowne, or shall be found, vntill tenn accors to a hundred pound bee made vpp: And it is ordred and agreed, and men chose to surueie eurie mans Lott of medow: And to Judge theirof, that eurie man may haue, as neare to equalitie as may in truth and faithfullnes be Judged of, by the men herafter mentioned, That is to say William Kerley Sen. Steeuen Gats, William Kerley Jur. and Ralph Houghton.

After fower accors to a hundred pound was Laid out and pfected, with the allowances, the Layers out called the towne together the 10th: of the 5th: mon 1655 who acted as followeth. It is this day ordred and agreed by a voat of the towne no man desenting, that the act of Laying out meddowes, In the first deuision, of fower accors to a hundred pound state, as it is alredie Laid out, the towne will maintain and defend, against all suits and encumbrances whateuer. And at the same time the same day, the towne drew Lotts. for a second deuision of medow of six accors to a hundred pound state. And the Layers out went afterward to Laying it out, but it would not hold out to giue to eurie one soe much, And theirfore the Layers out of medow called the towne togather againe, And the towne wholy disanuled what was done in that Later deuision of medow, because it would not reach to giue to eurie man, but many would haue beene without.

Quasaponikin and *Wataquadock* are named here for the first time. The contraction *Ponikin* appears first in 1718. This is uniformly the spelling used by the earlier clerks, who were familiar with the Indian speech, and by the best authorities since. *Ponakin* is a modern innovation, having no claim to be perpetuated. A similar name, *Quosopanagon*, was applied to a Groton meadow. Here the name attached to the broad area of intervale, the hill, and the brook, which retain it today. The published vocabularies of Indian words give no clue to its meaning, unless there is an echo of it in *Quascacanaquen*, which a writer in the New Hampshire Historical Society's Collections tells us means "entirely full of water."

The meaning, descriptive of the Bolton range of hills, hidden in the Indian word *Wataquadock*, has not been found, though long sought. Of local names about Lancaster none has experienced more varied spelling at the hands of clerks and historians. The later methods seem in no way improvements upon Ralph Houghton's first attempt to render into English syllables the word as he heard it from native lips, in 1653. In the town records we find *Wataquadoke* 1656 and 1659, *Wataquadocke* 1658, *Wadaquadock* 1718, all nearly the same in sound with the first above. Joseph Willard, Esquire, in 1826, preferred *Wataquodoc*. Reverend Peter Whitney gave us in 1792, *Wattoquottock!* It was not until the Indian tongue was forgotten in Lancaster, and the recorders were unusually illiterate, that such outré orthography as *Waterquaduc* and *Wattoquoddoc* crept in.

A leaf is here missing from the records. No contemporary notice is elsewhere found respecting this meeting of a board of arbitration, ten of whose "determinacions" are lost to our history. The provision in the covenant for the ending of disputes by arbitration was presumably the authority for assembling the board.

ARBITRATORS AWARD OR DETERMINACIONS.

11th *Complaint of Tho: Sawyer.* ffor Thomas Sawyers Complaint about his want of fiue accors of Entervaile Land, wee say it was Laid out by those apoynted by the towne according to order, And if he or any other may mesure their Land soe Laid out And accept vpon that ground, then all may as well haue Libertie to doe the same And then noe end will be Herin and theirfore we cannott alter it.

12th *Complaint about records for want of ye same.* ffor the Complaint of the want of recording Land in the towne booke, for help Herin, wee apoynt Ralph Houghton for that worke for the present vntill further order be taken.

13 *Complaint for want of Land Laid out.* Wheras diuers Complaints for the want of Land being Laid out according to their grant, wee Herby declare, that the towne is with car & what speed they may, to satisfie all those Complaints, in their Lawfull demands herein.

14 *Complaint of Jo: farer* ffor John ffarers Complaint for want of his accomodacions Laid out to him Considring his pson being soe Long hear, And also his expenc being as it was. wee cannot butt grant him his

hous Lott and Entervaile, and in Case he sell it or sett it to one the towne shall aproue of then he shall haue other deuisions acording to estat present eles[where].

15. *Conplaint about prudencialls afairs.* ffor the prudenciall afairs of the towne wee Conclud this. first the towne are to Consider what their occasions ar that shall be atended to their in. and writ it in their towne booke, And this being done then to Choose their select men to act their vpon according to the order of the Court.

16. *Complaint of John Rigbie.* for the Complaint of John Rigbie for the want of his Land Laid out, the answer is he shall haue his hous Lott when he shall axcept of the place and for his tenn accors of entervaile it is said to be Laid out, and for his medow that it shall be Laid out when he shall present his estate.

17. *Complaint of Jo: Johnson.* ffor the Complaint of Johnson for the want of Land acording to his estat wee Conclud he shall haue Land for fowertie pound estate.

18. *Complaint of Will Kerley.* ffor William Kerleys sen. Complaint which was about second deuision, wee refer him to the orders in the towne booke, with this proviso, that the deuisions therof shall bee by lott as in other deuisions.

19. *for Edward Breckes Lott.* ffor Edward Breckes Lott and his soons, wee determine that Edward Breck shall enjoy his Lott but for his son vnless he com and posess it within fower monthes, after intelligenc to him or his father of this determinacion or com and agree with the towne soe as they sufer not theirby, otherwis it shall be forfited to the towne.

20. *Allowanc of medo to diuers psons.* Concerning allowance of medow to diuers psons Complaining theirin, wee allow Lawrence Waters 4 fower accors, to Nathaniell Jossllin two accors, to Thomas Sawyer one accor and halfe, To James Atherton one accor, To John White fiue accors, all to com in the same order They drew at the first, And this to bee Laid out in the most Convenient medow yett vndisposed, And all the rest that haue receiued medow to stand as they are, only master Rowlandson is to haue fower accors and half for allowance as others haue.

21. *for the paying ye Laiers out of medo.* ffor the satisfacion of the psons that Laid out the medow, wee Conclude, They are to bring in their daies Labour to the towne as others doe about other occasions.

22. *Ministrs mantainanc.* Our answer to the pposition or querie about the ministrs mantainance our Conclusion is the towne shall presently begin and giue fiftie pounds by the yeare, And for the manor of the pay they ar to alow him their wheat at six penc p bushell vnder the price, it is at the bay, And soe for other graine by this pportion, And as god shall

bee pleased to enlarge their estat soe they shall enlarge theirin answrably, And this to be raised according to the order incerted in the towne Booke.

23. *difrenc about orders in the town book*. Wheras their was a diffrence amongst them Concerning sum orders in the towne book in deuiding of Land, our detirminacons are herin as followeth, Imprienis that for the first deuision of Entervaile Land eurie man shall pay one penny by the accor yearly to eurie thirtie pounds to all rats for Church and towne and what shall be wanting theirin shall bee made vp pporcioning eurie mans estat vpon goods and other improued Lands, And our Conclusion is that in other deuisions all men shall com theirto according to their estats.

24. *Ministry Land*. Wheras their was by an order of the towne fortie accors of entervaile Land giuen for the ministrie for ppetuity, buted and bounded though not Laid out, And wheras their was twenty accors of this giuen to Henrie Kerley without that due Consideracion as might haue beene, our determinacion is theirfore that the said Henrie Kerley shall relinquish this twentie accors vp for the end for which it was intended. And he shall haue Libertie to take vp twentie fiue accors of entervaile Land in Lew of that befor expresed in any place yett vndisposed, And for his expence and charge herin, he shall improue the said Land soe Long as vntill he shall bee satisfied for his charge soe expended, according to the towne order in that cas pviding. SIMON WILLARD

dated and Confirmed this 25th EDWARD JOHNSON
of Aprill 1656 1656 Witnes our hands EDMUND RICE

CONCORD WAY IN LANCASTER.

27 : 3 : mon : 1656. Wee whose hands are herevnto put being Chose by Concord and Lancaster, to lay out the Cuntrie highway betwixt the said townes within the bounds of Lancaster, haue acted and Concluded that the Cuntrie highway shall goe as foloweth : the place from whence we took our begining is at the highway Runing betwixt the Lot of John Prescott and John Mores Lott, And soe Runing on the east side the ministers house, and ouer the north Riuer by Lawrence Waters house, and soe ouer Penicooke Riuer neare to the house of Edward Breke, and soe ouer the Entervaile and through Swane Swamp where the towne hath alreadie marked out a highway for themselues and soe along to a litle pine tree on the north side of Wataquadoke hill, And soe along the old path, or wher may be most Convenient within the bounds of Lancaster.

GEORGE WHELLER JOHN SMADLEY
JOHN ROPER RALPH HOUGHTON

This, our earliest county road, started from the present highway somewhere near the cross roads in South Lancaster, and ran northerly to the first church, which crowned the highest ground in the middle cemetery, passing between that and the Rowlandson house to the shallows in the north branch of the Nashaway a few rods above Sprague bridge. Thence it followed very nearly the present line of road to the wading place about one hundred rods below the meeting of the rivers, and proceeded due east over Wataquadock, along the now nearly disused way, formerly known as the "Bay path," or "Sudbury road."

Swan Swamp. Though not proof positive that swans frequented the waters of Lancaster in the olden time, this name is quite good evidence that they were seen here at least occasionally. Nathaniel Morton, in the "New England Canaan," says: "And first of the Swanne, because shee is the biggest of all the fowles of that country. There are of them in Merrimack River and in other parts of the country, great store at the seasons of the yeare." If in the Merrimack, why not in the Nashaway, its chief tributary?

1656. The following documents, from the Middlesex Court Records and Files, afford brief glimpses of men and manners in Lancaster during the third year of its experience in managing its own affairs.

To Mary Gates of Lancaster.

By virtue heerof you are to apeere at the next Countie Court at Cambridge, to answer the complaint of John Prescott & James Atherton, for your sinfull cariage in the assembly one the lord's daye — heerof you are not to faille at your prill.

Datted this 27th: of the 11th: mo 1656.   SIMON WILLARD.

The deposition of John Prescott & James Atherton both of Lancaster.

Vpon a lords day att after exercise in the afternoone goodwife gats being called forth to giue satisfaccion for sum ofence done against Master Rowlandson, and she justifying herself, saying that she had formerly giuen him satisfacion, and in after Master Rowlandson replyed by sum arguments proving that she had not formerly giuen him satisfacion, her daughter Marie gats stood vp vncalled uerie boldly in the publique asembly contradicting our minister, when he denyed that goodwife gats had giuen him satisfacion, the said marie gats said yes and shee would take her oath of it.

This was taken vpon oath the 27th of the 11th mo. 1656, before me.

SIMON WILLARD.

Lancaster the 6th of the 11th mon 1656.

The deposition of Lidia Cibie Aged about 19 years. Vpon the Last Lord's daye goodwife gats being called forth in the publique Congregacion to acknowledge an ofence donagainst Master Rowlandson, I heard mary gats speake to Sergant Kerly that he would goe and speake, he said noe for it will giue ofence. Ofence—said shee, Lett those take ofence and be hanged all, If they will.

Sara Waters Aged 20 years witneseth, That shee heard mary gats at the same time speaking to Sargant Kerly. She said Lett them take ofence and be hanged all, If they will.

these weare both taken vpon oath the 27th of the 11th mon 1656 before me. SIMON WILLARD.

I Mary gates doe acknoleg that whearas I have spoke sumthing not long sence at this place that was mater of joste offence and uery sinfull, I am hertely sory for it and doe desire the Congregtion to pas it by, and I shall endever by the helpe of god not to alowe myself in any such practes.

this was acknoledged in publick in our hearing.

WILLIAM KERLY Juner
WILLIAM KERLY Sener
HENRY KERLY.

April 7 1657. This Court grants an Attachment agst Mary Gates of Lanchaster, and to Jno. Prescott a bill of costs for himselfe & witnesses being 24^s to be pd by the said Gates and shee is to appeare at ye next Court to Answ^r ye Compl^t of the said Prescott & James Atherton for her sinfull Cariage in the assembly on ye Lords day.

To the honoured Governour, Deputy Governour with the rest of the honoured magistrats assembled at the County Court holden at Charlestown the 16 of this instant Iune 1657, In most humble wise sheweth and complaineth, and . . [a line worn off in fold] . . petitioner Mary Gats of Sudbury lat of Lancaster was summoned to appeare at the County Court held at Cambridge the seaventh of Aprill last past and did not, your petitioner thought that full satisfaction had been giuen befor the honoured Maior Willard for the offence, also acknoledgement and satisfaction was farther rendered by your petitioner to all or any persons at lancaster, whom it might concern, further your petitioner was informed that if shee did appeare by an agent it might be exepted, hence what your petitioner did was out of ignorance and not of any contempt of athoryty or aversnes farther to acknolege the euill of my rash spech and shall be at your mercy, submitting to your fauorable sensur, allways praying for you.

MARY GATS.

23 ,, 4 ,, 1657. Mary the daughter of Steuen Gates of Lanchaster being complained of to this Court for bold and vnbeseeming speeches vsed

in the Publique Assembly on the Lords day and especially agst Mr Rowlason minister of Gods word there the evidence whereof appeareth by the testimony of Jno. Prescott, & James Atherton, Lidea Kibbie & Sarah Waters wch are on file with ye records of this Court, the sd Mary Gates appearing in Court freely, acknowledged her great euill therein, the Court admonished her, & ordered that shee should pay the Witnesses their charges & costs of Court.

Lancaster 24th 8^m 56. This may certifie the Honoured Court that wee have choose Ralph Houghton Clarke of the Writs. Witnes our hands

    Thomas Rowlandson John Rugg
    John Prescott   Thomas Sawyer

1656 28th May. "Lancaster alias Nashaway, Billeriky, & Chelmsford" were presented to the grand jury for not sending record of "theire meeting for nomination of magistrats ye year past," & the jury found a bill 7th of 2^d mo 1657.

1657. Whereas wee whose names are vnderwritten (being the freemen of Lancaster) were summoned by warrant to send some one to answer a presentment for our neglecting to send in o^r votes for Nomination of Magistrates, we have intreated John Prescott at psent Constable, to return our Defence vnto the Honoured Court, whereby we intreate the Honoured Court to consider that the Reason why wee sent them not was onely because wee were not called vpon according to order.

    William Kerly
    Thomas Rowlandson
    William (O) Lewis
    Thomas (F) Sawyer

23 : 4 : 1657. Steeuen Gates late const. of Lanchaster, being openly convicted in Court of his Breach of the law in not sumoning the freemen of that Towne to giue in their votes for nomination of magistrats, is fined according to law, ten pounds.

[Middlesex Court Records.]

1657. In answer to the peticon of Steeuen Gates, humbly desiring y^t no fine may be inflicted on him for his neglect in not warning the freemen to giue in their votes for magist^s, he being at y^t tjme sicke, & hauing pd tenn shillings for entering his peticon, the court graunts his request.

[Massachusetts Records.]

Vpon occasion & in answer to the peticon of Concord Lancaster &c, the Court . . . . . doe graunt to the inhabitants of Concord & Lancaster, and such as they shall associate vnto them, according to the tenor of theire peticon, liberty to erect one or more iron workes wthin the ljmitts of theire oune towne bounds, or in any comon place neere therevnto..

[Massachusetts Records.]

Works were soon in operation at Concord, and it seems certain that some attempt was made to establish in Lancaster the manufacture of iron from ores dug out of the bogs or fished from the ponds. Iron for smiths' use then cost over twenty pounds sterling per ton. The first forge in America had been successfully at work in Raynham for four or five years, and John Prescott, perhaps, ever watchful as he was of public needs, and stimulated by the high price, planned a bloomery in connection with his saw-mill, which probably stood on the site now occupied by the Bigelow Carpet Company's dam. This at least is certain: slag and cinders, such as accumulate at a forge, were once to be seen strewn about the embankment of a long disused dam in that locality. But bog ore, though found in various places near, was nowhere in deposits rich enough to make iron manufacture profitable.

COPPIE OF A PETTICION TO THE GENRALL COURT FOR A COMITIE.

To the Honoured Court our Honoured gouerner deputie gouerner with the rest of the magestrats the asistants and deputies

The humble petticion of the inhabitance of the Towne of Lancaster agreed on by a genrall voate of the towne whose hands are vnderwriten Sheweth, That wheras sundrie psones in this towne the Last year att the genrall Court by peticion, did obtaine the full Libertie of a plantacion to Choose selectmen and to order our prudencialls as other townes doe, suposing the towne to bee furnished for that purpose, But now vpon this short time of experienc this plantacion finding ourselues vnable to act and order our prudencialls by publique towne meetings, as a towne body by reson of many inconveniences and encumbrances which wee find that way, nor by sellectmen by reson of the scarcitie of freemen (being but 3 three in number) we want Libertie of Choic, And the Law requires (as your peticioners doe Conceiue) the greter voat of them that act to be freemen.

The premises being Considred your peticioners doe humbly Craue that the Honoured Court would be pleased to take our Condicion into their Considracion, and apoynt a comitie invested with power from the genrall Court to put vs into such a way of order as wee ar Capable of, or any other way which the Honoured Court may Judge safest, and best both for the present and future good, of vs and our towne and those that are to suceed vs, And such a Comitie soe apoynted and soe impowred, may stand till they bee able to make returne to the genrall Court that the towne is sufisiantly able to order our prudenciall afaires according as the Law requires, which if it shall please this Honoured Court to grant vnto vs, wee shall remaine further obliged, And as we ar in dutie bound Continue to pray for you.

COURTS GRANT OF A COMITIE.

Att a genrall Court held at Boston May 6th 1657. In answer to the peticion of the Inhabitance of Lancaster This Court Judgeth it meet to grant their request, And doe theirfore order and apoynt Maior Simon Willard, Captaine Edward Johnson and Thomas dainforth Comisioners, impowering them to order the afaires of the said Lancaster, And to heare and determine their seurall diffrences and greeuances which obstruct the present and future good of the towne, standing in power till they bee able to make returne to the genrall Court that the towne is sufisiantly able to order its owne affaires according to Law.

Vera Copia   THOMAS DANFORTH

ORDERS OF THE COMITIE.

The Comisioners apoynted by the genrall Court to order and setle the afaires of Lancaster, being asembled at John Prescots house September ye eight 1657 hauing heard the seurall informacions and Complaints of both pties, and reueued the records of the said towne, doe Judg meet to order and Conclud as followeth (i e)

   1. *Selectmen.* That master John Tinker William Kerley Sen John Prescott Ralph Houghton and Thomas Sawyer, shall bee and are herby impowered to order and manag the prudenciall afaires of the said towne, ffor this year next ensuing and vntill sum others be allowed and Confirmed by the Comisioners in their steed and place.

   2. *Encuragt master Rowlandson.* That the said Selecttmen take Care, for the due encuragment of master Rowlandson who now Laboureth amongst them in the ministrie of gods holy word, And alsoe that they take care for erecting a meeting house, pound and stokes, And that they see to the Laying out of towne and Countrie high waies and the towne bounds, and the making and executing of all such orders and by Lawes as may be for the Comon good of the plac (i e) respecting Corne feilds, medowes, Comon pasturag Land, fences, herding of Catell and restraint of damage by swine and for the recouring of thos fines and forfitures that are due to the towne from such psones as haue taken vp land and not fullfilled the Condicions of theire respectiue grants wherby the Comon good of the Plantacion hath beene and yett is much obstructed.

3. *Paymt. of towne debts.* That they take Care for the payment of all towne debts and for that end they are herby impowred to make such Levies or rats from time to time, as they shall see needfull for the discharge of the Comon Charges of the towne, And in Case any of the inhabitance shall refuse or neglect to mak due payment both for quality and quantitie upon resonable demand, they may then Levie the same by distresse, And are impowered alsoe to take 2^s mor and aboue such fine or Rate as is due to bee paid for the satisfacion vnto your oficer that taketh the distress for his paines theirin.

4. *manor of asesments.* That in all their asesments, all Lands apropriated, (Land giuen for addittions excepted) shall bee valued in manor following (i e) home Lotts the vnbroken att 20^s p accor and the broken vp at thirtie shillings by the accor the entervaile the broken at fowertie shillings the accor and the vnbroken at thirtie shillings the accor, and medow Land att thirtie shillings, and in all rates to the ministrie The home Lotts to pay tenn shillings p ann. according to the towne order. And this order to Continue for fiue yeares next ensuing, Alsoe that the selectmen tak spesiall Care for the preseruing and safe keeping the townes Records. And if they see it need full, that they pcure the same to bee writen our fairly into a new booke, to be kept for the good of posterity, the charge wherof to bee borne by the pprietors of the said Lands respectiuely.

5. *none freed from Rats vnless they relinquish vnder hand.* That noe man be freed from the Rates of any Land granted him in pprietie eccept he mak a release and full resignation theirof vnder his hand, And doe alsoe relinquish and surender vp to the vse of the towne, his home Lott Intervaile and medow, all or none.

6. *accomodacons for 5 or 6: be Left before 2 deuision.* That their be accomodacions of Land reserued for the meet encuragment of fiue or six able men to com and inhabit in the said place (i e) as may bee helpfull to the encuragment of the worke of god their, and the Comon good of the place, And that no second deuision be Laid out vnto any man vntill those Lotts bee sett apte for that vse; by the selectmen, that is to say home Lotts entervaile and medow.

7. *master Rowlandsons deed of gift.* The Comisioners doe Judg meet to Confirme the deed of gift made by the towne vnto master Rowlandson (i e) of a house and Land which was sett a part for the vse of the ministrie bering date 1th 6th mon 1657 vpon Condicion that master Rowlandson remoue not his habitacion from the said place for the space of three yeare next ensuing, vnlesse the said inhabitance shall consent theirto, And the Comisioners aproue theirof.

8. *Jo. Prescots highway.* That the highway Laid out through John Prescotts Land, be remoued vnto the place wher formerly it was Laid out.

9. *Steeuen gats hath noe right to a Lott.* That Steeuen gats hath noe right to those Lands claimed by him from this said plantacion.

10. *John Rigbe hath right to 10 acors of Intervale.* That John Rigbie hath right to tenn accors of Entervaile to be Laid out to him by the select men.

11. *Thomas Sawyer, 5 acors entervaile.* That Thomas Sawyer hath right to fiue accors of Entervaile to be Laid out to him by the select men.

12. *Jo: Mor 3 accors medo.* That John More shall haue three accors of medow Laid out to him by the selectmen to enioy the same to him and his heires for euer, on Condicion that he remaineth an Inhabitant in the said plac for three yeare next ensuing the Lords hand by death excepted.

13. *Lands bought by Master Tinker.* That those Lands bought by master John Tinker of goodman Knight bee Confirmed to him and his heires for euer. And that master Tinker be accomodated in deuisions of Land after two hundred pound estate.

14. *goodman Waters acomodacions.* That the selectmen Lay out vnto Lawrence Waters what he yett wanteth of his Just acomodacions in any place that is Comon, att the Choice of the said Waters. And that what Land the said Waters shall be without for more then six monthes after the date Herof he shall bee freed from the rates theirof pvided He shall neuer after make any claime theirto.

finally agst inmates. That none be entertained into the towne as inmates, tenants, or otherwise to inhabit within the bounds of the said towne, without the Consent of the selectmen or the maior pte of them, first had and obtained, and entered in the record of the towne as their act, vpon penalty of twenty shillings p month both to the pson that shall soe offend by intruding himselfe, And alsoe to the pson that shall ofend in receiuing or entertaining such pson into the towne.

Priualedges & voats. And that noe other pson or psones whatsoeuer shalbe admitted to the Inioyment of the priualedges of the place and towneshipp, Either in accomodaccions vots elections or disposalles of any of the Comon priualedges and interests theirof, saue only such as haue beene first orderly admited and accepted (as aforsaid) to the enioyment theirof.

By vs { SIMON WILLARD
EDWARD JOHNSON
THOMAS DANFORTH

SEURALL ORDERS OF THE SELECTMEN.

1. *about recording Land.* First of the 11th: mon. 1657: The Selectmen meet at John Tinkers house. They order that eurie inhabitant of the towne that hath Lands Laid out to them for tim past, They do bring a pfect List of quantitie qualitie plac and manor of Lying of their said

Lands with their seurall buts and bounds betweene this and July next to the Clarke of the Towne, who is apoynted by this order fairly to record the same, in a booke to be keept as the townes Records for after posterity, And to preuent any diffrence which may after arise through mistakes forgetfullnes or otherwise, in that pticuler, and the Clarke is alowed fower pence for recording eurie vpland Lott, and fower pence for eurie entervaile Lott, And for eurie accor of medow one penny, And for the Coping out of what hee recordeth, to those that desire it he is to haue halfe soe much as for recording, The like to be done by those to whom Lands be granted afterwards in one month after their Lands are Laid out.

2. *for want of Land according to grant.* That because some haue Complained they haue not all the Land Laid out that is granted to them, and som of their Lands are short of what they were Laid out for, And for which they Constantly pay rats, It is ordred that If any the inhabitance shall Complaine and make it out vpon Just proofe they are short of their due, in poynt of Lands, it shall bee made good to them in such place as is vndisposed of pvided all such Complaints be made beefore the Last day of September next, vnto the selectmen.

highwaies amply recorded. Eight of the 12th : mon 1657. The Selectmen meet at goodman Kerleys. They ordred that all highwaies Laid out and allowed for the towne and Countrie vse, be amply recorded, for posteritie, and the way markes bee yearly repaired by stakes or otherwise.

highway in Tho: Sawyers entervaile. That the ground Left fiue Rods widnes through goodman Prescots Entervaile for a way be staked out two Rods and halfe wid for a highway and soe much as is Left to bee dealt out toward the satisfiing of Thomas Sawyer his fiue accors wanting of his due of twentie accors entervaile, And granted by the Comittie.

gates in Comon feilds. Monday the 15th : 12 : mon 1657 The Select men meet at the house of Ralph Houghton. They agree that it is nesescarie that their bee fiue gates made and mantained at fiue seurall places in the entervailes on the east side of Nashaway Riuer, for the more Convenient pasing along the highwaies, which lyeth through the Corne feilds, where the fences are made against the Comons, And Comon pasturage Lands. To say, at the entrance of that Comon feild against good man Whits : two gates att the places where that highway paseth through the two outside fences. Three gates at the outside of the fences att the three places where the high waies enter into those feilds on both sides Nashaway Riuer on the South side of the North Riuer, and doe order, That those that are the pprietors of those Lands aforsaid doe Joyntly agree, And they or either of them are to make a gate att each place aforesaid, verie sufisiant, and vsfull hung and fitted by midsumer day next, And to mantaine the same from time to time, And the account of the charge theirof to be giuen into the towne, to bee paid and discharged by the towne.

Veiw way marks eurie march. That in march next and soe eurie yeare in the said month sum one man bee deputed, who hath beene formerly imployed in Laying out of ye highwaies, with one mor Joyned with him, to reveiw all highwaies apoynted or ordred for Comon vse, in and about the towne: And to see the way markes be sufisiant to be noted and knowne.

Second deuision. The Selectmen thinke meet and doe order, that soe soone as all Entervaile Lands belonging to the first deuision be Laid out, which is to bee done with all Convenient speed. That the towne doe Come all togather and draw Lotts for their second deuision of Entervaile which shall begine wher the first deuision ends and extend downe the riuer to the Still Riuer and soe beyond towards the plumtrees. And other places, wher entervaile is found vndisposed of as aforesaid, (not entrenching vpon any former order) vntill the whole deuision be Compleated

goodman whits gift of entervale. Monday ye first of the first mon 1657 & 58 the whole towne meet, and the orders made by the selectmen, was read to them They agree to all the orders except that of the gift to goodman White, And it is theirfore Crossed becaus he apeared not to speak in his owne Cause.

This plain record has been twice printed heretofore so as to wear an air of mystery which does not belong to it; the word "apeared" being transcribed as "feared."

John Rigbie. relese of half his Lott & his gift of medo. John Rigbie Laies downe half his hous Lott and entervaile. And reserueth tenn accors of each to him, And is allowed. And their is granted him a *Spong* of medow south of and buting on, the plumtree brooke and west of the highway Containing more or lesse two accors, soe far as it Rangeth north and south.

Spong or spung is a provincial term used in England to denote an irregular projecting portion of a field.

Mordicai Mukload his grant. Mordicai Mukload is admited an Inhabitant and granted tenn accors of vpland for a house Lott and tenn accors of entervaile

27 first mon 1658. The selectmen mett at goodman Prescots and Chose Ralph Houghton and Jacob farer to renew the markes of and for the highwaies: according to the order made the 15 : 12 mon last past no : 7th : order.

A TREATIE W^TH MASTER ROWLANDSON ABOUT HIS
SETLING.

Monday 3th: of the 3^d: mon 1658. On the Certaine intelligence of master Rowlandsons intent of remouing from vs, the selectmen, treated with him to know what his minde was: And his answer was his aprehentions were Clearer for his going, then for staying. They replied they feared his aprehentions were not well grounded, but desired to know his resolucion. He said his resolucions weare according to his aprehencions, for ott hee knew: Then the selectmen, Considering it was a case of nesesitie for the towne, to look out for other suply, they told master Rowlandson that now they did Looke vpon themselues as destitut of a minister, and should be forced to endeuor after sum other, soe discharging him.

debat with Master Rowlandson. ffriday the 14th: of the 3th: mon 1658. A mesenger Came from Belerica to fetch master Rowlandson away, vpon which the towne (hauing notice giuen them) Came togather, with intent to desire him to stay and setle amongst vs: And after some debate it was voated as followes,

1. *Voat for invitacon.* Whether it weare the mind of the towne, to invite master Rowlandson to abide and setle amongst them, in the worke of the ministrie — The voat was affirmitiue by the hands of all held vpp.

2. Whether it was their mind to allow him for his mantainance fiftie pounds a yeare, one halfe in wheat, sixpence in the bushell vnder the Curant prises at Boston and Charlstowne and the rest in other good Currant pay in like pporcion, or otherwise fiftie and fiue pounds a yeare, taking his pay att such rats, as the prises of Corne are sett eurie yeare by the Court. The voat was afirmitiue by the hands of all held vpp:

3. *gift of house and Land to master Rowlandson.* Whether they were willing that master Rowlandson should haue the dwelling house, which he Liued in as his owne pp right according to the deed made by the towne and Confirmed by the Comittie, with the poynt of Land estward and sum Land west and sum north of his house, for an orchard garden yards pasture and the like. This was put to the voate, and granted by the maior pte (and opposed by none but old goodman Kerley only their was a neuter or two) with this pviso. that it hindred not the buring place the highwaies, Convenient spac to passe to the Riuer, And the Land intended to Ly for the next minister, to bee reserued Convenient to the entervaile Lott now improued by Henry Kerley, all which was Left to the sellect men to Lay out according to their best discresion.

master Rowlandsons acceptance. And vpon this master Rowlandson accepted of the townes invitacion, And gaue them thankes for their grant, And agreed to the mocion Concerning his maintnance, And pmised to abide with vs in the best manor, the lord should enable him to improue his giftes in the work of the ministrie.

grant of sum entervaile to John White. Tusday 22th : of June the sellectmen meet at the meeting house all but goodman Kerley, and agreed That vpon serious Consideracion vpon the request of goodman White for the Land he hath plowed & fenced in the entervaile towards the still riuer (hauing entred damage for want of his right in after deuisions being demanded &c) it is granted he shall haue it as his pprietie in pte of his after deuisions according as it is now fenced being mesured to bee about seauen accors :

A MOCION ABOUT A SAW MILL MADE BY GOODMAN PRESCOTT.

Munday ye 15 : of the 9th : mon : 1658 att a training A mocion was made by goodman Prescott about seting vp a saw mill : That on Condicion goodman Prescott would sett vp a saw mill, for the good of the towne he should haue according to his desire viz : one pcell of Land Lying neare to his water mille Containing more or lesse one hundred and twentie accors ; bounded by the riuer and his owne Land, the end of a ledge of Rokes, and a stake, Joyning to his owne Land on the south west side of the mill pond : To bee to him and his posterity for euer in Consideracion abouesaid ; And is to be more exactly recorded when exactly knowne, alsoe that hee shall not be rated in any Rates for towne or Countrie for his sawes or saw mill, to be imposed by the towne, also for his said Land, he is not to pay any rats vtill it Com to bee improued, And then to pay as improued Lands vse to doe And vpon this grant goodman Prescott did pmise and engag to sett vp a saw mill, in the towne bounds, with all Convenient speed, And that the inhabitants of the towne, should bee suply with boards and other sawing on such termes as is vsually aforded att other saw milles in the cuntrie.

On Monday 17th : of ffeb : 1659 the Company granted him to fall pines on the Comons to suply his sawmill.

It was not unusual to transact town business on training days. Similar examples are found in the records of other towns. There were by law eight training days in the year, and every able-bodied male between the ages of sixteen and sixty was enjoined to be present for drill. These trainings were usually on Saturdays. The warning for a town meeting was a notice given by the constable in person to each voter, or from house to house. "Att a training" would therefore be a very convenient season for a special town meeting.

Before Prescott started his saw-mill, all houses of the town must have been rude structures of logs, hewn timber, stone and clay, for it was an impossibility to bring from the lower towns over the existing roads, and on the rude cart of the period, any large amount of sawn lumber. As lime was made only of oyster shells until about A. D. 1700, it was necessarily very costly. The first limestone discovered in the colony was at Newbury in 1697, and that in Bolton not much before 1736 probably, when Priest and Houghton's "Lime Kyln" is mentioned in records. Roofs were often thatched, following the English custom. Thus, in the inventory of Steven Gates' estate, A. D. 1662, we find the item "thatching tools, 3ˢ 6ᵈ." Chimneys were at first of logs well coated with clay, or of stone. The very old dwelling torn down in South Lancaster about 1812, behind the Moses Sawyer house, had stone chimneys, as did that of Manasseh Divoll on George Hill. When frame houses were built, the timbering was very heavy, commonly of oak, boarded and covered with "clove boards." One of the first roadways westward into the woods was known about 1700 as the "clabord path," and in the inventories of the period that essential instrument in the riving of staves, shingles, and clapboards, the *froe*, is often mentioned. It would be natural at first for builders to rest content with a single story, for few pioneers could afford more; but after 1658, with Prescott's saw-mill in successful operation, doubtless a few more pretentious structures arose. Daniel Hudson, a brickmaker and mason, was here resident in 1651. Nails, large and small, and all other articles of constructive hardware were made laboriously by hand upon the smith's anvil. Paint was unknown.

The complete destruction of all the dwellings in 1676, and the entire absence of any hint as to the construction or plan of a single building in the records of the day, leave us to pure conjecture as to their appearance. All we know about the Rowlandson house is, that it had one flanker and another in process of building, and Hubbard mentions "a leanter." Neither is there anything definite on record respecting the church, the garrisons, or dwellings of the second generation in Lancaster. Sawyer's garrison had "gates," which implies a palisade. Gardner's garrison had an elevated "watch box," "flanker," and a "parade," all which is meagre description. If, however, we examine the most ancient houses yet standing in various parts of the commonwealth, and the representations of older ones that have disappeared, we can form from their more uniform characteristics some reasonable opinion respecting the common style of early Lancaster architecture. In nine-tenths of the dwellings of that era in Massachusetts, as pictured to us in engravings, or the recollections of the aged, the roof will be found a modification of one of two forms. When the house was two storied in front, it was most commonly but one at the rear, the roof slope on that side extending down to within nine feet or less of the ground, sometimes with a change of pitch on a level with the front eaves. Another less common form was the gambrel roof used on both one and two storied houses. Plain two pitched roofs were quite rare except for small structures. Sometimes the upper story projected a foot or two over the lower. Porches or other irregular features were seldom seen. Generally one huge chimney ascended through the center of the house. When constructed with reference to defensive purposes it was usual to line the walls with brick or flat stone, to make them bullet-proof. Doors were unpaneled, with heavy wooden latch and a string hanging outside to lift it by. Windows were square holes in the walls protected by a board shutter, succeeded later by small leaden sash with little diamond-shaped panes of greenish glass. There are those living who remember such sash; notably one in the Gates Tavern. The last log house in

Lancaster was probably that of Perley Hammond, the mulatto blacksmith, which stood near the west end of the Rigby, and on the Boylston road.

about bridges. Monday the 3th: of the 11th: mon 1658. The selectmen mett at Thomas Sawyers and ordred ffor the Bridges ouer nashaway and the north riuer. It is agreed, That they that are on the neke of Land, doe make a cart bridge ouer the north riuer by goodman Waters, And they on the south end doe make a cart bridge ouer nashaway about ther wading place att their owne Charges.

SUM ORDERS OF THE COMITIE P'CURED BY MASTER TINKER. PETICION TO THE COMITIE.

To the worshippfull maior Simon Willard Captaine Johnson and master Thomas danforth Comitie for the affaires of Lancaster.

May it please you to vnderstand that since your session with vs, and Comision granted to such as you weare pleased to intrust in the prudencialls &c: the Lord hath succeeded our endeuours to the setling (wee hope) of master Rowlandson amongst vs, And the towne in some scilenc at least, and we hope in a good preparatiue to after peace, yett is it hard to repell the boylings, and breaking forth of som psons dificult to please and sum pettie differences, will arise amongst vs, pvide what wee can to the Contrarie; wherfore bee pleased to Consider.

1 *querie*. whether our power alreadie giuen bee not sufisiant, to add a small penaltie to the breach of our orders made for the good of the towne each neighbor &c eles it is a sword-toole and no edge.

2 *querie*. Iff wee may not receiue power from you to hear and determine of diffrences amongst vs vnder twentie shillings damage otherwise the opressed in small things beares his burden because tis a greater burden to goe far for ease

3 *querie*. If our power reach not to giue, grant. Lotts deuisions, addicions &c of Lands medowes &c: If for good to the whole and ptes &c which wee see great need theirof.

4 *querie*. Iff wee may Choose an artist amongst ourselues or other our neighbours to Lay our townes bounds, And make our returne theirof to acceptance: because master Thomas danforth and the worshipfull maior Willard canott be obtained, or either of them.

Honoured gentellmen be pleased to resolue these Cases and vouchsafe vs an addicion to our power where defectiue in any of theis, as without which wee are, or seeme, of litle Curage, and by which through gods asistance wee may bee theirs and yours humbly to serue

JOHN TINKER.

Answers to the Formencioned Queries

In answer to the within named queries, the Comitie doe make returne as ffolloweth

To your first. That it is in the power of the selectmen to impose any meet fine for the breach of any their prudenciall orders not exceeding twentie shillings for one offence.

To your 2ᵈ That If the towne please to nominat, three meete psons to bee your Comisioners for ending finall Causes and present them to the Countie Court they may their bee alowed for ending any Case vnder fowertie shillings.

To your 3ᵈ. That it shall bee in the power of the sellect men and not in the hands of the Inhabitance who may make their adresse to the Comitie in Case of any greeivance

To yᵉ 4ᵗʰ. That it is not in the power of the Comitie to determine but in Case it bee done they shall further the acceptance theirof to their power.

giuen vnder our hands att Boston
22ᵗʰ 9ber 1658

SIMON WILLARD
EDWARD JOHNSON
THOMAS DANFORTH

A RECORD OF THE HIGHWAIES TO BE FAIRLY DRAWNE IN THE RECORDS AS FOLLOWETH.

Cuntrie way. One way for the Cuntrie Lyeth: from the entranc in to the towne on the east pte from Wataquadocke hill, downe to the Swann Swampe, and ouer the wading place through Penicooke riuer: that is by the indian warre [weir] and soe along by master Rowlandsons ground and the riuer and againe vp to goodman Waters his barne betweene old goodman Breckes lott and that which was Richard Smithes now in the posession of John Tinker. To bee as it is staked out, att the Least fiue Rods wide. on the neck, and to be as wide as can be on the east side the riuer vnder tenn Rods and aboue fiue, and soe from goodman Waterses ouer the north riuer, vp by master Rowlandsons the breadth as is Laid out and fenced and marked and staked vp to goodman Prescotts Ry feild and soe betweene that and John mores lott and Crosse the brook and vpp betweene John Johnsons and John Ropers Lotts fiue Rods wide; And soe beyond all the Lotts into the woods.

This is the highway laid out by the Concord and Lancaster Committee, previously commented upon. This description, however, starts from the eastern end and extends the road half a mile further, the last section being the same way used at present, from the Atherton Bridge road west, at right angles with South Lancaster street, over Roper's Brook and up the hill at the school-house.

Way to quasaponikin medow. one way: from goodman Waterses barne to quasaponigin medowes before the houses of goodman gates and both goodman Josllins &c: as it is Laid out and marked: fiue rods wide and in the enteruaile 2 rods wide.

This is essentially the present street from Sprague Bridge to the North Village cemetery, and the meadows beyond.

To quasaponikin hill. one way: from goodman Breckes house through the end of his ground, and Ralph Houghtons James Athertons goodman Whites and goodman Leweises &c, to quasaponikin hill fiue Rods wide.

The same highway is used now, along the east side of the Neck.

To the mill. one way to the mill att the heads of the Lotts of John Prescott Thomas Sawyer Jacob ffarer &c fiue Rods wide from the Cuntrie highway to the mill.

This is, with slight changes at some points, the street from the county road first noted, to the Prescott mill site in Clinton, which was on the brook just below the factory near the foot of Water street.

Street in y^e south end of y$_e$ towne. one way Called the Street or Cross way: from goodman Kerleyes entervaile and the rest of the entervaile Lotts: And soe south beetweene the double rang of Lotts: fiue Rods wide and soetowards washacome when it is past Jacob ffarers Lott: And alsoe Itt runes thes^ame widnes beetweene the house Lotts and entervaile lotts northward to the wallnut swampe:

This is now known as the Back Road, extending from Walnut Swamp along the eastern base of the George Hill range, past the school-house, and so south on a direct course for Washacum Ponds.

from the Cuntrie highway to ye entervaile of Jo: Prescott soe to Wataquadoke. one way from the mill way att the end of goodman Prescotts Ry feeild, to the Entrance of his entervaile fiue Rods wide, And through the entervailes ouer Nashaway Riuer and the Still riuers, to the outsid fenc. of Jacob ffarers Lott, two Rods and half wide.

This is the road from South Lancaster street over the Atherton Bridge. A portion of it, east of the river, was discontinued many years ago.

Way to the plumtrees & groten. One way: from that entervaile way downe along all the entervailes to the Still riuer and towards grotten on the east side of the riuer two rods wide.

The Plumtrees Meadows were in Harvard. This road had to be discontinued because of frequent damage by freshets, and the present highway to Harvard, on higher ground, took its place.

1658. Several facts respecting the family of the first minister of Lancaster are found in the autograph report of administration, and accompanying agreement below transcribed from the Middlesex Court files. It is noteworthy that Master Joseph Rowlandson's mother and brother could not write their names.

Sept ye 10 58   Wheras Mr Joseph Rolenson had letters of Administraĉon granted him by the Court held att Cambridge Aprill 57 in refference to the estate of Thomas Rolenson Senr. late of Lankester deceased. This is to testifie the said honor^d Court, that the said Administrator together with the relict of ye sd Rolenson & the rest of his Childeren haue mett together & haue agreed concerning the distribuĉon of the said estate vnto eache of o^r full satisfacĉon & content and this wee doe testifie vnder o^r hands & desier it may be recorded for ye securitie of ye said Administrator.

                                         the marke of (Er) BRIDGETT ROLENSON
                                                                             widdow
        Signed in ye p^{r}sence   the marke [R] of THO. ROLENSON
of vs   THO. BRADBURY   RICHARD WELLS
           JOHN FLYN   JOHN EATON
                                               JOSEPH ROWLANDSON

In all these particulars at o^r meeting at Salisbury the 10th Sept 58 wee were fully satisfied as followeth.

Imp. That ten pounds were due to the Administrator from the estate vpon a cleare accompt.

It. That more than one yoake of oxen should not be mentioned in the Inventory forasmuch as the other yoake was giuen to the three Children of the Deceased in his life time though vnknowne to the Administrator when the said inventory was made.

It, That out of what remained after these deductions the widdow of the Deceased should receive her thirds, the eldest son (consideration had of what estate he had from the now Deceased in his life time) should receive from the Administrator sixteen pounds — twenty pounds to the two daughters wherein they receive equal shares, And that which remains is the Administrators portion.

This was the result of our agitation, and accordingly I haue acted in the Distributions that haue beene, and am ready to fullfill what remains at any time — who Desire to remaine   The servant of my mother and Brethren in what I may.

JOSEPH ROWLANDSON

1658. John Whettcombe for and in consideration of three swine killed and spoiled by his three sonnes, doth hereby promise to pay vnto Steven Gates the sume of forty fiue shill. in wheate wthin a week after michael tyde next 1658 to be paid at his house in Sudbury the s^d Steven allowinge for the carriage of the wheate tenn shill 6^d.

    Dat apr 2, 1658   JOHN WHETCOM

28,,10, 58 Jno. Whetcombe owned this bill in Court to be his act.

THO: DANF: Record^r

To the honor^{ed} County Court at Charlestown. The humble Petison of Jno. Whetcome humbly sheweth. That whereas yor Petitioner hath set his hand to a note to pay fortie and fiue shillings to Stephen Gates of Sudbury. It was through my age and weakness that I did not consider of it that I had no right to pay anything to him, before he did duly make it apeare that I had damnified him, he did complaine before the deputie Gou^r his wor^{pp}, that I or my Sonnes had killed and spoyled three of his swine in the woods, And made as if we stole them & with many threats which did somewhat amaze yor petitioner so that I could not declare my case which is such as I have now gotten to be drawne vpp fairly in wrighting, by which it may appeare to this honor^d Court that I had not wronged Stephen Gates nor was indebted to him anything for wch I should agree to pay him anything. Wherefore yor petitioner being aged & weak and mean in estate hath wronged himselfe and family in loss of so much, besides by this means of giueing satisfaction there is an imputation of theft cast vppon mee and the family of yor petitioner (to y^r great Greef being inoscent in that respect) and we are much defamed in our names and creditt, and therefore do humbly request this honor^d Court that our case may be considered, and my bill may be suspended vntill the next County Court and that then the case may be fully heard on both sides and determined accordinge to euidenc and equtie and yor petition^r shalbe redy and willing freely to yeald vnto what is right and shall thankfully remain

                      Yo^r wor^{pps} humble servant

JOHN WHETCOMBE
[Middlesex Court Records.]

The court decided that the bill must be paid.

ORDERS OF THE SELLECTMEN

monday the 7th: 12th: mon 1658 the selectmen meet att goodman Prescotts all except goodman Kerley.

1. *highway by goodman Kerley.* They Consider againe about the highway along by goodman Kerley: And they Conclude it the best way and doe order that John more John Rugg and the rest apoynted to mend that highway, doe chuse the best Range betweene the range of the Lotts, from the Corner of goodman Smithes Lott to the Corner of John Ruges on a line, and the brooke And to cut vp the brush of it, to make good that highway and that the way extend on the Lott of John Tinker soe far as sume Corner or Elboe of the brook doe ly Comon to the way and he to bee meetly satisfied for it

2. *The invitacion to maior Willard gent.* They thinke meet and doe order that a leter of invitacion bee sent to maior Simon Willard, to com to inhabit amongst vs, with such motiues Concerning accomodacions as hath beene formerly ppounded, and the hands of the select men afixed, And a copie of it reserued.

3. *about sum Land taken from Tho Sawyer, at Nashaway bridg.* They order that John More and Jacob ffarer take notic of what Land is taken out of Thomas Sawyers entervaile by the way to the bridge ouer Nashaway riuer: And make report to the sellectmen that he may bee satisfied for it, And alsoe what is they think meet for him to haue in Lew of it to be Confirmed.

5. *yt Jon: more mak known &c* That John more mak knowne wher he desires his defects of entervaile, And to bee satisfied, what is meet If in such places as is not Laid out or sequestred.

6. *about mster Rowlandsons Rate.* That master Rowlandsons Rate bee made for the Last half yeare past to pay him twenty seauen pound tenn shillings and for eurie following half year soe much att Rates as paid to the Cuntrie Rats: And that soe much be aded for the Last half year what was short taking in the ouer pluses of the former Rates to make vp towards it what that will reach.

7. *Jacob ffarer his lott altred.* That Jacob ffarer on his request, hath his hous Lott altred att one Corner, to say; the south west Corner shall runne out twentie Rods and the south est so much in: And he is to Leaue a Rode spac for a foot way between his house lott and Thomas Sawyers:

Munday 7th: 1st: mon 1658 (9?) The select men meet att Ralph Houghtons except goodman Kerly.

Order about Ensigne noice. They order that when Ensigne Noyce Comes to Lay out the towne bounds goodman Prescott do goe with him to marke the bounds, And Jobe Whetcombe and young Jacob ffarer to

Carie the Chaine, And such other as Ensigne Noyce shall desire If need bee, And that a bargain bee made first betweene him and the selectmen, in behalf of the towne, for his art and paines.

orders for Layers out of Lands and lotts. They doe Conceive it meet when any Lands ar granted to be Laid out to any inhabitant, the Layers out to bee directed by the selectmen where and how, to preuent after inconveniences.

Noyes' original return, in Massachusetts Archives, cxii, page 115, is as follows :

Aprill 7th. 1659 In obedience to the order of the honoured generall Court to the now inhabitants of lancaster layd out ye bounds of lancaster accordinge to the sayd grants, wee begane at the wading place of nassua riuer and rune a lline three mille vpon a west north west poynt one degree westerly, and from the end of ye three mill we rune two perpendicular lines beinge fiue mills in length each line, the one line runing north north est one degree northerly, the other line running south south west one degree southerly wee made right angls at the ends of the ten mille line, runing two perpendicular lines, runninge both of them vpon an east south east poynt on degree esterly, one of the sayd lines beinge the north line wee did rune it eight mill in length the other being the south line, wee did rune it six mill and a halfe in length and ther meeting wth the midell of the line, which is the line of the plantation granted to the petitionrs of Sudbury whos plantation is called Whipsuffrage and so runinge their ljne four mill wanting thre score perches to the end of their line at the nor west Angle of Whipsuffrage plantation and from the sayd angle of Whipsufrage runing six mille and three quarters ther meeting with ye fore sayd east end of the eight mile line and soe period all the sajd lines and bounds of lancaster which sayd grants rune eighty square milles of land this by me THOMAS NOYES

The deputyes approue of this returne. our Honord Magists consenting hereto.   14 October 1672.   WILLIAM TORREY *Cleric*

The magists consent hereto prouided a farme of a mile square 640 acres, be layd out wthin this bounds for the countrys vse in such place as is not already Appropriated to any — their brethren the deputyes hereto consenting. And that Major Willard, Ralph Houghton & Jno Prescot see it donne.

Consented to by ye deputyes   EDWD RAWSON *Secretary*
18 , 8 , 72   WILLIAM TORREY *Cleric*

It will be seen from above dates that the survey ordered in the grant of 1653 was not made until nearly six years thereafter, and when made, was not approved formally until thirteen years more had elapsed. The final provision for a state farm may have been duly carried out, but there is no allusion to it whatever found in any town or colonial record. Joseph Willard, Esquire, notes a tradition that the mile appropriated to the state was laid out in some tract of little value in the south part of the town.

Noyes' survey is explicit, and its lines can readily be traced in the boundaries of the towns that have been shaped within its area, as the map at page eight shows. The result was not a rectangle ten miles by eight, as the lost deed of Sholan and the court's order specified; because when Noyes had run the south line six and one-half miles he suddenly encountered the north line of the Whipsufferage plantation, afterwards Marlborough, a line seven miles in length laid out several years before. Neither was the original Lancaster a trapezoid, as Joseph Willard, Esquire, supposed, but an irregular pentagon. Its area by Noyes' record would have been exactly eighty and two-tenths square miles. But old surveys generally were liberal in measurement, and Lancaster's affords no exception to that rule. This is partly due to the "allowance" usual in such surveys, of about one rod in thirty for swag of chain and irregularity of ground. It is possible that the choice of "Jobe Whetcombe & young Jacob ffarer to Carie the Chaine," was based upon some known talent of theirs in that art. One thing is certain, the ten mile line of 1659, in modern maps stretched to over eleven miles, and the other lines followed a similar proportion. Noyes ran his ten mile line twenty-three and one-half degrees west of a true north, but this is not necessarily unaccordant with the terms of the order of the general court, the words north, south, east and west, being commonly used in a relative sense for northerly, etc. Possibly some fixed point was given in Sholan's transfer determining direction, and certainly Sholan's heirs were in the vicinity to watch that the intent of the deed was not transcended.

The wading place of the Nashaway. Before the arrival of the Englishman with his axe, doubtless all the streams of Lancaster bore seaward a much less variable volume of water, and that perhaps fifty per cent. greater in amount than since the hills and swamps were shorn of forest covering. Men living have conversed with those who claim to have seen alewives and trout in streams now, save in winter and spring months, known only as dry gravel beds. Hence wading places even for horsemen and cattle were infrequent in the rivers, and became important localities in our early annals. One of these appears to have been selected by Sholan and King as the centre of the township, and from it Noyes was obliged to begin his survey. The Nashaway is no respecter of any man's metes and bounds, and in process of time we find our careful historian, Joseph Willard, searching for this lost wading place, and finally deciding that it must have been "near the present mill bridge." To accept this would be to charge Noyes and his chain bearers, first, with making his three mile line considerably too short, and, secondly, with fixing his south line full three-fourths of a mile nearer the *centre* than his north line. Thomas Noyes was too experienced a surveyor to do this. Measurement upon the map shows that the "meeting of the waters" is very near indeed the middle of a north and south line through the old township, and but little over three miles from the original western boundary. Our mutilated town records seem to afford a clue leading in the same direction. In the transcript of the oldest records of the proprietors, Prescott's "Entervail Lott" is described as "on the west side of Nashaway Riuer part whereof *Lyes between . . . . is named in the court Grant for the center of the town at the meeting of the riuers*";—the provoking blank indicating where some words were illegible to Caleb Wilder when copying the original book. Thus the evidence seemed likely to remain forever imperfect; but, fortunately, John Prescott, alone of the early proprietors, was so careful a man of business that he had all his land grants and contracts duly recorded in the County Registry by Ralph Houghton, in 1669, and there the missing words are found to be "*the wading place which,*" and the word "*at*" to be an error for "*and.*" As the description of Prescott's interval proves it to be the same generally known today as the Thayer interval, we must conclude that Noyes' starting point was a wading place that existed very near indeed to the site of the Atherton Bridge.

2 : 6 : 1659. Lanchester is pressented for want of weights and meassures according to ye Standard & for want of A Sealler.

Lanchester is pressented for daffect in a highway in their owne bounds toward ye Baye.   Wittnes William Lewis

[Middlesex Court Files.]

To the constable of Lanchaster. You are required to Warne some of yor Towne to appeare at ye next County Court to be held at Charl-Towne the 21st of this instant June, then and there to Answ^r for ye defect in the highway between yor Towne & ye Bay & for witnes Wm Lewis & hereof you are to make a true returne vnder yor hand, & not to faile.

dat. June 1, 1659   By Thomas Danforth *Re*

Also yor miller for want of scales & weights according to law.

[Middlesex Court Records.]

1659 June 21. Lanchaster is Injoyned to repayre the Highwayes within their bounds leading towards Concord, & in such places as Concord with y^m shall Judge most convenient, to be done before the next County Court at Camb^r, on penalty of ten pounds fine ; also they are to pvide thems. of weights & measures for town standards, before the next Court.

[Middlesex Court Records.]

Mr Danforth.

Sir acording to yor warant we haue made choyce of Goodm. Lewis to serue on the Grand Jury and Nathaniell Joslin for the pettie Jury and it is the request of the Towne that it may be spared from the servic of Pettie Jurors wch we intreat if it be in yor pow^r to do it yo^{r}selfe, if in the Court then to ataine it for vs & we shall euer remaine yor obliged

Lancaster 1mo 1659   John Tinker

in the behalfe of the Towne of Lancaster, few weak & 34 miles of.

[Middlesex Court Files.]

ORDERS OF THE SELECTMEN.

a repeale of a former [order] about phibiting of inhabitanc. Munday the 4th : 5th : mon. 1659. The Selectmen meet at John Tinkers house and doe order That notwithstanding, that former order that their should not bee taken into the towne aboue thirtie and fiue families (the right vnderstanding of which is not soe clearly expresed) itt hath beene sinc ordred by the towne and by the Comitie alsoe, that fiue or six families more then wear then in being should be admited for the good of the towne and church soe further it is Conceiued by the selectmen to be most for the good of the towne, that soe many inhabitance be admited as may bee meetly accommodated, pvided they are such as are acceptable, And theirfore that former order is repealed and that admitance bee granted to soe many as shall stand with the discrescion of the selectmen, And are worthie of acceptance according to the Comities apoyntment.

goodman Wilder selectman. 26 : 4th : mon 1659. Master Tinker who was one of the Selectmen apoynted by the Comitee, to order the afaires of this towne, he hauing remoued his dwelling to Pequid, the rest of the selectmen peticioned the Comitie that good man Willder might bee apoynted by them to act as a sellect man which was granted.

ORDERS & DIRECTIONS GIUEN TO RALPH HOUGHTON ABOUT THE LAYING OUT THE 2 DEUISION OF MEDOW.

Munday the 5 : ffebruarie [1659] the towne met at the house of Maior Willard to Consider of a way to sett forward a 2 deuision of medow; And forasmuch as their was by a former act of the towne way made for the efect the work of Laying out a second deuision of medow first by surveying the medowes and men Choise to doe it theirfore the towne put it to voat whether that way should stand or noe which voate was as ffolloweth.

They that are minded to Carie an end the 2 deuision of medow acording to the true intent of the order formerly agreed on by the towne, And heare Read before the towne, for the manor of it, only a new tim sett for the accomplishment of it, in Regard the tim that was sett is past, only the towne hath their Libertie to chuse new men and to agree with them vpon as easie termes as they can, They that are thus minded Let them manifest it by holding up their hands, the hands held vpp were 14. They that are otherwise minded Lett them manifest the Contrary by holding vp their hands, the hands held vpp were 16 : which being done this following voat was Confirmed by the towne. If the towne bee minded that a man shall be made Choice of, and agreed with, forthwith to goe on with Laying out the 2 deuision of medow, acording to such orders and directions the towne shall agree of to bee his Rule theirin, and that 4 acres of medow to 100^{lb} estate be Laid out and to begin in such a place and soe to proceed from medow to medow acording to such instrutcions as the towne shall giue in writing this was Confirmed by a voat none descenting.

A mocion was made by sum that If there was any medow Left comon at after the 2 deuision was finished, that then such as did draw but litle medow by deuision might haue sum helpe and in answer wheruuto this following voat past in the towne. They that are in a minde that when a 2 deuision of medow is Laid out of 4 acres to 100^{lb} state, If any be left such as are in want and haue but a litle medow by Lott acording to order of the towne shall haue sum suply out of the Remainder of the medow that is such as haue home Lotts and beare a compitant charge in the towne this ordred by a voat of the towne to bee entred into the towne booke as an act of the towne.

to george Benit. Nextly a litle medow at Chesquonopog pond was granted to georg Benit for his full proporcion to a 2 deuision of medow which was due to his grandfather Richard Linton

medo granted to such as haue it in their 2 deuision of vpland. Nextly it was granted that such as haue medow in their 2 deuision of vpland haue their Libertie to take it for pte of their 2 deuision of medow and to take soe much Lesse where their Lot falls.

Surveiors order. Nextly it is ordred that the Layer out of this 2 deuision shall and is herby impowred to Carie an end the worke of this 2 deuision and to Call forth men eurie day soe many as he thinks hee Can dispatch their Lotts and they are to atend the worke and not depart vnlesse the Layer out giue way theire vnto, And the Layer out of medowes is to haue a care acording to his best discresion that eurie mans Lott may be made equall in qualitie, as neare as he can acording to his discresion and If any man neglect to atend the worke when he is Called by the Layer out, hee shall forfite double to an ordinarie daies wage that soe the surveier may hire one in his Roome, that soe the worke may not be neglected,

Ralph Houghton chos Surveior. And Ralph Houghton is Chosen to Carie an end the worke and he is to haue 3^{s} an acre paid within a month after the worke is done in marchantable wheat or indian Corne and this worke to bee finished by the 24 of June:

grant to the maior to exchang medo. Nextly Libertie was granted to the maior to haue 10 acres of medow or soe much as hee may giue to Simon Gats and Thomas in way of exchange for their medow at the Still Riuer and plum trees, And hee is to allow acre for acre at the brooke medow in that medow next to the pond to bee deuided in this 2^d deuision.

directions wher to begin and how to pceed. Itt is ordred that the 2 deuision of medow shall begin at the northermost medow at the plumtrees and soe to Lay out all the plumtree medowes, And soe to go to the great pond medow at the northermost end of it in sum small peices betweene

the brooke medow and the pond medow, And when the pond medow is
Laid out, then to begin at the northermost slipe of medow at the bar hill
And soe to Lay out all the nearest medowes at the bare hill and 2 small
peices that lyes south from goodman Whits second deuision. And then
to follow the brooke eastward vntill all the bare hill medowes be Laid out.
And then to begin at the furthermost medow at the north end of Long
hill, And soe follow the medow westward vntill it com to the meadow
neare to bar hill where John Whetcombe mowed. And then to begin at
the north end of goodman Whellers medow and Lay out what is medow
fit to mow towards master Josllins house and the medow by the bay path
on the west sid the Long Hill and soe to a medow east sid the Long
Hill. And soe to the medow that shuts vp to the bay path from Wataquadoke to begin at that end next to the bay path and to Lay out soe
much of it as is fit for medow acording to the discresion of the Layer out
And soe to follow that medow to goodman Sumners medow and the medows their that are Laid out, And then to goe to the medow that which is
Comon by John Mors house, And then to follow the brooke what is Comon below where Malbrow path Croseth the brooke, And then to begin at
the south end of goodman Ropers medow and to Lay out such as is fitt
for medow their and then to two Litle medowes neare to Malbrow path
And then to begin at the east end of the medow vnder the side of the pin
swampe, And then to sum medowes to the southward of that neare to the
2 deuision of vpland of goodman Gats vntill 4 acres to 100^{lb} state bee
made vp, And If any other medowes shall be discoured they are to be
Laid out in the Ranges wher they fall acording to the discresion of the
Layer out.

Which being finished and all the orders and instructions aforsaid
agreed on, and the Lord being sought vnto for his blesing vpon his owne
ordinance Lotts were taken as followeth without any disturbance or dis-
traction :

William Kerley sen	1		John Whetcombe Ju	15
Ralph Houghton	2		Steeuen Gats Sen	16
Mstr Joseph Rowlandson	3		John More	17
William Leweis	4		John Houghton	18
Edward Breeke	5		John Smith	19
John Prescott	6		Jacob ffarer	20
John ffarer	7		John Roper	21
Edmund Parker	8		Gamaliell Beman	22
John Johnson	9		Mordicai Muke Load	23
Thomas James	10		Thomas Josllin	24
Phillip Knight	11		Nathaniell Josllin	25
Jonas ffairbanke	12		John Whetcombe Sen	26
Thomas Sawyer	13		James Atherton	27
John Leweis	14		Richard Wheeler	28

William Kerley Ju	29	Henrie Kerly	35
Jerimiah Rogers	30	Thomas Willder	36
Lawrence Waters	31	John Rugge	37
Daniell Gains	32	Roger Sumner	38
John White	33	James Butler	39
John Rigbie	34		

PRESCOTT'S SAW-MILL CONTRACT.

Know all men by these presents that forasmuch as the Inhabitants of Lanchaster, or the most part of them being gathered together on a trayneing day, the 15th of the 9th mo. 1658, a motion was made by Jno. Prescott blackesmith of the same towne, about the setting vp of a saw mill for the good of the Towne, and y^t he the said Jno. Prescott, would by the help of God set vp the saw mill, and to supply the said Inhabitants with boords, and other sawne worke, as is afforded at other saw mills in the countrey, In case the towne would giue, grant, & confirme vnto the said Jno. Prescott, a certeine tract of Land, lying Eastward of his water mill, be it more or less, bounded by the riuer east the mill west the stake of the mill land and the east end of a ledge of Iron Stone Rocks southards, and forty acres of his owne land north, the said land to be to him his heyres and assignes for euer, and all the said Land and eurie part thereof to be rate free vntill it be improued, or any p^t of it, and that his saws, & saw mill should be free from any rates by the Towne, therefore know ye that the ptyes abouesaid did mutually agree and consent each with other concerning the aforementioned propositions as followeth.

The towne on their part did giue, grant, & confirme, vnto the said John Prescott, his heyres and assignes for euer, all the aforementioned tract of land butted & bounded as aforesaid, to be to him his heyres and assignes for euer, with all the priuiledges and appurtenances thereon, and therevnto belonging to be to his and their owne propper vse and behoofe as aforesaid, and the said land and eurie part of it to be free from all rates vntill it or any pt. of it be improued, and also his saw, sawes, and saw mill to be free from all town rates, or ministers rates, prouided the aforementioned worke be finished & completed as abouesaid for the good of the towne, in some convenient time after this present contract covenant and agreem^t.

And the said John Prescott did and doth by these psents bynd himself his heyres and assignes to set vp a saw mill as aforesaid within the bounds of the aforesaid Towne, and to supply the Towne with boords, and other sawn worke as aforesaid, and truly and faithfully to performe, fullfill, & accomplish, all the afore mentioned pmisses for the good of the Towne as aforesaid

Therefore the Selectmen conceiuing this saw mill to be of great vse to to the Towne, and the aftergood of the place, Haue and do hereby act to rattifie and confirme all the the aforemencc͡oned acts, covenants, gifts, grants, & immunityes, in respect of rates, and what euer is aforementioned, on their owne pt, and in behalfe of the Towne, and to the true performance thereof both partyes haue and do bynd themselues by subscribing their hands, this 25th day of february one thousand six hundred and fifty nine   JOHN PRESCOTT

The work aboue menccõned was finished according to this couenant as witnesseth.   RALPH HOUGHTON

Signed & Delivrd In presence of   THOMAS WILDER
                                                                THOMAS SAWYER
                                                                RALPH HOUGHTON.

The above covenant has disappeared from the Town Records, and is transcribed from the Middlesex Registry, III, 400.

1659. *To the Honored Generall Court assembled at Boston.* The humble petition of John Prescot of Lancaster humblye Sheweth, That whereas y^r petitioner about nine or ten yeares since, was desired by the late hon'red Governour, Mr Winthrop, wth other Magistrates, as also by Mr Wilson of Boston, Mr Shephard of Cambridge with many others, did lay & marke out a way at ye north side of the great pond & soe by Lancaster, which then was taken by Mr. Hopkins & many others to bee of great use ;   This I did meerly upon the request of these hono^red Gentlemen to my great detrim^t, by being upon it part of two Summers not only myselfe but hiring others alsoe to helpe mee, wherby my family suffered much :   I doe not question but many of ye Court remember the same, as also that this hath not laine dead all this while, but I haue formerly mentioned it, but yet naue no recompence for the same ; the charge whereof came at 2^s p day to about 10^{li}. it is therefore the desire of y^r petitioner y^t you would bee pleased to graunt him a farme in some place undisposed of, which will engage him to you, and encourage him and others in publicq͂e occasions, & y^r petitioner shall pray &c.

The Comittee consideringe the grounds of this pet. do Judge meet that the Court be pleased to grant him 100 acc^{rs} of land, to be layd out adjoyneing to the lands that are layd out by ord^r of this Court to that Plantation

                                        THOMAS DANFORTH
                                        ANTHONY STODDARD
                                        ROGER CLAP

The deputies approue of the returne of the Committee in answer to this Pet. desiringe the consent of or honor^d magist^s hereto.
                                        WILLIAM TORREY *Cleric.*

Consented to by ye magists.   Edw Rawson *Secret.*
                                        [Massachusetts Archives, CXXI, 31.]

1660. In obedience to the grant of the honoured generall Court held at boston the 18th of October 1659, layed out to John Prescott of Lancaster neare adjoyning to the west line of Lancaster bounds his farm contayninge one hundred acres joyning to a great pond [Washacum] on the northeast and allso joyning to a brooke (running out of the sayd pond) on the south east with four acres of medow joyning to the sayd pond and six acres of medow being vpon the sayd brooke — this being exactly meassured by me vnderwritten the 15 of January 1660

THOMAS NOYES

[Massachusetts Archives, XLV, 81.]

1660 August 26. Roger Sumner was dismissed, that with other Christians at Lancaster, a church might be begun there

[Dorchester Church Records.]

1662 April 1. Lanchaster and Marlbury being presented for defect in weights & measures &c, are enjoyned to make returne to ye next Court at Charlestowne that they are prouided according to law on penalty of forfeiting forty shillings a peice to ye Tres'ry of this Coun.

[Middlesex Court Records.]

1661 April 2 William Lewis of Lanchaster is released from all ordnery trayneings, paying fiue shill. p Ann. to ye millitary Company of ye Towne where he dwells.

[Middlesex Court Records.]

1662 Oct Lawrence Waters of Lanchaster is released from all ordnary trayneings paying fiue shillings p Ann. to ye millitary Company of ye towne where he dwells.

[Middlesex Court Records.]

SEURALL ACTS AND ORDERS OF THE TOWNE IN THE YEAR 1663.

The towne being Called together orderly by the townsmen to consider of seurall things that were propounded to theire Consideracion namely to peticion the Comitie to meet and to haue a hearing of seurall actions of the townesmen since they did betrust them to act as townsmen in this towne, And If the Honoured Comitie see Cause to Returne Libertie into the towns hands, againe to act in their owne prudencialls as other towns and seurall other proposisions, which were propounded to the towne, the Lecture day before the towne meeting which are here following vpon Record.

The towns mens declaracion to the towne. To our Brethren and neightbours the inhabitance of this towne of Lancaster, by the pvidence of god, fforasmuch as for the tim being the townsmen of this place are not called by the inhabitance as in other towns, which as we Conceiue, by the mocion and allsoe by sum expresions of seurall of our Brethren and neight-

bours that theire is not such a louing Concurance, as wee could desire,
That If it bee your desire to haue the Libertie to Chuse oficers, and to
order the prudencialls of the towne as other towns; If our indeuors herin
be of vse to you, And alsoe accptable to you wee desire to blesse god for
it, but If not wee desire not to Creat trouble to ourselues and greife to our
Louing Brethren and neightbours, but Rather Chuse this Louing tender to
you, which is as you know the betrust Comited to vs was by a Comitie
apoynted by the Honoured genrall Court, which If it bee your desire, wee
shall Louingly and Cordially Joyne with you to peticion the Honoured
Comitie to apoynt a meeting and to haue a hearing, of what hath beene
acted by the townsmen heare, since they Comited the care of the prudencialls of this place to vs; And If any bee greiued at any thing that hath
beene acted, that then and theire they may be eased. And If the Comitie
please to Returne Libertie in to the towns hands wee hope it will bee as
accptable to vs as vnto your selues, And If this be your desire as aforsaid,
we Conceiue this to bee the only way to ataine it.

dated this 3 : 11 : mon : 1663   Simon Willard
                                  John Prescott
                                  Thomas Willder
                                  Roger Sumner
                                  Ralph Houghton

SEURALL PROPOSISIONS TO THE TOWNE BY THE TOWNS MEN.

Theis seurall proposisions were made to the towne being orderly asembled to that end.

1 John Prescott saith hee neuer drawed medow for his estate on the
towne booke, but yett notwithstanding he hath 12 acres of medow; tho 15
acres would haue beene his due by his estate only he hath 12 acres of
swampe which hee hath paid as much Rats for as tho it had beene medow,
which he accounts a double wronge to him, his desire is that the towne
would Consider it, he is willing to take the 12 acres of medow for medow,
and soe to pay for it, And the swampe for soe much medow as it is worth,
according as the interuaile swampe is ordred in the 2 deuision that is fower
acres in Lew of an acre of medow in the 2 deuision :

This p'posision was granted by the towne fully soe that the said John
Prescott hath with the aforsaid swampe acording to his valueacion of it,
his full pportion of medow that his estat would haue drawne in the first
deuision of medow, this was granted 2 : 12 : m 1663.

2 John Prescot desired 12 acres of medow to bee Laid out to him or
his asignes that hee bought of John Caudall, it being soe that eurie man is
serued with medow in his first deuision.

The towns grant was that the said John Prescott should haue the 12
acres of medow which hee bought of John Caudall it being soe that a true

title theirvnto did apeare, Though his ingenuitie Lead him to Lett it Ly vntill all the first deuision was serued with medow, this was voated and none descented, And it is herby ordred to bee Laid out to the said goodman Prescott or his asignes, in a peice of medow aboue good man Willders at the ponds their being 4 acres as it was formerly Laid out for daniell allin And a litle peice of medow at the south end of the bar hill, And the Rest in a Corner of the great medow at the pond medow, this was granted the 2 : 12 : mon 1663.

3. That the towne would thinke of sum way to Rectifie Lands in the 2 deuision in Regard of sum inconveniencies that are fallen out accedentally.

The grant of the towne was that maior Willard Roger Sumner and Ralph Houghton are by a voat of the towne, Chose to pvise the transactions of the 2 deuision, And to put things in to such [shape] as may be for the Comfort and peace of the towne for the present and future, And to make Returne theirof to the towne that soe way may be made for the Recording Land in the 2 deuision, this was granted the 2 : 12 : mon : 1663.

4 Proposition to the towne was that the towne would Consent that John Houghton might haue Libertie to Lay downe a halfe home Lot being that he had a lott and halfe granted by the towne, this was granted by the towne, 1 : 12 : mon : 1663 :

5 proposition to the towne was to Consider what to doe about the minister's Land in the posesion of John White, this was agreed on by a voate of the towne as followeth : Those that are in a minde that Henrie Kerley shall haue that intervaile Lott which was intended for the vse of the ministrie, which soe much difrence hath beene about, together with a home Lott, which he is to take vpp in sum place yet undisposed of, for peace sake this wee tender in Case it will be accepted of, otherwise the Case to stand as it doth at present betweene vs ; And the towne to pceed as they see Cause or as Counsell may advise for their Recouring their owne interest theirin. this was voated and none descenting but John Prescott and Lawrence Waters who voated neagatiue, but at the same tim Henrie Kerley being present would not acept of it.

Theirfore the towne made Choice of John Prescott and John More and by a voat of the towne they were impowred to act in behalfe of the towne, And to psecut the towns Case Concerning the Recouring the towns Land stated for the vse of the ministrie and kept byake from the towne by Henrie Kerley notwithstanding such Louing tenders as hath beene made by the towne. And the towne pmiseth to beare the Charge herof, And they are to vse all such means as their discresion may Lead them to, or as Counsell may advise them to, this was Confirmed by a voat of the towne : 2 : 12 : mon : 1663

but presently the same day before the towne the pprosision aboue said of the towne, to Henrie Kerley to giue him the intervaile Lott and vpland

Lott aforsaid was accepted of by Henrie Kerley, And granted by the towne for the acceptance theirof witnes my hand Henrie Kerley.

6 act of the towne was that goodman Prescott goodman Willder and goodman Roper are Chosen to veiw a towne way that Lyeth betweene the Lott of John Roper and that which was John Johnsons Lott And to see what defect may be in it And make Report to the towne what is needfull to bee done, that soe Course may be taken theirin. this was voated by the towne.

The town way here designated was the first over the George Hill range, that which turns from the main road by the school-house.

7 John Prescott and Ralph Houghton are made Choice of to veiw sum waies on the neke that are desired by sum and denyed by others, they are indiferenly to see the waies and to heare what is to be said by both parties, And to make Report to the towne: that soe due course may be taken theirin for the best good of all, And John Roper is Chosen a third man this was voated by the towne The 2 : 12 : mon : 1663

8 The towne granted to James Butler a halfe home Lott, And he is to haue 10 acres of vpland for a halfe home Lott and twentie acres of vpland for a halfe home Lott of intervaile, And to take it where it is not disposed of, neither to any pticuler pson or in the Stated Comon, And he is to haue other acomodacion suitable acording to his estate.

9 Itt is ordred by the towne that all gifts grants acts orders Conclusions and Records, acted ordred or Recorded, by the towne Townsmen or Comitie, shall bee and is herby Confirmed and Ratified by the towne, from the begining of the plantacion to this day : this was voated and Confirmed none descenting this 2 : 12 : mon : 1663.

10 Itt is ordred by the towne and voated that the Comitie apoynted to haue the ouersight and Charge of Rectifiing the 2 deuision shall and is herby desired and impowred to see theis acts of the towne, at theis towne meetings theis two daies entred and Recorded into the towne booke

Lastly the towne agreed to Chuse townsmen and did Chuse maior Willard John Prescott Thomas Willder John Roper and Ralph Houghton townsmen for a whole year next insuing after the date herof.

And Ralph Houghton Chosen Clarke by the towne for this yeare And is to haue 2^{lb} : 18^s : for his Labor theirin.

The power of the townsmen from the towne, is to order all the prudenciall afairs of the towne only they are not to dispose of Lands And they ar to further a 2 deuision of medow to bee Laid out.

Theis seurall acts of the towne in this page, And sum on the other side that beare the same date with this, was agreed on by the towne, the day before; the towne being then Legally asembled, to Consider on this day aboue writen.

AN ACT OF CONFIRMACION FROM THE COMITIE

Theirfore it is ernestly desired that the Honoured Comitie would be pleased to put forth their power, to Ratifie and Confirme this act of Confirmacion of the towne, And alsoe to giue Libertie to the towne to Chuse townsmen within themselues, soe Long as your selues se a louing Concurance theirin, among ourselues, And in soe doing your worships will ingage vs yours in all Christian seruice.

dated at Lancaster 6 march 1664-65

gentlemen and louing freinds

Wee haue alltho through straits of tim but breifly pvsed [*perused*] and considered what you haue aboue presented, And doe with much thankfullnes to the Lord accknowledge his fauor to your selues, And not only to you but to all that delight in the ppitie [*prosperity*] of gods people and children, in your louing Complyance togather, that this mercie may bee continued to you is our ernest desire, And shall be our praiers to god, And wherin wee may in our Capasitie Contribut their to wee doe acount it our dutie to the Lord and you, And for that end doe fuly Concure and Consent to your pposalls for the Ratifying of what is, And for Libertie among yourselues, obseruing the directions and Lawes of the genrall Court for the election of your selectmen for the future

dated ; 8 : 1 : $\frac{64}{65}$
           SIMON WILLARD
           THOMAS DANFORTH
           EDWARD JOHNSON

aceptance to goodman Hudson. Saturday 26 : 9 : m : 1664. The towne meet at the meeting house to Consider about seting forward a second deuision of medow, And good man Hudson being newly Com vp to inhabit desired acceptance to the prieueledges of a townsman, And his mocion was granted and acceptance giuen by the towne.

grant to Ralph Houghton. Libertie was granted to Ralph Houghton to Lay downe an acre of medow at the great pond medow and take it vpp in that medow by John mors house by a voat of the towne.

grant to goodman Rogers. The towne gaue Libertie to goodman Rogers to take in a litle Corner of the Stated Comon, Leauing out soe much of his second deuision vpon the pine hill neare toquˆasaponikin brooke and to be mesured by the surueiers soe that the Comons may not sufer damage.

Libertie to mordicai. The towne gaue Libertie to mordicai mukeloade to bring in 50^{lb} estate to enter into the towne booke to draw Land and medow by in a second deuision And to haue Comon Right suitable.

grant to James Butler. The towne gaue Libertie to James Butler to haue a Rode of vpland in breadth, to set a fence on at the side of the seauen acres of Interuaile which he bought of goodman Josllin.

way cros the neke. The towne fully impowered John Prescott John Roper and Ralph Houghton to veiw the high way Crosse the neke to quasaponikin, And to Lay it out If they se cause.

grant to goodman Prescott. The towne gaue Libertie to goodman Prescott to take up a slipe of medow ground Runing through the most part of a great pine plaine that Lyeth sutherly of his Corne mille, which he is to haue in Leiw of two acres of medow, formerly granted him in a corner of the great pond medow which was granted vpon the account of John Cowdall and he is to take two acres Lesse their.

grant to Master day. 2 ffeb : 1664, at a genrall towne meeting It was vpon the Receit of a leter from master Steeuen day of Cambridge granted that the said master day should haue a hundred acres of vpland twentie acres of it for a house Lotte and to pay 10ˢ a yeare as other men doth and fowertie acres of it in Leiw of an Interuaile Lott and to pay as other men doth for an interuaile Lott, And fowertie acres in Lew of a 2 deuision and to pay as other men doth for Land in the 2 deuision And this Land to be Laid out neare to Washacombe near to the outside of the bounds and he is to haue noe other acomodacions in the towne but only that hundred acres as a farme.

2 deuision of medow confirmed. It was ordred by a voate of the towne that the second deuision of medow acording as it is alreadie Laid out is herby Ratified and Confirmed : 2 : 12 : m : 66.

grant to goodman Sawyer. It was granted that goodman Sawyer should haue six acres of Land Laid out to him Joyning to Washacombe litle pond for and in Consideracion of three acres of Interuaile that he wanted in mesure vp nashaway Riuer. 2 : 12 : m : 66.

1667. *To the Honoured Countie Court majestrats and grand Jurie.*
The humble petition of Sargant Willder for and in behalfe of the Inhabitants of Lancaster hñbly sheweth. That forasmuch as the towne Lyeth vnder a presentment for want of a stoke of powder and other Amunition acording to Law, And also the Honoured generall Court hauing made epesiall pvision and giuen strict charge to the chiefe oficer of eurie Companie to be pvided acording to Law, it must be confesed to our greife that wee are defectiue, tho means hath been vsed by the townesmen and course taken for the pviding of a town stoke yett notwithstanding by Reson of the scarcite of powder and the Low Condicion of seuerall of the inhabitants part is wanting, but by the helpe of god wee will indeuor a Restoracion thereof and alsoe of such defects as may be found in the Companie for want of armes and amunicion acording to Law · Therefore your humble peticioner

humbly craueth that the honoured Court would be pleased to consider our Low Condicion and not ad a burden to the weake by imposing a fine, but be pleased to exercise pacience toward us in granting a litle time vntill the fruits of this year be mad, and in the meane time wee will be endeuoring to furnish ourselues in the best manor the Lord shall enable vs. And without ceasing pray for the p^ritie and saftie of the Honourable Court and Cuntrie. by mee THOMAS WYELDER
Lancaster this 30th of 1 m 1667.

[Middlesex Court Files.]

TOWNE GRANTS 3 : 12 : MO : 1667

Jo. Roper his grant for highway. It was granted that goodman Roper should haue twelue acres in the Comons where it is not stated Comon, or otherwise granted or Laid out to any other man which he is to haue in Leiw of damage done in his home Lott by Regulating a highway which damage was Judged by a Comitie that was apoynted by the towne to veiwe it, to be fower acres in that place, And theirfore it was Judged three acres for one being he was to haue it Remote, And the highway was to Ly as it is now staked out in his Lot to the Comons.

Groten way altred. The towne was willing If groten Consent with vs that the Cuntrie way as it is Laid out about the swampe at the maiors Intervaile be Laid downe, And the Cuntrie way to Run through the maiors Intervaile where the towne high way Runs to the plumtrees this is Consented to by the towne and Confirmed by a voate.

Jo: Houghton's grant. It was ordered by a voate of the towne that John Houghton should haue Libertie to fall Timber in the Comons for his trade vse, And If he take the barke of it, And sett his marke vpon it, Then it is not Lawfull for any to take or make vse of any such Timber.

goodman Whellers grant. Good man wheller desired the towne to giue him a litle peice of Land Lying by the side of Nashaway Riuer a litle aboue Johns Jumpe which was granted by the towne 2 : 12 : m : 1668

1668, 27 May. On the motion of Major Symon Willard, on the behalfe of the towne of Lancaster, that the leter L_c be the allowed brand marke for the sajd towne of Lancaster, the Court orders the same so to be.

[Massachusetts Records.]

SEUERALL TOWNE ACTS MADE 2 : FEB : 1669 AS FOLLOWETH :

order inioyning psons to atend y^e publique meting. And at the same meeting it is ordered by the towne that eurie setled inhabitant atend the publique meeting of the towne eurie yeare the first munday in februarie by 10 : of the cloke then and theire at the meeting house or other place of publique meeting to atend the publique ocasions of the towne vpon penultie of Loosing their voate in such transactions of the towne, that may be acted by the towne in their absence and alsoe pay 2 shillings to the vse of the towne to be leuied by the Cunstable in Case it be not paid without, vnlesse sum thing more then ordinarie doe apeare to preuent theire being theire. And such as haue any thing to suiest to the towns Consideracion, whether it concerne the towne in generall or any pticuler persons case or Condicion, such persons to bring it in to the Clarke or selectmen of the towne to take a Record of them that soe theire may be order atended for the more speedie Isuing of busines by the towne, And that the towne Chuse moderators to that end, to Consider what is nesesarie to be done And to se that order be atended, And that nothing be acted after sun sett, this was voated and Confered by the towne.

The latter portions of this act are interesting as foreshadowing the formalities that govern the calling and management of our modern town-meeting; while the first provision, read in the light of recent experience, seems fully worthy of being rehabilitated.

ORDERS ABOUT MAKING AND MAINTAINING HIGHWAIES

7: & 8: 12: mon: 1669. It was ordered that the making and Repairing of highwaies the Charge and Cost theirof shall be Raised from the Rateable estate of the towne, namly Catell and Land and other estate as it is to the Cuntrie Rate, And medow as it is to the ministers Rate this was Confirmed by a voate It is alsoe agreed by a voat that the Last yeares worke to the high waies shall be Regulated by this Rule aboue writen. And that all highwaies for towne and Cuntrie or any perticuler pson that is alreadie Laid out or to be Laid out shall be made and maintained vpon a publique charge, acording to the order aboue expresed this was Confirmed by a voate.

order about the 2 bridges. And it is alsoe agreed and ordered by the towne that the two bridges alreadie built namly nashaway bridge and that by goodman Waterses are to be maintained and vpheld by the publique towns Charge, acording as the towne order prouides for in making and maintaining other highwaies. And the time to begin is this 2 of februarie, 1669 about the maintaining and vpholding the bridges, (only) If the towne thinke it may be for the saftie of the north bridge that the Cages be put downe, that then they shall be sett downe vpon the nekes Charge the first convenient optunitie, this was alsoe Confirmed by a voate.

burning woods & veiwing fenc to be paid by ye towne. It was ordered that the burning of the woods and veiwing of fences, the Charge theirof be paid by the towne in the same way as the Charge of the highwaies is defraid this was alsoe Confirmed by a voate.

grant to goodman Leweis of medow. In Reference to goodman Leweis Complaint about his second deuision of medow, the towne being willing to helpe him with sum alowance, And after seuerall waies ppounded to that end & yet the end Could not with saftie and Conueniencie be atained, seuerall of the Inhabitance ofered to Contribut freely out of their owne proprieties, And to take soe much Lesse in theire deuision where it falls in the medow that is Comon, namly the maior giues an acre adioyning to his owne at the brooke medow And three quarters of an acre at the froge hole. Goodman Prescott halfe an acre Coperall More halfe an acre John Houghton halfe an acre George Benit halfe an acre goodman Sumner halfe an acre goodman Rogers a quarter of an acre goodman Beman a quarter of an acre Ralph Houghton halfe an acre vpon Condicion the maiors three quarters at frog hole be giuen to John Leweis, And by the Consent of the towne this is to be mesured out of the comon medow as sone as their may be a convenient optunitie: this was confirmed by a voat of the towne.

SEUERALL OTHER ACT[S] OF THE TOWNE IN THE YEARE 1670: 7: & 8: 12: MO.

Jo. Houghtons grant. It was granted John Houghton to Lay downe twentie acres of second deuision Land for a high way on the south side of deans brooke, And to take it vp againe in a plaine neare his medow this alsoe was Confirmed by a voate of the towne.

Deans Brook seems to have derived its name from that Samuel Dean who signed the town covenant in 1653, but has no after connection with Lancaster history. The brook retained the name for a hundred years, but before 1760 became known as "Gutteridge," or Goodridge Brook, from a family that lived on the hill half a dozen rods north of the railroad bridge over the highway between Clinton and Lancaster.

Order about Land Lying in comon to Seuerall towards Washacombe. The towne ordered that goodman farer goodman Wheeler goodman fairbankes goodman Rugge Thomas Willder and Henerie Kerley haue theire Libertie to Lay downe their Land ppounded for, lying by georges hill, prouided they all agree, otherwise they are inioyned by this order to lay out their Lotts by the Last of March or otherwise to pay all such damages as any pticuler man in the Companie shall sustaine, And they haue theire Libertie to take theire Land in sum other place or places, this was Confirmed by a voate.

Order about Com. medow. The towne ordered that the towns men as a comitie should modle out a way for the deuiding of the Comon medow, And in Convenient time to present theire thoughts to the towne and to be inquisitiue of psons to find out what medow their may be Comon within the towne, And If any know of any comon medow, they are to make Report to the towns men. this was Confirmed by a voate.

alowance to abra. Joslin for a highway. Munday 30 : 11 : mon 1670. The towns men meet at maior Willards house and ordered to alow Abram Josllin for a highway taken out of his land at long hill, Lying by his house to the medowes at Long hill, and alsoe the Cuntrie way, And he is to haue two acres for one and Ralph Houghton is to Lay it out as speedily as may be.

george adams grant. Munday 6 : 12 : mon : 1670. In Reference to george Adames proposision to the towne about sum Right to a lott of twentie acres which was formerly laid out by master day After serious Consideracion and debate about it, the towne thought he might haue sum Right theirvnto, And haue granted him sixtie acres of vpland in Consideracion theirof And he to pay for land improued and Catell and other Ratable estate, to all publique Charges, And he is to haue Comon priuiledge, for feeding Catell only ; together with timber and fire wood for theire owne vse in the place, but noe other Right to any other Lands either in Comon or to draw by deuision, the said george togather with his sonn John, both of them ingageing for them selues their heires and asignes neuer to disturbe or trouble the towne or any man in the towne about any former Rights titles, or Charges expended in or about the plantacion or any Lands theirin Contained the said Land to be Laid out where it is Comon Land southward of washacombe great feild neare to the Line of the plantacion And he to be subject to towne orders.

GEORGE ADAMES
his ◊ marke
JOHN ADAMES
his 2 marke

The twenty acres claimed was on George Hill, being the lot next and south of the trucking-house site, and assigned as a home lot to Jonas Fairbanks.

This closes the entries in the town book by Ralph Houghton, although in the Book of Lands his signature is attached to records until the year of the massacre, 1675 ; and again upon the resettlement in 1680 and 1681 his pen was resumed in behalf of the town, as appears by a petition to the General Court. The next year another was chosen clerk. Ralph Houghton's term of service, including the four years while the town was deserted of its people, was twenty-six years, 1656–1682. He was a good penman and an able man of affairs. If any of his townsmen wanted a will written, or to deed land to another, or to send a petition to Court, Ralph Houghton's pen was certain to be summoned for the work. He was among the first to attach his name to the covenant, and, though a young man, took at once a prominent place in the councils of the plantation. He seems to have had entire charge of the business of the proprietary for over thirty years, surveying and recording each man's share in the several divisions. He lived upon the east side of the neck, not far probably from Nicholas Frost's residence, but upon which side of the highway the records do not tell us.

Cyprian Steevens succeeded Ralph Houghton as clerk, the following return of his election being from the files of the Middlesex County Court.

To the Hono[rd] County Court. These are to giue you Notice that Cyprian Steeuens is by y[e] Inhabitance of Lancaster chosen to be Clarke of y[e] writs for lancs[tr] June·14th 1682.
20 .. 4 .. 82   as Attests GAMALIEL BEAMAN
   Allowed in Curiam F. B. R.   Constable of Lancs[tr].

Of Steevens' town records none are extant. He was, however, probably clerk but three or four years. He served in the capacity of Constable for several years, and returns and letters of his are not rare in the County and State archives. His penmanship and rhetoric were florid rather than elegant, and his official signature was sometimes a marvel of elaboration. Cyprian Steevens was the youngest son of Col. Thos. Steevens of Devonshire, England, and came from London in 1660. January 22, 1672, being then about twenty-two years old, he married in Lancaster, Mary, the daughter of Major Simon Willard. Their children were Mary, born Nov. 22, 1672; Dorothy, —; Simon, born in Boston, 1677 or 8; Elizabeth, born about 1681; and Joseph, —. As in 1693 his wife is named Ruth,

he must have contracted a second marriage. The time and
place of his death are not matters of record, but his name
appears as witness in Lancaster as late as 1713. His
career, as deduced from the court files, gives evidence of
more energy than discretion. At one time we find the
Natick Indians complaining that he had far exceeded his
constabulary authority in levying upon goods of theirs,
and he was compelled by General Daniel Gookin to refund.
Within a year thereafter he is convicted of selling powder
and shot and three gallons "of strong liquors which they
brought in wooden Bottels of about one galon a peece," to
a party of Indians hunting " up in the woods near Watchuset." Some years later he is again in trouble, having
permitted the escape of a ruffian, Robert Crosly, who had
assaulted Steevens' neighbor, Philip Goss, then living just
across the river on the Rowlandson estate. He was even
accused of being in collusion with Crosly, but the worst
that was proven against him, was a too great unwillingness
to face a brace of loaded pistols and a sword in the hands
of a desperate privateersman. This fault he condoned
speedily by pursuing the rascal to Dorchester, and bringing him to justice.

Upon his marriage with Mary Willard, her father, the
Major, partly in exchange for lands which Steevens owned
at Dunstable and partly in way of dowry, deeded to his
son-in-law

<blockquote>all ye Houseings, Barns Stables, orchards Lands, Entervailes, Meadows
lyeing and being in Lancaster according to their severall Butts & bounds as
followeth, viz: the House Lott formerly called Major Willards whome
Lott, bounded by ye North Riuer South & ye Night Pasture east and y^e
Country highway North, & West by the highway that Leads to ye North
Riuer. . . . . . .</blockquote>

Thus the original lot of Lawrence Waters upon which
the first dwelling house in Lancaster was probably built,
came into the possession of its sixth owner in 1673. The
house that could be a home to Major Willard's large family

must of necessity have been commodious, but it was moreover a garrisoned house, and in 1676 sheltered for six weeks eight families and a guard of soldiers. It was probably of stone or brick, for when abandoned, it was partially demolished by gunpowder, which would hardly have been used if fire alone could have effected destruction. Within a few rods of Cyprian Steevens' home and garrison was the bridge, and in sight, across the river, little more than a rifle shot off, stood the church and the Rowlandson garrison in 1675.

All town records failing until 1716, the miscellaneous documents which follow, culled from many sources, are transcribed to make these annals continuous.

1669, 2, 6. The grand jury presents "Lankester * * for want of sufficient bridge ou^r Still Riuer in ye way to groaten in Major Willards land Witnes   Henry Carley   Willm longly."

[Middlesex Court Files.]

1670. Whereas Abraham Joslyn dyed not longe since at sea of from ye Coast of Virginia in ye Ship ye Good Fame of New York, but before his decease made a will the wch hath beene approu^d by ye oath of Two persons who are witnesses therevnto, wherein he disposeth of his estate in Nashawaye & elsewhere in his Maj^{ties} Colony of the Massachusetts, vnto his wife & children, These presents may certifye all whom it doth concerne that ye said will hauing beene proued as aforesaid remaines vpon Record with ye rest of ye wills and Testaments of such as doe happen to dye wthin this the Province of his Royall Highness . . . . . .

New York 17 April 1670.

[Middlesex Court Files.]

To the Hon^d County Court of Middlesex now assembled at Cambridge this 4 of 8 mo 1670. The petition of Jeremy Rodgers of Lancaster Humbly Sheweth, That yor petition^r being for seuerall years together one that did officiate (vnder the Comand of the Hono^d Major Willard) as an Sergant In the millitary Company at Lancaster and that with good acceptanc & approbation of the said maj^r and Company yet at last by the Company I was dismissed of the said office for reasons best knowne to themselues not for any neglect or misdemeanor In my place that I know off. or y^t euer I was chardged with, yet sinc then the sucseding officers haue called mee to bear armes as a com̃on souldier in the said company wch as I haue ben informed Is contrary to the custome and law of armes and for aught

I haue heard or can learne not the practice of the country to beare armes as a comon souldier whervpon I did not appeare, and when theire officer came to straine vpon my goods, wee came to an agreement to referre the matter to the Hon^r Maj^r gen^{rll} [*Leverett*] Maj^r Willard, Maj^r Lusher, Capt. Mason and Capt. ffoster, who all but Capt. Mason mett at the Maj^r Genr^{lls} house In may Last, who Heard what was said on both sids (though more might be said but I am desirous rather to forbeare than to offend or greiue any). But those Hon^d ffrends and Gentleⁿ vpon what they then heard did judge and advise that the fines should bee forborne and not taken, and also that there being noe law here extant to free such a one from training did advise that I should address myself to this Hon^d Court whom they doubted not but would grant mee a free dismission, o^r Honrd maj^r Willard then willing and Consenting thereto. My humble petition vnto yor worships is that you would bee pleased to take it into yor Consideration and grant mee this favor to be freed from training in that Company at Lancaster where I haue been an officer, for your petitioner shall notwithstanding bee Ingaged to serue the Country and your worships according to my power and abillity In what I can, and euer pray for yor peace and prosperity long to continue . . . .

To the Honoured Countie Court at Charlestowne.

This may Certifie the honoured Countie Court that I henerie kerley of Lancaster (though vnworthie) yet hauing the Comand of this militarie Companie laid vpon mee, And accidentaly vnderstanding that Jeremiah Rogers Senior hath Recourse to the honoured Court to procure a fredome from militarie traininge, though he did not aquaint me nor the Companie therewith, the truth is If the honoured Court should see cause to fre him before his making his peace with the Companie, it will tend much to the destrucion of peace and order in the Companie and force me togather with the Rest that are in ofise, in the Companie to lay downe our places, their hath beene soe much provocacion on his part not only to vs, but alsoe to the Companie in generall in the managing of this his controuersie so vnwarantably taken vp, the truth of the whole mater being by the Companies order drawne vp to informe a Comitie desired to arbitrate the case, a true Copie wherof the honoured Court is desired to peruse and therein you will haue a full declaracion of the case : And herin I shall not trouble the honoured Court any further but Rest your humble servant.
    LANCASTER this 20 : 4 mon : 1670.

To the worshippfull our honoured major generall Leveret, maior Willard and maior Lusher, togather with our two worthie and highly esteemed frends Captaine Mason of Watertown, And Captaine ffoster of Dorchester who are a Comitee humbly desired by Sargant Kerley on behalfe of himselfe and the military Companie here at Lancaster and our neighbor Jeremiah Rogers, to here and determine a difrence depending betweene the said Jeremiah Rogers and the Companie; our Ernest Request is that your worships would be pleased to pardon our boldnes as also to pitie what you see of weaknes in this our present declaration wherin we desire truly and fully to discouer the truth of the case as alsoe the condition of this small Companie for seuerall years, since Sergant William Kerly who now liues at Marlbrow, did leaue vs. Honoured gentlemen, be pleased to take notice that sinc the said Sargant William Kerly did Remoue his dwelling from among vs this Companie hath made choise of seurall to ofisseat in the place and ofice of Sargant, though litle apearance that was pmising for the manageing of that soe great a betrust, it is not our desire or endeuor to slight one or any pson or talant but freely and truly to informe yourselues with the stat of things, the truth of what we here asert is well known to our honoured Major Willard who hath not bene wanting to put forth himself to helpe the Companie in poynt of exercise, but the want of psons fitly qualified to take the Charge of the Companie was much bewailed by general sober minded and well atested psons; sum years agoe within the time aforementioned, our neighbor Rogers was made choise of and did ofiseat for sum Considerable time, and in the time of Sargant Willders being Comander in Cheife, though seuerall in the Companie were vnsatisfied with the said Sargant Rogers and the grounds they aledged was that it was not a legall choise in Regard it was not atended acording to Law but that we that bore arms and were in the feild then, did voat and sum that had Right to voat had no notice of the Choise: and also did not apprehend him fitly qualified for the place, and this coming to the ears of the aforsaid Sargant Willder did fully manifest himself vnwilling to ofiseat any longer without a new choise and sum of the Companie do afirme that Sargant Rogers did alsoe discouer himselfe to be of the same mind but most of the companie doe afirme that he did not manifest any thing to the contrary. And therevpon the Companie went to choise of two Sargants, and Sargant Willder was againe Chosen to be Cheife oficer & John More for a Sargant to asist him. And why our neighbor Rogers should vpp a conceit that he was turned of, and alsoe a preiudice agst the Companie and not to atend to ofiseat in the place of a Sargant, nor to come in the place of a privat souldier we know of no militarie custom for the same, wee desire not to put him to trouble nor charg, but desire that quiet and order may be preserued in the Companie and the said goodman Rogers being present with the Companie this 16 day of Mar beinge a training day, vpon sum discourse about sending downe it was moued that sum thing might be proposed in Reference to the ending the diference at home, it was desired that our neighbor Rogers would mension his greiuances to the Companie that so It might be they might be taken of, that so there might be a comfortabl Composure of the diference, and he desired y^t ye Companie on their part would first declare & it was manifested by the Companie that they had nothing against him but only his absenting from publique trainings, but he Refused to aquaint the Companie with what was an obstruction in his way, but would declare it when he cam before yourselues, and it was Replyed that his motion would not be Regular to declare that against vs or of vs that he would not declare to vs: And so leauing the case with yourselues, acording as you may se cause to judge and the Companie haue made chois of Sarjant Kerly and Sarjant divole on the Companies behalfe to atend your meeting and to manage this case and further shall not trouble your worships but pray for the good guidance of y^e in this case.

[Middlesex Court Files.]

The documents in the case of Lancaster versus William Lincoln, found in Middlesex Court files, disclose the method used to get rid of undesirable immigrants.

1671. *ffor William Linkcorne.*

Be it knowne to you that the townsmen take ofense at you in Regard you haue not atended the towns order though you were made aquaint therwith. before your coming into the towne, therefore you may expect the order to be put into execution which will not bee to your profit, for the penaltie of your intruding yourselfe into the towne is twentie shillings p month, which will be a burden it may be too heavie for you though procured by yourselfe.

ffor William Lincorne.

fforasmuch as you haue aproued yourselfe an intruder into this towne of Lancaster without consent. contrarie to order, Therefore in his maiesties name you are Required to withdraw yourselfe and family, and to depart the towne forthwith, in Regard the towns men, vterly disclames you an inhabitant, And herein faile not at your prill — dated this 25 of Aprill 1671. By order of the townsmen   RALPH HOUGHTON

This was Read to William Lincorne at his house and a true copie deliuered to him in the name of the townsmen, the 28 : 2 mon : 1671.

         By vs   RALPH HOUGHTON
                       JONATHAN WHETCOMB

Ralph Houghton & Jonathan Whittcom weare sworn the 29th 2 mo 1671 before me   SIMON WILLARD, *asistant*

To the Constable of Lancaster or his deputie.

You are in his maiesties name Required to atach the goods, and for want thereof the bodie of William Lincorne, And take bond of him to the value of twentie pounds for his apearance at the next Countie Court holden at Cambridge the 4th day of Aprill next after the date hereof, then and there to answer the complaint of the townsmen of Lancaster or any one of them as an Aturney for the Rest in behalfe of the towne for his forcing of himselfe into the towne as an Inhabitant Contrarie to an order of the towne, the penaltie of which is twentie shillings a monthe to any such as soe doe, the payment wherof Is by him denyed tho legally demanded, and herin faile not but make a Returne vnder your hand. dated the 23 of march 1671.   By the Court   Ralph Houghton R.

  This Atachment was serued and bond taken this 24 of March 1671 By me.   GAMALIELL BEMAN
Constable of Lancaster.

  The deposision of Ralph Houghton aged about 47 yeares, Witnesseth that the Last Spring of the yeare, I met with William Lincorne in our towne and he being a stranger I inquired of him what his ocasion was their and he told me he was about to hire a farm of master Kimball in the towne, and I told him of our towne orders which did impose a penaltie of twentie shillings p month to any that should com to inhabit without the consent of the townsmen, And advised him to goe to the townsmen & haue their aprobation before he made any contract with master Kimball, and he told me that he had bene with three of the townsmen who were met vpon sum other ocasion and they had apoynted him a day when he might come and haue a full meeting, and be heard, but he did not atend that meeting: And further this Deponent saith not.

  1672, 7 May. Whereas the honoured Major Willard, Mr Thomas Danforth wth the late Capt Johnson, haue, by order of this Court, binn a comittee to order the prudentiall affaires of Lancaster for many yeares, Lancaster hauing binn setled for seuerall yeares, & as the sajd comittee informes, many yeares since binn trusted by them & able to mannage their owne affaires; the sajd towne of Lancaster now humbly desiring the Courts favour, that the Comittee, for their great pajnes & service for so long a season, may be thankfully acknowledged & dismist from future trouble in such respect, & themselues betrusted, as other townes are, to mannage their owne affaires, the Court judgeth it meet to grant their request heerin.

[Massachusetts Records.]

To the honourable the Govr the Deputy Govr magts & Deputyes assembled in the gen^{r}all Court.

  The Petition of Jno Prescott of Lanchaster In most humble wise sheweth, Whereas ye Petitio^r hath purchased an Indian right to a small parcell of Land, occasioned & circumstanced for quantity & quality according to the deed of sale herevnto annexed and a pt thereof not being legally setled vpon me vnlesse I may obteyne the favo^r of this Court for the Confirmation thereof, These are humbly to request the Courts favo^r for that end, the Lord haueing dealt graciously with mee in giueing mee many children I account it my duty to endeauo^r their prouission & setling and do hope that this may be of some vse in y^t kind, I know not any claime made to the said land by any towne, or any legall right y^t any other persons haue therein, and therefore are free for me to occupy & subdue as any other, may I obteyne the Courts approbation. I shall not vse farther motiues, my condition in other respecks & w^t my trouble & expenses haue been according to my poor ability in my place being not altogether vnknown to some of ye Court.

That ye Lords p^rsence may be with & his blessing accompany all yor psons, counsells, & endeauo^rs for his honor & ye weale of his poor people is ye pray^r of

Yo^r suppliant. JOHN PRESCOTT Senr

17 : 3 : 1672 read and referred to ye Comittee,

In Refference to this Petition the Comittee being well Informed that the Pet^r is an ancient Planter & hath bin a vsefull helpfull & publique spirited man doinge many good offices ffor the Country Relatinge to the Road to Conecticott, marking trees, directinge of Passengers &c and that the Land Petitioned for beinge but about 107 Acres & Lyinge not very Convenient for any other Plantation, and only accomodable for the Pet^r we Judge it reasonable to confirme the Indian Grant to him & his heyres if ye honor^d Court see meete.

The Deputyes approue of the returne of the Comittee in answer to this pet: o^r Honor^d magis^ts consenting hereto.	EDWARD TYNG GEORGE CORWIN HUMPHREY DAVIE

W^M TORREY *Cleric*

29 May : 72. Consented to by ye magists

EDW RAWSON *Secret.*

Attention was called to the above petition by the Honorable Samuel A. Green. Both petition and deed are among the Shattuck Manuscripts in the possession of the New England Historic, Genealogical Society. The grantor was James Wiser, alias Quanapaug, that brave Christian captain of the Nashaways, whose timely warning of the impending danger might have prevented the massacre of February, 1676, had the colonial authorities paid proper regard to it. The land joined Prescott's farm at Washacum previously granted. The railroad buildings and tracks at Sterling Junction occupy a portion of it.

In the Middlesex Court Files are several papers relating to Elizabeth Parker's illegitimate child, and Edmund Parker's neglect of Sabbath day ordinances. The more important of them are here transcribed, not only to record town action, but because they afford a picture of what was probably the most abjectly wretched home in Lancaster.

For Decon Parkes & the selectmen of Roxbury.

You are herby to take notice that the selectmen of the Towne of Lancaster haue made Application vnto the Court of this County held yesterday being the 18th of June where they manifested themselues onwilling to Receue into their towne a Bastard Child born of the body of Elizabeth Parker in your towne & now sent with the mother to liue in the towne of Lancaster with Edmund Parker who is a very poor man & vnable to mainteyne his owne family much less the said Bastard Child & its mother, the Court haue heard their Complaint & ordered that the selectmen of Roxbury do take care to prouide for the mainteynance of the said Bastard Child according to Law. This at y^r Request I thought meet to certifie you, Mr Danforth being not psent to giue you a Copy of ye^e Courts order.

June 19th: 1672. Yr louing friend

DANIEL GOOKIN C.

To the Constable of lanchester or his deputy.

You are in his majesties name [*several words illegible*] the child of Elizabeth Parker with the mother vnto Roxbury where it was born vnles the grandfather Edmund Parker will vndertake to secure the town of Lanchester to the sattisfacion of the selectmen whereof you are not to faile this 29 of 4 mo 1672, this is a trew coppy.

SIMON WILLARD *assistant.*

The following is neither signed nor dated ; it is in Ralph Houghton's handwriting.

Worshipful and honoured gentlemen.

Wee have Receiued a letter bearing date the 30: 5 m: 72, wherby wee vnderstand your worships wanted information in Regard you had the report only of one partie in Reference to the bastard child borne at Roxberie, for had your worships bene well informed and well considered the trouble it hath caused in our pore towne, wee supose the curant of your advise wonld haue Run an other way, for besides the infamie of hauing a bastard, legaly fathered vpon another towne as apears by the order of the honoured Countie Court at boston prouision being made theire for the keeping of it, and the townsmen willing and forward to take care of and for it, that If the said maintainance ordred were to scanty they would vse means to make it vp by the towne, and yet notwithstanding all this, that the Reputed father which is soe able to haue kept his owne, should violently and forcibly If not fraudelently thrust it vpon vs, it being soe that he did know that the townsmen had warned Edmund Parker, him that tooke the child to the contrarie before they had made any Contract about it, wee conceiue had the like bene done to your towne, your worships would haue bene of an other mind and haue looked at yourselues caled to stand vp in your towns defence against such a wrong and the sence your worships had of the pore infants sufering would haue moued you to haue advised the Right owner to haue kept his owne and not to haue exposed it to an other jureney and the hazard thereof, and had your worships knowne the pore man's incapacitie for such a thing in Respect of his habitation is soe mean that when it Raines their is noe drie plac in it and many times forced to goe to other houses for shelter and for lodging, but one pore bed for himselfe his son and daughter all to lodg in or sleep by the fire, soe that before she went from him to liue in service it was said they all lay togather, which ocasioned her to ly at neighbouring houses and soe her time was lost & she became a burden to her father and other neighbours, wher she haunted, and then she went to service; and also the mans ill disposition in Refranc to the ordering of his family, which was but one son who is about 20 years of age, and all the means the towns men from time to time can vse would not be available to cause him to get his said son a litle learning nor to atend to the publique ordinances on the Lords day, soe as that it is said and credibly Reported that he hath not bene at meeting a whole year and when delt with. full of froward and peevish and provoking language, and that is the best that can be expected by the townsmen's endeuors with him, therefore the townsmen humbly craue the asistance and helpe of the next honoured Countie Court herin and alsoe to judge whether this man be fit to take more young ons in to his family, and alsoe in Referenc to the Charg that must of nessesitie be forthwith expended in building and for lodging and other nesesaries fit for a woman that giues sucke and such a child that soe their liues are healthey, may not be exposed to danger and the towne to quiet, we supose your worships will judge the burden too heavie for this pore towne. and not countinance the Reputed father in such an vniust imposition, but to lay the charg vpon him who is soe able to beare it, and says it shall be *here* tho it cost him £100, or otherwise that the Countie may Contribut herin or that the honoured Countie Court would be pleased to free our towne of guilt in case either the mother or child sufer or pish. And soe crauing pardon for our boldnes herin we Rest yours in subiection to law and order.

1672 Oct 1. The Court hauing considered the Complaynt of Lanchaster selectmen referring to the Bastard Child of Silvanus negro, late serv^t to Deacon Wm Parks of Roxbery, and entertained by Edmund Parker of their Towne Contrary to their order & notice giuen them. notwithstanding the vnsutable prouision y^t he hath for the entertainm^t thereof as they informe, Do order that during the abode of ye said child in y^t place, the selectmen shall take care that it be prouided for in all respects as humanity and religion requires, and that the said Parker shall giue them bond with sufficient suretyes to the vallue of 100£ for to saue the Towne harmless & to pay all disbursments for the prouission of the said child, or otherwise the sd Parker shall return it to Roxbury, there to be prouided for according to the order of Boston Court.

LANCASTER this 13th 11mo: 1672
A bill of charges drawne vp by the townsmen in Reference to the bastard child of Elizabeth Parker.

1	The Cunstable and Ralph Houghton themselues and horses attending Charlestown Court where the child was fathered vpon Roxburie	0 : 11 : 0
2	Goodman Prescott going to Nonacoyecos for a warant to convey the child to Roxbury	0 : 1 : 0
3	Going downe to Roxburie to carry the child and its mother, 2 men and 3 horses	0 : 16 : 0
4	the Cunstable and goodman Prescott attending Cambridge Court by their order in Reference to making prouision for her child	0 : 16 : 0
5	to Jonathan Whetcombe for a horse to nonacoiacus	0 : 1 : 0
	tot	£2 — 5s

1673   1st of 2 mo.— LANKESTER
Wee doe present daniell James for living from vnder famely government.   Witnes   John More & John Prescot Senr
[Grand Jury presentments — Middlesex Court Files.]

To the Cunstable of Lanchaster.
In his majties name you are required to warne Edm: Parker & his sonne Abram to apeare at ye Court to be held at Charlstowne the 16th of this instant December to ansr for neglect of Gods Publ worship on ye Lds Dayes & for witnesses Jno Prescot Senr & Henr Kerly, Also Jon Addams to answer for lying & false dealing & for witness Jonathan Prescott & John Diuell & hereof you are to make a true returne vndr yor hand and not to faile
  dat 4 : 10 : 73   THO DANFORTH R

Edmund Parker and his son and the witnesses to his case wer warned to apeare at the Court acording to this warant. Jon Adams was absent and could not haue warning but the others were warned as aforsaid.
  8 : 10 : 73   By me   JONATHAN PRESCOTT *Cunstable.*

To the Honoured Countie Court at Charlstowne.
The humble Request of the townsmen of Lancaster in Reference to Edmund Parkers presentment sheweth that the witnesses namly John Prescott sen who is aged and infirme and not able to atend the court being

winter season, the grand jurie man did informe the said Parker that If he did not Reforme his not coming to meeting he must present him, but he did not Reforme neither hath bene at meeting, neuer since the last Court, he semeth to plead his pouertie and want of cloathes but in answer to that he hath land and catle sum what considerable and himselfe and his son able bodied for labor, and no after charge only his daughter and her bastard which he violently tooke in, contrarie to the towns order and much endeuors against the same which the honoured court is well aquainted with: in Reference to his son it is the greife of many in the towne, and the townsmen, that he hath had noe beter educacion: the towns men haue laboured with the said Parker to get his son some learning and to send him forth to publique catechising but all in vaine, but haue had many froward peevish expresions from him, soe that he hath wearied them out. They liue miserable vncomfortable liues both for food and cloath, and lodging. it is Reported that all the sleepe they haue is siting by the fire vpon a bloke, and all through his owne froward imprudent cariage. theirfore it is the humble Request of the townsmen that the honoured Court would be pleased to asist the townsmen in this bussiness either by sentance or counsell or what way soe euer may be most conducing to the poore mans welfair and his sons. And in soe doing the honoured Court will ingage the townsmen as in dutie bound euer to pray.

By order of the townsmen

LANCASTER 13: 10 mon: 1673. RALPH HOUGHTON *Clarke*

LANCASTER the 4th 2 mon: 1674

To the Honoured Countie Court siting at Cambridge the 7th of Aprill 1674.

The townsmen of Lancaster, In faithfullness to our neighbour Parkers soule and body both, doe count it their dutie to giue sum informacion to this honoured Court. it being soe that their indeuors at home hath bene fruitlese. And they wearied out with pevish, froward provoaking expressions, when they haue laboured to psuade him to put himselfe and family into a more comfortable way of liuing, for it is hard for the honoured Court to conceiue how vncomfortably the pore man liues both in Respect of food cloathing and lodging tho he hath land and catle considerable and a strong yong man to his son and noe other charge but what he hath needlesly and indiscreetly brought vpon himselfe in taking in his daughter and her bastard child forcibly against the towns order soe that through his owne indiscretion he hath brought a great burden vpon himselfe, If not vpon the towne, the towns men from time to time hath laboured with him in Reference to his son to gett him sum learning and to bring him vp to sum honest imployment acording as the law prouids or to sufer them to doe it, but nothing would prevaile with him. but as it is signified to the honoured Court by a presentment it is certainly knowne among vs that his son hath not beene at meeting at the worshipe of god this seuerall yeares only sum few sabothes about a yeare senc, And he himselfe hath not beene in the meeting house for sum considerable space of time which is to our greife, nor about the house in the time of publique worshipe saue sum few sabothes a late And what his Reson is wee know not, And his not coming into the house makes the case doubtfull to the witnesses as to take a posetiue oath that he doth not com. And herin your worships haue a true Relation of the case in Reference to our neighbour Parker. Crauing Pardon for our boldnes herin we shall not trouble the honoured Court any further at present.

  Subscribed by order of the townsmen   RALPH HOUGHTON

  1674 April 7th. Edmund Parker of Lanchaster appearing before the Court & being convicted of neglect of Gods worship in Publ on the Lords dayes both himselfe & family was admonished. And the Court do comend it to the care of the selectmen of y^t place dilligent to inspect his family and observe their manners for the future, and in case that they find not an amendment in those charges whereof he hath been now convicted they are then hereby ordered and impowered to dispose of his sonne to service where he may be better taught & governed, and in case that threw stubbornnes of father or sonne, they be obstructed herein, that then they informe ye Court or some of the magts thereof who will take order therein as the law directs.

  1674, Oct 6. The Comittee nominated Aprill 73 for laying out ye highway between Groton & Lanchaster are againe desired and impowered by this Court to attend ye same and Capt James Parker is to appoynt time & place for their meeting.

              [Middlesex Court Records.]

  This committee had taken action the year before, and the following report of their doings is found in "The Early Records of Groton," by the Honorable Samuel A. Green.

  Wedensday 4 of June 1673 fforasmuch as the countrey hye way as it was formerly layd out by Lankaster and groaten vpon seuerall yeares triall, proued to be very insufficient and very difucult to be made passable in regard it was for the most part lyeing in the Intervailes wheirin their are seuerall soft places and litle brookes vpon which bridges and other mater for making the same passable is apt to be raised and torne vp by floods and vpon experiance of the same Lancaster made aplication to groaten for Remouing of the said way to Run more vpon the vpland which was Readily atended and John Prescott seni= and Roger Sumner for Lancaster and sergent Parker and corperall Knop for groaten wer chuse committe by both to townes to lay out the said hye way as aforsaid which was atended the day aforsaid as followeth (viz) first within the bounds of groaten they toke their begining at their meeting house to the mille of Jonas Prescott by Matthias ffarnworths his house six Rods wide turning of out of the common mill way near twenty Rod aboue the mille and then it Runs 4 Rode wid through the land of the aforsaid Jonas Prescott acording as it is described by trees marked by the men aforesaid and from the said Jonas Prescotts land to penicooke Riuer in Lancaster through swan swamp 6 Rod wide as it is already marked out by the comitte aforsaid and from the way aforsaid butting upon Penicook near to the night pasture wading place, they tak the way as it is left in width through the Intervayle and ouer nashaway bridge and soe to the meeting house and as it is to be vnderstood that the way within lancaster bounds Runes neare the mideway betweene the brook medow and plumtrees medowes ouer a hill called Mahaneknits hill and soe along on the vpland to the pond path as it Runes near to the Still Riuer medow and Josiah Whits medow vntill it come to the Swan Swamp path as aforsaid and to the confirmation hereof the comitte aforesaid haue here vnto put their hands the day and year aboue said

            JOHN PRESCOTT
            ROGER SUMNER
            JAMES PARKER
            JAMES KNOP

1674. General Daniel Gookin says of the Nashaway Indians "These have been a great people in former times but of late years have been consumed by the Maquas wars and other ways; and are not above fifteen or sixteen families."

LANCASTER IN PHILIP'S WAR.

1675.   ffrom Nashowah Allies [*alias*] Lankester 16th : Augst 1675.

Honoured Sir

. . . . . last nightt aboutt seauen A Clocke we martched Into Nashowah wheare we are Att Presentt butt shall as soone as the Constable Hajth prest vs a dozen Horsses; Proseed for groatton & so to Chenceford; according to the ord^{rs} Major Willard gaue me yesterday Att Quoahbauge; . . . . . our Major hauejng A Seartayne Intelligence of a Considerable Party of Indians y^t haue gathered toogather a littell aboue Chensford which I hope wee shalbe vp with this Night or to Morrough at furthest & if it pleese God I come vp wth them god assisting me I wjll Cloosely ingadge wjth them, & god Spearing my life I shall as oppertunity gives leave Acquaintt yor honor off my Actjons; I Have wth me butt 60: Men at Present; . . . .

SAMUELL MOSLEY

The above is extracted from a letter of the noted Captain of dragoons to Governor Leverett, in Massachusetts archives LXVII, 239. Six days later, Sunday, August 22d, the Indians having warily avoided an encounter with the dragoons, and got in their rear, made a raid upon Lancaster. Gen. Daniel Gookin states that this bloody foray was headed by a one-eyed chief of the Nipmucks, named John Monoco, "who lived near Lancaster before the war began," and that he had twenty of Philip's men with him. Mrs. Rowlandson writes :

Those seven that were killed at Lancaster . . . . upon a sabbath day, and the one who was afterwards killed upon a week day, were slain and mangled in a most barbarous manner by one eyed John and Marlboroughs praying Indians, as the Indians told me.

The charge against the Christian Indians was maliciously untrue, as proven upon their trial. The scene of the murders was at the north end of the settlement, the house of the MacLouds being in the neighborhood of the North Village cemetery. The names of the slain were:

<blockquote>
George Bennet,   Mordecai MacLoud,
William Flagg,   Mrs. Lydia MacLoud,
Jacob Farrar, Jun.,   Hannah MacLoud, aged four
Joseph Wheeler,   years,
                      An infant MacLoud.
</blockquote>

Flagg was a soldier detailed for duty here, from Watertown. Wheeler was not a Lancaster man, but probably of Concord.

ffor the Honoured Countie Court siting at Cambridge.

I was desired by a poore widow whose husband was slaine by the Indians here and hath 5 small children left with her; by a law of the countrie shee should haue brought in an Inuentorie of her husbands estate, but such are the deficulties of the time, and alsoe the trouble of her litle children that shee could not posibly with any saftie com downe; her name is Lidia Benet, And alsoe a Scotsman Mordicai Mukload who alsoe was slaine and his wife and children, and his house and goods all burned: he hath a brother suruiuing, both of them had a desire to haue com downe with their Inuentories but both of them haue Catle in the woods, but know not whether the Indians haue killed them or not, and therefore they humbly desire the honoured Court not to looke vpon them as contemners of authoritie but giue them liberty vntill another Court and in soe doing, the honoured will ingage the widow and fatherless children as in dutie they are bound to pray for the honoured Court.

Lans 2 : 8ᵐ : 1675   Subscribed by RALPH HOUGHTON
                                      Clarke of the writs
[Middlesex Court Files.]

The bold incursion of one-eyed John was but the prelude to the fearful tragedy of February 10th. Of the plan for the destruction of Lancaster in all its details, even to the very day assigned for its accomplishment, the colonial authorities were fully advised; yet so far as any records show, with a neglect that seems criminally strange, they did almost nothing to ward off or meet the blow. Of the aboriginal possessors of Nashaway none, unless Sholan, better deserves to be honored among us than that Indian scout, whose courage, skill and fidelity should have saved the town from the massacre of 1676,—James Quanapaug, alias James Wiser, alias Quenepenett, or Quannapohit. This Christian Indian was so well known for his bravery, capacity and friendship for the English, that Philip had marked him for martyrdom, and given orders accordingly to some of his lieutenants. The governor of the Colony about the same date, commissioned him and a fellow Christian named Job Kattenanit, from Natick, for the dangerous venture of visiting the Indian camps to bring back information of the numbers and plans of Philip's forces. These two men, the historian William Hubbard tells us, "through the woods, in the depths of winter, when the ways were impassable for any other sort of people," sought the Nipnet outposts, and "ordered their business so prudently as that they were admitted into those Indian habitations as friends and had free liberty of discourse with them." They were closely watched, however, threatened, and but for a powerful friend would have been slain. In Quanapaug's own words :—

> Next morning I went to One-eyed John's wigmam. He said he was glad to see me :— I had been his friend many years & had helped him kill Mohaugs :— and said nobody should meddle with me. I told him what was said of me. He said if any body hurt me they should die . . . . I lay in the sagamores wigwam ; and he charged his gun, and threatened any man that should offer me hurt. . . . . And this Indian told me they would fall upon Lancaster, Groton, Marlborough, Sudbury and Medfield, and that the first thing they would do should be to cut down Lancaster bridge so to hinder their flight and assistance coming to them, and they intended to fall upon them in about twenty days time from Wednesday next. . . . .
>
> [James Quanapaug's Information.]

Quanapaug finding that he must soon meet Philip, and having effected the main purpose of his errand, evaded his suspicious foes by a cunning stratagem, and on the 24th,

11th mo., 1675, brought to his employers, the Governor and Council, full knowledge of the hostile forces and their fell intent. The emergency demanded speedy energy; it met inaction. Rumors of coming woe meantime stirred the air in the Nashaway valley. The chief military officer, the minister, and other leading citizens went to the Bay to awaken the Council from their lethargy and beg for help. It was too late. February 9th, 1675-6, about ten o'clock at night, Job Kattenanit, the second spy, completely exhausted, dragged himself to Major Gookin's door in Cambridge. He had deserted wife and children, and alone travelled upon snow shoes through the pathless wilderness from New Braintree, a terribly fatiguing march of eighty miles, to save his English friends. James Quanapaug had foretold that on the morrow the blow would be struck at Lancaster. Let Daniel Gookin tell Job's story, and the fulfillment of the prophecy.

He brought tidings that before he came from the enemy at Menemesse, a party of the Indians, about four hundred, were marched forth to attack and burn Lancaster, and on the morrow, which was February 10th they would attempt it. This time exactly suited with James his information before hinted, which was not then credited as it should have been; and consequently no so good means used to prevent it or at least to have lain in ambushments for the enemy. As soon as Major Gookin understood this tidings by Job, he rose out of his bed, and, advising with Mr Danforth one of the Council that lived near him, they despatched away post in the night to Marlborough Concord and Lancaster, ordering forces to surround Lancaster with all speed. The posts were at Marlborough by break of day and Captain Wadsworth with about forty soldiers marched away as speedily as he could possibly to Lancaster (which was ten miles distant). But before he got there the enemy had set fire on the bridge: But Capt Wadsworth got over and beat off the enemy, recovering a garrison house, that stood near another bridge, belonging to Cyprian Stevens, and so through God's favor prevented the enemy from cutting off the garrison, God strangely preserving that handful with Capt Wadsworth, for the enemy were numerous, about four hundred, and lay in ambushment for him on the common road, but his guides conducted him in a private way and so they got safe to Cyprian Stevens, his garrison as above mentioned. But the enemy had taken and burnt another garrison house very near the other only a bridge and a little ground parting them. This house burnt was the minister's house Mr Rolandson wherein were slain and taken captive about forty persons, the minister's wife and children amongst them.

[Daniel Gookin's History of the Praying Indians.]

The narrative of Mrs. Rowlandson, a sufferer in the tragedy, is a source of much of our knowledge of the horrors of that day. For two hundred years her little book has kept hold upon popular favor, and twenty or more editions testify the public appreciation of its simple eloquence. It need not be quoted here. Other briefer contemporary records of the massacre are:

1. William Hubbard's, in "A Narrative of the Indian Wars in New England," 1677.

About the 10th of February after, some hundreds of the Indians, whether Nipnets or Nashaway men is uncertain, belonging to him they call Sagamore Sam, and possibly some of the stoutest of the Narrhagansets that had escaped the winter brunt, fell upon Lancaster, a small village, of about fifty or sixty families, and did much mischief, burning most of the houses that were not garrisoned: And which is most sad and awful to consider, the house of Mr Rowlandson, minister of the said Lancaster, which was garrisoned with a competent number of the inhabitants; yet the fortifications of the house being on the back side closed up with fire wood, the Indians got so near as to fire a leanter, which burning the house immediately to the ground, all the persons therein were put to the hard choice, either to perish by the flames, with the house, or to yield themselves into the hands of those cruel savages, which last (considering that a living dog is better than a dead lion) they chose, and so were forty-two persons surprised by the Indians, above twenty of the women and children they carried away captive, a rueful spectacle to behold; the rest being men, they killed in the place, or reserved for further misery: And many that were not slain in fighting, were killed in attempting to escape. The minister himself was occasionally absent, to seek help from the Governor and Council to defend the place, who returning, was entertained with the tragical news of his wife and children surprised, and being carried away by the enemy, and his house turned into ashes. yet it pleased God so to uphold his heart, comforting himself in his God, as David at Ziklag, that he would always say, he believed he would see his wife and children again, which did in like manner soon come to pass within five or six months after; all, save the youngest, which being wounded at the first, died soon after among the Indians.

And such was the goodness of God to those poor captive women and children, that they found so much favor in the sight of their enemies, that they offered no wrong to any of their persons, save what they could not help, being in many wants themselves. Neither did they offer any uncivil carriage to any of the females, nor ever attempted the chastity of any of them, either being restrained of God, as was Abimeleck of old, or by some other accidental cause which withheld them from doing any wrong in that kind.

Upon the report of this disaster, Capt. Wadsworth, then at Marlborough, with about forty resolute men, adventuring the rescuing of the town that was remaining: And having recovered a bridge, they got over safe, though the planks were pulled off by the enemy, and being led up in a way not discovered by them, they forced the Indians for the present to quit the place, after they had burnt and destroyed the better half of it. Yet afterwards it not being judged tenable, it was abandoned to the pleasure of the insulting foe.

2. A letter written February 10th, 1675–6, by Thomas Hinkley, then in Boston, to his wife; printed in the appendix, page 436, to Nathaniel Morton's "New England's Memorial," edition of 1826.

Dear Heart:

Since my last inclosed which I broke up to signify to thee, not to expect my coming home this week, Job the other Indian spy, sent out as I have before said, is last night returned to Capt. Gookins & informs, that the Narragansets are got to the Quabaug Indians four hundred of them & three hundred of the others as I mentioned heretofore & informs that six of Eames his children, the owner of the house burnt at Sudbury of which before, are with the Indians, and the Indians intend marching this day three hundred of them to fall upon Lancaster alias Nashaway. Post was sent by Capt. Gookin and Mr Danforth last night, midnight for eighty troopers & forty foot thereabout & at Marlborough to hasten to Lancaster for their relief, but whether they came time enough is not yet known. A post came thence today to inform, a great many Indians were at Lancaster bridge: and the smoke of some houses fired there appeared to him as he came. The good Lord fit us for his pleasure.

3. A True Account of the most Considerable Occurences that have happened in the Warre between the English and the Indians in New England. London 1676.

. . . . . . the Enemy visited us, and assaulted Lancaster, a small Town, in which the Inhabitants, having retired into some fortified Houses and deserted the Rest, the Indians burnt those, and assaulted the Garrisoned Houses, but were not able to carry any of them but one. wherein were 42 Persons 12 men, the Rest Women and children of whom they slew several, and carried the Rest Prisoners: The House was the Ministers, one Mr Rowlandson, whose Wife and Children they carried Captive (which are since returned to us) . . . . . . on the 11th of May two of our Captives were returned by Ransom from the Indians who had been taken at the Destruction of the Town of Lancaster: the one of them the Sister of the Wife of Mr Rowlandson Minister of the Place: and another Woman taken out of the same House . . . . . . About the time of that Thanksgiving the Son and Daughter of that worthy Minister of Jesus Christ, Mr Rowlandson, who had been Captives since the Burning of Lancaster were returned by Ransom. She wandered with an Indian Woman from the Rest of the Indian Company (by whom she had been detained) three Days in the Woods, having Nothing to eat all that time but green Hurtleberries: with which she was sustained till she and the Woman arrived at our English Town of Providence, and so got Home.

4. News from New England being a True and last Account of the present Bloody Wars, &c. London 1676.

. . . . . . in a Town called Nashaway which they set Fire to, and burnt to the Ground, taking no less than 55 Persons into their Merciless Captivity. . . . . of these 55 Captives, the Minister of the Towns Relations made no less than 17 of them: viz, Mrs Rowlandson the Ministers Wife, and three of his Children, her Sister [*Elizabeth Kerley*] and seaven Children, and her Sister Drew [*Hannah Divoll*] and four Children. . . .

Another pamphlet published in London late in the same year, entitled "A new and further Narrative of the State of New England," copies its facts from the preceding.

A LIST OF THE CASUALTIES FEBY 10 167$\frac{5}{6}$. COMPILED FROM ALL KNOWN SOURCES OF INFORMATION.

Killed in Rowlandson Garrison.

Ensign John Divoll.
Josiah Divoll, son of John, aged 7.
Daniel Gains.
Abraham Joslin, aged 26.
John MacLoud.
Thomas Rowlandson, nephew of the minister, aged 19.

John Kettle, aged 36.
John Kettle, Jr.
Joseph Kettle, son of John, aged 10.
Mrs Elizabeth Kerley, wife of Lieut. Henry.
William Kerley, son of Lieut Henry, aged 17.
Joseph Kerley,   do.,   aged 7.
Mrs Priscilla Roper, wife of Ephraim.
Priscilla, child of Ephraim, aged 3.

                                                              14

Carried Captive from Rowlandson Garrison.

Mrs Mary Rowlandson, wife of the minister, ransomed.
Mary Rowlandson, daughter of the minister, aged 10, ransomed.
Sarah Rowlandson,   do.,   aged 6, wounded & died Feb 18.
Joseph Rowlandson, son of the minister, aged 13, ransomed.
Mrs Hannah Divoll, wife of Ensign John, ransomed.
John Divoll, son of Ensign John, aged 12, died captive?
William Divoll,   do.,   aged 4, ransomed.
Hannah Divoll, daughter of do, aged 9, died captive?
Mrs Ann Joslin, wife of Abraham, killed in captivity.
Beatrice Joslin, daughter of Abraham,   do.
Joseph Joslin, brother of Abraham, aged 16.
Henry Kerley, son of Lieut Henry, aged 18.
Hannah Kerley, daughter of do.,   aged 13.
Mary Kerley,   do.,   aged 10.
Martha Kerley,   do.,   aged 4.
A child Kerley, name & age unknown.
Mrs Elizabeth Kettle, wife of John, ransomed.
Sarah Kettle, daughter of John, aged 14 escaped.
Jonathan Kettle, son of John, aged 5.
A child Kettle, daughter do.   20
    Ephraim Roper alone escaped during the assault.   1
                                                                    35

Mrs. Rowlandson writes: "Of *thirty-seven* persons who were in this one house, none escaped either present death or a bitter captivity save only one." Most authorities are united, however, in stating the number of the garrison as 42. Seven persons are therefore unaccounted for in above list.

Killed outside of Rowlandson Garrison, being all of South Lancaster.

John Ball.
Mrs Elizabeth Ball, wife of John.
An infant child of John Ball.

Jonas Fairbank.
Joshua Fairbank, son of Jonas, aged 15.
Ephraim Sawyer, aged 26.
Henry Farrar.
Richard Wheeler.
A man mentioned by Mrs Rowlandson, but not named.   9

Captive.
Two of John Ball's family names unknown.   2
                                                         ––
                                                         11

The whole number of casualties being 55, nine remain not ascertained. A soldier from Watertown aged 20, named George Harrington, was killed near Prescott's Mills a few days after the massacre, and John Roper was killed the day the town was finally abandoned by all its inhabitants, March 26, 1676.

A special session of the General Court was called by Governor Leverett, Feb. 21, and among the orders passed were these:

> It is ordered, on request of Capt. Scyll, that the comittee for the warr doe forthw^th send twenty pounds of tobacco & three gallons of rume for the supply of the company that now resides at Lancaster.
>
> [Massachusetts Records.]

> 25th February   Mr Roulison not being disposed to accept of the motion of ye Court to goe out wth the forces as preacher, it is ordered, that Mr Samuel Nowell be intreated to goe vpon that service. . . . . .
>
> [Massachusetts Records.]

So great was the terror inspired throughout the Bay towns by the quick succeeding Indian raids of this period, that it was seriously proposed to abandon and fence out Lancaster, Groton and other outlying towns by a stockade eight feet high and twelve miles in length, from Watertown to Wamesit. [*Mass. Archives*, LXVIII, 174.] Three pounds per head bounty was voted by General Court for the killing or capturing of "sculking Indians," and the following is found, crossed, in Massachusetts Archives, LXIX, 43:

August 12 1676. The Councill doth hereby declare that if any person or persons Volunteers of this Colony shall bring in ye body of Philip sachem dead or alive they shall haue for y^r reward   50£
    & for Sam Sachem of Lanchaster   20£
    & for Jno [*Monoco*] of Lanchaster   10£

To the Honor^d Governor.
    The Information of Hugh Clarke Sheweth. That hee being the last weeke vpon the Scout wth Capt. Gibbs, through the woods about Lancaster, Concord, Sudbury &c, they found seuerall houses deserted, hauing corn in them & Cattle about them belonging to the late Inhabitants thereof who for feare left theire habitations, wee brought in about thirty ffive head of Cattle into Concord which wee founde, & left about 60 bushells of corn in one house: So that the Enemy haue a very great advantage, in recruiting themselues thereby wth provisions: and the English wilbee exceedingly straitned without some expedient bee founde out for prevention thereof: by drawing in the corn & cattle from the out ffarmes or otherwise as yor Hono^r shall thinke meete
    ffeby 23 1675 6

In another hand, in the margin opposite the statement about "60 bushells of corn," is written, "in Kettls farme"—"it is so in several others."

    Ordered by the Councill that the Secretary give forth warrants to the Constables of Concord & Sudbury requiring them forthwth to impresse 8 carts in each Town for the bringing down of the goods of such persons of Lancaster as being bereaved by the late hand of god are disenabled from continuing there wch carts shall be delivered to Ralph Houghton & Deacon Sumner of Lancaster to be imployed as above
    24 feb 1675. past p Councill E. R. S.
                                    [Massachusetts Archives, LXVIII, 142.]

To the Honer^d Gournor and Counsell
    The humble petition of the poor destressed people of Lancaster, humbley sheweth, that sence the enemy mad such sad & dismall hauocke amongst our deare ffreinds & Bretheren, & we that are left who haue our Liues for a prey sadly sencable of Gods Judgm^{ts} upon us, this with the destresse we are now in dus embolden us to present our humble Requests to yor Honors, hoping our Condisions may be considered by you & our Requests find exeptance with you, our stat is very deplorable, in our Incapasity to subsist, as to Remoue away we can not, the enemy has so Incompased us, otherwise for want of help our catle being the most of them caried away by the barberouss heathen, & to stay disinabled for want of food, the Towns people are Genrally gon who felt the Judgm^t but light,

& had theyr catle left them with theyr estats, but we many of us heare in this prison, haue not bread to last us on mongth & our other provision spent & gon, for the genrallyty, our Town is drawn into two Garisons wherin are by the Good favours of yor Hon^{rs} eighteen soulders, which we gladly mayntayn soe long as any thing lasts, & if yor Honors should call them of, we are seartaynly a bayt for the enemy if God do not wonderfully prevent, therefore we hop as God has mad you fathers ouer us so you will haue a fathers pitty to us & extend your care ouer us who are yor poor destressed subjects. We are sorowful to Leaue the place, but hoplesse to keep it unlesse mayntayned by the Cuntrey, it troubles our sperits to giue any Incuridgm^t to the enemy, or leaue any thing for them to promot their wicked designe, yet better saue our Liues then lose Life & Estat both, we are in danger emenent, the enemy leying Aboue us, nay on both sids of us, as dus playingly Apeare. our womens cris dus dayly Increase beand expresion which dus not only fill our ears but our hearts full of Greefe, which makes us humbly Request yor Hon^{rs} to send a Gard of men & that if you please so comand we may haue Carts About fourteen will Remoue the whool eight of which has been presed long at Sudburry but nevr came for want of a small gard of men, the whooll that is, all that are in the on Garison, Kept in Major Willards house, which is all from yor Hon^{rs} most humble servants & suplyants. JACOB FFARRAR

Lancast^r March 11th 16$\frac{75}{78}$

JOHN HOUGHTON Senr
JOHN MOORE
JOHN WHITTCOMB
JOB WHITTCOMB
JONATHAN WHITTCOMB
JOHN HOUGHTON Junr
CYPRIAN STEEVENS

The other on Garison are in the like destresse & soe humbley desire yor like pitty & ffatherly car, haueing widows & many ffatherlesse chilldren. the Numb^r of Carts to Carey away this garison is twenty Carts.

Yo^r Hon^{rs} Humble pettisioners.

JOHN PRESCOTT Senr
THO. SAWYER Senr
THO. SAWYER Junr
JONATHAN PRESCOTT
THO WILLDER
JOHN WILLDER
SARAH WHEELER wid
WIDOW FFARBANKS
JOHN RIGBY
NATHANIELL WILDER
JOHN ROOPER
WIDOW ROOPER

[Massachusetts Archives, LXVIII, 156.]

The whole is in the handwriting of Cyprian Steevens.

A short naratiue of what I haue atended vnto by the councill of late since I went to releiue Groatten the 21 : 1 : $\frac{75}{76}$. I went to Concord, & devided the troope committed vnto me from Esex & Northfolke, into three pt^s one to garde the carts, presed from Sudbury, one pt. for the carts presed from Concord, both to Lancaster, & one pt for the carts that went from Charlestowne & Wattertowne, that went volintiers or wear hiered, when I had sent them to ther seuerall placeses I came downe, beinge the 22 : 1 : 75^6 : & went to Concord the 25 : 1 : $\frac{75}{76}$ when I came ther, I inquiered how it was with Lancaster, the answer was they weare in distrese, I psently sent 40 horse theiyr to fetch away corne, & I went that night to Chellmsfoord to se how it was with them, they Complayned, Billerikye Bridge stood in great need of being fortified. I ordered that to be don, allso they told me, that the Indians made two great rafts of boords & rayles, that they had gott that laye at the other syd of the Riuers. I ordered, 20 soulldiers to go ouer & take them, & tourne them downe the Riuer or preserue them, as they se cause. the 27 of this Instant I went from Chellmsfoord to Concord agayne, when I came ther, the troopers that I sent to Lancaster last, had broght awaye all the people ther but had left about 50 bushells of wheat & Indian corne. Yesterdaye I sent 40 horses or mor to fetch it awaye, & came downe from Concord, this daye I expectt they will be at Concord. Some of the troope I relesed when this last worke was don, the other I left order to scout ahead vntill they heer frome me agayne. I thought it not meet to relese more, when we stand in need of men. my desier is to know what I shall do herin. Concord & Chellmsfoord looke euery daye to be fiered, & wold haue more men but know not how to keepe them nor paye them.

Your humbl servant

29 : 1 : 76.   SIMON WILLARD

The above letter has been printed in the "Willard Memoir," but in modern spelling. The original is in Massachusetts Archives, LXVIII, 186.

1676, April 25. Major Willard dyes at Charleston, buryed 27th

[Diary of Samuel Sewall, I, 12.]

1676. RANSOMING THE CAPTIVES.

Mr Rowlandson minister of Lancaster (a pious and good man) having his wife, children & several friends in Captivity among the enemy . . . . himself and several other ministers in his behalf had some time since petitioned the Council to use what means they could for the redemption of his wife &c. Which the Council consented to and in pursuance thereof ordered Major Gookin to endeavour to procure at Deer Island one or two Indians that for a reward might adventure to go with a message to the enemy to offer for the redemption of our captives, particularly Mrs Rowlandson. But although the Major went to the Island and did his utmost endeavours to procure an Indian to adventure upon this service at that time yet could not prevail with any; so the matter lay dormant a good space of time. But on the 23^d of March some friends advised Mr Rowlandson to make another petition to revive the former motion; which he did that day. The Council declared themselves ready to promote it and send a message if any could be procured. Major Gookin who stirred up Mr Rowlandson hereunto was informed that one of the Indians lately brought down from Concord named Tom Dublet alias Nepponet had some inclination to run that adventure; of which the Major informing the Council they ordered Capt Hinchman to treat and agree with him which he accordingly did and brought him up from Deer Island some few days after; and he was sent to Major Gookins at Cambridge, where he was according to the order of the Council, fitted and furnished for this enterprise; and had a letter from the Council to the enemy concerning the redemption of the Captives, and upon Monday April 3^d he was sent away from Cambridge upon his journey, and he did effect it with care and prudence and returned again upon the 12th of April with this answer in writing from the enemy.

[Daniel Gookin's History of the Praying Indians.]

Letter sent by Tom Dublett. For the Indian Sagamores & people that are in warre against us. Intelligence is come to us that you have some English, especially women and children in Captivity among you. We have therefore sent the messenger offering to redeem them either for payment in goods or wampum or by exchange of prisoners. We desire your answer by this our messenger what price you demand for every man woman and child, or if you will exchange for Indians. If you have any among you that can write your answer to this our message, we desire it in writing; and to that end have sent, paper pen and incke by the messenger. If you lett our messenger have free accesse to you, freedome of a safe returne, we are willing to doe the like by any messenger of yours, provided he come unarmed, and carry a white flag upon a staffe, visible to be seene, which we take as a flag of truce, and is used by civilized nations in time of warre, when any messengers are sent in a way of treaty, which we have done by our messenger. In testimony whereof I have set my hand & seal.

JOHN LEVERETT *Govr*

Boston 31 March 1676. Passed by the Council

EDWARD RAWSON *Secy*

[Massachusetts Records.]

Answer brought back April 12. We now giue answer by this one man, but if you like my answer send one more man besides this one Tom Nepanet, and send with all true heart and with all your mind by two men, because you know and we know your heart great sorrowful with crying for your lost many many hundred men and all your house and all your land,

and woman, child and cattle, as all your thing that you have lost and on your backside stand.

SAM <i>Sachem</i>
KUTQUEN <i>and</i>   PETER JETHRO
QUANOHIT <i>Sagamore</i>   <i>Scribe</i>

Mr Rowlandson, your wife and all your child is well but one dye, your sister is well and her 3 child. John Kettel your wife and all your child is all well, and all them prisoners taken at Nashua is all well.

Mr Rolandson se your louing Sister his hand C Hanah

And old Kettel wif his hand †

Brother Rowlandson, pray send thre pounds of Tobacco for me if you can, my louing husband pray send thre pound of tobacco for me.

This writing by your enemies
SAMUEL USKATTUHGUN <i>and</i>
GUNRASHIT. <i>two Indian Sagamores</i>

This letter is printed in S. G. Drakes' "Biography and History of the Indians of North America." The original has not been discovered.

Mr. Rowlandson had meantime interested Mr. John Hoar of Concord in his behalf, a man who had won to himself the entire confidence of the Indians, by deserving it. His friendly and brave interposition perhaps availed more towards the recovery of the captives than all the colony's power or the governor's diplomacy. Tom Dublett, alias Nepanet or Nepenomp, was again sent, and with him Peter Tatatiquinea, alias Conway, with a letter from the Council of which no copy is found. They brought back 27, 2mo 1676, a second reply from the chiefs, written by James Printer, an Indian who had passed sixteen years apprenticeship in Samuel Green's printing office in Cambridge. The original is in the Massachusetts Archives, Hutchinson Papers, II, 282.

ffor the Governor and the Council at Boston.

The Indians, Tom Nepennomp and Peter Tatatiqunea hath brought us letter from you about the English Captives, especially for Mrs Rolanson; the answer is I am sorrow that I haue don much wrong to you and yet I say the falte is lay upon you, for when we began quarel at first with Plimouth men I did not think that you should haue so much truble as now is: therefore I am willing to hear your desire about the Captives. Therefore we desire you to sent Mr Rolanson and goodman

Kettel: (for their wives) and these Indians Tom and Peter to redeem their wives, they shall come and goe very safely: Whereupon we ask Mrs Rolanson, how much your husband willing to giue for you she gaue an answer 20 pound in goodes but John Kittels wife could not till. and the rest captives may be spoken of hereafter.

In Massachusetts Archives, XXX, 201, is the Council's response.

To the Indian Sachems about Wachusets.

We receiued your letter by Tom and Peter, which doth not answer ours to you: neither is subscribed by the sachems nor hath it any date, which we know your scribe James Printer doth well understand should be. wee haue sent the s^d Tom & Peter againe to you expecting you will speedily by them giue us a plaine & direct answer to our last letter, and if you haue anything more to propound to us wee desire to haue it from you under your hands, by these our messengers, and you shall haue a speedy answer. Dated the 28th, April, 1676.

Mr. Hoar accompanied these messengers, bearing twenty pounds in money and goods raised by several Boston gentlemen for the ransom of Mrs. Rowlandson. May 2d, his purpose happily effected, Mr. Hoar with the two Nashobah messengers brought the redeemed captive from Wachusett to Lancaster, and the day following arrived in Boston. Monday, May 7, Tom Dublett was again on the path to Wachusett, accompanying Mr. Seth Perry, a messenger with written instructions for his own guidance and the following letter to the sachems:

These for the saggamores about Watchusets, Phillip, John, Sam, Washaken, Old Queen & Pomhom.

Wee received your letter by John Hoare, who went vp to yow wth the messengers, Tom & Peeter, being sent to yow from Mr Roulandson. Our expectations was, that yow would lett vs know vpon what condition yow would release to vs all the English captiues among yow. Our minde is not to make bargaine wth yow for one & one, but for altogether. Vnto this, which was our cheife buisnes, yow send vs no answer, which wee doe not take kindly, for this way spends much time. In your letter to vs yow say yow desire not to be hindred by our men in your planting, pmising not to doe damage to our tounes. This is a great matter, and therefore cannot be ended by letters, without speaking one wth another; we haue therefore sent to yow. once more, to lett yow know our minds wth all speed. If yow will send vs home all the English prisoners, it will be a great testimony of a true heart in yow to peace, which yow say yow are willing to haue; and then, if any of your sachems and Councellors will come to vs at Boston, or els to Concord or Sudbury, to meet with such cheife men as wee shall send, wee will speak wth yow about your desires, and with true heart deale wth yow. This way is the best way; therefore send speedily to vs, whither yow will accept it or no. If yow vnderstand not our full minde, Seth Perry, whom we now send wth this letter, will declare it more plainely. And wee doe hereby grant & promise, that all such as yow shall imploy in a treaty wth vs shall be safe & free to come & goe, on condition that our messengers also shallbe safe wth yow

  May the 5th, 1676.   By the Court EDWARD RAWSON, *Secret*
 [Massachusetts Records.]

A verbal message seems to have been returned appointing a meeting, and Jonathan Prescott was sent the following Thursday, with a letter of elaborate instructions for his own conduct, and the following:

To the Indian sachems. Yow know wee sent our messengers according to your desire, and wee very true heart, but yow no giue vs answer in writing, by our messengers, as yow promise; wee now send these our men, Peeter Gardiner & Jonathan Prescott, to know your minde, whether yow willing lett vs haue our weomen & children yow haue captives; and if yow haue any proposall to make to vs, wee willing to heare yow; and if yow come yourselues, wee send some of our sachems to treat yow at Concord, or some other place where best, and yow haue safe conduct; for wee very true heart, and yow tell your people so.

    By the Court   EDW: RAWSON *Secret*.
 [Massachusetts Records.]

The story of this meeting, and of colonial ingratitude to a faithful and brave copper-colored Christian, was told eight years later in a petition found in Massachusetts Archives, xxx, 279.

Aprill the second 1684. Wheras wee Peeter Gardner, Daniel Chamney, & Jonathan Prescot were Imployed By the Hono^red Council sometime in May or June 1777 [6] to goe vp among the enimy Indians that then quartered in the woods About Watchuset in order to procure the deliuery of Inglish captiues, Wee doe Certify that Thomas Dublet alius Nepanet was our interpreter & helper in that Affayre, And that hee had beene a jorney before that time to treat wth the enimy & had procured them to meet vs aboue twenty miles from ther quarters, for the sachems met vs betwene Concord & Groaten; and at that time old Goodman Morse of Waterton was deliuered to vs & brought home & haueing By order paid fower pounds for his redemption wch Thomas Nepanet had bargained for in his former jorney. And we further say y^t the said Tom Nepanet carried it faithfully in that matter & Deserues satisfaction for his Trauille & Aduenture in y^t dificult time & we vnderstand hee hath receiued no satisfaction for that seruice hitherto, therefore wee humble conceue the Hono^red Councill should consider him and order him to receue thirty or forty shillings for that Hazardoes seruice: And In testimony of the Truth of this certificate wee whose names are aboue exp^rssed haue herevnto sett o^r hands the day & yeare aboue written. To bee p^rsented to the Honble Gouernor & Councill of the Massachusetts Colony; by the pson concerned. JONATHAN PRESCOTT

[*Endorsed*] DANIEL CHAMNE

At a Council held at Boston the 8th May 1684 In Answer to the petition of Tho. Dublett Indian & in sattisfaction for his paynes & trauile about ye procurm^t of Goodman Morses freedom from ye Indians: tis ordered that ye Tresurer giue him two Coates.

past E. R. S.

Mr. Hoar, three pounds ten shillings of the Money ordered you from Mr John Hubbert Must be remitted into the hands of Jonathan Prescot to compleat Payment for Goodwife Divell to ye Indians.

Boston 13 Ap. 1676. JOSEPH DUDLEY
by order of the Councill

[Massachusetts Archives, C, 189.]

In a letter from Rev. Thomas Cobbet of Ipswich to Mather, called " New England's Deliverances," being No. 76 of the Mather Manuscripts in the Prince Library, is some information respecting the Lancaster captives not elsewhere to be found.

. . . . . . May the 12th Goodwife Diuens [*Divoll*] and Goodwife Ketle vpon ransom paid, came in to Concord, and vpon like ransom presently after John Moss of Groton and Lieftenant Carlers [*Kerley's*] daughter were set at liberty, and nine more without ransom . . . .
. . . . Mr Rowlinsons daughter was brought to Seaconke by a captiue squa, that got away from the Indians, and got home after Mr Rowlinsons son and his sister Diuens [*Divoll's*] daughter, vpon theyr ransoms paid, were brought to Major Waldrens. And about July 11th Goodwife Ketles elder daughter, about 17 y old, got away from the Indians to Marlborough bringing her little sister vpon her back almost starued . . . . .

In Massachusetts Archives, LXX, 125, a petition and accompanying papers add to our knowledge of this subject.

To the honored General Court now sitting at boston October ye 15th, 1684.
    the humbl petision of Onesiphoras page of Salsbury humbly Sheweth. That wheras about the Latter end of the Late warr with the Indians several captives wear brought in at Maj^r Waldrons & Mr Peter Coffens, among wch wear the Sons of Mr Rolenson & of the widow Divel: which 2 Captives your petisioner was sent to redeem, by the widow Wells of Salsbury who was sister to Mr Rolenson: & when yor petison^r came there the Ransom of Mr Rolenson's son was pay^d by the Gentlemen of the place, so yor petioner had only to do with the other (to witt) the widow divels son: for whose Ransom yor petioner gaue his bill of four pounds to Mr Coffen, & afterwards Mr Rolenson moued the Counsell about it who wear pleased to vndertake the paying of the sd four pound . . . . .

    Boston 21st May 1677. On the motion & Information of Mr Rowlison that Goodwife divall's son hath binn redeemed from his Captivity for which fower pounds was promissed by Left. Peter Coffyn & by his Agent demanded of the sayd Goodwife Divall; who hauing lost hir husband & three of her children: being very low & vnable to make payment, It is ordered that if the sayd fower pounds be not already ordered to be discharged It is now ordered that Left Peter Coffyn placing the sayd sume on the countreys Account and, It shall be allowed him. That this is a true Copie,
                          Attests   EDW^D RAWSON *Secrety*

By summer time the Sachems were pretty thoroughly humbled, as is shown by the following letters coming from Shoshanim, alias Sam, the chieftain of Nashaway, who had "insulted over the English, and said if the English would first begge Peace of him, he would let them have Peace, but that he would never ask it of them." These letters are printed in Samuel G. Drake's "Biography and history of the Indians of North America." It is not known where the originals are.

To all Englishmen and Indians, all of you hear Mr Waban Mr Eliott.
    July 6 1676. Mr John Leverett, my Lord, Mr Waban, and all the cheif men our Brethren Praying to God: We beseech you all to help us: my wife she is but one, but there be more Prisoners, which we pray you keep well: Mattamuck his wife we entreat you for her, and not onely that man, but it is the Request of two Sachems, Sam Sachem of Weshakum, and the Pakashoag Sachem. And that further you will consider about the making

Peace: We haue spoken to the people of Nashobah (viz Tom Dubler and Peter) that we would agree with you and make covenant of Peace with you. We haue been destroyed by your souldiers, but still we Remember it now to sit still: do you consider it again: we do earnestly entreat you, that it may be so by Jesus Christ. O let it be so: Amen Amen.

       MATTAMUCK his Mark N
       SAM SACHEM his Mark X
       SIMON POTTOQUAM *Scribe*
       UPPANIPPAQUUM his C
       PAKASHOKAG his Mark &

My Lord Mr Leveret at Boston, Mr Waban, Mr Eliott, Mr Gookin, and Council, hear yea. I went to Connecticot about the Captives, that I might bring them into your hands, and when we were almost there the English had destroyed those Indians. When I heard it I returned back again: then when I came home, we were also destroyed: After we were destroyed then Philip and Quanipun went away into their own Countrey againe: and I knew they were much afraid, because of our offer to joyn with the English, and therefore they went back into their own Countrey, and I know they will make no warre: therefore because when some English men came to us Philip and Quanipun sent to kill them: but I said if any kill them, Ill kill them.

                SAM SACHEM
 Written by SIMON BOSHOKUM *Scribe*

The Council replied — That treacherous persons who began the war and those that have been barberously bloody, must not expect to haue their lives spared, but others that have been drawn into the war, and acted only as souldiers submitting to be without arms & to live quietly & peaceably for the future shall haue their lives spared.

Finally, perhaps under some false promise, or hope that the pardon offered might be extended to them, or being worn out with privations, the sachems came in at Cocheco in September and gave themselves up. A letter of Thomas Cobbet to Increase Mather, in Massachusetts Archives, Hutchinson Papers, II, 288–9, has this mention of Monoco at that time.

 . . . . . . Ye blasphemous speeches of one eyed John vttered at Groton to Capt Parker in ye heareing of Diuerse: Boasting how many places he had Burned, & saying he would burne Concord, Watertown, Charlestowne &c Adding: And Me will doe, what me will: these were spread before ye Lord, & pleaded that he would plead that cause of his soueraignty

Against that wretch: wch he did in September 76, who when taken at ye Eastward . . . . . & standing bound ready to bee put aboard ye vessel prouided to send him & others to Boston, he suddainly fell a singing in his humbling posture: & being asked by one of ye souldiers who was there to guard y^m, why he sung: replied: me must sing or dye: ye souldier replying y^t if he were so Afraid, why did he come to ye English, he answered, y^t no man brought him thither but Englishmans god Alone brought him to that end: and was afterward executed at Boston. . . . . . .

1676 Sept 26. Tuesday Sagamore Sam & Daniel Goble is drawn in a cart upon bed cloaths to execution . . . . . One eyed John, Maliompe Sagamore of Quapaug, General at Lancaster & Jethro (the Father) walk to the gallows.

[Diary of Samuel Sewall, I, 22.]

The stern, even-handed justice of the judges is attested by this record. Daniel Goble, thus executed with the murderers of the women and children of Lancaster, was a soldier, the ringleader in an atrocious murder of Indian women and children, during the popular excitement succeeding the Indian massacres. The sad story touched Lancaster, in the person of one of its most promising young men, and must not be passed over here.

"Wee the Grand Jury for our Soueraigne Lord the King doe Present & Indict Nathaniell Wilder of Concord [*Lancaster*] in the County of Midlesex in New England for that he not hauing the feare of God before his eyes & being Instigated by the Divil wth other his Accomplises at or on the 7th of August last, at or neere to Hurtlebury hill, in the woods in the precincts of Concord or neere therevnto did murder & kill three Indian weomen & three Indian Children contrary to the peace of our Soueraigne Lord the King his Crowne & dignitye the law of God & of this Jurisdiction. The Jurors ffinds this beill and leue hime to ffurther triall.

RICHARD CALICOTT fforeman in the name off the rest off the Jurey.

[*Endorsed*] They finde a speciall vierdict. If being present & seing the fact done & concenting, it be murder then we find him gilty according to Inditement, if not not gilty.

To the keeper of the prison in Boston.

You are hereby in his majty^s name, required to take into yor safe custody the persons of Daniel Goble, Stephen Goble, Nathaniel Wilder & Daniel Hoare & them safely keepe, in order to their tryall for killing of seuerall Indians weomen & children wch they owned, and see that they be forth coming at the next court of Assistants, or whenever the authoritys shall giue further order, dated in Boston the 11th day of August 1676.

   By order of the Councill   · Edw^D Rawson *Secrety*
[Massachusetts Archives, xxx, 209, 211, 221.]

The four soldiers were convicted and sentenced to death.

11th Oct 1676. Upon the humble peticon of Daniel Hoare & Nathaniell Wilder, presented to this Court, acknouledging the justice of this Court, & begging pardon for their liues, the Court haue granted their petition, and accordingly doe remitt the sentence of death passed against them, and order, that they pay prison chardges and tenn pounds apeece money, halfe towards the charge of witnesses, to be payd to the Tresurer of the country. and the other halfe to Andrew Pittime, & Swagon, ye Indians prosecuting against them : on payment whereof they are dischardged.

            [Massachusetts Records.]

1676 Sept 6. In answer to the petition of Ralph Houghton of Lancaster it is ordered that the peticoner be payd for his disbursements mentioned in his petition by the executors of the late Tresurer . . . . his oune rate amounting to six pounds to the country being discompted.

            [Massachusetts Records.]

1676 Oct. 12. This Court being informed by certifficat vnder the hand of Capt. Daniell Hincksman, that when he was out in the service of the country at Lancaster, they had occasion to make vse of an oxe for a supply of the forces vnder his comand, which sajd oxe was vallued. by indifferent persons, at fiue pounds in country pay, on a motion made in behalfe of the ouno^r of the oxe John Houghton, it is ordered, that the Tresurer of the Country make payment to the sajd Houghton for the sajd oxe accordingly.

            [Massachusetts Records.]

1676 Oct 12. In answer to the petition of Lawrence Waters of Lancaster humbly desiring the favour of this court to order the payment of his accounts mentioned in his peticon of seven pounds fiueteen shillings & fower penc, or thereabouts, due him from the country, his rate of forty two shillings being deducted, the ballance may be pajd him, being aged & blind, &c, it is ordered that the Tresurer make payment to the peticoner the sume aboue mentioned, prouided that if it is belonging to the old Tresurer and not charged in his account, that he passe it to the new Tresurer.

            [Massachusetts Records.]

1677 Oct. 22. The Court on vejw of widdow Wheelers bill, of Lancas-

ter of disbursements, signed by the comittee for y* Country, doe order & grant her payment from the Tresurer of sixe pounds nine shillings & eight pence.
[Massachusetts Records.]

1678. November 23. Dyed Mr Joseph Rowlandson the worthy & faithful Pastor of Weathersfield about y* 47 year of his age. He dyed Suddenly & his death was much Lamented & there was great cause, espec. at this time wⁿ God is calling home his Embassaders apace besides others to pour of his Displeasure vpon y* Country.
[Bradstreet's Journal.]

Reverend Joseph Rowlandson had been called to Wethersfield, Connecticut, as colleague to the Reverend Gershom Bulkeley, in April, 1677. November 24, 1678, is usually given as the date of his death.

Among the Shattuck Manuscripts of the New England Historic, Genealogical Society is the report of a Committee dated Cambridge, 28 : 1^m. 1676, appointed to propose means for the security of the frontier towns. It was therein recommended :

That such townes as Lankester, groaten & marlborough that are forced to remoue ; and haue not some aduantage of settlement (peculiar) in y* bay, be ordered to settle at y* frontire townes that remain for their strengthening ; and y* people of y* said townes to which they are appointed are to see to their accomodations, in y* s^d townes.

Few of the Lancaster refugees but had relatives or friends in the lower towns, and in their banishment they became widely scattered. Most of them, however, longed to return to their dearly bought lands on the Nashaway, and those who had found temporary resting places in Sudbury and Concord may have visited the ashes of their homes from time to time. So soon as their savage enemies had been subjugated, they moved to the resettlement, and as at first, sturdy John Prescott led the van.

1679. *To the honored County Cor^t sitting at Cambridge October 7.* 1679

Ye humble petition of those whose names are here vnderwritten y* Inhabitants of Lancaster before o^r remouall from thence by reason of y* late warres, in o^r owne & others behalfe, y* pprietors of y* said place as followeth. Whereas there was an order made the Last hono^red generall Co^rt y^t places deserted should not be againe Inhabited, till the people first make application vnto the Gouno^r & Council, or to the County Co^rt w^thin whose Jurisdiction they be, for a cōmittee to order matters concerning ye place, as in the said Law is expressed, wee yor petitioners wth diuers others purposing (if ye Lord please) to returne to Lancaster from whence wee haue beene scattered, doe humbly request this Co^rt that they will be pleased to nominate & appoint an able & discreet Cōmittee for that end, who may wth all conuenient speed attend the said Buisnes that soe wee may pceed to settle the place wth comfort & encouragement & yor petitioners shall pray for the Lords gracious psence wth you in all yor Administraċons

[*Added in another hand.*]
And the persones which we vnder[writ] doe nomenat if this honered Court sc caus to aproue of them is Decon Ward of Marelborogh, leutenant haines of Sutbery and cornit Woodes of Concord.

JOHN PRESCOT Senior
JOHN MORE
THOMAS SAWYER Sener
JOHN RUGG
JOHN PRESCOTT Juner
JONATH PRESCOTT
THOMAS WILDER
THOMAS SAYER Juner
JOSIAH WHIET

[*Endorsement.*]
7:8:79. In answ^r to ye motion of ye within named subscribers, the Court do nomenate Capt. Prentice, Deacon Stone, & Corporall Wm Bond to be a Cōmittee to settle ye rebuilding of Lanchaster as the order of Court provides. Capt Prentice to appoynt ye time & place of meeting & all persons concerned accordingly to attend.

[Middlesex Court Files.]

The action of this Committee seems not to have been made matter of record. Lancaster had inhabitants and recorded births, in both 1679 and 1680.

1681. *To the Honoured generall Court now siting at Boston our Honoured Gouernor, deputie gouernor Assistants and deputies.*

The petition of the poore Inhabitants of Lancaster humbly Sheweth. That whereas your poore petitioners by the late Indian warr were much Ruined, our houses and other buildings and fences burned, and most of our substance wasted and som of our Children slaine and som caried into Captiuity by the enimy and som neuer Returned, and we with the Rest forced to fly for our liues and to leaue our places of liuing to seeke shelter in other townes where we could, And haue gone through many straits and dificulties vpon that acount, soe that few townes in the cuntrie haue sufered the like, And now through the good hand of god about 17 or 18 families haue againe Returned with a desire to build the plantation againe and through many dificulties, by Reson of our pouertie, are about building and fencing that soe they may provid bread for their families, and not be troublesom and burdensom to other townes which of nesesitie must haue bene If we had Continued where we were, and this yeare the honoured tresurer sent his warant for a Cuntrie Rate, And tho it be but a litle, yet to our greife we must say we are not able to pay it. Theirefore your poore petitioners humbly Craue this Honoured Court to Remit this Rate and grant an exemption from Cuntrie Rats for the future for som years, soe many as this Honoured Court may Judge meet. And in soe doing you will oblige your poore petitioners as in dutie we are bound for euer to pray for a blessing vpon all the Concerns of this Honoured Court.

This petition by a generall voice and voate of all the inhabitants was desired to be drawne subscribed and presented By me.

RALPH HOUGHTON

The magists Judge meet to grant ye petitioners exemption from Country Rates for this yeare & the next, their bretheren the deputyes hereto consenting.

EDWARD RAWSON *Secretary*

17th ffeb^r 1681. Consented to by the deputies
WILLIAM TORREY *Cleric*

[Massachusetts Archives, CXII, 330.]

1681 Dec 20, The Deposition of Tho: Wilder aged 37 years sworn, sayth that being with Jno Prescott Senr About six houers before he died he ye sd Jno: Prescott gaue to his eldest sonn Jno: Prescott his house lott with all belonging to ye same & ye two mills, corn mill & saw mill with ye land belonging therto & three scor Acors of land nere South medow & fourty Acors of land nere Wonchesix & a pece of entervile called Johns Jump & Bridge medow on both sids ye Brook. Cyprian Steevens Testifieth to all ye truth Above writen.

Sworn in Court. J. R c

[Middlesex Court Files.]

Upon ye 7th of April 1683 LANCASTER.

A Jury of Inquest was Caled to giue in their virdict concerning ye vntimely death of John Whitcomb, we whose names are vnderwriten doe by what we vnderstand by ye brother of ye deceased by name Jonathan Whitcomb and one more by name George huse who was standing on ye shore and saw how ye said John Whitcomb felle into ye water, do here vnanimously giue in our virdict thus. that ye sd John Whitcomb and Jonathan Whitcomb being bringing some hay ouer ye riuer vpon two canooes indeavoring to pull them ouer by a rope which was fastned to a bough at ye riuer side, but ye cannooes sinking ye said John Whitcomh falling into y^e

riuer was by a prouidence of god drownded in pennecuk riuer ye 7th of this instant Aprill.

JOHN MORE Senr	JOSEPH WATERS
THOMAS SAWYER Senr	JOHN BEAMAN
JOHN RUGG	JAMES SNOW
THOMAS SAWYER Junr	JAMES HOUGHTON
JOSIAH WHITE	JOHN HOUGHTON Junr
DANILL HUDSON	

John Moor Sen fforeman & the rest of the subscribers the Jury of Inquest vpon the vntimely death of John Whetcomb late of Lancaster appeared before me Pet: Bulkeley Assist, & made oath that the premises contain a true Acco of the cause of the death of sd Whetcomb according to their judgmt & conscience

June 18 1683   PET BULKELEY *Assist*
[Middlesex Court Files.]

LANCASTR May ye 28 1684. The Towne being mett together vpon adjornment of ye publique meeting. The towne made choyse of Josiah White and gave him order to gather in all ye Ratts Due from al y^t live out of towne to ye meeting house & ministry in this last years Ratts, this was Confirmed by a voat of ye towne

		money ss. d	lbs ss d	
Henry Kemball	to ye meetinge house —	00 - 03 - 03 &	1 - 06 - 04	in pay
Thomas Swift	to ye meetinge house —	00 - 01 - 04 &	0 - 11 - 00	
Stephen Waters	to ye meetinge house —	00 - 00 - 10 &	0 - 06 - 08.	
				ministers
Edmond parker	to ye meetinge house —	00 - 01 - 03 &	0 - 10 - 04.	0-11- 0
Archelos Corser	to ye meetinge house —	00 - 00 - 04 &	0 - 03 - 08	0- 8- 4
Daniell gains	to ye meetinge house —	00 - 00 - 08 &	0 - 05 - 04	0- 8 0
Simon & Thomas gatts	———	00 - 03 - 03 &	1 - 06 - 00	
Adm^r Major Willard	———	00 - 05 - 02 &	2 - 01 - 04	
Mr Robinson	———	00 - 01 - 01 &	0 - 08 - 04	
for William Lewese	———	00 - 03 - 03 &	1 - 06 - 04	0-16- 0
John Lewes	———	00 - 00 - 08 &	0 - 05 - 01	0-16- 0
Christopher Lewes	———	00 - 00 - 06 &	0 - 04 - 00	
for Mordeca Mukload	———	00 - 00 . 08 &	0 - 05 - 04	0- 5- 6
for John Divole	———	00 - 01 - 00 &	0 - 08 - 04	
Thomas hares	———	00 - 00 - 08 &	0 - 05 - 00	0-10- 0
Jeremiah Rogers	———	00 - 02 - 11 &	1 - 03 - 04	0-19-10
Jonas fairbank	———	00 - 02 - 02 &	1 - 17 - 04	
George Adams	———	00 - 00 - 08 &	0 - 05 - 00	
for ben allin	———	00 - 00 - 05 &	0 - 03 - 08	0- 4- 6
Lauranc Waters	———	00 - 02 - 07 &	1 - 0 - 10	1-17- 0

     By order of ye Towne.   JOHN HOUGHTON

To the Honoᵇˡᵉ Generall Court assembled in Boston the 10ᵗʰ *Septembr.* 1684.

Josiah White, in behalfe of the Town of Lancaster, now vpon a re-setlement, humbly Prayeth this Honoᵇˡᵉ Courts order (if it may seeme good,) for the confirmation and strengthening of the vote passed by the Town as aboue written, That all those who are Proprietors of Lands lying within sd Town although not dwellers there, may be assessed in proportion to yᵉ value of their Estates as the Inhabitants are, towards the erecting of a meeting house, maintenance of a minister & other publique charges, the rate for this yeare being made as aboue: And that you please to order the levying of the same.

The magists haue voted that In answer to the Request of the present Inhabitants resident at Lancaster, this court doth order that all psons or their heirs executors or administrators that are propriters of lands there being grants of that towne, shall pay their proportion to a town Rate, for erecting a meeting house, & mainteynance of A minster in yᵗ towne according as other, the inhabitants yᵗ are pʳsent ther do pay for the same sort of lands.

The magists haue past this their Brethren the deputyes hereto consenting 15 September 1684.   EDWARD RAWSON *Secretary*

Consented hereto by yᵉ Deputies, prouided that all persons & estates, be assessed by a due proportion to said Rates
                                      L HAMMOND *p order*.
[Massachusetts Archives, CXII, 366.]

We must rely upon so late an authority as Reverend Timothy Harrington for the information that, "after the resettlement, divers gentlemen for the space of seven years supplied the pulpit." He names in a note "Mr. Carter, Mr. Wooddroffe, and Mr. Oakes." The last was perhaps Edward Oakes who was graduated at Harvard college in 1679. William Woodrop was a non-conformist deprived of his benefice in England, A. D. 1662. Samuel Carter, graduate at Harvard, 1660, was the son of Reverend Thomas Carter of Woburn, and a teacher there. He married Eunice Brooks in 1672. In 1688 Henry Kerley deeds his lands on George Hill to him, but he may have been resident here at an earlier day. In 1692 he was settled in Groton, and died there in 1693, aged fifty-three, leaving four sons and three daughters, whose numerous descendants figure prominently in the town's history.

1684. Henry Kerly, heretofore leiftenñnt at Lancaster, now remooved, & marrjed at Marlborow, is appointed ensigne to the trajne band there in ye roome of his brother, deceased there.

[Massachusetts Records.]

1688. Josiah Whetcomb is allowed 20 shillings to be paid by the County for killing one growne wolfe in ye Towne of Lancaster.

Nathaniel Wilder is allowed forty shillings to be paid by the County for killing two growne wolves in the Towne of Lancaster.

John Womsquam Indian is allowed ten shillings to be paid by the County for killing one growne wolfe in the Towne of Lancaster.

[Middlesex Records. Court of Sessions.]

A law of 1653 established a bounty of 30 shillings for each wolf killed by a white man, 20 shillings if killed by an Indian; the county treasury refunding 10 shillings of this amount to the town in either case. For one hundred years this law was little modified except by an increase in bounty, though after 1718 the Indian hunter was placed on an equality with the Englishman. For whelps and cubs the premium was commonly half that paid for full grown beasts. The head of the animal whether wolf, wild cat, catamount, or bear, had to be brought to the local constable, who cut off the ears and buried them to guard against fraud.

LANCASTER DURING KING WILLIAM'S WAR. 1689-1697.

The deep scars left by Philip's war had not disappeared before the outlying towns of New England were again menaced with the horrors of savage warfare. Among the New York colonial Manuscripts is a letter from Capt. Francis Nicholson, of which the following is an extract:

BOSTON August the 31st 1688.

. . . . . Soe next day I went through Groton and Lancaster where the people were very much afraid (being out towns) butt I told them as I did other places that they should nott be soe much cast down, for that they had the happinesse of being subjects of a victorious King who could protect them from all their enemies. . . .

LANCAST^R ye 3^d of July: 1689.

Whereas we ye Inhabitants of sd Lancaster being under som fears of being surprised by ye Indians we being by foremer experience sencsible of theire mallice and crueltie: and being at present destitute of any officers in power to order ye millitary afairs of ye towne they doe mutually Nominate Mr Thomas Wilder for a Leauten^t and sergeant John Moore to be ensigne and doe hereby adress our selues to our hon^{r}ed Councill for allowance and confirmation of ye same.

By order of ye Towne   JOHN HOUGHTON *Cler*

The above nomination of officers are allowed in their Respective offices by the Representatives   July: 5: 1689
Attest   EBENEZER PROUT *Clerk*
Consented to by the Governor and Councill.
I^{SA} ADDINGTON *Secry*
[Massachusetts Archives, CVII, 171.]

1689 3^d July. An Order was despatcht to Cap^{ne} Tho Prentes rallying his Troop this day at Cambridge to send out two partys of twenty each out of his Troop well appointed wth armes and Amunition, one party for

Dunstable and ye other for Lancaster for the Reliefe and succor of those places, to scout about the heads of those Towns and other places adjacent to discover and observe the Enemys motion, and to take surprise or destroy them as they may have opportunity.

[Massachusetts Archives, LXXXI.]

LANCASTER May 6 1689.

The Inhabitance of sd Lancaster meeting together according to advice from ye hon^{r}ed Councill giuen at Boston May 2^d 1689 doe accordingly chuse & impowre Mr Ralph Houghton to serue with ye Councill on ye Townes behalfe as occasion shall Require, which was confirmed by a voate of ye Towne:

as attests   JOHN HOUGHTON *Towne Cler*

2dly The Townes desire and expectation is that our hon^{r}d Gou^r and Assistants that were ellected by the fre men of this colloney, in May 1686 or so many of them as by ye said hon^{r}d gou^r and Company shall be Judged meete to gether with the Deputies that shall be sent downe from ye seuerall Respectiue Townes shall Reassume and exercise ye gouernment as a gen^{r}ll Court according to our Charter for the yeare Insuing or untill that orders from his highnes ye Prince of Orange appeare for the setlement of ou^r affaires, which was declared by a voate of the Towne:

as attests   JOHN HOUGHTON *Town Cler*

[Massachusetts Archives, CVII, 15.]

Wednesday, Dec. 3, 1690.

A church is gathered & Mr John Whiting ordained Minister at Lancaster. Mr Sam Whiting gives him his Charge, Mr Estabrooks gives the Right hand of Fellowship: Mr Brinsmead and others there.

[Diary of Samuel Sewall, I. 337.]

John Whiting was the second son of Reverend Samuel Whiting, minister of Billerica for fifty-five years. He was, when ordained here, twenty-six years of age, having been graduated at Harvard college in 1685. His wife was Alice Cook of Cambridge. Timothy Whiting, the head of the family that came to Lancaster from Billerica nearly a century later, was the direct descendant of Oliver, the brother of Reverend John Whiting. According to Reverend Timothy Harrington, "In Feb., 1688, Mr. John Whiting was invited to preach on probation." Joseph Willard, Esq., from some original source not now accessible, quotes the additional information that at the same date the town voted to build a parsonage to be paid for:

one eighth in money; the rest, one half in work, and one half in corn, viz. Indian, one third, and English two thirds, at country price, or other merchantable pay . . . . At a town meeting Jan. 3, 1690, agreed to make conveyance to Mr Whiting of the house and land formerly granted by the town. And the town the same time went out of the house, and gave Mr John Whiting possession thereof in behalfe of the whole above written, formerly granted by the town.

[History of Lancaster, 63.]

April 7, 1692, Jonathan Prescott of Concord conveyed a piece of intervale land "on ye west side of North River near to ye bridge in ye County Road" (Atherton's) to the town, acknowledging this consideration :

Promoting the ministrie of the Gospel in ye Town of Lancaster, Desiring & Endevoring the settlement of Mr John Whiting Pastor There by Enlarging His accomodations There in s^d Lancaster, & 5£ p^d by John More Senr Thomas Wilder & John Houghton in ye name of Inhabitants of Lancaster.

[Middlesex Registry.]

1690. Lancaster was represented among the sufferers in Sir William Phips' mismanaged and disastrous expedition against Canada. Endorsed on a list of Phips' captains, in Massachusetts Archives, XXXVI, 134, is "Lt. Willard of Lanchaster" [Benjamin], and the names of five soldiers are known from a petition of their heirs, in 1738, for land grants, viz :

Joseph Atherton, John Pope,
Jonathan Fairbank, Samuel Wheeler,
Timothy Wheelock.

1690. *To the Honrd Lift Gourn^r & Counsell of Massachutts Province New England, Grace Mercy & peace be multiplied to ye worthy Gentlmⁿ of ye Assembley.*

The humble Petition of Cyprian Steevens humbly sheweth that being Constable in year 1690|1 that yeare sevrall psons moued some to Canady & to other parts & no estate to be found, my Humble Request is that yor Hon^s will Consider yor Petitin^r that he may not pay out of his own Estate, for that wch was other men's dues. Yor Petitin^r also Relating to his office that yeare has been a great suffrer, haueing two Ratts to colect namely tweenty Ratts wch was Graine, & two & a halfe money, the scarcity of y^e on & not haueing the other, ye Loss in a great meashur became ye Constabl^s, now yor petition^r humbley Craues yor Hon^rs favour that you will please to Graunt him a clearence from Mr Tayler Treasur^r so shall he be oblidged to pray for yor Hon^rs peace & prsprty

               Yo^r supleant serv^t   CYPRIAN STEEVENS

                          LANCASTER June 4th, 1695.

A List of ye names of those p^rsons that moued from ye Town of Lancaster of wch sum are Dead, in ye yeare 1690.

Also ye Loss of 16 wolues by a mistake of Major Phillipses Clarke

Emp^r Joseph Watters,	18	"	Cyprian Steevens	7 - 3
Cyprian Steevens	17	"	Willm Huttson	4 - 3
	1	15	"	Sam^ll Wheeler	4 - 1
			Benjamin Willard	4 - 4
			Joseph Watters	6 - 6
			Nath^ll Harwood	3 - 10
			Sam^ll Sumner	5 - 4
			Arthur Tooker	4 -

  A true Acount as Atests   1 ,, 19 ,, 7
              CYPRIAN STEEVENS
                                 Constable for Lancaster

We whose names are vnder written do Atest to y^e mouall or death of y^e p^rsons Aboue written & wer in sd Constables Rates in y^e yeare 1690

           JOHN MOORE Senr   } *Selectmen for y_e Town*
           JOSIAH WHITT Senr   }
           JOHN MOORE Junr   }   *of Lancaster*

June 8th 1695 Read in the house of Representatives.

[*Endorsed.*] June 8th : 1695. The Selectmen of the town of Lancaster haueing sent under their hands to excuse the Constable, severall being dead & Remooved that the Rate was laid on Voted—that it is due from the Towne and that the Selectmen Assess the said Town for said Summ
                                    W^M BOND *Speaker*

  [Massachusetts Archives, CI, 33.]

1691. Simon Davis & Ensign Humphrey Barrett of Concord, John Howton & Nath^ll Wilder of Lancaster & Boaz Brown & Thomas Williams of Stow, are by this Court appointed a Comittee to lay out a convenienhigh way from Concord according to Law, for theire direction in the matter, and to make theire report to ye next Inferior Court for ye County of Midd^x.

                                  [Middlesex Court Records.]

George Nube being called into Court to Answer for horrid wickedness and profaneness laid to his charge he appearing & ye witnesses sworn ye case was committed to ye Grand Jury.

George Nube of Lancaster being Indicted by Grand Jury for high handed contempt of God's Word, Reproaches of ye ministers & calling them liars Drunkards and Whoremasters, and for a practice of high handed Debauching as by his own confession & profane neglect of Gods Publick worship on ye Lords daies, & Appearing before ye Court to make answer thereto dos stand Legally Convicted thereof: Is sentenced to be severely whipt on his naked body twenty stripes & to give bond in 20£ for his good abearance & appearance ye next Court to be held for their Majties in Cambridge & to stand committed till this sentence be performed & to pay costs.

The documents in the case of Lancaster *vs.* George Newby are quite voluminous, including two piously penitent petitions of the culprit, praying to escape the whipping post. Much of the evidence is unfit for print. The accusation of the town fathers was as follows:

The Declaration of Jno Moore Senr, Against George Newby Humbly Sheweth to this Honer^d Court, this sd Newby since he came to ou^r Town, he has endeavrd to Pervert all thats Good and has been a Leader to all maner of evill, Paying nothing to church nor state, Greatly wronging most men that Deale with him, but that wch I most would signifie to yor Hon^{rs} is sd Newbys most profainly spaking & sliting of that most worthy Peice of worke the Asembly of divines, even the Catechism, sliting the holy Bible & the Embasingers of Jesus Christ, saying that they were Drunkerds, Lyers, & whorem^sters, with many other Gross Villineys which Inlarges my heart to Pettition yor Hon^{rs} as you are our ffathers & soe wayting on you for support, that such a felow may be Removed from us Under which Protection & Blessing our Little Israel here in Lancaster may be Ingaged to pray for yor Hon^{rs} peace & pr^sperity from your Humble servt.
[Middlesex Court Files.]

1692. The following letter from Maj. Thomas Hinchman, at the time in command of all forces in this part of the Province, gives a clear view of the unhappy condition of Lancaster and her sister towns; daily expecting invasion by savage enemies and almost powerless for defence against them, yet forbidden by a special act of legislature from removing. The document is in Massachusetts Archives, XXXVII, 340:

May it pleas your Honors.
    Yo^r advice of the 14th Instant of ye probable Advancing of ye Enemy west^{wd} I haue Received & Render humble thanks for the same. Yo^r con-

cernednes for y⁰ security of these parts Intimated will quicken vs to
speciall vigilancy & also Incorages mee earnestly to pray yᵗ sould^rs to y⁰
numb^r of at least 60 may, (if yor Hono^rs see meete) be speedily sent vp,
for without such a supply of men I cannot conceive how wee can be defended in case of an Attack by y⁰ enemy : our men must work this suñer or
starve in winter, & y^r hard labour in y⁰ day renders ym verry vnfit to watch
every 3 or 4 nights as many must do if they go to Garrison, & if they stay at
y^r house they must expose to be made a sacrifice : I Hope y⁰ Hon^rd Councill
will consider yᵗ whereas y^r are but 10 small towns in my Regiment 6 of y^m
are frontiers & as for Sherbon I can procure no men frō y^r, my ord^rs will
not be obey^d, becaus y^r is no militia setled, Among y^m, & no settlement or
directions how I may procure sould^rs frō y⁰ seuerall Towns, & also prov.
[*provisions*.] I hope y⁰ Councill will also remember yᵗ seuerall sould^rs in
this Regmt are sent Eastw^d. O^r people groan vnder y⁰ Burden they ly
vnder for want of sould^rs frō y⁰ Bay parts, & y^rs. I Intreat o^r case may be
Considered as yor wisdom shall direct & Compassion to vs shall Incline
you. All y⁰ Inhabitants of dunstable excepting 2 familys desire to draw
off, viz Jno Sollendine & Thos Luñ whose Garrisons are nere to each
other, these seem wiling to —— themselves with 10 or 12 sould^rs. I desier
an ord^r to Capt. Parker for sum shott who hath a Quantity of y⁰ Countrys
stock in his hand. I am advised yᵗ Lancaster hunters haue lately seen a
cōpany of Indians near Wachusett y⁰ number of yᵗ is reported to be
about 300. yy report themselves to be Albanians, Senecas Maquas wth y⁰
western or Connecticut Indians. This vnusual Confluence of so many
Indians makes many to suspect & fear a design agst vs. I doubt not but
y⁰. Councill will satisfy themselves about it. The sould^rs yᵗ I Desier will
be needed in Chelmsford, Groton & Lancaster. Thus H^d Gentlemen I
haue been bold to craue at yor hands w^thout y⁰ least Intention to dictate
to my superiors but humbly to submit all to yor pleasure, & craue pdon of
my simplicity & plainnes. I am not capable at present of a personall
waiting vpō you, otherwise I could more pticularly spread before you o^r
nakedness & y⁰ extream danger of destruction yᵗ wee are in if not better
defended then at present wee are.

         I am y^r Hon^rs Humble Servtt
Chelmsford, 12 April, 1692.   Tho Hinchman

Of the murder of the Joslin family by Indians, July 18, 1692, no contemporary mention is discovered. The victims were :

Killed.

Mrs. Hannah Whitcomb, widow of Jonathan.
Mrs. Sarah Joslin, wife of Peter.
Three young children of Peter Joslin.

Captive.

Elizabeth Howe, sister of Mrs. Joslin.
Peter, son of Peter Joslin, aged 6 years; killed shortly after.

April 17, 1701, a resolve was passed in General Court allowing three pounds eighteen shillings to Mr. Thomas Howe, " he haveing Paid so much for the Redemption of Elizabeth Howe who was Captive to the Indians." She returned from Canada in 1696, being then about twenty years of age, and married Thomas Keyes Dec. 23, 1698.

1694. *To his Excelency y^e Gou^r Sr Will$_m$ Phipps Kn^t &c the Honrd Councill & Representatives conveaned at Boston : ffeb : 14th: 1693 4.*

The Humble Petition of Jno Houghton in behalfe of the Inhabitants of y^e Towne of Lancast^r: Humbly Sheweth, That wheras y^e sd Inhabitants of Lancaster haue both formerly and of late been exposed to very great troubles & charges by Reason of ye Long continued war with ye Indians: seuerall persons being killed by them & others haueing Lost great part of theire estate by them: & also by being so long Nessessitated to liue in Garison where neither men nor women can doe but very litle towards ye supply of theire familyes; theire being so mutch time spent in watching warding & many allarrums that haue been amongst us & that which is more ye dayly feares we were exposed to in ye Dangers which atended us in our labours, being for so long a time constrained to get our bread with ye perill of our liues: wherby many are brought to extreame poverty, not knowing how to get either food or cloathing for themselues or famillys: also ye great charge expended in building Repairing & maintaining so many Garissons: eight of which being allowed by order: ye charge of sd Garissons being very considerable: also in ye midest of theese troubles we haue beene at great charges in ye setlement of our towne: it being wholly Destroyed ye last warr: & and yet we are in great feares notwithstanding ye present peace we being so few in number & so unable to defend ourselues.

You^r Peti^{rs} Humble Request to yor Hon^{rs} is that you would consider the prmisses & Relieue sd Inhabitants by Granting them som considerable allowance for ye charges expended in ye building & Repaireing sd Garissons, acording as you^r Hon^{rs} in wisdom and Justice shall see meet & heerby your Pet^r together with ye Rest of the Inhabitants of sd Lancaster shall be the beter Incouraged to conflict with ye many Diffucaltyes we are Incident to & farther oblidged as in Duty bound euer to pray: &c:

          JNO HOUGHTON in behalfe
March 3^d, 1693|4   of the Inhabitants of Lancast^r

In answer to the aboue Petition & for the incouragment of the Inhabitants of Lancast^r, referring to their great charge in fortifiing themselues in this Troublesome time the house of representatiues do vote that the said Town be allowed them Twenty pounds out of ye next assesment & sent up to his ex^{lly} ye Gouer^r & Councill for theire Concurrance & Consent.

NATH: BYFIELD *Speaker.*

Oct^{br} 20th 1694. Vot^d a Concurrance by the Council.

IS^A ADDINGTON *Secret.*

[Massachusetts Archives, C, 466.]

1695. On a certain Sabbath of this year, the date of which is not on record, Abraham Wheeler, when on his way from the garrison to his own house, was mortally wounded by an Indian lying in wait for him. It has been stated that Wheeler lived upon Wataquadock. This location of his home is proved an error by these items in the inventory of his estate, presented in Middlesex Court, Nov. 6, 1695, by his widow Tabitha :

To House Lott 12 acres & houseing upon it.
To three acres of Intervale swamp *at ye Riuer by ye house.*

[Middlesex Probate Files.]

1697. 12th May. Hañah Dustan came to see us. . . . She saith her Master, whom she killd, did formerly live with Mr Roulandson at Lancaster.

[Diary of Samuel Sewall, I, 453.]

Sabbath Septr 12. We hear of the slaughter made at Lancaster yesterday.

Septr 13. At Roxbury Mr Danforth tells me that Mr. Whiting, the Minister, was dead and buried : Indians shot and scalped him about noon.

[Diary of Samuel Sewall, I, 459.]

May, 1697. In the latter end of this month a woman the wife of Lieftenant Willder distrode her self in a fit of mellancholly. She was in her Life time esteemed a truly pious woman By them y^t knew her.

Sept. 1697. On the Saturday following the Indians did a great deall of mischief at Lancaster, they beset the towne about noon. Burned 10 houses, killed and captivated about 20 persons of which the chief was the Reverend John Whiting pastor of ye church of Christ there.

[John Marshall's Diary in possession of the Massachusetts Historical Society.]

On September 11 a party of the enemy came upon the town of Lancaster then prepared for mischief by a wonderful security, and they did no little mischief unto it. Near twenty were killed and among the rest Mr John Whiting the pastor of the church there. Five were carried captives, two or three houses were burnt and several old people in them. Capt. Brown with fifty men pursued them till the night stopped the pursuit, but it seems a strange dog or two unknown to the company did by their barking alarum the enemy to rise in the night, and strip and scalp an English captive woman and fly so far into the woods that after two days bootless labour our men returned.

[Cotton Mather's Magualia, II, 639.]

In Massachusetts Archives, II, 257, is a letter from Governor William Stoughton to the Governor and Council of Connecticut, from which this is an extract:

BOSTON Sept. 14, 1697.

. . . . Upon ye 11th instant a party of Indians to ye number of about Forty as was judged, about twelve o clock the same day, Surprized and kild about 26 persons at Lancaster, of which the minister of the Town was one, burnt two Garrison houses and two Barnes, the Garrisons being left open and ye Inhabitants surprized in their Fields: there is a party of men out in pursuit of ye Enemy. . . . .

A LIST OF CASUALTIES SEPTEMBER 11, 1697.

Killed.

Reverend John Whiting, aged 33.
Daniel Hudson.
Mrs. Joanna Hudson, wife of Daniel.
Two children of Nathaniel Hudson, grandchildren of Daniel.
John Scate, *Skait* or *Skeath*.
Mrs. Scate, wife of John
Mrs. Hannah Rugg, widow of John, and daughter of John Prescott.
Joseph Rugg, son of Hannah, aged 29.
Mrs. Rugg, wife of Joseph.
Three children of Joseph.
Jonathan Fairbank, aged 31.
Grace Fairbank, daughter of Jonathan.
Jonas Fairbank, son of Jonathan.
Ephraim Roper.
Mrs. Hannah Roper, second wife of Ephraim.
Elizabeth Roper, daughter of Ephraim, aged 14.

Captives.

Joanna, daughter of Daniel Hudson, aged 37.   Killed (?) in captivity.
Elizabeth, daughter of Daniel Hudson, aged 39.   do.
Mrs. Mary Fairbank, wife of Jonathan, returned January, 1699.
Mrs. Wheeler, Tabitha, widow of Abraham (?).

Mary Glasier, returned January, 1699.
Ephraim Roper, son of Ephraim, aged about 12, returned.
John Scates' son.
Hannah Rugg, daughter of Joseph.   8

Rev. Timothy Harrington in his Century Sermon includes among the captured "a son of Joseph Rugg," which is probably an error of gender, as Hannah Rugg is the name of a Lancaster prisoner, 1699. Harrington also names Joanna and Elizabeth Hudson as killed. If killed, their relatives did not know the fact nearly three months later, as will be shown below.

Reverend John Whiting's residence was on the lawn of the Col. Fay estate, a few feet south of the well which is still in use. The house stood until early in the present century, a path bordered with huge button-wood trees leading from the front door to the highway south. The inventory of his estate sums £221 9^s, a large amount in those days; and the articles of household furniture indicate a degree of luxury in living quite unusual in Lancaster. Mistress Alice Whiting doubtless was much envied the possession of "a pair of Blew Curtains & Vallens," valued at 1£ 10^s,—"a silver cup & three silver spoons 2£ 10^s,"— and "4 blew cloth chaires & 2 plaine great chaires." The "Books" were estimated worth 7£ 14^s. Twin children, "Alice & Fanie," nearly three years old, died May 19, 1697; and Eunice, aged 1 year, survived the father but two months. In 1701 the widow married Reverend Timothy Stevens.

Daniel Hudson, a brickmaker and bricklayer from Watertown, was admitted an inhabitant in 1664. When he made his will two years before his death, he was in possession of two house lots of twenty acres each, namely: the John Moore lot and Gibson's Hill, which last he purchased in 1670 of Major Simon Willard. In short, he owned the upland from the Rowlandson Garrison site to Mrs. Ware's corner. The exact position of his house is not discovered. He had at least five sons and five daughters, and those surviving signed an agreement December 2d, 1697, from which are transcribed these provisions:

> For our sisters' wearing clothes We mutualy agree to leave them undivided at present . . . . hoping that one of them namely: either Johanah or Ellizabeth may be yet alive : . . . . . also in case that either of our said sisters shall by God's goodnes be againe Reduced from Captivity, that then we do farther oblige ourselves as aforesaid to allow & pay unto either of them that so Returne her portion doubly.

John Skeath, "a cordwainer from Boston," married Sarah the daughter of Lawrence Waters. As he, in connection with his brother-in-law, Stephen Waters, owned lands in Lancaster, it seems not improbable that the victim recorded as John Scate, may have been his son John, born in 1659.

Mrs. Hannah Rugg had been widowed less than a year, and Joseph perhaps lived with his mother upon the John Rugg home lot which bordered the south side of the road that climbs George Hill, forty rods north of the schoolhouse. The captive girl, Hannah, had not returned fifteen years later.

Jonathan Fairbanks was a son of that Jonas who was slain in the massacre of 1676, and dwelt somewhere near the southerly end of the George Hill range. From his inventory he seems to have been a blacksmith. Two children, the oldest and youngest, escaped capture. The two slain were under eight years of age. If the evidence of a gravestone in the old burial ground may be accepted, the boy Jonas lived four days after the Indian raid.

Ephraim Roper was the same who escaped from the Rowlandson garrison in the massacre of 1676, and was son of John Roper, killed that year. He was about fifty-three years of age, and had served as a soldier under Captain Turner in Philip's war. Hannah was his second wife, and widow of Stephen Goble, hanged for murder in 1676. His house was garrisoned, situated on the George Hill road a little west of the school-house, and probably on the north side of the way. An item in the bill of the administrator, Nathaniel Wilder, against Ephraim Roper's estate, was for the fee "pd to Jonathan Prescott for curing one of ye Daughters of ye said Dec^d of a wound Received by ye Indians 7^{br}, 97," but whether this was Ruth, aged 16, or Bathsheba, the younger, is not intimated.

CASCOE BAY, ye 17 January 1698|9

The names of the Captiues Rec^d aboard the Province Gally from the Indians.

    Mary ffarbankes of Lancaster
    Mary Glasser of Lancaster . . . . .

The names of the Captiues yett in the Indians hands.
    Ephraim Ropper of Lancaster Gon to Allbanie.
    Hannah Rugg of Lancaster Gon to Allbanie. . . . .

[Massachusetts Archives, LXX, 398.]

To the Honble The Lt. Govr. Council and house of representatives in Gen^{ll} Court assembled this 5th of June 1701.

The Petition of Captⁿ. Thomas Brown humbly Shewth. That yor Pet^r in the Month of Sept. 1697 when the Indians alarmed the Towne of Lancaster, was comanded by Maj^r. Tyng with a Company of Solders to pursue them, and in that pursuit and Expedition lost a very good horse of about Tenn pounds value and never yet had any satisfaction for the same. Yo^r Pet^r hopes yor hon^{rs} will consider the premises, and recompence yor pet^r by allowing him the value of his loss, purely sustain^d in the Countreys service, or w^t oth^r compensation yor hon^{rs} shall see meet;

[Massachusetts Archives, LXX, 527.]

1697. To the Rt. Hon^{rable} the Lieut Govr the Hon^{ed} Councill &^a Representatives Convened in Gen^{rall} Assembly at Boston October 13 1697

The Humble Petition of John Houghton in behalfe of the Inhabitants of the Towne of Lancaster Humbly Sheweth That fforasmuch as the Righteous God hath permited the heathen Indian Enemyes to kill and destroy many of our people in a cruell & barbarous maner both formerly and lately to the great terror & amazement of those that survive & to our great Loss & Damage & especially in having our minister taken away by such a awfull stroke, we greatly feare we shall not prevaile with any to com & setle with us in the work of the ministrey because of the present troubles & also we being left few in number & brought very low by the long continued troubles, all which is Ready to cause us to dispaire of any Longer Continuance in said Towne except we may have som encouragement & Relieffe. Which moveth yor petition^r Humbly to Request your hon^{rs} to consider our distressed condition & that our part of the tax last granted may be Remitted there being so many of the persons on whome it was levied & their estates destroyed & that we may be freed from paying taxes Whilest we Remaine under such troubles, & that if we may be p^rmited through Gods goodnes to continue there for the future we pray that we may have your hon^{rs} advise & help in the procuring & setlement of a minister, without which we cannot at present of ourselves do it, & that we may be supported with souldiers, for we are no long^r able of ourselves to beare up under such a Wasting, & desolating War, all which being by your Hon^{rs} considered, it is hoped you will se meet to grant our Request as above which will greatly encourage said Inhabitants & yor petition^r as in duty bound shall pray &^{tra}

JOHN HOUGHTON.

[*Endorsed.*] In ye House of Representatiues, Oct: 19: 1697 Rec^d. Read ye 26th Oct, 97. In ye house of Representatiues Voted. That for encouraging & enabling ye said Towne to get a Minister: y^t there be Twenty pounds payd out of ye publick Treasury of this prouince to ye minister y^t shall be procured to liue there for ye first year.

Sent up for Concurrance   PENN TOWNSEND *Speaker*

In Council. 26th Oct. 1697,   Voted a concurrance

ISA ADDINGTON *Secy*

[Massachusetts Archives, XI, 125.]

1699, Dec 12. Josiah Whitcomb on behalfe of Lancaster Informed the Court that they are provided wth sufficient pound & stocks and weights and measures for which they stand pr'sented for ye want of; the Court accepting of his Information they are dismist he paying fees of Court.

[Middlesex Court Records.]

In a note to "A Century Sermon," Reverend Timothy Harrington gives the names of three ministers who were temporarily in Lancaster between 1697 and 1701. They were: John Robinson, afterwards minister in Duxbury, 1702-1739, graduated at Harvard, 1695 ; Samuel Whitman graduated at Harvard, 1696, and a Mr. Jones. Harrington says : "Mr. Jones was invited to settle, but difficulties arising, his Ordination was prevented, and he removed." Joseph Willard, Esq., suggests that this may have been John Jones, graduated at Harvard, 1690. If so, he was never ordained elsewhere. Harrington adds: "In May 1701, Mr. Andrew Gardner was invited to preach, and in September following was invited to settle in the Ministry."

The following gives evidence that Mr. Gardner was at once placed in possession of his predecessor's house and lands:

March 21st 1701, Alice Whiting, "widow & Relict to the Reverend Mr John Whiting late minister of the Gospell at ye Town of Lancaster," ——— in consideration of sixty pounds in money paid, sold to —
Thomas Sawyer Juner and John Houghton Senr and to all and every the rest of the Inhabitants of said Lancaster . . . . my Dwelling house at said Lancaster with ten acres of upland adjoining to it lying on the west side of the River neer to s^d Thomas Sawyers house and bounded northerly and southerly by two highwayes and westerly it comes to be narrow neer to a point and easterly it is bounded by a little common upland that lyeth betwixt it and som medow of Thomas Sawyer Senr . . . . also about six acres of Interval Land more or less which said Inhabitants formerly purchased of Lieut. Jonathan Prescott: and is bounded by said Sawyers medow west, Sam^{ll} Prescotts Land north, the highway south, and at the eastward end it comes near to a point. All which house and land were formerly given by said Inhabitants of Lancaster to ye late reverend Mr John Whiting some time Pastor of ye Church of Christ there.

[Middlesex Registry.]

THE ADDITIONAL GRANT.

1702, Nov. 6. A Petition of the Town of Lancaster, Praying Liberty to purchase of George Tahanto, Indian Sagamore, a Certain Tract of Land lying adjoining to the West end of sd Township betwixt that, and Wachusets Hills was sent up from the Representatives with the orders of that House in answer to the Same, That a committee be appointed by this Court to go upon and take a view of the Land petitioned for and to make their report to the next session of this Court. The Petitioners to defray the Charge of the said Committee. Which Petition and Order being read at the Board the said Order was Concurred with: and Collo. Tyng Major Thos Browne and Capt James Minott, with such others as the Representatives shall think fit to Name were appointed by this Board to be a Committee for the affair afforesaid.

[Massachusetts Records.]

The land thus petitioned for, had been bought and bonded more than a year before. The original petition has not been found. A copy of the Bond made by John Houghton is among the papers of Joseph Willard, Esq.

Know all men by these presents, that I, George Tahanto, Indian Sagamore, for and in consideration of what money, namely, twelve pounds, was formerly paid to Sholan, my uncle, sometime sagamore of Nashuah, for the purchase of said township, and also forty six shillings formerly paid by Insigne John Moore and John Houghton of said Nashuah to James Wiser, alias Quenepenett, now deceased, but especially for and in consideration of eighteen pounds paid part, and the rest secured to be paid, by John Houghton and Nathaniel Wilder, their heirs, executors and assigns forever, a certain tract of land on the west side of the westward line of Nashuah township, adjoining to said line, and butts southerly for the most part on Nashuah river, bearing westerly towards Wachusett Hills, and runs northerly as far as Nashuah township, and which lands and meadows, be it more or less, to be to the said Insigne John Moore, John Houghton, and Nathaniel Wilder their heirs and assigns, to have and to hold forever. And I the said George Tahanto, do hereby promise and engage to procure an order from the honored General Court, for their allowance and confirmation of the sale of said lands as aforesaid, and also that I will show and mark out the bounds of said land in convenient time, not exceeding four months, and also to make such deeds and conveyances, as may be necessary for the confirmation of the premises, and that also I the said George Tahanto do by these presents fully ratify and confirm, all & every, the said township of Nashuah alias Lancaster to the inhabitants and proprietors thereof according as it was formerly granted to them or their ancestors by my uncle Sholan, and laid out to them by Ensign Thomas Noyes, and confirmed by the Hon. General Court. For the performance of all the abovesaid, I, the said George Tahanto, have set my hand and seal, this twenty sixth day of June, in the 13th year of the reign of our Sovereign Lord, William the Third over England, &c. King, Anno Domini, 1701.

        GEORGE TAHANTO his O mark
        MARY AUNSOCAUMG her) mark
Signed and sealed in presence of
   JOHNWONSQUON his) mark
   JOHN AQUITTICUS his | mark
   PETER PUCKATAUGH his P mark
   JONATHAN WILDER
   JOHN GUILD.

No action seems to have been taken by this committee, or by the general court until 1711, and the bounds of the grant were finally settled in 1721, under which dates further records will be found.

LANCASTER DURING QUEEN ANNE'S WAR. 1701-1713.

1703. To his Excell[cy]: Joseph Dudley Esq[r]: Capt: General and Governor in Chief in and over the Province of the Massachusetts Bay in New England and Vice Admiral of the same, The Hono[ble]: her Majties: Council of the sd Province, and To the Hono[ble] House of Representatives convened in General Assembly for the sd Province.

The Humble Petition of several of the ffreeholders Proprietors & Inhabitants of Lancaster within the sd Province, whose names are hereunto subscribed, Sheweth—That in or about the year 1653, The Inhabitants of the sd Town did agree amongst themselves to pay to and for the Use of the Minister of the sd Town the sum of Ten shillings a year in consideration of their home Lotts, and if that should fall short of a maintenance, then to make up the same by an equal Rate upon their Goods and other Improved Lands in such way and order as the Country rate was raised. Which way and method was equal so long as the Inhabitants of the sd Town continued upon their home Lotts. But now so it is may it please yo[r] Excell[cy]: and Honors: That several of the sd Inhabitants are removed from their home Lotts (which are left destitute & unimproved, & thereby disenabled to pay any rate att all) to their second Division of Lotts which pay no Rates, and the charge of the Maintenance of the sd Minister wholly falls upon yo[r] Petitioners to their great wrong & damage, and if not timely remedied by yo[r] Excell[cy]: & hon[rs]: will be a standing & intolerable inconvenience & matter of Division in theyr Town, for that they are not able to bear the Charge thereof. And for as much as the sd Town had never any settlement made by Law, but such an agreement as above sd which is neither binding nor equal and whereas sd Town cannot agree among themselves how to raise their ministers sallary, yo[r] Petitioners Therefore humbly pray That yo[r] Excell[cy]: & Honors will be pleased to take the Premises into yo[r] serious Consideration; and settle the maintenance of the minister of the sd Town in such methods & ways as to yo[r] Excell[cy]: and Honors, shall in yo[r] great wisdom seem to be most equal

just & Right & which may be binding upon them & their posterity for
ever, and yor Petitioners as in duty bound will ever pray &^{tra}

BENJAMIN BELLOWS	NATHANIEL SAWYER
JOHN JOHNSON	JOSEPH WHELOCK
JOSEPH GLAZEAR	JOHN GLAZIER
SIMON STEEVENS	GEORGE GLAZIER
NATHANIEL WILDER	THOMAS ROSSE
PETER JOSLIN	SAMUEL PRESCOTT
JOSIAH WHITE	EPHRAIM WILDER
SAMUELL BENNETT	NATHANIEL HUDSON
WILLIAM DIVOLL	SAMUEL CARTER
JONATHAN WHITCOMB	DANIEL RUGE
	CYPRIAN STEEVENS

[*Endorsed.*] In the House of Representatives, June 2^d 1703. Resolved, That inasmuch, as the Inhabitants of the Town of Lancaster within mentioned were driven out by the Enemy, and the Place wholly Deserted: Their former Agreement for the maintenance of their Minister is now null and void, and they ought to Proceed to Levy their ministers Rate upon their Inhabitants in equall Proportion as the Law Directs.

Sent up for concurrence.   JAMES CONVERSE *Speaker*.

die predict, In Council Read and past a concurrance
                                ISA ADDINGTON *Secty*.

In the House of Representatives, Septr 7. 1703.

Upon the Reading and Considering of the Petition on the other side, ordered, That the ministers salary in the Town of Lancaster be Levyed, and Collected of the severall Inhabitants by the same Rules, and in the same Proportions with the Province Tax; for this present yeare.

Sent up for concurrence.   JAMES CONVERSE *Speaker*.
[Massachusetts Archives, XI, 183-4.]

The foregoing petition marks the beginning of an important change in the growth of the town. In days of peace the movement of increase had been steadily westward, and even the bloody lesson of the massacre of 1676 had not availed to disturb the centre of population materially; though a few families collected along the sunny side of the Wataquadock range, and on the hills east of Still River. But each succeeding Indian raid emphasized more strongly the fact, that, in a military point of view, George Hill was a very unsafe position. A retrograde movement along the eastern highways took place, and, clustering about central garrisons, fast growing families shaped the little villages that in a generation or two were to be excised from the original grant as the townships of Harvard, Bolton and Berlin.

1703. *To his Excllency Joseph Dudley Esq. Capt. Generall & Governour In Chiefe &c* tra: *the Honrable Council & Representatives of her Majsties Province of Massachusetts Bay In New England Convened in Generall Assembly the thirteenth Day of August* 1707.

 The Petetion of Joseph Wilder of Lancaster Humbly Sheweth, That yor Petetioner In ye yeare 1703 being ordered by Capt Benjamin Willard to Provide twenty paire of good Snow Shoose for ye use of his souldiers which Accordingly was nineteen paire of them provided, four of which Coll Jonathan Tyng sent for & had them for ye expedition to Wenepissiockett: the others were Delivered by said Capt Willards order to his men & used by them In Scouting about ye frontiers. Your Petetioner Disburst Considerable of his owne money towards the procuring of these, to ye persons that made them, & is threatened to be sued for ye Remainder, & In case he should, must unavoidably pay it, which will be apparent wrong. Your Petetioner expected that Coll Tyng would have Taken care they should Long eare now haue been paid for, but hitherto never Received one peney. If Coll Tyng ever Received any pay for ye foure paire first delivered yet nothing hath been allowed to them that made them, but what your Petetioner disburst as abovesaid, which is greatly to theire wrong & Damage & if not in a short time Remedied Will proove a Greivance. Your Petetion^r therefore Humbly Prayes that your Excellency & Hon^{rs} would consider ye Premisses & order that your Petetion^r may be paid out of the Publique Tresury what is Justly Due for said Snow Shoose which at foure shillings a paire as was then alowed amounts to ye sum of foure pound fifteene shillings that so ye persons concerned may be paid without further Trouble or delay, And your Petetioner as In Duty Bound Shall ever Pray &c ^{tra}:

JOSEPH WILDER.

In the House of Representatives
 Nov: 4: 1707. Read & Comitted. 25 Read & Resolved That the sum of ffour Pounds and fifteen shillings be allowed & Paid out of the publick Treasury to Joseph Wilder the Petitioner in full for the snow shoes above mentioned. Sent up for concurrence.

JOHN BURRELL Speaker

Novr 26. 1707.
 In Council Read & Concurr^d   ISA ADDINGTON *Secry*.

LANCASTER 7th Decm 1703.

To Sargent Joseph Wilder. You are here by ordered by vertu of an order to me from his exc^lly to teake care of ye solders now under my comand in Lancaster and upon eny amurjences that eny towne be detrod by ye enemy you murst command all under my command in groton and persew after them according to your best understanding and keepe our solders in good order til further order from me or other of your Seupeirior ofesers.

      Your friend. BEN^IA WILLARD *Capt.*

and further you are here by ordered to prouide forthwith twenty pair of snow shoes. fail not.

      Your friend BENI^A WILLARD *Capt.*

[*Endorsed.*]   ROXBURY. 24. Novr 1707.

The above order was present^d to mee this day, and I do allow it to be in persuance of my orders to Captain Willard at the time.

            J. DUDLEY.

[Massachusetts Archives, LXXI, 378.]

Pursuant to comand from his Excellency bearing date April 15th 1704 for the Settleing of Garrisons in ye Towne of Lancaster & ordering men to ye Same, Wee the subscribers do hereby Direct & Comand you ye Inhabitants of s^d: Lancaster to Repair to you^r Severall Garrisons according to appointment as followeth & Attend you^r Duties therein. Dat. 20th April 1704.

on ye east side of ye River			Bare Hill	
John Moore & Jonathan Moore	}		John Priest Senr	2
Allowed a Garrison ye said	} p^esons		John Priest Ju^r	1
John Moore Comander —	}	2	John Warner	3
Jonathan Moore		1	Caleb Sawyer	2
Willm Sawyer		1	James Atherton S^r	1
Joseph Sawyer		1	James Atherton Ju^r	1–10
Josiah Wheeler		1		
John Hinds		2	Simon Willard & Benjamin Bellows allowed a Garrison said Simon Willard Comand^r	1
James Keyes		1–9		
			Benjamin Bellows	1
Josiah Whetcomb sen^r allowed a Garrison himselfe Comander		2	John Willard	1
Josiah Whetcomb Ju^r		1	Joshua Atherton	1
David Whetcomb		1	Henry Willard	1
Hezekiah Whetcomb		1	James Houghton	3
Jacob Houghton		1	Joseph Hutchins	1
Henry Houghton		1	Joseph Waters	1
John Wilder Ju^r		1–8	Hezekiah Willard	1
			James Smith	1–12

Capt Thomas Wilder & John Houghton sen.r allowed a Garrison Cap.t Wilder Comand.r — 3
John Houghton S.r ——— 2
John Wilder j.r ——— 2
Jonas Houghton ——— 2
Robert Houghton ——— 2
John Rugg ——— 1
Thos: Wilder ——— 1
Beatrix Pope Widow
John Houghton j.r ——— 1
Joseph Houghton ——— 1–15

on y.e west side Nashuway River M.r Andrew Gardner & Thomas Sawyer Ju.r a Garison
Thomas Sawyer Comander — 3
M.r Gardner ——— 1
Jabez Fairbank ——— 1
Nath.l Sawyer ——— 1
John Harriss ——— 1
Daniell Rugg ——— 1
Sam.ll Prescott ——— 1– 9

Gamaliell Beaman ——— 2
John Beaman sen.r ——— 1
James Snow S.r ——— 2
James Snow Ju.r ——— 1
Jeremiah Willson ——— 1
James Buttler ——— 1– 8

at y.e Corne Mill
John Prescott Sen.r ——— 1
John Prescott Ju.r ——— 1
John Keyes ——— 1
Ebenezer Prescott ——— 1– 4

on y.e West Side Penicook River Called y.e Neck Serg.t Josiah White a Garrison p.esons Himselfe Comander ——— 3
Joseph Wheelock ——— 1
John Glazier ——— 1
George Glazier ——— 1
Joseph Glazier ——— 1– 7

Leu.t Nath.ll Wilder a Garison himselfe Comander ——— 3
Sam.ll Carter ——— 1
Ephraim Wilder ——— 1
Thomas Ross ——— 1
John Carter ——— 1– 7

Ensigne Peter Josllin a Garison himselfe Comander ——— 1
Will.m Divoll ——— 1
John Beaman Ju.r ——— 1
John Johnson ——— 1
Cyprian Steevens ——— 1
Simon Steevens ——— 1
Sam.ll Bennitt ——— 1
Jonathan Whetcomb ——— 1
George Hervey ——— 1– 9

JONATHAN TYNG.
THO: BROWNE.
JOHN LANE.
JERAHMEL BOWERS.

[Copy of a document in possession of Dr. John S. H. Fogg of South Boston.]

The locations of these garrisons can be fixed approximately only, by the known residences of the householders belonging to them.

1. Those in John Moore's garrison lived on the Marlborough road in the southeast part of Bolton, near the district now called Fryville. The graves of the brothers John and Jonathan Moore are in the burial ground on the old road to Hudson.

2. Those composing the Whitcomb garrison lived also in Bolton, toward the northeast corner. Families descended from them resided there until recently.

3. The Priest garrison was at the easterly side of Bare Hill in Harvard.

4. The Josiah White garrison was upon the east side of the Neck, where Edward Houghton now lives.

5. Those belonging to Peter Joslin's garrison lived along the highway from the Sprague Bridge to the North Village. "*Hervey*" is an error for Hewes.

6. Those forming the Simon Willard garrison dwelt along the road through Still River village.

7. Capt. Thomas Wilder's garrison was on the Old Common north of the highway, and, according to Joseph Willard, Esquire, about twenty rods in rear of the house known as the Dr. David Steuart Robertson place.

8. The six men whose names are headed by that of Gamaliell Beman, had homes upon the east slope of Wataquadock Hill. In the descriptions of their lands frequent mention is made of "the cold spring" and "the hill where Simon Pipo had a planting field."

9. Reverend Andrew Gardner lived by the well a few rods westerly from the house of the late Colonel Francis B. Fay; Samuel Prescott, across the road south; Thomas Sawyer, where his venerable descendant, Mrs. Sally Case, resides; Nathaniel Sawyer and Jabez Fairbank, half a mile westerly in the Deer's Horns neighborhood.

10. The Prescott garrison site is in Clinton, southeast of and very near the crossing of High and Water streets.

11. Lieutenant Nathaniel Wilder's home was upon the slope of George Hill, next his father's home lot. His brother Ephraim lived near, and his brother-in-law, Samuel Carter, on the farm now owned by Frank D. Taylor. Thomas Ross lived half a mile north on the first lot of John Smith.

> July 30 1704, Sab. morning or Monday morning Indians invaded Lancaster Killed 2 or 3 persons burnt ye Meeting house and some other houses.
> [Journal of Reverend John Pike.]

This assault was made Monday, July 31st, very early in the morning. The casualties were: Lieutenant Nathaniel Wilder, mortally wounded near his own garrison; he died the same day. Abraham How, Benjamin Hutchins and John Spalding, killed. The last was one of Captain Tyng's soldiers; How and Hutchins were Marlborough men.

> On Monday morning past, the enemy French and Indians, fell upon Lancaster, about four hundred of them, assaulted six garrisons at once, where the people defended themselves very well, until assistance came in from all parts, by the governors order, so that in the evening there were three hundred men in the town. And the enemy was beaten off with loss, but are yet hovering on the head of those towns, to make some further impression, if not prevented.
> [Boston News Letter, October 30, 1704.]

The account given by Samuel Penhallow in his "History of the Indian Wars," is most relied upon for the details of this affair. Reverend Timothy Harrington impugns the accuracy of his statements respecting "the mischiefs done in this town by the enemy," but he borrows most of his own relation from that history, which is as follows:

> The French in Canada were now forming another design on North Hampton, of which we had seasonable advice: . . . . Their whole body was seven hundred, with two Friars, under the command of Monsieur Boocore who in their march began to mutiny about the plunder they had in view, and expected to be master of, forgetting the proverb about dividing the skin before the bear was killed. Their dissention at last was so

great, that upwards of two hundred returned in discontent. However the rest came on, and sent scouts before to observe the posture of the English, who reported that they were as thick as the trees in the woods. Upon which their spirits failed, and more of their number deserted. They then called a council of war, who resolved to desist from the enterprise. Yet some staid, and afterwards fell on Lancaster and Groton, where they did some spoil, but not what they expected for that these towns were seasonably strengthened. Capt. Tyng and Capt. How entertained a warm dispute with them for some time, but being much inferior in number, were forced to retreat with some loss: yet those that were slain of the enemy, were more than those of ours. One of them was an officer of some distinction which so exasperated their spirits that in revenge, they fired the Meeting House, killed several cattle and burnt many outhouses. . . . . It was not then known how many of the enemy were slain it being customary among them to carry off their dead; however it was afterwards affirmed, that they lost sixteen besides several that were wounded. . . .

[Penhallow's Indian Wars.]

To his Excellencie Joseph Dudley Esqr. Capt. Generall and Governour In Chief in and over Her Mjties province of the Massachusetts Bay in New England &^{c}. and to the Honourable Her Majties Council and Representatives in Great and Generall Court assembled. 9^{br} 8th 1704.

The Petition of Thomas How of Marlburrah in the Behalf of himself & Company. Humbly Sheweth, That Whereas, at the time that Lankester was assaulted by the french and Indian enemies, your petitioner and company (to it) about thirty, did emediately Issue out, and were a means vnder God, to preserue many persons liues & estates, in sd Towne; with the loss of two men of said company, and defended sd Towne from the Insults of so cruel and barbarous an enemy. And after wch There was found on the Spot where seueral barns were burnt, the bones of Sundry of the enemy y^t were slain by your petitioners & company, besides many more supposed to be wounded, wch the enemy drew off, and altho your petitioner & company recouered no scalps, yet being very cleer and plain (to it) of the enemies being slain as afore^{sd}, your petitioners; do Therefore pray that your Excellencies, & Honours would please to consider the premises, and Grant them such Compensation as in your Wisedom shall seem mete &c. And yor Petition^r shall as in Duty, pray &^{tra}

THOMAS HOW for himself & Comp^a

In the House of Representatives

Novr 8: 1704 Read. Resolved That the sum of Ten Pounds be allowed, and Paid out of the publick Treasury to Captn Thom. How, to be equelly Distributed amongst the Petitioners, as a Token that this Court Takes notice of, & well accepts, their good service, abovementioned.

Sent up for concurrence. JAMES CONVERSE *Speaker*

In Council. Nov. 10. 1704.
Read and pass[d] a concurrance.   ISA ADDINGTON *Secry*.
[Massachusetts Archives, XXX, 498.]

To his Excellency Joseph Dudley Esq : . . . . . *Nov* : 18 : 1704.
 The Humble Petition of Capt. William Tyng Sheweth, That just before the mischief was done at Lancaster, yo[r] Petitioner was in Boston, and by his Excellency was ordered down forthwith to his Post, to go by Dunstable and thence to Lancaster, which yo[r] Petitioner accordingly did and rode thither upon his own Horse, which he turned into a pasture there, and the next morning the Horse was by the Indians taken out of the sd pasture & driven into the woods, when they killed and ate the sd Horse. And Farther yo[r] petitioner Sheweth That one John Spalding who was a soldier under his command was killed in that action and his Gun taken by the Indians, and he being a very good soldier (tho a youth,) & the Gun being his ffathers who is very poor, yo[r] Petitioner therefore humbly prays this great and General assembly to take the premisses into Consideration and that he may have such satisfaction & recompence made him for the loss of his Horse, and the ffather of the young man for the loss of his Gun as to this great & General Assembly shall seem meet, and yo[r] Petitioner shall pray &c   W[M] TYNG

 [*Endorsed*.] In the House of Representatives. Nov. 18 : 1704. In Answer to the Petition on the other side Resolved, That the sum of Four Pounds be allowed and Paid out of the publick Treasury to Capt. William Tyng the Petitioner — And the sum of Twenty Shillings to John Spalding father of John Spalding dec[d] mentioned in the Petition.
 Sent up for concurrance . . . .   JAMES CONVERSE *Speaker*
[Massachusetts Archives, LXXI, 105-6.]

 Oct. 25. 1704. Mr Andrew Gardner minister of Lancaster, coming down from y[e] watchbox in y[e] night wth a darkish coloured gown was mistaken for an Indian & solemnly slain by a sorry souldier belonging to y[e] Garrison nomine Presket.
[Journal of Reverend John Pike.]

 I now return to the westward, where, on the 25th of October the enemy did some mischief. Lancaster was alarmed, and the alarm was the means of the untimely death of the Rev. Mr Gardiner their worthy pastor.
 Several of the inhabitants who belonged to the garrison, were wearied by hard travelling the day before, in pursuit of the enemy. This caused this good man out of pity and compassion to watch that night himself : accordingly he went into the box which lay over the flanker, where he staid till late in the night ; but being cold (as was supposed) he was coming down to warm himself, when one between sleeping and waking, or surprised through excess of fear fired upon him as he was coming out of

the watch house where no man could rationally expect the coming of an enemy. Mr Gardner, although he was shot through the back came to the door and bid them open it for he was wounded. No sooner did he enter, but he fainted away: As he came to himself, he asked who it was that shot him, and when they told him, he prayed God to forgive him, and forgave him himself, believing that he did it not on purpose; and with a composed frame of spirit, desired them that bewailed him not to weep, but pray for him and his flock. He comforted his sorrowful spouse, and expired within an hour.

[Samuel Penhallow's History of the Indian Wars.]

On *Wednesday* night an Englishman was killed in the Woods at *Groton* by the Indians, which were afterwards descryed in the night by the Light of their Fires by a Person Travailing from *Groton* to *Lancaster*, and judged they might be about Thirty in number: pursuit was made after them but none could be found.

[Boston News Letter, October 30, 1704.]

From the diary of John Marshall, of Braintree, in the library of the Massachusetts Historical Society, we learn further that the man "killed and scalped by the Indians, belonged to the town of Groton, his name was davis: a very usefull man and much Lamented." This was probably Samuel Davis, who married Mary Waters in Lancaster, A. D. 1656, and lived here for a time.

On Thursday night the Reverend Mr Gardner Minister of *Lancaster* was unfortunately shot by the Sentinel on the Watch, supposing him to be an Indian climbing over the Walls of the Fortification: of which wound he died in an hours space or little more.

[Boston News Letter, October 30, 1704.]

Boston. In our Numb. 28, As we then received it, we gave you the Account of the Death of the Reverend Mr *Gardner*, Minister of *Lancaster*: and having since had a perfect and exact Account of the same, from Eye and Ear Witnesses: we thought it expedient to insert it here, to prevent various reports thereof: And is as follows — That a man being Killed the day before between *Groton* and *Lancaster*, and the Indians having been seen the night before nigh the Town, Mr. *Gardner*, (three of the men belonging to his Garrison being gone out of Town, and two of the remaining three being tyred with Watching and Travelling in the Woods after the Indians that day,) being a very careful as well as couragious man, concluded to Watch that night himself; and accordingly went out into the little Watch-house that was over one of the Flankers, and there stayed till late in the night; whence and when he was coming down, (as it was thought,) to warm him. The man that shot him, who was not long before sleeping by the fire, came out, and whether between sleeping and waking, or surprized with an excess of fear, fired upon him as he was coming down out of the Watch-house, through a little Trap-door into the Flanker, where no man having the exercise of his Reason could suspect the coming of an Enemy, or suspect him to be so, when in a clear Moonlight night he was nigh him. Mr *Gardner* (though his wound was in his breast, being shot through the Vitals) came to the door, bid them open it, for he was wounded; after he came in, he fainted away, but coming to himself again, asked who it was that shot him, and when they told him, he prayed God to forgive him, and forgave him himself, for he believed he did not do it on purpose; and with a composed Christian frame of spirit desired them that were bitterly lamenting over him, not to weep but to pray for him, and comforted his sorrowful wife, telling her he was going to Glory, advising her to follow him; and in about an hour Dyed, leaving his sorrowful friends to lament the loss of so worthy and desirable a Person.

[Boston News Letter, November 20, 1704.]

The coroner's inquest entirely exonerated Samuel Prescott. The verdict of the jury is probably somewhere extant, but has escaped search. Joseph Willard, Esquire, basing his statements upon that document, tells us that Prescott was the sentinel on duty, pacing his beat on the parade, when, dimly seeing a supposed enemy coming out of the upper flanker, he challenged him twice. No response being given, his suspicions were confirmed and he fired. His neighbors declared him guiltless even of careless haste; but they could not lift from his life the self-imposed burden of bitter regret. His home was but a few rods away, and he could not step from his door, or look out from his windows, but his eyes encountered the scene of that pitiful tragedy. He soon removed to Concord, selling his pleasant home to Reverend John Prentice. Mr. Gardner was the son of Captain Andrew and Sarah (Mason) Gardner of Brookline, and a graduate of Harvard college in 1696. He was in his thirtieth year, when his promising life was cut short.

To his Excellency, Joseph Dudley Esqr Captain Generall & Comander In Chiefe in & over his Maj^ts Province of ye Massachusetts Bay In New England &c: his Maj^ts Hon^rable Councill & Representatives Convened In Generall Assembly at Boston October 25 1704.

The Petition of ye Inhabitants of ye Towne of Lancaster in ye Province, Humbly Sheweth That whereas yor Petitioners the destressed Inhabitants of said Lancaster being under ye Awfull Rebukes of Gods hand In ye manifest Token of his Displeasure against us, In p^rmitting those Barbarous Heathen to be such a Scourge to us whereby in ye Sumer past we have Sustained such Losses by them that therby we are greatly Impoverished and destressed & som of us almost Ruined as to our estates having little or nothing left for our present Sustenance and much less able to Contribute to Publique Charges, the Towne having lost severall hundreds of pounds estat by ye Indians in theire last attack together with ye loss of our meeting house being burnt by them, & more particularly that late awfull stroak of Gods Hand ye Last weeke in ye Loss of our Reverend Minister who was every way Worthy & desirable, whose Loss is Ready to sink our spirits, also we haveing been at great charge formerly in settleing ye ministry & haveing one minister slaine by ye Indians & now another Taken away by a more awfull stroake we are still left destitute & have all againe to procure which will be great charge & we feare with much dificulty all which Layes us under an Inability of performing what is Required of us, Reffering to our Publique Charges. The p^rmisses being considered by your Excellency & Hon^rs with many other Reasons that might be alleadged we Humbly Crave that ye late Tax set and proportioned upon said Towne being ye sum of eighty six pounds may be Remitted or such an abatement thereof made & Granted to sd Town as yor Excellency & Hon^rs Shall in Wisdom see to be Reasonable & Just & such Protection and encouragement afforded for ye future as may be necessary, & yor Petitioners better enabled to beare up under ye many Difficultyes we are dayly exercised with & ffurther obliged as in Duty bound ever to pray : &c :

  In behalfe of ye Inhabitants of Lancaster
Novb^r ye 2^d 1704.   JOHN HOUGHTON
               JONAS HOUGHTON

[*Endorsed.*]
  In the House of Representatives Dec : 28 : 1704.
  Resolved, That the sum of Forty Pounds be allowed and Paid out of the publick Treasury to the Town of Lancaster towards Building a Meeting House as soon as they shall have Erected a frame for the same and Paid the Taxes already laid upon them.
            JAMES CONVERSE *Speaker*.

In Council. 28. Decr. 1704. Read and Concurred.
            ISA ADDINGTON *Secry*.

[Massachusetts Archives, CXIII, 363.]

To His Excellency Joseph Dudley Esqr Captain Generall & Comander in Chieffe &c: In and over her Maj^{ts} Province of ye Massachusetts Bay, in New England her Maj^{ts} Hon^{r}able Councill & Representatives of sd Province Convened In Generall Assembley at Boston: October: 25th, 1704.

Wheras Wee the Subscribers having Lately Preffered a Petition to your Excellency And Hon^{rs} In behalfe of ye Inhabitants of Lancaster, In short Representing The present destressed Condition of said Towne & on that account Humbly Praying for ye Remission of ye late Tax of eighty six pounds sett upon sd Towne or for an abatement of ye same, & being since Informed by Capt Thomas How of Marleborough that you desire a more particular Accompt of ye late Losses sustained by severall persons in said Towne this last Sumer by Damage don by ye Indians we have accordingly sent you an accompt thereof as followeth.

July ye 31st 1704 ye Indians besett the Towne in severall places & particularly Lieut Nath^{ll} Wilders Garrison where early in ye morning one of ye Indians shott him In the thigh of which wound he dyed ye same day, & ye Indians killed of his cattell six oxen five cowes 3 calves sixteen sheep twelve swine & burnt his Barne & about 12 load of good English hay.

Of Ephraim Wilders one ox 2 calves 3 cowes one horse 15 sheep 2 swine one good dwelling house with 2 fires.

Jonathan Wilder two oxen one horse.

John Carter 3 oxen one cow one horse 3 swine.

Sam^{ll} Carter 3 oxen one cow one horse 2 calves 2 swine one good Dwelling house with 2 fires.

Thomas Ross one cow 2 calves one swine one dwelling house with one fire.

John Houghton Jun 3 swine one large dwelling house* with 3 fires, belonging to him & Phillip Goss & about sixteen pounds of Personall estate belonging to sd Houghton burnt in sd house.

*This house was probably near or upon the site of the Rowlandson garrison, John Houghton having married Mary, widow of the elder Philip Goss, who bought the Rowlandson estate in 1687.

George Hewes two oxen 2 cows.
Sam^{ll} Bennitt 3 oxen 2 cows.
Jonathan Whitcombe 2 sheep.
Simon Steevens one Horss.
Jonas Houghton one Ox.
Jabez ffairbank one new barne with about 8 loads of good English hay.
Thomas Sawyer Jun one heiffer.
John Preist Jun one heiffer.

All which creatures were then killed by ye Indians & Housing burnt by them & many more creatures wounded & Severall Horses that cannot yet be found, though some of the men that have been out have found where som horsses have been killed and Rosted, also those cattell are yet preserved are in great hazard to be lost for want of Hay, especially many of those on ye yeast side of ye River, for most of ye Inhabitants on y^t side have had but little or no help or protection in there Garisons but have been necessitated to watch & ward a third part of their time at least, besides Ranging the woods after when Rumours & Allarms have hapened so that neere halfe our time is spent in actuall service & when we are about our own work we cannot keep to it, but lose a great part of what we Labour for being forced to get our bread with ye pril of our Lives which hang in Doubt continually & but little peace day or night & many of us have formerly been greatly Impoverished by ye Indians, & see no probability but if they can againe it will be so for the future, & having lost our meeting house being now burnt by them this sumer which is a Generall loss, & also ye los of our late minister so. that we are on all accounts as new beginers, & under such discouraging circumstances that our spiritts are Ready to sink & almost dispaire of subsisting another yeare except we may be under beter circumstances, but still under God Relying on your favourable protection & Relieffe hoping for ye Remission of ye said Tax prayed for in the afforsaid Petition, which if it be granted will not Respond a sixth part of ye loss & damage we have lately sustained. So leaving ye Premisses to your favourable consideration wee Remaine.

Your Excellencys & Hon^{rs} most Humble Servants to Comand.

November 15 1704.

THOMAS WILDER
JOHN HOUGHTON Jr
JONAS HOUGHTON.

[Massachusetts Archives, CXIII, 365.]

To his Excellency Joseph Dudley Esqr Governour, the Honorable Council and ye Representatives siting in Boston June ye 27 1705

The humble petition of Mary Gardner of Lancaster humbly Sheweth That whareas thare was yesterday an acount laid before ye Court signed by ye worshipfull Colonell Tailer of money dew to me from ye country for entertaineing of souldiers & damage done by their horses who at coming up to Lancaster when ye attaque was made upon it by ye enemy, who in a hurry put theare horses in to a field of ry whareby an acre was imediately destroyed, for which damage & entertainment of souldiers this honerable hous saw cause to alow me but fifteene shillings when besides that, they drank a barell of boyled Cyder & a barell of strong bear. Besides Mr Gardner his going out Chaplin with ye army in that expedition after ye enemy for all which we have Received nothing. Your humble petitioner being a desolate widdow prayeth y^t Justice may be done her & that she may have Dew recomepence for those things which ye country is more able to bare them then herself who hath alwayes bin & is ready to undergoe any trouble laid upon her for yᵉ service of yᵉ country. Your Granting my petition herein will Greatly obliege your Humble pet'ioner.

MARY GARDNER.

In Council; June. 29. 1705. Read & sent down
[*Endorsed.*]

In the House of Representatives June 29: 1705. Resolved That the sum of Three Pounds, 4 shillings & six pence; be Allowed & paid out of the publick Treasury to Mary Gardner the Petitioner as a full Consideration for the Petition on the other side:

Sent up for concurrence.   THOMAS OAKES *Speaker*

June, 29. 1705. In Council. Read & concurred.

ISA ADDINGTON Secy.

[Massachusetts Archives, LXXI, 157-8.]

1704|5. An Acompt of funeral Charges &c of John Brabrook a soulder under yᵉ comand of Capt. Willᵐ Tyng, who Deceased March 31ˢᵗ 1704⁵.

		l	s	d
Imprimis	To Dressing his lame leg &c —	,,	12ˢ	0
	To Nursing & Charges when sick —	,,	6	,,
	To funeral Charg. viz graue clothes & Drink —	,,	18	,,
	To yᵉ Coffen & Grave —	,,	10	,,
			2	6

EPHRAIM WILDER
JOSEPH WILDER

[Massachusetts Archives, LXXI, 128.]

An acompt of funeral Charges: &c: of John Carter a souldier under yᵉ Comand of Capt. Willi Tyng who deceased March yᵉ 26 1704|5:

Imprimis, To two Jurneys to Concord for yᵉ Doctor —	0 = 7 = 0
To one Jurney to Boston for things for said Carter in his sickness —	0 = 11 = 0
To nursing one week —	0 = 10 = 0
To 4 Gallonds Wine at —	0 = 15 = 9
½ a barrill Syder —	0 = 4 = 0
To Sugger, fruit & Spice —	0 = 5 = 6
To 6 paier of Gloues —	0 = 9 = 0
To yᵉ Coffen and Graue —	0 = 8 = 0
	£3 = 10ˢ = 3ᵈ

NATHANIEL SAWYER.
EPHRAIM WILDER.

[Massachusetts Archives, LXXI, 129.]

1705 Oct. 15. Three men are carried away from Lancaster from Mr Sawyers Sawmill.

Oct. 16. Hear the bad news from Lancaster.
[Diary of Samuel Sewall, II.]

Mention is found of Thomas Sawyer's mill upon Dean's, now called Goodridge Brook, as early as 1699. It was upon the site of the present dam near the Deer's Horns school-house. The three captives were Thomas Sawyer, Jr., his son Elias, a youth of sixteen, and John Bigelow, a carpenter of Marlborough. Samuel Sewall's, being a contemporary record, is no doubt correct, though Reverend Peter Whitney in the History of Worcester County places the scene of the capture at Sawyer's garrison house. A younger brother of Elias, about fourteen years old, escaped through a window, it is said, when the others were captured. From Whitney's history we derive the romantic story of the elder Sawyer's rescue after he had already been tied to the stake for torture. A friar successfully excited the superstitious fears of the savages by brandishing a key, and threatening with it to unlock the door of Purgatory and thrust them into its eternal fires, if they did not release their prisoner to him. He was probably incited thereto by the French Governor, who wished to avail himself of Sawyer's promised skill in the construction of a mill upon the Chambly. The mill built,—the first in all Canada,— Thomas Sawyer and Bigelow came home. Elias was detained a year longer, to run the mill and instruct others in the art of sawing. The grave of Thomas Sawyer is in the old burying ground. He died " September 5th 1736, in ye 89th Year of his Age."

1705. *To his Excellency Joseph Dudley Esq: Capt. General and Governor in Chief, To the Hono^{ble} the Council and House of Representatives now in General Court assembled in and for her Majties. Province of the Massachusetts Bay in New Engl^{d}, November the* 29th 1705.

The humble Petition of several of the Inhabitants of the Town of Lancaster whose names are hereunto subscribed. Sheweth. That yor

Petitioners dwell on the West side of the River ffronting towards the Enemy and have suffered very much and are diminished in their number several heads of ffamilies having been cutt off within these few years and when the Enemy were there about 17 or 18 months ago they burnt down the Meeting house which always stood on the West side the River. Now so it is (may it please this great & General Assembly) that those of the Inhabitants who dwell on this side the River (several of whom are removed for fear of the enemy even to the bounds of Marleburrough) use all their Endeavour to have the Meeting house built on this side whereas the Meeting house Ground & the Ministerial Land & Meadow are both on the other side, and moreover should the Meeting house be built on this side, the Enemy might come when the Inhabitants were att Meeting and destroy the whole Western part and secure the Bridge so that nobody should be able to resist them or Relieve their ffriends. But the Meeting house being built on the West and Exposed side (as it used to be) the Inhabitants on that side are a Guard to the others on this side as well as to themselves, notwithstanding these reasons (which yor Petitioners humbly hope will have their due Consideration in this Hono^{ble} House) they of this side having never had a man kill^d in the service, are grown so numerous, that they out vote yor Petitioners, and carry it against them att their Town Meetings.

Yo^r Petitioners therefore humbly pray That yor Excellency and Hono^{rs} would please to take the premises into yor serious consideration, and to Grant an order or vote of this Hono^{ble} House for the final ending of this Controversy and the Rebuilding of the Meeting house in its usual place. And yor Petitioners shall ever pray &c

SAMUEL BENNETT	PETER JOSLIN	JOHN PRESCOTT Senr
SIMON STEVENS	JOHN BEMAN jun^r	CYPRIAN STEVENS
BEZALIEL SAYWIAR	WILLIAM DIVOLL	JOHN PRESCOT jun^r
EPHRAIM WILDER	JOHN JOHNSON	JOHN KEYES
JONATHAN WILDER	BENJ^A BELLOWS	NATHANIEL SAWYER
THOMAS ROSS	JOSEPH GLAZEIR	JOSIAH WHITE Jr
	JONATHAN WHITCOMB	JOHN HARRIS
	PHILIP GOSS	GEORGE HUES

Nov. ult. 1705. In Council Read & ordered That Jonathan Tyng, James Converse, Thomas Browne and James Minott Esqr^s. be a Comittee to hear the Allegations of both parts of the Town referring to the situation of their Meeting House, Jonathan Tyng Esqr. to appoint the time & place for the Committee^s meeting. And to Report their doeings to this Court at their next Session.

ISA. ADDINGTON Secy.

In ye house of Representatives voted a concurrence.

THOMAS OAKES Speaker

[Massachusetts Archives, XI, 200.]

Besides information of general interest given in the matter and by the signatures of this Petition, the clause which asserts in effect that not one man had been killed by the enemy on the east side of the river, is important, as helping to prove incorrect the statements of our historians that Richard Wheeler had a garrison at Wataquadock, and that he with Jonas and Joshua Fairbank were killed there in the massacre of 1676; and that Abraham Wheeler was slain there in 1695.

1706. *To His Excellency Joseph Dudley Esqr Captain Generall & Governour In Cheefe: &^{c}: Her Majesties Hon^{r}able Councill & Representatives of the Massachusetts Bay In New England, Convened in Generall Assembly at Boston: May ye 29th: Annoque Dom: 1706.*

Wheras it appeares that som of the Inhabitants of the Towne of Lancaster have made Application to your Excellency & Hon^{rs} concerning the place of Setting the Meeting house In said Towne & that a comittie hath been appointed to Consider thereof but not knowing how far they have proceeded therein nor what complaints have been made wee have thought It our duty to acquaint this Great & General Assembley with a breviate of the Townes Proceedings, Refferring to said meeting house & first at a Towne meeting appointed by ye selectmen of said Towne in order therto the 16 of October 1704 the Towne then voted to build a meeting house and agreed on ye demencions thereof unanimously, but when it came to be voted where it should stand about 4 or 5 persons Declared their dissent against it, but the Rest of the persons present at said meeting (or ye most of them by far) to ye number of neere 30 agreed to set sd house on ye East side of ye River on or neer to a plaine knowne by ye name of bridcake plaine in the most convenient place, but those which were dissatisfied objected that ye meeting was not Legall because only warned by the selectmen & not by warrant by the hand of ye constable, to Remove said objection the selectmen consented to warne another meeting to consider what was farther necessary to be don, Refferring to ye building of a meeting house & accordingly gave out warrants to ye Constables, to warne the Inhabitants to meet on Munday the 14 of May 1705, which was accordingly don & the Inhabitants of said Towne being com together after severall other things agreed upon, they came to discourse about ye place of seting the meeting house & having som debate theire were some that declared theire Dissent against any vote passing Referring to a meeting house, Resolving as they said that nothing should be don about it (without a comittie(except it be set on the place it last stood, but notwithstanding the Towne thought they were in theire way to try it by vote (as had formerly been used about our former meeting house & consonant with the first agreement of ye plantation about a meeting house) & accordingly voted by papers to set it on the East side of the River as neer to it as conveniently can be which was don by a majo^r vote neer Double to those that then appeared against it. afterwards at a Towne meeting October ye 8th, 1705: upon due warning given to consider about building the meeting house & how to Raise a Rate for it & first as to ye house notwithstanding a former vote about ye demencions thereof the Towne now agreed by a vote to build it Larger, also at another meeting November ye 19th 1705, it was againe voted as to ye place of setting sd house & by a major vote agreed to set it on ye east side of ye River on ye place concluded on by the former votes. In all which transactions the Towne have Indeavoured to accomodate ye whole as neer as may be & apprehend they have taken Right methods in Improving theire Liberties & followed the directions in the Law for the ordering & managing theire own prudentialls by a major vote, & this matter Refferring to a meeting house we think to be very essentiall & of great moment & a thing wherein every one ought to be privilidged with what convenience may be & which is the very thing cared and provided for in ye first covenant & agreement of ye Plantation about a meeting house, that it might be sett in the most equall & convenient place that may be advized by them, which is all we still desire & accordingly have endeavoured to follow ye stepes of our predessessors without being sencible of breaking any Law or wronging any persons among us, so humbly Craving your favourable construction of all our proceedings herein, & praying your Excellency & honors would Indeavour that peace with truth & equitie may be promoted amongst us we Remaine your most Humble Servants according to our Capacitie.

THOMAS WILDER
JOHN WILDER
JOHN HOUGHTON
JOSIAH WHETCOMB   } Selectmen

The said John Houghton subscribes to all above written except, what was don at said meeting Novemb^r the 19th 1705, at which meeting he was absent

[Massachusetts Archives, XI, 209.]

John Houghton, as town clerk, appends a certified copy of "the townes first agreement about a meeting house."

To his Excellency Joseph Dudley Esq. Captain Generall and Governour In Cheife &c. Her Majesties Hon^rable Councill and Representatives convened In Generall Assembley at Boston May ye 29th 1706.

Wheras som of ye Inhabitants of the Towne of Lancaster have manifested theire Disattisfaction with the Proceedings of said Towne Refferring to the Building of a Meeting house & have addressed themselves to y^e

Generall Court & have obtained a Comittie to Consider of ye premisses which Comittie (som of them) have had ye Reasons of ye Townes Proceedings therein in som measure laid before them which we hope & believe are suffisient to evince the equitie of ye same but what Influence they have had we know not, therefore we have thought it Necessary to acquaint this Great & Generall Assembley with som of many that might be alleadged, & first as to ye place of setting said house the Towne have considered the Circumstances of the case & have condisended (for ye convenience of ye Minister & those on ye west side of ye River) to set it neere a mile to ye westward of ye Center of ye Township & Inhabitants, there being neere two thirds of them that live on the east side of the River & neere two thirds of all publique charges are borne by them & neere two parts of ye Lands ly on ye East side & almost all the medowes so that that side not onely is, *but forever is like to be the bigest by far*, neither will the setting of a meeting House where the Towne have voted it disoblidge those on ye west side for neere halfe of them will be almost, if not altogether as nere to ye place now voted as they were to ye old place & the other but little farther from it, & there is above twenty famillies on ye east side that yet will be neere as far agen from ye meeting house as the farthest of those on ye west side, of such as are made further off by setting it on ye East side the River, & wheras som suppose it will be too far from ye minister we know not as yet how far that will be for the Towne have agreed to give him a hundred pound to settle himselfe & if it be his pleasure to live where he now doth (which is scarcely a mile) the Towne is not in fault about it, & as for setting a house on ye west side the River, the Towne can not comply with it *having lost two already burnt by the enemy on that side*, & therefore think it not prudence to build thereon againe, it being apprehended to be a very dangerous place & if there be any that is more safe & also more convenient for ye whole Towne then we apprehend it both our prudence & Duty to build it there, & whereas the most of them that seeme to be most avers to the Towns proceedings have declared it is because they are contrary to ye first agreement of ye Towne about a meeting house or else they could Redily comply, so on the contrary we apprehend what ye Towne have don herein is wholly consonant with said agreement as may be made appeare, the essence whereof is only this: viz to set it in the most equall and convenient place that may be advized & concluded by the Plantation, & if we must be compelled to set up a meeting house on ye place it last stood, then the neerest of all ye famillies on ye east side of ye River will be as farr if not farther from said House than the farthest of those that live on ye West side, except the Mill & we think they ar not farther from ye new place then they are from ye old, so that considering all our circumstances we apprehend we have don nothing to wrong any person but Indeavoured to accomodate the whole as neer as may be, so hoping that this Generall Court will not Infringe us of the Liberties & Privilidges Granted us by the Generall Courts Grants &

the Laws of this Province, for us to manage our owne affaires which being acted according as we conceive according to said Grants & Laws wee hope will be very much for yᵉ future peace & welfare of our towne, which wee hope & believe this Generall Court will alwayes be Ready to promote & hereby encourage us under those many Difucalties, we are Continually laboring under & be farther oblidged as in duty bound ever to pray &c : & Remaine your Excellencies & Honors most Humble Servants. In behalfe of yᵉ major part of yᵉ Inhabitants of Lancaster

JOHN HOUGHTON
THOMAS WILDER
JOSEPH WHEELOCK   } *Comittee*
JOSIAH WHETCOMB
JOHN WILDER

[Massachusetts Archives, XI, 208.]

The first clause printed in italics above, as the yet unfulfilled prophecy of one esteemed very wise in his generation, is commended to the attention of the Lancastrian towns east of the Nashaway, for their encouragement. The second passage italicised proves that the first church was burned by the savages, and probably during the abandonment of the settlement, 1676-9, being rebuilt upon the same spot about 1684. This has been noted in correction of popular belief and previous printed statement, by Reverend Abijah P. Marvin, in his history of Lancaster.

Wharas by the prouidence of God by sicknes I could not atend the commit at Boston yet I thout good to let thos that are concarned under stand my mind about that mater refaring to the seting of the meting houes of lankestr, that the most conuenient place for the inhabitance will be on the est sid of the riuer ner to or wher I under stand the town hath voted it.

Dat March 3 1706   THO: BROWNE.

CONCORD June. 5. 1706.

This may certifie whom it may concern, that whereas the subscriber was chosen one of a committee to make report where Lancaster meeting hous might most conveniently stand for the benefit of the inhabitants his opinion was that it should be on the est side of the town.

                JAMES MINOTT

[Massachusetts Archives, XI, 210.]

LANCASTER June y* 4 1706.

The Inhabitants of y* east side of y* River in said Towne met together to choose a Comitie to send to y* great and Generall Assembly now sitting: said Court having notified them to appeare that so a hearing of y* matter Refferring to y* place of setting up a meeting house in said Lancaster might be had said Inhabitants thought it necessary (the better to acquaint said Court) to measure & see the difference of y* Length of y* way from the houses in that part of y* Towne called y* neck to y* place where two of y* Comittie made theire Report the meeting house should stand & to y* place where y* Towne have voted it to stand & where y* other two of y* Comittie apprehend it most convenient, & find that neer one halfe of them are considerably neerer to y* Latter & the Rest of them but little farther from it than they are from y* place Reported to y* Court, & the farthest of them not fully two miles from y* place the Towne have voted it, except y* mill, & the Inhabitants on the East side of y* River must notwithstanding above 20 famillies of them go farther than any of y* west side & many must go twice, & some neere three times as far though the meeting house should be set where it is voted, so that we do not take the house from them on y* west side as they would Intimate, nor have we don anything but what was apprehended to be designed when y* last meeting house was built: for although then severall voted to set it on y* east side, yet the major vote carried it on y* west side y* River so all was quiet with this expectation and generall discourse, that the next we built should be set on y* east side without obstruction, therefor think it strange to meet with so much trouble about it from some of those on y* west side of y* River.

THOMAS WILDER
JOHN HOUGHTON
JOHN WILDER   } Comittie
JOSEPH WHEELOCK
JOSIAH WHETCOMB

[Massachusetts Archives, XI, 210.]

Province of Massachusetts Bay.
To his Excellency Joseph Dudley Esq. . . . . May, 29. 1706.

The Humble Petition of several of the Inhabitants of the Town of Lancaster whose names are hereunto subscribed in behalf of themselves and the Rest of the Inhabitants on the West side of the said Town. Sheweth, That yo[r] Petitioners presented a Humble Petition to this Great and General Assembly at their sessions in November last referring to the situation of their meeting house praying that it might be settled where it formerly stood (vizt: on the west, and most exposed side,) as is most convenient both for minister and people, as was fully set forth in sd Petition, to which yo[r] Petition[s] refer, the Consideration whereof yo[r] Excellency and Hono[rs] referred to a Committee of four Gent[n], two whereof vizt: Col. Tyng and Major Converse (who knew the Circumstances of the matter) were clearly for having it built on the West side, but the other two vizt: Major Browne & Capt. Minott who were strangers, refused to Concur with them so that nothing was then done. Yo^r Petitioners therefore humbly pray this Great & General Assembly would please to putt a final End to this affair which has been very troublesome & expensive to yor Petitioners and to Determine & appoint the place where theyr meeting house shall stand. And yor Petitioners (as in duty bound) shall ever pray, &c^{tra}

CYPRIAN STEVENS
JOHN PRESCOT
PETER JOSLIN
JOSIAH WHITE
EPH^M: WILDER

Verte

[*Endorsed.*]

May, ult. 1706. In Council. Read, & Resolved That both parts of the Town of Lancaster be heard before the whole Court on Friday the 7th of June next by their Committees, referring to the situation of their meeting House, and that they be notifyed to attend accordingly.

Sent down for concurrance.   ISA. ADDINGTON *Secry.*

In the House of Representatives June 1: 1706. Read and Resolved a concurrence.   THOMAS OAKES *Speaker*

12, June, 1706. In Council. Upon a full hearing of both parts of the Town of Lancaster by their Committees, Resolved That the Meeting House be Erected and set up at or near the place where the old Meeting House stood, and has been twice before built.

Sent down for concurrance.   ISA. ADDINGTON *Secy.*

In the House of Representatives June 26: 1706. Read & not agreed, & Comitted.

June 28: Upon a full Hearing, of both parts of ye Towne of Lancaster by their Comittees, & ye pleas made, by and in ye behalf of ye sd West side, vizt, y^t upon the setting sd house in ye old place they were obliged to pay for their house Lotts extraordinary to ye support of sd House & Ministry: And ye East side pleading the Rationality of ye Rebuilding of ye Meeting house on ye East side; In regard of ye danger where it stood formerly, & the dissasters that hath befallen them there: & y^t it is contrary to ye vote of about two thirds of ye Inhabitants, that met at a Legall Towne Meeting warned & held for the determining y^t affair in their Towne; & seeing most of the first planters children being remoued to ye east side Resolved, that ye meeting house be erected & sett at ye place, where ye Towne last appoynted, it should be sett upon ye East side of ye Riuer & y^t ye obligation layd upon ye sd House Lotts extraordinary shal be for euer hereafter null & voyd: & y^t said Land be rated to the ministry & sd House according as ye Townes other Lands Improved; by ye Income, as ye Law provides for Towne Rates.

  July 5 sent up for concurrence   THOMAS OAKES *Spkr*

 July, 13th 1706. In Council; Read and not concurred.

                  ISA ADDINGTON *Secy.*
 [Massachusetts Archives, XI, 207.]

To his Excellency Joseph Dudley Esq. Captain Generall and Governour in Chiefe &c: . . . . . .

 The Petition of John Houghton of ye Towne of Lancaster Humbly Sheweth. That Whereas som of ye Inhabitants of said Lancaster on ye West side of ye River have applyed themselves to the Generall Assembly Manifesting theire Dissattisfaction with ye Townes Proceedings Refferring to ye place of setting theire meeting house & his Excellency & Councill having sent to said Towne to stop theire proceeding theirin till the said Generall Court shall give theire Direction concerning it, In obedience whereunto said Towne have Desisted & have don nothing to it since the Spring so that ye frame is much damnified by ye weather, & ye People under great disadvantage for want thereof, having for above this two yeares been necessitated to meet (on the Sabath) at the Ministers House which will not containe halfe ye Inhabitants but many of them must stand abroad in all weathers which is very greivious, nor can they heare the minister with that benifitt that otherwise they might, & if they may not forthwith go on to finish said House they must still be under the same uncomfortable circumstances this winter also: as for ye distance of ye inhabitants on ye west side the River from ye place where the frame now standeth the farthest of them is but about two miles, & there is above 20 famillies on the east side that the neerest of them will still be at least three miles from it & som 4 or 5, & were it not to accomodate those on the west side as neere as may be, said meeting house should have been sett neere a mile more eastward to com to ye center of ye Towneship & Inhabitants, your Petitioner therefore Humbly prayes that your Excellency & Hon^{rs} would take ye Premisses into your Consideration & Grant that the former Restriction may be taken off & all obsticles Removed, Refferring thereto, which tis hoped will be much for ye peace & encouragement of said Inhabitants & farther oblidge yor Petitioner as in duty bound ever to pray &c:

                  JOHN HOUGHTON.

 Nov: 1: 1706, Read In the House of Representatives. Ordered that the Prayer of sd Petition be Granted.

  Sent up for concurrence.   THOMAS OAKES *Sp.*

 Nov. 2, 1706. In Council Read & Concurred.

                  ISA. ADDINGTON *Secy:*
 I consent to the within order.   J. DUDLEY.

An interesting picture for those who have eyes to see, is framed in this simple letter of the old town's clerk — a pleasant picture, wherein the shadow of a severe asceticism is perfused with the glow of heroic faith — a picture of the Sabbath in Lancaster one hundred and seventy-five years ago — fifty and more of our sturdy progenitors at stated hour, some on horseback with wife or daughter on pillion behind them, most afoot, with guns on shoulder, wending their way at the head of their families from widely scattered homes towards a common centre — from Prescott's Mills and Bare Hill, from the Neck and Bridecake Plain, from Quasaponikin, Wataquadock and far-away Kequassagansit, little processions of God-fearing people clad in leather and homespun, coming through storm or sunshine, in winter's snow or spring mire, and gathering about the parsonage at the road crossing in South Lancaster; filling its rooms to overflowing, and huddling about its open doors to catch in listening ears and carry away in retentive memories the fervid exhortations of young master John Prentice, the new minister.

The frame, "damnified" by two years' storms, was now quickly covered in, and peace reigned in the church. Very few facts can be gleaned from contemporary records about the edifice, except that Robert Houghton was probably chief architect and builder; the town voting him twelve acres of land "for work don by him at the meeting house," and twenty-five acres "for making the pulpit." His brother John seems to have been a peace maker in the controversy, and is credited with the gift of the site for the building, while Thomas Wilder gave land opposite for the burial ground, now known as the Old Common Cemetery. Reverend Timothy Harrington tells us that Mr. John Prentice began preaching here in May, 1705, was offered a settlement February, 1707, and was ordained on the 29th of March, 1708. Joseph Willard, Esq., in his history of Lancaster gives some information respecting Mr. Prentice's family which, he is careful to state, was derived from the investigations of another. His informant was largely in error, if we may believe the results of more modern research. Reverend John Prentice was born in Newton about 1682, being the son of Thomas, Jr., and Sarah (Stanton) Prentice. His father died in 1684. His grandfather was the captain of cavalry famous in Philip's war, who was alive at the time of his grandson's settlement in Lancaster, but died at the age of ninety, July 6, 1710, "in consequence of a fall from his horse while returning from public worship." John Prentice, according to the Roxbury church records, was married to Mrs. Mary Gardner, Dec. 4, 1705. His faithful ministry in Lancaster ended with his life, Jan. 6th, 1748.

1707   LANCASTER August y⁰ 19 1707.
May it Please your excell⁷. About four of the Clock afternoon.

 Wee are sorry that we have Such News to acquaint you with, in y⁺ in our Persuit & Engagement with yᵉ enemy we lost 2 men of marlborough besides Wilder which was taken which is Killed; one of Lancaster and one of marlborough is wounded: we overtook them about 8 or 9 mile wide of Lancaster this day about 9 a clock this day where we fought them about 2 hours the enemy haveing a great advantage of us when we come up with them; there being about thirty of them as we suppose, at Length we wholly routed them and took all their packs and provision & have Slain Severall of them without any doubt, but we had not Time to find them. we have sent about thirty men to waylay them or head them if they can, being in great hast we subscribe
        Your excelly⁸ Most Humble Servᵗˢ,
Praying your further directˢ.   THO: HOWE
             JOSIAH CŌVERSE
[Massachusetts Archives LI, 174.]

 On Monday last the 16th currant. Thirteen Indians on the Frontiers surprised two men at their labour in the Meadows at Marlborough about four miles distant from the body of the Town, took them both alive; and as they parted out of the Town took a woman also in their marching off, whom they killed. How, one of the Prisoners broke away in a scuffle, and brought home the Indians Gun and Hatchet, and acquainted the Garrison and Inhabitants, who speedily followed them, and were joyned by 20 from Lancaster, being in all 40 odd, came up with the Enemy who were also increased to 36 and on Tuesday at ten of the Clock found them, and in two hours exchanged ten shot a man in which skirmish we lost two men and had two slightly wounded, and no doubt we killed several of the Enemy, whose Tracts of being draggd away we saw, but recovered but one of them, tho tis probably conjectured, that we killed 10 or 12 at least; we took 24 of their Packs, and drove them off their ground, and are yet pursued by two Parties of the Forces from Lancaster and Groton; at our Forces overtaking and attacking the Enemy they barbarously murdered the Captive.

[Boston News Letter, 25 August, 1707.]

Parties of hostile Indians had been continually hovering about the settlement, and on the 16th of July, 1707, had killed Jonathan White, a son of Josiah, and brother of Captain John White. The captive mentioned above as "barbarously murdered," was also a Lancaster man recently removed to Marlborough, by name Jonathan Wilder, whose father, Lieutenant Nathaniel Wilder, had been slain in 1704. He was twenty years of age. The other victims were: Richard Singleterry and John Farrar killed, Ephraim Wilder and Samuel Stevens wounded severely.

Ensign John Farrar was of Lancaster birth, being son of Jacob Farrar, Jr., who was killed in the massacre of Aug. 22, 1675.

Ephraim Wilder was brother to the captive, and it is probable that the detailed account of the affair given by Reverend Timothy Harrington in the Century Sermon, was derived from him. He lived until 1769, dying Dec. 13th of that year, aged 94. The place where the skirmish was fought is in the northwest corner of Sterling, and to this day is called the Indian Fight.

1708. *To his Excellency Joseph Dudley Esq. Captain Generall and Governour In Chiefe &c: . . . . Boston: June ye 10th: 1708:*

The Petition of Samuell Brigham of ye Town of Marleborough In behalfe of Severall Persons Inhabitants of Marleborough & Lancaster: Humbly Sheweth, That Whereas somtime in ye Month of August Last past, In an Engagement with ye Indian Enemy, In ye woods beyond Lancaster, besides other Damages not here mentioned; Ephraim Wilder of said Lancaster was then wounded being shot through the thigh which wound was Considerable Damage to him in Loss of time being ten weeks beside ye paine of said wound & cost of cure, which was foure pounds ten shillings, as may appeare by the Docters Bill for sd cure, also there was one Gun lost being caried away by y‍ᵉ enemy which Gun belonged to John ffarer of Marleborough who was then slaine, & his widow & children Left in a Low condition, y‍ᵉ Gun was worth at y‍ᵉ Least fourty shillings which yoʳ Petitioner prays may be alowed to said Widow; there were two Horses killed and two wounded, one that was killed belonged to Jonathan Brigham being worth eight pounds & the other valued worth foure pounds belonged to Samuell Ward one of y‍ᵉ Horses wounded was Joseph Newtons his charge of cure & Damage was at least twelve shillings, the other Horse wounded belonged to Oliver How whose charge for cure & Damage was twenty shillings, ther was also somthing Considerable expended as was Necessary for y‍ᵉ Decent Buriall of three Persons Slain in said Engagement.

Your Petitionʳ therefore Humbly Prays that your Excellency & Honʳˢ would take the Premisses into your serious Consideration & Grant such Reasonable alowances to y‍ᵉ Parties concerned as above mentioned: as In your Wisdom shall seem Just & Equitable & your Petitioner as In Duty Bound Shall ever pray &c.   Samᴸᴸ. Brigham.

House of Representatives, June 16. 1708. Read & Resolved: That there be allowed & Paid out of the Publick Treasury, as follows, vizt:

To Ephraim Wilder for the cure of his wound the sum of three Pounds and for the losse of his Time, charges &c five Pounds.

To the widow of John Farrer for a Gun lost Thirty shillings.

To Jonathan Brigham for a Horse killed four Pounds.

To Samˡˡ Ward for a Horse killed Two Pounds.

    Sent up for concurrence, 16 June 1708

                       Thomas Oliver *Speaker*

In Council   Read & concurrᵈ   Isa. Addington *Secret*

                     Concord June 8 1708.

These may Certify whom it may concern there is due to me for Medicine dressing & curing of a wound in y‍ᵉ thygh of Ephraim Wilder of Lancaster which he Received by a shott from y‍ᵉ Enemy in a late engagement some time in August last under y‍ᵉ conduct of Let Brigham of Mlbrow, y‍ᵉ sum of four pounds tenn shillings as atests

                       Jona. Prescott *Chir*.

[Massachusetts Archives, LXXI, 454 et. seq.]

In Massachusetts Archives, LXXI, 421–3, is a petition from Samuel Stevens dated Nov. 10, 1707, asking aid, "his hands being both shott by y‍ᵉ enemy & lost many joynts which has Greatly disinablᵈ him as to his caling, being a Joyner." Twenty pounds was voted him and a pension, at pleasure of the government, of forty shillings per annum.

1709. *To his Excellency Joseph Dudley Esqr Capt General and Govern^r in Chief in and over her Majesties Province af the Massachusetts Bay in New England, and to the Most Honorable Gen^t of her Majesties Council, with the Honor^{ble} Gent of the house of Representatives.*

 Humble Pettion of us Whose Names are Under Written humbley Sheweth, we Inhabiting on ye West part of ye Town of Lancaster being ye extreame front, & haveing Subsisted Capt Willm Tyngs men, are kept out of our Money to our Great damage, sume of us haueing Rec^d nothing since Apr^{ll} 28th 1708. Which to last April maks a full yeare besids old arers of no smal sum. Sume of us being poor & Under Ingagmts wch cannot be answered for Want hereof wch exposses to ye penalty of ye law, we haue now to Adress ourselves but to yor Hon^{rs} as ye fathers of our Israel, hoping you will Vouhsafe to help us, that our Money so well deserved, Being alowed but 3^s ye week a man, may be more easchy com at & not to pass through ye hands of perticuler men, wch has greatly hurt us sum years past, if your Hon^{rs} se cause to Graunt yor Pettin^{rs} what we pray for, will lay us Under obligations to pray for yor Hon^{rs} peace & Pr^{s}perity.

       Yo^r most humble Servts
 Oct 28 1709.

           JABEZ FFAIRBANKS
           JOSEPH HUTCHINS
           JOHN GLAZEAR
           JOHN PRESCOT
           CYPRIAN STEVENS
           SIMON STEVENS
           JOSIAH WHITE
           NATHANILL SAWYER

[*Endorsed.*]

 In the House of Representatives. Novr. 10: 1709. Read and ordered, That the Treasurer, be Directed, to make no Paymts either to Col Tyng, or his son Maj Tyng, for any Demands they haue to make, upon the Treasury, for any sum or sums due to them, untill they Produce Discharges, under the hands of the Petitioners, for the sums due to them, for their Billetting Souldiers (by their order,) unto this present year 1709. And That the sd Col. & his son, do notify the severall Inhabitants of Lancaster, Grotton Dunstable &c, That haue by their order Billetted, Souldiers to meet with them some time in this present month of November, at some certain place in the respective Towns, that they make up their amounts & Take Discharges from the Severall Inhabitants, for their Billetting Souldiers for the time afores^d.

 Sent up for concurrence.   JOHN CLARK *Speaker*

		lb	s	d
due to Jabez ffairbanks for Billeting of men under the command of Capt William Tyng in the years 1707 & 1708 —		9 ,,	16 ,,	10
due to John Prescott —		2 ,,	12 ,,	4
due to Joseph Hutchins —		1 ,,	19 ,,	8
due to Nathanael Sawyer —		2 ,,	8 ,,	9
due to Cyprian Steevens —		6 ,,	19 ,,	6
due to Simon Steevens —		1 ,,	17 ,,	8
due to Josiah Whit —		2 ,,	8 ,,	0

LANCHASTER twenty first of November 1709
Then received of Captain William Ting for subsisting men under his command in full from the beginning of y^e world to the twenty eighth of Aprill one thousand seven hundred and nine by us the subscribers

NATHANIEL SAWYER
CYPRIAN STEUENS
SIMON STEUENS
JOSIAH WHITE
JABEZ FAIRBANK
JOHN PRESCOTT
JOSEPH $\overset{his}{+}\underset{mark}{}$ HUCTHINS

[Massachusetts Archives, LXXI, 565-8.]

The first page of the Church Records, begun by Reverend John Prentice after his settlement, contains a copy of the Covenant. There are no minutes of church meetings before 1728, all earlier records being those of baptisms and admissions to the church.

LANCASTER CHURCH COVENANT.

Renewed March 29 1708 *before the Ordination of the Revd John Prentice.*

We whose Names are hereunto subscribed being Inhabitants [of the] Town of Lancaster in New-England, Knowing that we [are] prone to offend & Provoke the most high God, both in heart [word and deed] through the Prevalence of Sin that dwelleth within us, & [through] Temptations from without us, for which we have great [reason to] be Unfeignedly humbled before him from Day to Day do [in the] name of our Lord Jesus Christ, with Dependance upon the Assistance of his holy Spirit, Solemnly enter into Covenant with God, & one with another according to God, as followeth.

Imprimis That having Chosen & taken the Lord Jehovah to [be our] God, we will fear him, cleave to him in Love, & serve [him in] truth with all our hearts giving up ourselves unto him [as his] People. In all things to be at his Direction & Sovereigne [disposal], that we may have & hold

Communion with him as [members] of Christs Mystical Body, according to his Revealed will [unto our] Lives End.

2. We also bind ourselves, to bring up our Children & Servants [in the] Knowledge & fear of God, by holy Instructions according to our abilities, & in Special by the Use of orthodox Catechisms [that] true Religion may be maintained in our families while we [live] yea and among such as shall Live when we are dead & Gone.

3. And we further promise, To Keep close to ye truth of Christ, endeavouring with lively Affection towards it in our hearts, to defend it against all opposers y^{r}of, as God shall call us at any time thereunto, [which] that we may do, We Resolve to use the holy scriptures [as our] platforme, whereby we may discern the mind of Christ [and not the] New found Inventions of men.

4. We also Ingage our selves to have a Careful Inspection of our own hearts, viz, so as to Endeavour by the Virtue of the [death] of Christ, the mortification of all our sinful Passions, [worldly] frames & Disorderly affections, whereby we may be withdrawn [from] the Living God.

5. We moreover Oblidge our selves (in the faithful Improvement [of our] ability and opportunity) to worship God according to all the particular institutions of Christ for his Church under Gospel Administrations [with] Reverent attention unto ye word of God, to pray unto him [with] Praises, and to hold Communion each with other, in the [use of] the seals of the Covenant, namely, Baptism & ye Supper of [the Lord.]

6. We Likewise promise, That we will peaceably submit [unto the] Discipline appointed by Christ in his Church for offenders, obeying (according to ye will of God) them that have the Rule over us in the [Lord.]

7. We also bind our selves to walk in Love one towards another endeavouring our mutual Edification, Visiting, Exhorting, Comforting, [as occasion] serveth, and warning any Brother or Sister which offendeth [not] divulging private offences Irregularly, but heedfully following the Precepts laid down for Church dealing Matth. 18, 15, 16, 17. [While for]giving all that do manifest unto the Judgment of Charity [that they] truly Repent of their miscarriages.

Now the God of peace that brought again from the Dead Our Lord [the] great shepherd of the sheep through the Blood of the Everlasting [Covenant,] Make us perfect in every good Work to do his Will, working that which is well pleasing in his sight through Jesus X to whom [be] glory for ever & ever. Amen.

Words printed in brackets are in place of those worn from edge of leaf. The writing is that of Mr. Prentice, and at the end he signed his own name, and wrote below it the names of seven of his church, perhaps at that time the only male members. They were: Thomas Wilder,

John Houghton, Josiah Whetcomb, John Wilder, Jeremiah
Willson, John Rugg, Jonathan Moor. Twenty-five other
names have been signed on the same, and four on the
opposite page, from time to time, as they became members
of the church; for example, Major Samuel Willard's, who
joined Nov. 18, 1733, and that of Joseph Wilder, Jr., who
was admitted April 14, 1734. A majority seem not to have
signed this copy of the covenant.

1710. *Middlesex ss. To her Majesties Honrable Justices of said County
of Middlesex convened in Quarter Sessions at Charlstowne, March
ye 13th 1710/11.*

The Humble Request of The Inhabitants of ye Towne of Lancaster
as ffolloweth. That forasmuch as said Inhabitants have for several yeares
past Sustained Great Damage by Reason of Many Cattell & Horses belonging to other Townes being brought to feed (in ye Sumer Season) on
our Comons, although ye owners of said cattell have no Right therin &
Some of our Inhabitants that live neer the outskirts of ye Towne have
from time to time for several yeares past Received such cattell under their
care & Inspection, whereby we are not only Damnified In our feeding
land, but also most of our out medows are quite Ruined & so eat up that
we can get but very Little Hay, but shall unavoidably leen our cattell.
For Prevention of the Like Damage for ye future ye Inhabitants of said
Lancaster at theire Towne Meeting May ye 22^d 1710, Voted & ordered &
ye Selectmen of said Towne have Acordingly agreed & concluded that
from & after ye first Day of April next beinge ye yeare of our Lord 1711 if
any Person or Persons inhabitants of said Lancaster shall Presume to take
in any such cattell as above said whose owners have no Right nor Privilege in said Comons, & shall Keep such Cattell to Run at Large to ye Damage of ye Towne as abovesaid, every such Inhabitant so doing shall be
Lyable to pay as a fine (to ye use of the Towne) five shillings pr head for
every such beast so taken & Kept by them to feed on said Comons as
abovesaid, which in behalfe of ye Inhabitants of said Lancaster is hereby
presented to your Hon^{rs} Humbly praying your alowance & approbation of
ye same that so it may be binding to all ye Inhabitants of said Lancaster
in all Respects as the Law Dirrects in such Cases, that may be approved
off by your Hon^{rs} & Remaine

Your Hon^{rs} most Humble Servants.

THOMAS WILDER
JOHN HOUGHTON } *Selectmen*
JOSEPH WILDER
JACOB HOUGHTON

[Middlesex Court Files.]

CHARLESTOWN, Mar 13 1710/11.

The Court having Inspected the by Laws of the sd Town of Lancaster as on file allow of the same for this year.

[Middlesex Court Records.]

1710–11. *Middlesex ss. To her Majesties Hon^rable Justices of said County of Middlesex Convened in Quarter Sessions at Charlstowne.*

March ye 13th 1710 11. Pursuant to a summons Wherein ye Selectmen of ye Towne of Lancaster or some of them are Required to appeare at said Sessions to Answer to a Presentment of said Towne for want of a Schoolmaster. These are Humbly to acquaint your Hon^{rs} that before the presentment wee had appointed a Towne Meeting in order to ye procuring of a Schoolmaster & accordingly have agreed with Mr. John Houghton Senr. for the yeare ensuing who is now actually Ingaged for & in said work, & hath formerly been Imployed by the Towne in said service & Instructed some in Writing but under our present Dangerous Circumstances it is very Hazardous sending our children to schoole Living so scattering, yet we are willing to do herein what Possibly is to be done, not onely to answer ye Law but for our own benifitt & therefore Humbly pray there may be no farther Proceedings upon said Presentment.

Dated LAN^R. March ye 9th 1710/11.

pr yr Hon^{rs} most Humble Servants

THOMAS WILDER
EPHRAIM WILDER } Selectmen
JOSEPH WILDER
JACOB HOUGHTON

[Middlesex Court Files.]

CHARLESTOWN Mar. 13 1710/11.

The Selectmen of Lancaster appearing in Court to answ^r their presentment of their Town for want of a schoolmaster and representing to ye Court their circumstances and their care for Instruction of youth, the Court accepts the same and allow thereof till further order of this Court as on file.

[Middlesex Court Records.]

1711   A LIST OF THE FRONTIER GARRISONS REVIEWED BY ORDER OF HIS EXCELLENCY THE GOVERNOUR IN NOVEMBER 1711.

No.	Garrisons	Families	Inhabitants	Souldiers	Souls
1	Heze Willard	3	4	1	8
2	Mrs Houghton	4	5	1	25
3	Capt Wilder	7	11	1	47
4	Mr Houghton	2	4	1	13
5	Mr White	6	8	2	38
6	Lieut Joslin	3	3	2	18
7	Mr Bowers	3	7	1	9
8	Mr Bennet	3	7	0	34
9	Mr Stevens	4	4	2	19
10	Mr Prentice	2	2	3	9
11	Ensg Wilder	4	4	2	18
12	Mr Sawyer	5	7	1	23
13	Mr Prescot	3	4	2	15
14	Mr Beaman	3	4	0	14
15	Mr Snow	3	4	0	18
16	Henry Houghton	3	2	0	15
17	Mr Preist	6	7	0	25
18	Caleb Sawyer	2	3	1	11
19	Wm Sawyer	3	3	0	12
20	Mr Whitcomb	4	4	0	17
21	Mr More	1	1	0	8
22	John More	2	2	0	7
23	Mr Houghton	1	1	1	3
24	Mr Wilson	1	3	0	11
25	Jo Whitcombe	2	2	0	7
26	Mr Wheeler	3	4	0	19
27	Mr Fairbank	2	5	0	15
27		83	111	21	458

[Massachusetts Archives, LXXI. 876.]

1711.   At a town meeting held February 5, some action was taken favoring the acquisition by the town of the land bonded by Tahanto in 1701, and ninety-eight of the inhabitants signed the following contract:

Know all men, that we the subscribers being desirous to purchase a tract of Land which lieth on the West side of Lancaster, which lands have formerly been petitioned for to the General Court, and which the Inhabitants of Lancaster are still in pursuance of and their petition is still with the General Court for granting the same, and considerable money having been paid to George Tahanto and other Indians, towards the purchasing of said lands though not yet consumated, We, the subscribers, do hereby bind ourselves and our heirs to pay each one his equal share of the purchase of said land, and all charges that have or shall be expended about the same, and to run equal hazard of obtaining said land, provided that if said land be obtained, we shall each one have an equal share and the said money to be paid before the 5th of March next, and shall subscribe hereto on or before the 15th of the present month or else lay no claim to said land.

Feb. 15, 1714, a committee was chosen to apportion this land, forty acres of the best ground being allotted to each share.

LANCASTER November 21 and 22, 1711.

Whereas we the subscribers namely Jonathan prescott John Farnworth and Sam^{ll} Jones are a Comity Appointed to vew a tract of Land petitioned for by ye Inhabitants of Lancaster and to make Report theireof to the Genarall Court or Assembly for theire farther Consideration, and we have Accordingly been upon ye spott the Days above Dated and proseded their upon as foloweth.

Imp^r we began at ye northwest corner of the proper Bounds of Lancaster plantation and from thence Run a Line upon a north west point or neer theirabouts along by ye southwest sides of Masapauge & unkachewalunck ponds extending said line three miles & from thenc we made an angle Runing neer upon a south west poynt Crosing a River caled ye North River & so Ranging along over Hills Caled manosok Hils sd line being about six mils in length till it meets with ye middle branch of Lancaster River at or neer a litel Hill on which ye Indians had marked a tree for a corner of said Land. Being neer five mils wide at the Southerd end bounded partly by the River & partly by Capt. Davenports farm to the South west corner of Lancaster old bounds the land Included within these lines is Rocky and mountinous and very poorly acomodated with medow.

JONATHAN PRESCOTT.
SAMLL. JONES
JOHN FFARNWORTH

In the House of Representatives Mar: 20: 1711.

Ordered that the Tract of Land as above Described be added & Confirmed to the Town of Lancaster, as part of that Township.

Sent up for concurrence. JOHN BURRILL *Speaker*

In Council, 21, March, 1711. Read.

In the House of Representatives Oct: 25 : 1712.

Ordered that the Vote of this House above written be Revived & sent up for Concurrence.

JOHN BURRILL *Speaker*

[*Endorsed.*]

1713. June 5, 1713. In Council

Read and Ordered That the Tract of Land as within described be added and confirmed to the Town of Lancaster as part of that Township, not prejudicing any former Grants.

Sent down for concurrance. ISA. ADDINGTON *Secy.*

In the House of Representatives June 8 1713 Read & Concured.

JOHN BURRILL *Speaker*

[Massachusetts Archives, CXIII, 633.]

1715. To the Hon^{rable} His Majties Justices of the County af Middlesex Convened in Quarter Sessions at Charlestown December. ye 13th 1715.

These are to acquaint your Hon^{rs} that for as much as we understand that the Towne of Lancaster is under Presentment for want of a Grammar Schooll & some of ye Selectmen of said Towne are Required to appeare in order to Answer thereto we have accordingly appointed Capt. Joslin & Mr Hooker Osgood to Inform your Hon^{rs} that we having no Grand Jury man had no knowledge of ye Presentment till we were summoned to answer, yet nevertheless the Towne for these severall months have Indeavored to Procure a schoole master that may benefit ye Towne & answer ye Law, & have agred with a young Gentleman Viz : Mr Perpoint of Roxbury who had now Probably been actually in said service but his Indisposition of Body hinders ; we would crave leave further to acquaint your Hon^{rs} that we are humbly of oppinion that we are scarcely Liable to Presentment for we have but very Lately had ye number of families ye Law Requires, & a considerable number of them are either single Persons widows or poor families noways able to Contribute to ye Charge nor yet subsist without Reliefe, therefore Humbly pray that no fine may be Imposed upon us, nor be as yet enjoined to be constantly provided with a Grañer Schoolemaster but that a writing schoole may answer till our number be Increased. In behalfe of the Selectmen of Lancaster.

JOHN HOUGHTON

Dated LAN^r Decemb^r ye 12 1715 *Town Clerk*

1715. CHARLESTOWN Dec 13 1715

Capt. Joslin & Mr. Hooker Osgood of ye Selectmen of Lancaster appearing to answer their prsentment for want of a grammar school, Informing the court they have agreed wth young Mr Pierpont who had been with y^m actually but is fallen under indisposition of Body by reason of sickness & expect him speedily, the court accept the sd answer and are dismist paying fee.

[Middlesex Court Records.]

The law of 1647 enjoins that "where any towne shall increase to ye number of 100 families or house hould^{rs} they shall set up a grammer schoole, ye mr thereof being able to instruct youth so farr as they may be fited for ye university." This law was in force, and the above action of the court fixes approximately the population of Lancaster at this date.

1715. Notandum, August, 4th 1715, Att a Church meeting att ye house of John Prentice, Captain Peter Joslin & Joseph Wilder were chosen to ye Deacons office in the Church of Christ in Lancaster & accepted of said office.

[Lancaster Church Records.]

Where not otherwise stated, the following pages in the town's records are by the hand of Joseph Wilder, Sen., proprietor's clerk.

1716. Monday Feburary the 4th 1716/17. att a Meeting of the Propratee of Lancaster it being there Stated Meeting. and first made Choyce of Jabaz ffairbank as Moderater for Said Meeting Then severall Propozitions was Read before the Town brou into ye Selectmen

I Towit the proposition of Nahum Ward Desiers that the Hiway that Leyeth by his Hous may be altered on ye South Side the brook & Lye a little Higher & it will be upon as good Land & as Neer to pass to where it now Lyes on Divols Land

2. Josah White Desiers the Town would Grant Liberty that two gates may be sett up on the hiway through his entervail according to a former order in ye Town

3. John Houghton Senr Desieres the Town would Let him have the entervale aboue the Red Spring which was formerly granted to Danil Gaines to make up his entervale Lott the said Houghton haveing Purchased said Gaines Second devition entervale Lott & Cannot find where it was Laied out : or if he Cannot have sade entervale Then that the Town would Grant him some other land in Lew there off

4. Then Jonathan Houghton desiers the town to Grant him Liberty to Cutt 3 or 4 hundered pine trees & draw the Turpentine, s^d pines desiered ar ajoyning to Som Land of his fathers on ye west side the hiway that Leeds to Thomas Wilders.

The collection of turpentine and manufacture of tar in the New England pine forests had become an important industry, and these products an article of export to Great Britain. So early as 1703 legislation was demanded to prevent the destruction of trees by those engaged in the public forests collecting turpentine.

5. Ebenezer Wilder desiers the Town would Grant him fifty three acres of Land, or there abouts partly leyed out by him soposed to be but a part of what was purchesed by him of John Addams; or Els that the Town would appoint som meet person to state and make bounds with him as Neer as may be according to what is Written the bounds being som of them Lost.

6 Jonathan Moor desiered the Town would Grant him a hiway through ye Land of Willm & Joseph Sawyer formerly Granted & Laied out to bare hill Medows.

7 the propozition of John Goss desiers the hiway that goes from the Scar bridge to the mill may go up by the River & so com in to the path after it com up the Hill

8 a Clame was Made by Severall Persons Represented by frances fullom to wit as followeth.

We the subscribers whose Names are under Written

	£ s d
Daniel How upon the Right of Capt Henry Carley —	100 - 0 - 0
John Barns upon the Right of Capt Henry Carley —	050 - 0 - 0
James Keyes upon the Right of ——— Roper —	050 - 0 - 0
John Shermon upon the Right of John Moor —	
Benjamin Bayley upon the Right of John Houghton —	020 - 0 - 0
David Church on ye Right of Capt Carley —	050 - 0 - 0
David Church upon the Right of Edward Breck —	050 - 0 - 0
John Booker upon ye Right of Robert Houghton —	
Simon Gates upon the Right of Steeven Gates —	314 - 0 - 0
Isaac Hunt upon ye Right of Samuell Bennit —	030 - 0 - 0
Sam^{ll} Wright upon ye Right of Cypran Steevens —	040 - 0 - 0
Fra Fullam upon ye Right of George Adams —	

Do Hereby Demand all & every of our Respective Rights & Divisions of in & unto all Rights & Devitions of Lands Made or to be Made in that tract of Land Last Granted by the Great & Generall Court of the Province of the Massachusets Bay in New England the 27 of May 1713 to be added & Confermed to ye Town of Lancaster as part of that Townsheep in which Tract of Land we have & Clame our Just Rights of property in proportion as being Invested with the oRiganal Rights in said Town of Lancaster

    JOHN SHERMON SAM^{LL} WRIGHT
    DANIL HOW   FRA FULLAM
    JOHN BARNS   DAVID CHURCH
    JAMES KEYES   BENJ BAILY
    SIMON GATES

In the second place they Granted the Proposition of Nahum Ward refering to ye Hiway.

Thirdly they Granted Josiah White Leberty to set up Gats in the Hiway foure years

forthly they Granted the proposition of John Houghton Refering to Ganes Entervail that it lie aboue the Read Spring provided it be not found to be all Ready Laid out els where

In ye 5 place In answer to the Proposition of Jonathan Moor they Made Choyce of Left John Houghton Ensigne James Wilder & Josiah Wheeler to be a Commity to vew ye way proposed for by Jonathan Moor from his Hous to barehill Medow, & pertequlerly through ye Land of Willi^m & Joseph Sawyers Land to See if there be need there of: & if needed to Lay out ye same & make a Report to the Town.

Sixtly They Voted that Ebenezer Wilder have sixty-three acres of Land in full of what was purchased by him of John Adams where he hes now Layed it out by Jonas Houghton Juner: with alowance for a hieway through a part of it

Seaventhly they voted that they will Lay out ye Stated Comon on ye west side the River & appointed Jonas Houghton Ju. to be the servaier & that Eph Wilder & Joseph Wilder assist him therein & make a Return to the ajornment of this Meeting

Eaightly they voted that ye first Monday of March next be the Meeting for Choosing of Town offisers.

Ninthly they voted that John Houghton Ephriam Wilder James Wilder & Joseph Wilder should Treet with the Noninhabitance Refering to there Right

In ye Tenth place, There was a motion made in sd Meeting that ye Stated Common & other Commons should be divided: but was left to Consederation

There was allso then a Return made to the Town by a Commity who sent to vew ye Land of Edmund & Ebenezer Harris & to se how there bounds was betwene them & the Stated Common & Reported thus that they had made bounds, from Ebenezer bemans Corner to ye Corner of John Benit Layed out to ye Right of Mucklode takeing in ye swamp to the Harrises as it is now marked John Benits Corner being a little pine & so Runs to a popler takeing in a Smal Corner of Land to Ebenezer Harris & from thence it Runes to a Red Oke at ye hiway on ye west side of the hiway & so to a Red Oke. one the east side ye way & so runs to a white oke & so to another white oke & so to Ebenezer Bemans Corner. Note allso that ye line from Jonn Benits Corner Runs straight to the ould Corner of Ebenezer Harris Land being a pine. Said Report was Excepted by the Town and ye Meeting was ajorned by the Moderater to ye fifth day of March next following.

March ye 5 1716/17. The propriaters of the Town of Lancaster Meet at the Meeting hous upon ajournment from ye forth of February & first took into there Consederation the Motion & Clam Made by Seaverall persons Represented by Cpt frances Fullum upon ye 4 of february last past of and in a tract of Land purchased by the Inhabitance of Lancaster of Goorge Dahannata & other Indins & since aded & confermed to ye Town of Lancaster by the Great & General Court, agitated the Same & Concluded that they towit the proprieters of the Town of Lancaster haue no Right nor Enterest in sd Land purchased of ye Indiens by any former Rights of the Town of Lancaster & allso further Conclude & agree that they will haue nothing to do with ye said Land in point of devition upon ye OReginall Rights of said Town. But Conclude that it be to ye Inhabytance of said Town of Lancaster who purchased ye same, set off as a propriaty ye first tusday of March 1715-16 as their proper Right & propriety to order Divide Improve & despose of the same according to there enterest therein by purchas as ye Law in that case hes made provition.

Secondly They Made Choyce of Mr John Houghton & Jabaz Fairbank to give an answer to ye Non Resodance Refering to there Clame.

thirdly they Chose Jonas Houghton Ju to be a Servairer to Lay out Land in ye old Town Bounds

forthly The Town Made Choyce of John Houghton Nathanil Sawyer Jonas Houghton & Joseph Wilder to be a Committy to Mesuer & find out ye Lotts formerly Layed out in Quasaponacin & make Report to ye Town as soone as may be

fifthly that ye Stated Common Extend half a Mile wide till ye first or loer line com to ye River

6 They Granted a half devision of Land in the undevided Land in Lancaster to be divided by the same Rule as formerly & that they begin to Lay out the first of May next & not before

7 They Granted Eaighty acres of Land to John Houghton Sr for Serveing as Clerk & Makeing of Rates, Lying aboue ye Red Spring if found out of ye Stated Common

8 They Town Granted six acres of Land to John Wilder & foure to James Wilder for alowance for a hiewaie through ye Land of John Wilder from ye Corner of his Land till it Comes to ye Land of Joseph Wilder & from ye Land of Joseph Wilder to ye hieway that Comes from Marlburrow

Lastly they ajorned the Meeting to ye 8 of april being the Second Monday of sd month.

1717. April ye 8 1717 on ajornment from ye 5 of March the Town Meet at ye Meeting House and first John Goss Proposed to have ye Hiway moved that Goeth to ye Mill the Town made Choyce of John Wilder Sr & Robard Houghton to be a Commity to vew ye same & make Report to ye Town

2 Samuell Warner put in a proposision to ye Town Requesting them

to Grant a Hiway to Pin hill medow: the Town thereupon made Choyce of Jonas Houghton Sr David Whetcomb & Jacob Houghton to be a commity to vew y⁰ same & make report to y⁰ Town at there next Meeting.

3 They proceeded to y⁰ Reading of som Lands to wit y⁰ Land of Edward Phelps Simon Steevens & Joseph Sawyer & Joseph Hutchins: James Atherton Ju objected against sd Hutchinses Land, Laying som Clame there to

4 The Comitty, to wit Ephriam Wilder Jonas Houghton & Joseph Wilder Present^d a plat of y⁰ Stated Common to y⁰ Town which they were ordered to Measuer Lyeing on y⁰ west side y⁰ River: the town after som descors Gave order that y⁰ same Comitty Measuer y⁰ Stated Common on y⁰ Neck side y⁰ River & then ajorned y⁰ Meeting to that day fourtnite being y⁰ 22 of sd Month at 8 of y⁰ Clock in y⁰ Morning.

April y⁰ 22th 1717 The Town Meet on Ajornment from y⁰ 8 of sd Month 1 Upon y⁰ Report of a Committy sent to Vew y⁰ Way to Prescotts Mill towit upon y⁰ proposition of John Goss & y⁰ Town Voted that said Hiway be moved & lie by y⁰ River — Provided said way be kept four Rods Wide from y⁰ Scar bridge till it com to y⁰ Hill from y⁰ top of y⁰ River bank: and after it amount said Hill to Lye where it shall be most Conveniant to y⁰ Town till it Com to sd Mill sd Goss to Cleer said Rode when that Committy shall stake it out.

The scar bridge and the road crossing it were disused more than one hundred years ago. The highway came down the hill not far from the scar known as Emerson's Bank, and over a bridge a few rods down the river from the present northern end of High street in Clinton.

2. y⁰ Town voted that y⁰ Hiway to Whashacom be four Rods Wide

3. The Town Gave leve that Samuel Rugg Have his Land Recorded that was Granted to His Father as it was Layed out by Capt Wilder

4. Y⁰ Town Voted that no Land be laid out from Pin hill Medow to barehill Roode with out an alowance in it for a hiway of foure Rods wide where it is likely to be wanted

5. They Voted that y⁰ fifth devision be not entered upon till y⁰ first of September next

6. they voted that y⁰ Town Books should be searched to see what persons have Layed out there full Right & who have not & no person to lay out any more Land till he have under the hands of such as shall be Chosen: what his orejonall Right is & how much he hath Laied out & how much he hath to laye out & then made Choyce of John Houghton S^r & James Wilder to search said Town Books & Give forth a Counts: to be payed by such as improue them

7 They exsepted ye Return of ye Commity who was sent to Lay out ye Stated Common

8 They Voted that all those Persons who have Layed out Land in ye Stated Common should hould ye same as it is Layed out.

9 They voted that the Stated Common be divided according to the Interest

10 They voted that no person Cut any timber on ye Stated Common otherwise then under ye like penalty as by Law provided for Cuting on other mens Land till it be Layed out.

1717.   CHARLESTOWN April 30 1717.
Lancaster Selectmen are allowed to enter theire Caution agst one Robert Hues being an Inhabitant of their Town having by their Lawfull Officer warned him to Depart theire Town as per theire Caution allowed on file.
[Middlesex Court Records.]

To the Hon^{a}ble Justices .... March y^e 13th 1716$\frac{17}{17}$.

May it Please your Hon^{rs}, that whereas the selectmen of the Towne of Lancaster Did in December last past by an order to Josiah White Constable, Warne Robbert Hues to depart out of y^e Bounds or Limits of said Lancaster & accordingly said Constable on y^e 4th of said December did warne said Robbert Hues forthwith to Leave said Towne & also made Returne of his so doing to ye selectmen & they also Did notifie your Hon^{rs} Desiring that an entry thereof might be made: that so the Towne might not be Lyable to be at ye Charge for his maintenance in case he should come to want Reliefe, but understanding said notification was not accepted, because not signed by the constable, wee have herewith presented to your Hon^{rs} ye sd selectmens order to said Constable with his Return upon it signed by him, Humbly Requesting it may be Received & Entered & said Towne of Lancaster secured from being Chargeable with ye maintenance of said Hues, we apprehending that our former notification was agreeable with ye Law.

JOHN HOUGHTON
JAMES WILDER   } *Selectmen*
JOSEPH WILDER

Dated Lancaster March 8 1716/17.

1717 August..... and allso we present ye town of Lancaster for neglecting to repair ye great bridge in sd town neer ye meeting house . .
[Middlesex Court Files.]

Tusday august ye 29th 1717. In a meeting of ye Propriaters of Lancaster warned by a Warrant from Justice Thomas How Esqr first Made Choyce of John Houghton Sr for a Moderater & then Suspended the forth devision till the next february meeting:

Lancaster February the 3 1717/18 att the Stated Meeting for propriatie, Made Choyce of Capt Peter Joslin for a Moderator for Said Meeting : & then Receved in Sum Propozitions towit first the propozition of the Reverend Mr John Prentice Requesting the propritie to appoint som meet persons to State the bounds betwixt the land his Hous now Stands upon & the Land Called the Minesteeriall Land

Reverend John Prentice, June 1, 1708, had purchased of Samuel Prescott, the unfortunate man who by accident killed the Reverend Andrew Gardner, "all his houseing, Lands and meadows." The deed includes "one upland house Lott by estimation Twenty acres more or less lying on the West side of the River on the North side of the Lott of Thomas Sawyer, bounded south by said Sawyer's Lott : North & West by the highway." This was the "Rye Field," so called, of the first John Prescott, and somewhere near the easternmost end of it stood Samuel Prescott's house. In 1841 or 1842 a large and undoubtedly ancient house, known as the Dr. Atherton mansion, was here torn down by Deacon Charles Humphrey, and the present house erected upon its site. That old house, which Dr. Israel Atherton possessed through his marriage with the widow of Dr. Stanton Prentice, may have been, in whole or in part, the house of Reverend John Prentice above alluded to. The *ministerial land* included the grounds to the north recently purchased by Eugene V. R. Thayer.

2 the Harrises Requested the Town would throw up the Hiway through there Land from the other Hiway to butlers feeld

3 Danil Preest Requested the Town would Give him one acre of Land by his Barn.

4 Samuell Carter Requested the Town would Grant a Comitty to vew the Hiway through plumtrees & Stake it out

5 Caleb Sawyer & Jabaz ffairbank Requested that the Town would grant them libertie to set a fence upon the towns Land to fence in there Medow which lyeth upon the north branch of bare hill brook

6 John Prescott Requests the town would Grant a hiway from his Land att the Slabbin to his medow Called prescots Medow

And 1 in answer to the propozition of ye Revered Mr Prentice the

Pŕop'tors made Choyce of John Wilder Sr Jonas Houghton Sr & James Wilder to be a Committe to vew & Stake said bounds.

2 in answer to the propozition of Edmund & Ebenezer Harris the Town voted to give said Harrises the Hiway proposed for provided the said Harrises Cleer the owld bering feeld & Keep it well subdued five years

3 they Granted the propozition of danil Preest:

4 the town in answer to the propozition of Samuell Carter then made Choyce of John Houghton Esq John Wilder Sr & Jabaz ffairbank to be a Committy to stake the hieway through plumtrees entervail as neer where it was first Layed out as they can, by the best Enformation they can Gitt

5 the town Granted the propozition of Caleb Sawyer & Jabaz fairbank & Gave them liberty to set there fence upon the towns Land for the fenceing there Medows.

6 The town Granted a hieway in answer to the propozition of John Prescott from his Land to the loor end of the medow Called preescots meedow neer where the path now goes to witt the parth called the dugway

7 Vpon the Report of a Committy sent to vew the Land in ponacin & Reporting that they can find but fifteen acres of Entervaill Left for Jabaz fairbank the town voted that ye said Jabaz fairbanks should haue thirty acres of Land to make up said entervail where he shall find it in Land not yet Layed out

8 they voted that the forth devision be sospended till the ajornment of this meeting and then the Moderator ajorned the Meeting to the 17 day of february Currant.

Monday February the 17 : 1717/18 the town meet att the meeting house and ajorned the meeting to the Last wensday of March next coming at 8 of the Clook in the Morning & also defered the forth devision till then : & also warned a town meeting to be on the 1 monday of sd mrch for the Choyce of town offisers

The following records are in the hand of John Houghton, Esq., town clerk.

Monday ye 10th of March 1717/18 The Inhabitants of Lancaster Met at the Meeting house in order to Consider about Building ye Neck Bridge by Night pasture : & first chose John Houghton Senr Moderator for sd Meeting & then Discoursed about ye Demenssions of sd Bridge : & concluded it should have 5 Trussells, & to be a foot Higher than before, to make good buttments : & to be 13 foot wide between ye posts which are to be of sound oak & so ye Caps and braces : and to brace into ye Posts above ye caps & Down into ye^e Mudsells which are to be 40 foot Long & to cover sd Bridge with good Plank or Logs, as they which Build it shall count best, & voted to give 35 pounds to them that should build it, according to sd Demensions one halfe when it shall be Raised, & the other halfe when it is finished: and then Chose three Men: viz: John Houghton Senr Josiah White & James Wilder: to Lett out sd Bridg & it to be finished at or before the first Day of August Next: the Town to help to Rais it & nextly chose Samuell Bennitt Senr to be of ye Comittie in stead of John Wilder Senr.

1718. Wednsday ye 26 of March 1718 the Town met at ye Meetinghouse upon ajournment of theire Late ffebruary Meeting: Capt Joslin being Moderator: & first some Lands of John Houghtons & Jabez ffairbanks were Read; and also some Lands Laid out by Benjamin Bellows to ye Right of Stephen Gates: but Simon Gates Made some objetions against that Laid out by Bellows being 100 acres mostly beyond cannoo brook all being third Divission:

Next the allowance for ye highway through Quassaponikin Intervall was Read & voted (as followeth) that they should have two acres for one allowed them and so proportionable (to such of them as have had no allowance already) & Liberty to Lay it out either in ye Stated Comon or other undivided Land as they please & then some other Land was Read: viz: seventy one acres for ye Carters; one acre & quarter for elias Sawyer; 5 acres & halfe for James Snow; and nine acre & halfe to James Atherton: & seventy four acres to Nath Hapgood; all third Divission. & then gave the Committie appointed about ye Highway at ye Plumtrees; power to Lay or State ye said Highway where it may be Most Convenient for all Concerned. & nextly appointed James Wilder Josiah White & John Houghton Jur a Committie to Lay out ye Highway from ponikin Intervall to Whites Pond & to mens Land in that part of ye Towne: & the way from ponikin Brook Down to Cumbery Intervals & medows; & then added John Houghton Senr to James Wilder & Jonas Houghton Senr; to state ye line betwixt Mr Prentices Land & ye ministrey Land; & then adjourned sd ffebruary Meeting untill ye second wednesday in May next at 10 of ye Clock in ye forenoon then further to Consider of, & give oppertunity for Reading of more Lands in order to Record; & for what is necessary & proper to be done. Also upon sd wednesday ye 26 of sd march 1718: ye Proprietors in ye Stated Common in ye old Township of Lancaster Met at ye Meeting house: upon Due warning given in order to Chuse a Clerk for said Propriety: & to Consider & agree of a Method for ye Dividing of sd Common: as set forth in said warning & other affairs therein Mentioned: & after some Discourse Proceeded to ye choice of a Moderator John Houghton Senr: & then accordingly Chose Joseph Wilder Clerk of sd Proprietors in said Propriety: & because there was Severall Proprietors Missing the sd meeting was Adjourned till ye second wednesday in May Next; which would be ye 14 day of said Month & to meet at 12 of ye Clock.

Wednesday the 14 of May 1718 the Town met at ye Meetinghouse according to adjornment of theire Town Meeting of ye 26 of March Last & also upon ye account of warning given for Choice of a Representative, & first Chose John Houghton Senr Moderator for sd meeting, & nextly Chose John Houghton Ju^r Representative to serve for the yeare ensuing: & nextly voted to have Mr Samuell Stow for a Schoolmaster for ye yeare ensuing, beginning the first Day of May Currant & to allow him 40 pound for ye yeare: or proportionable for what time he shall Serve: & to Raise the same by the Next Invoice, & then voted that ye 35 pound Granted or allowed for building ye Neck bridge be Raised by ye last Invoice: & then granted a Town Rate of 7 .. 12 .. 0 for Defraying of Towne charges, Viz: 5 pounds for ye Representative John Houghton Ju^r & twenty five shillings for edmund Harress for sweeping the meetinghouse, & 12 shillings to Mr Osgood for going after a scholmaster & for payment of the Assessors & then Granted a highway Rate of 20 pounds.

Wednesday ye 20th of August 1718: The Inhabitants of Lancaster met at ye Meetinghouse upon Due warning Given, In order to give in an Invoice of Polls & estates for ye Province Tax & other The Assesments arising in sd Town for ye yeare ensuing: & Accordingly then The Selectmen took Account of what they could obtain: & afterwards a writing sent by Mr Prentice to be Comunicated to ye Towne was Read in which after his Desiring the Towne to Consider his Present Circumstances & what Need he was in of some help by the Towne he Requested that some Addition Might be Made to his Sallerey: & after Considerable Discourse about it: it was thought it might be better to appoint a Meeting purposly for to Consider of it: & in ye Meantime to Request a Contribution for his present Reliefe: & accordingly appointed or Desired John Houghton Senr to acquaint ye Congregation of it the next Sabaoth Day: to Desire such as were willing to do it that Day fourtnight; & then appointed that Day Month to be a Meeting for the Consideration of sd Sallery & accordingly then ye Towne met at ye meetinghouse (being Legall warned thereto) & first Chose John Houghton Senr MoDerator for sd meeting: & after some Discourse Relating to ye pmisses the Towne seemed Inclined to make some Addition to sd. Sallery & some expressed theire thoughts what sum to Add thereto, & after some Tryall by vote, & not effecting ye matter, it was voted whether the Town would add fifteen pounds & so make ye sd Sallery 85 pounds a yeare which was voted in ye affirmitive upon ye Consideration that Bills of Creditt were of so Low a value: & to Continue to be paid Anually till such time as the Creditt of them was better: or some other Method of traffique betwixt man & man found out that might be more Reasonable in equity to Remidy that Inconvenience: as the Town may Consider & Conclud thereof.

Then follow records in the hand of Joseph Wilder, proprietors' clerk.

May the 14 1718 the proprietors being meet att the meetinghous in Lancaster Capt frances fullam Requested sd proprietors that they would appoint a Comittie to accompanie him to se his Clame of 200 acres of Land at Whashacom hill which he purchased of John addames & was Confermed to George & frances addams by the Generall Court the town in answer to sd Request voted that John Houghton Sr Capt peter Joslin Capt Eph Wilder Ensigne James Wilder & Joseph Wilder be a Comittie to treet with sd Capt fullam in the towns behalf & to see the Land Clamed & to do what they apprehend to be Resonable & just be tween him & us the sd propriators of Lancaster : & then ajorned the meeting to the next morning to eaight of the Cloock

In 1672 " John Addam" was granted 100 acres of land by the General Court, described as " lying at Weshecum nere the south side of that pond." The town had also given George & John Adams in exchange for a twenty acre lot on George Hill claimed by them, 60 acres near "Washacombe great field."

May the 15 the proprietors of Lancaster being meet Conclude & agree that those persons who have Layed out there third devision in the Stated Common or any part there of have libertie to Lay out there Stated Common in undevided Land & to Lay 3 acres for one they aquiting the Stated Common of the fifth devision it being a devision granted upon the Stated Comon

2 they agree to Chuse a Comittie to make an Equallity as to quantitie & quallitie to every proprietor according to his Right, who shall make his Choyce in the Stated Common where he will laye it

3 that the Rule for the Standard be Justice Houghtons lott Compared in its own Quallitie to geather

4 they Conclude that every four pound of town Right draw one acre according to that Standard

5 they Conclude that all persons who have a desier to Lay out there fifth devision in undevided land haue a libertie so to do & to Lay out three acres for one & to find it them selves & to Lay it out by the Comon Servaiers as former devisions

6 they Conclude that if any two or more persons shall applie themselves to the Comittie for Servaiers for one pece of Land then it shall be desided by a lott who shall injoy it & the other to make a new Choyce

7 they Concluded to Chuse three men for a Comitty and then made Choyce of John Houghton Sr Capt Peter Joslin & Hooker Osgood to be the Committy

8 they Concluded to Leve six acres of Land for a training feeld by the Hiway below Thomas Sawyers door to be Layed out by the Committy for that vse

9 they Concluded to Give Joseph Wilder 3 acres of Land in the Stated Common att ye Walnut Swamp to Ly to gether with the Rest of his devision on sd Common which they give him leve to Lay there, He giveing the Propriaty thre acres in the Lew there of by the Hiway neer Justice Houghtons barn to Ly Com̃on for a training feeld.

10 they Conclud that Mr John Prentice haue ten acres in the Stated Common Layed out to him where he shall chuse the same before any other person begin

11 the Conclud that the Committy begin to Lay out the stated Common the next Monday: Lastly that the forth devision be defered till the first of Ocktober next and then to begin all the perticulers aboue sd ware voted destinctly & caried in the affermitive.

John Houghton, Senior, was Town Clerk in 1718-19, but the following record is in the hand-writing of his son, Jonathan.

Monday ye 2^d of march, 1718/19. the Inhabitants of Lancaster meet at ye meeting House, according to apointment in order to Choose Town officers &c: & first chose

1 Capt Ephraim Wilder moderater for said meeting, & then next a warrant was Read for Choice of a Grandjuror, & accordingly ye Town was warned p Sam^{ll} Willard Constable to Choose one,

2 & then ye Town proceded to ye Choice, & Chose John White the person to serve on ye Grandjury for ye year ensuing.

3 the Town proceded to ye Choice of Selectmen, & Chose John Houghton Sr. Capt Peter Joslin Josiah White Jonas Houghton Junr & Joseph Wilder Selectmen for ye year ensuing

4 the Town Choose John Houghton Sen. Town Clerk, & then voted to choose assessors

5 voted & chose John Keys Joseph Wilder & Jacob Houghton Assessors for ye year ensuing.

6 the Town voted & chose Daniel Rugg Jonathan Houghton & Hezekiah Whetcomb Constables for ye year ensuing, & then ye Laws enjoined to be Read were Read in said meeting

In 1712 it was enacted that "the laws against drunkenness prophaneness and other immoralities . . . . be solemnly read by the town clerk in each town at their anniversary town meeting in March."

7 The Town voted & chose Servaires of Highways, namely George Glazier Jonathan More Jonathan Sawyer & Oliver Wilder.

8 The Town Chose James Wilder Town treasurer.

9 the Town Chose Josiah White & Samuel Warner Tything men

10 The Town Chose Bezaleell Sawyer & Thomas Carter fence vewers

11 the Town Chose Hooker Osgood Jur. John Hinds Junr Daniel Houghton & John Goss Hawyards.

12 the Town Chose Thomas Carter Sealler of Leather.

13 the Town Chose Jonas Houghton Junr Gager—and then ye meeting was adjorned to ye second Wednesday in may next at thre of ye Clock in ye after none.

Next follow records by Joseph Wilder, clerk of proprietors.

Monday February ye 2 1718/19. The Town or Propriators thereof mett at the Meeting Hous being Warned there to by a Warrant from Justice Houghton Esqr for the Continuance of February Meeting for the Reeding of Lands the Granting of Hiwaies and the Confirming the same it being the first Monday of Feabruary being the Anual Meeting for the ends before Mensoned and first made Choyce of Joseph Wilder for a Moderator of said Meeting: and then Red som Lands in order to be Recoarded

3 They voted that all afairs or things that Consern Propriatie that any person or persons shall desier to haue transacted att the anule Febary Meeting or any ajornment there of shall be sesonablyly brought in to the Propriators Clerk who shall post the same in a Notification in Som Publick place fourteen dayes att leest before said meeting or any ajornment there of

4 They voted to Chuse a Committy to vew such Hiwayes as was then proposed for & to stake out such as should be thought Needfull & to make Report to the propriaty of there doings therein att ye ajornment of this Meeting: towit a Hiway proposed for by Joseph Wilder att ye Walnut Swamp by Ebenezer Wilder & Thomas Carter att Jonson Medow by Jeremiah Wilson att Broad Medow hill, by David Whitcomb & others from Wadaquadock Brook to the Bay Rood & from John Whetcombs to Jonas Houghtons and that they also vew and state ye bounds betwixt the Land which Joseph Wilder Bought of George Glazier and ye Swan Swamp Roode

5 They made Choyce of Nathanil Sawyer Ensign John White & Ebenezer Wilder to be a Comitty for ye ends aforesaid: and also to stake out the hiway from the Rolly Hill to Justice Houghtons feeld. There was then Left to Consideration a proposition of Elias Sawyer Refering to som Entervail now in his posesion which was purchased of Capt Kerly there being no Recoard to be found of it he Requests that it may be Reconed as it is bounded in said deed of Kerlies and also the proposion of Jonas Houghton for a Recompence for mesoring of the Stated Commons & those asisted him and then the meeting was ajorned to ye second Wednsday of May next at Eaight of ye Clock.

1719. The copye of ye notification Lancaster April ye 29 1719 To the Proprietors of Lancaster Conformable to your Stated Rule for ye Governing of your Meetings these are to inform you that besides what was left for your Consideration to ye ajornment of your Last Meeting to the thirteenth of May next at 8 of ye Clock Caleb Sawyer proposes for a hiway through the Land of Danil Hutson & John Preest to his Medow: it is also desiered by severall that the owners of ye Walnot Swamp lott be indented with that the Hiway which Lyeth by the north entervail may cross the sd Lott into ye new hieway marked out by the Committy which Croseth the River neer sd Lott

JOSEPH WILDER *Clerk*

May the 13 1719 The Propriaters being mett upon ajornment from the second of Feb. & first voted that the Land which Lyeth free in the Swan Swamp & is not yet Layed out be Stated & Staked out for a Hiway as neer the Extent of the Bredth Proscribed in the Town Book for ye Same as may be

2 Voted to Chuse three men as a Committy to Stake it out and then made Choyce of John Houghton Esqr Capt Ephriam Wilder & Mr Joseph Wheelock to be a Committy to Stake it out

3 They took in to Consideration the proposall of Jonas Houghton and voted to give him five shilling per day for mesoring the ye Stated Common & those who asisted him three shillings per day: the whole amounting to fourtie four shillings & voted to pay them in Land att four shillings per acre

4 They Receved the Report of the Committy appointed to vew som hiewaies proposed for & to state the bounds between the Land of Joseph Wilder & the Swan Swamp Rode and first exsepted there Return of a Hiway from Mordacoy to Wakapaket brook & Confermed it for a hiway as it is marked out exsepting in the Land of James Wilder & he to haue libertie if it be for his advantage to moue it more northward: the Report of the Committy was as ffolloweth

Tusday April the 25 We began at the Swan swamp and Ran a straight line from the end of Glazers Dich to a white oke Stump below Benjamin Bellows Hous which we accounted to be the Corner and Staked out the Same. And then Proseeded to vew the Hiway through the Stated Common to Wakapakit Brook, and we Judge it most Conveniant that it Run from the Entervaill up by the lott of Joseph Wilder through the land of William Divoll Edward Hartwill Ebenezer & Edmund Harrises till it Coms to the Corner of Joseph Wilders Land that he purchased of Jabaz fairbank & then Runing Round sd Corner of Joseph Wilder through the Land of John Warner & then Croses a Corner of Joseph Wilders Land to the Land of James Wilder & through that to the Land of Josiah Wheeler & through to the Land of Josiah Wheeler to the side of Gateses Land & so through a pece of Common Land to Bellowses Corner being his West Corner & from thence Ran down betwixt the Land of Justice Houghtons Land & the Land of John Harris Crossing a little Corner of sd Houghtons Land to Wacapacit Brook:

JOHN WHITE
EBENEZER WILDER

a true Copy of sd Report Entered by me.

JOSEPH WILDER *Clerk*

Lastly they voted that the Committy afores^d determine how much every man is damnified by said Hiway Runing through there Land & what Recompence they shall haue per acre for what is taken from them and such persons to have liberty to Lay it out such alowance in undevided Land so soon as it is Known as Land in other devision are Layed out and then the Meeting was desolved: the Return of a hiway

Lancaster may the 15 1719 we John Wilder Jonas Houghton & Jacob Houghton being Chosen and appointed a Commity to Lay out the waies from the Randevou tree to the medows down that brook as also up the Brook to John Sawyers and from thence to ye medows at the north east Corner of the Town as it is now staked out wee haue accordingly done the same and for what Land we haue taken of sd Sawyers hom place we haue alowed him two acres of Land on the west side the Brook below ye hous provided he leve Room for a Convenient hiway between [sd land] and the hill one west side.

JONAS HOUGHTON JACOB HOUGHTON this Return was exsepted and Confermed

The *Rendezvous tree* was in Harvard.

A COPY OF THE NOTIFICATION.

To the Proprieters of Lancaster these may informe you that the things to be Considered att your next meeting upon the first of February next are the Propozition of Joshua Atherton and Joseph Hutchins for a hiway to brook medow and the medows ajasant thereto also the said Atherton Requests that ye Second devision entervaill and Conveniancy belonging to the estate of his father and also the second devision Land of William Lewes now in his posession may be put upon Record there being non as yet to be found of them the propozition also of Elias Sawyer for the like for that ye Conveniancy which his father purchesed of Capt Kerley may be Recorded according to the tenure of said deed January the 15 1719/20   JOSEPH WILDER *Clerk*

LANCASTER February the 1st 1719/20 att a meeting, of the proprieters first made Choyce of Jabaz ffairbank for a Moderator and then in the first place Granted a hiway to brook medow & the medows ajasant in answer to the propozition of Joshua Atherton & Joseph Hutchins towit to pinhill and to a medow of aaron Willard and a medow called pollopod and down the west side of brook medow till it com to the Land of John Willard and then made Choyce of Capt Wilder Josiah White and Joseph Wilder to be a Committy to Lay it out thre Rods in wedth and make Report to the propriete

2 They Granted the Propozition of Joshua Atherton Refering to His Entervaill and the Land that was William Leweses

3 They Receved and Exsepted the Return of a Hiway att ye barehill Medows of a Committy to witt John Wilder Jonas Houghton & Jacob Houghton which was as followeth Lancaster May the 15th 1719 we John Wilder Jonas Houghton & Jacob Houghton being chosen a Committy to Lay out ye waies from ye Randevo tree to the Medows down that Brook as also up the Brook to John Sawyers and from thence to ye medows att ye North East Corner of the Town as it is now staked out and marked, Wee have accordingly don ye same: and for what Land we haue taken from John Sawyer att his Hous place for ye benifit of sd Hiway we haue alowed to him two acres of Land on the west side ye Brook below his house provided he Leve Room for a Conveniant Hiway between said Land and the Hill on the west side of the same. JONAS HOUGHTON
JACOB HOUGHTON

this Return was Exsepted and Confermed by a vote. and then ye meeting was ajorned to ye second Monday of March next:

JOSEPH WILDER *Clerk*

A COPY OF THE NOTIFICATION.

To the Proprieters of Lancaster these are to notifie you of what may be laied before you att the ajornment of of your February Meeting upon the second Monday of March next att eaight of the Cloock, towitt the Propozition of Hooker Osgood for a Hiway betwixt the Lott of Justice Houghton which was Hutchsons and his own and so in to ye wods and for alowance for what he has wrought in said way and also for a small slip of Land by the minesteeriall medow upon Certain Conditions as may be then offered: also the Propozition of Josiah White for a Record of the Hous Lott which he now lives upon and also Severall other peces of Land layed out to his Grandfather John White which there can be no Record found of: and that he may haue libertie to make a new Record of a pece of Land att the bare Hill according to a platt Lately taken of it: the old Record being so dark that it is not so Intellegable as he desiers Ebenezer Wilder also for the tenpound Due to him from the Town that He will take it in Land if the Proprietie se meet: also the propozition of Josiah Wheeler that a Hiway through ye Land of Sumner and Townsend might haue the marks Renewed Townsend also desiers that the hiway may be remoued in his Land for his better Conveniancy; also that the hiway betwixt the Justices feeld and the Rooty hill might be marked out and layed so as might be most Conveniant Lastly the propozityon of Jonas Houghton that he might haue a little strip of Rockey Common Land lying upon Vans hill for what is due to him for nine daies work att a Bridge over ye north River:

LANCASTER February the 27 1719/20   JOSEPH WILDER *Clerk*

"*Vans*," i. e., Vaughans Hill, is in the north part of Bolton.

1720. A Memorial of William Tailer Esq. in Behalf of the Committee appointed to lay out two Towns to the Westward of Groton, Shewing that the Committee in Surveying the Land appointed for the Town of Lancaster of a Grant of Land made by the General Assembly to the said Town, The Committee appointed to survey it stating the Course left it to be run by the said Town, and the said Town running the same upon a Point of the Compass different to what the said Committee had determined and that the said return is confirmed by the General Court: That thereby a Grant of Land mad to the Town of Woburn, & another to the Town of Dorchester are pushed into the Plan designed for one of these new Towns. Which will prove prejudicial to the whole Province as well as to the said intended new Towns if not remedied.

BOSTON July 21 1720. Signed By order of the Committtee Wm Tailer.

In the House of Representatives July 22 1720. This House having Information that Jonathan Prescot Samuel Jones & John Farnsworth a Committee formerly improved by this court, to view a Tract of Land petitioned for by the Town of Lancaster & make Return, & who did report the Bounds for a Tract of Land but only assigned the Points of the Compass, whereby to mark them out wch the said Town of Lancaster have since done but have not duly followed the Directions of said Committees Report:

Ordered that Cpt. Peter Rice, Cpt. Jonas Prescot, & Mr William Ward be a Committee, to run & mark out the Lines & Bounds, of that Late Grant to Lancaster, Pursuant to the directions in the Report of the said Committee, and make Report of their Doings to this Court the next Sessions. The surveyors and Chainmen which they shall improve to be under oath. The charge of the Committee & Survey to be born as shall be directed by this court. In Council read & concurred.

        Consented to.   SAMLL SHUTE

[Massachusetts Records.]

Whereas we the Subscribers being a Comittee ordered by the Honble Court at their Session, began July 13 1720 to run the line and mark the bounds of the late Grant to Lankaster :—Pursuant to the directions in the report made by a Comittie formerly sent forth by this Court to vew the afores^d track of land

1720 Sepr 13. Pursuant to which order we proceeded as viz: Imp^s we began at a heap of stones, shewn us to be the N. West Corner by

Lankaster old bounds, thence runing a line three miles giving the allowance of aboute one rod in thirty, for Swagg of chaine & uneven ground, upon a N West point according to a true meridian, at the end of which line we where two hundred & thirty rods from the Kachewalunck Pond, spoken of in afores^d Comittees report as passing along by.

2dly At the end of the three miles we made an angle runing a line (six miles & a hundred rods wth the allowance as afores^d) S. West crossing the North river & over some of the monosek hills untill we met wth the middle branche of Nashaway river: thence making the land five miles, two hundred and eighty rods wide, and where without the tree spoken of in the report (so marked by the Indians for a S. West corner) aboute three hundred rods. Thus finding a disagreement between the lines and points given and things mentioned as bounds in ye report of ye afores^d Comittee for in runing the two lines mentioned we came not near ye pond & other bounds, but leaving out the quantity of a Thousand five hundred & twenty three acres. and likewise taken in at the S. West corner two thousand acres wch Lankaster men claim not. Likewise considering where that report speaks of but two lines. He that runs by the bounds must of necessity make four or five lines all wch things makes thes bounds & ye points with their length of lines impossible to reconcile. And being directed in our ord^r to have regard to ye lines & bounds mentioned in ye afores^d Comittees report: We therefore make our report as above mentioned leaving it to this Honble Court to determine as they in their wisdome see cause.

      Remaining in Submission.

           PETER RICE } Comittee
           WILLIAM WARD

[Massachusetts Archives, CXIII, 649-50.]

A Petition of the Inhabitants of Lancaster and Proprietors of Lands purchased of George Tahanto an Indian Saggamore &c: Shewing, that whereas the General Court did in the year 1713 make a Grant and Confirmation of the said Lands to them as it was set forth and described in the Report of a Committee sent by the Court to View and Lay out the Same, That in the year 1720 A vote was pass^d for altering the Bounds of the said Land. In which Vote it is asserted That the people of Lancaster did not fairly and Truely, represent their Bounds and the Lines of their old Township, They are ready to prove by the affidavits of Two of the said Committee (which consisted of but three persons) That their Lines were truely and faithfully run, and therefore praying that this Court would Confirm to them The Grant of the sd Land as made in the year 1713.

1721. In the House of Representatives Jan 15th 1721.

Whereas this Great and General Court did at a Session held at Boston the 29th of May 1713 pursuant to a Report of Cpt Jonathan Prescott

Messrs Samuel Jones & John Farnsworth a committee appointed by their order, that a certain Tract of Land should be added and Confirmed To the Town of Lancaster, as part of that Township, not prejudicing any former Grants. The aforesaid Tract of Land beginning at the Northwest Corner of the proper bounds of Lancaster plantation (Then so Call[d]) and from thence to run a Line upon a Northwest point or near thereabouts, along the southwest side of mashapoag & Uncachewalunk pond extending said Line three miles and from thence a Line running near upon a Southwest point crossing a River called the North River and so ranging along over Hills Called Monosuck Hills Said Line being about six miles in Length till it meets with the middle Branch of Lancaster River at or near a Little Hill where is a Tree mark[d] by the Indians for a corner of the sd Land being near Five miles wide at the southward and bounded partly by the River and partly by Cpt. Davenports Farm to the southwest Corner of Lancaster old Bound, and whereas two of that Committee have been lately upon the aforesaid Tract of Land & viewed the same and do declare upon oath that they are no ways apprehensive that they were deceived, or Imposed upon by Lancaster men or misled in that matter and they marked a Tree upon the Westerly side of sd pond upon the Brink thereof as a mark to the sd Lands, and that it was their True intention that the Land at that end should be three miles in Weadth whether it should fall short or come beyond said mark It no ways appearing that that Report was Grounded on Misrepresentation of the Inhabitants or proprietors of Lancaster but on the contrary, that they fairly shewed the committee, The Bounds and Lines of their old Township; Resolved That that Tract of Land which was confirmed to the Town of Lancaster by this Court anno 1713 and described in the return signed by the aforesaid Jonath[n] Prescott, Samuel Jones & John Farnsworth be and Remain to the Proprietors of Lancaster and their assigns for ever by Virtue of the aforesaid Grant any former act or Resolves of the Court to the Contrary notwithstanding.

In Council Read, & Concurr[d]

Consented to   SAM[LL] SHUTE

[Massachusetts Records.]

1721 June 21. In the House of Representatives: Whereas by the Resolve of the Court relating to some Lands formerly belonging to the Town of Lancaster but since taken into the New Township at Turkey Hills lying on the West side of Groton and now ordered to belong to the Proprietors of Lancaster, many persons that drew their Lots in the new Town and paid their money therefor will be Great Sufferers for that they will fall within the tract of Land, now settled upon Lancaster unless this Court make some Reparation.

Ordered That the former Committee that laid out the new Town be Impowered to lay out an Equivalent to those persons whose lot fell within that tract of Land now settled in the Proprietors of Lancaster and Report

their doings to this Court at their next Session. In Council read and
concurred Consented to SAM[LL] SHUTE
[Massachusetts Records.]

March The 14th 1720 The Propriety being Meet first voted that Elias
Sawyer haue lebertie to Lay out and Enter to the Estate of William Kerly S[r] The Conveniance belonging Said Kerlys estate in the place where
he now Clames it or elswhere not infrenging upon former Records: this
was voted and Caried in the affermitive

2 it was put to vote whether Josiah White haue Lebertie to make a
Record of his Land at the Barehill according to a plat then presented
taken by Jonas Houghton Sirvaier and was Caried in y[e] affermitive

3 it was put to vote whether Josiah White haue Lebertie to Record
his Hous Lott and Intervail Lott according to y[e] Grant of them and also
the Second Devision of Intervaill and upland where it is now Clamed according to the Severall Devision[s] to the Estate of John White his Grandfather not enfrenging upon former Records and it was Caried in the
affermitive

4 They made Choyce of Jabaz Fairbank Nathanil Sawyer and Samuell
Carter to be a Committy to vew a hiway proposed for by Hooker Osgood
and a hiway up to wacapacit hill and a hiway to Wonksacoxet Hill and if
they find them nesesary for the benifit of the Town to mark them out and
Make Report to The Propriety and also to mark out a Hiway to Whashacom all Redy; Granted of four Rods wide and make a Returne here of
that it may be put upon Record

5 They Granted Jonas Houghton S[r] Six or Seaven acres of Land
upon the top of the Southermost Vans Hill for to Sattisfie him for nine
dayes work don at the bulding of a Bridge over the North River Neer Mr
Osgoods

6 They voted that Left John Houghton En[s] James Wilder and Josiah
Wheelor to be a Committy to markout a Rode or Hiway from Marlburow
Rode to four mile brook and also to moue the Hiway by Towsends if it
be Conveniant and also from Justice Houghtons to Wadaquadock; and
then ajorned the meeting to y[e] 18 of may next

May y[e] 18th 1720 The Proprieters being Meet att the Meeting Hous

1 Herd an acount from a Committy sent out to vew som Hiwaies pe-
tisoned for on the west side of the River and voted to give said Commity
Power to mark out said waies and give the accounpt of them to the Propri-
etrs Clark that they may be Recorded and that they also take an account
of what, and how much said waies Takes of from perteculer mens Land
and what they shall be alowed there for per acer in undevided Land to be
Layed out to them as other Lands in the Town The Committy being Jabaz Fairbank Nathanil Sawyer & Samuell Carter; Reserveing a Saveing for
agreved Persons to applye them Selves to the Propriety for Remidy Said

waies aboue mensoned to be for the most part three Rods wide and wider where the Committy shall se it needfull which was voted and Caried in the efermitive:

2 They voted to send a Committy to vew the Hiway propounded for by Cp^t Joslin at the Walnut Swamp and then made Choyce of Jabaz fairbank Nathanil Sawyer and Samuell Carter to be the Committy; & also to Stake out or marke the way Called the Street along by the North Intervails

3 They voted that the slip of Land left by the Committy between the Land of Samuell Carter & Oliver Wilder from the hed of the Lots to the hiway that goes to Wacapacit should ly for a hiway

Samuell Carter and Danil Rugg then appeared before the Propriety and Consented and a Greed that the aboue said way Should Run down between their House Lots to the way Called the Street Takeing on Rod out of each mans Land the way to be two Rods wide & the Propriety accepted it accordingly.   JOSEPH WILDER *Clerk*

This Record fixes the age of the road that goes up the hill a little to the north of the George Hill School-house. Samuel Carter owned the lands on the north side of this highway, his father Samuel, a minister from Woburn, having purchased two lots of Capt. Henry Kerley in 1688. He lived on the site of, or perhaps in, the very old house torn down two or three years ago, known as the Captain Ephraim Carter house. Daniel Rugg lived on the south side of the road, owning the original home lot of 20 acres assigned to his father, John Rugg, in 1654.

A COPY OF THE NOTIFICATION JANUARY THE 20TH 1720/21

To the Propreters of Lancaster In observance of your order and Costom: These may Inform you that the Propozition of Capt Joslin for the Remoueval of a hiway in Quasaponacan: David Whetcomb & John Prescott for Lebertie to Servay fourty acres of Land Lying in two peces neer the hed of Rigby Brook as neer as may be where it was formerly Layed and that a new Reccord may be made thereof the old marks being most of them Lost and the Record being so dark that the bounds cannot be found thereby also of Josiah Willard and Joseph Atherton that ye Hiway to Groton may be marked out and a Rode from that to the hed of Joseph Athertons Lott; and Josiah Wheelor for a Hiway to Hog Swamp; and John Benit for Leberty to Set a fence upon the east side of the River in Quasaponacan in the Hiway upon the River Bank; and Josiah White that

Ebenezer Wilder may be payed the Debt which he Clameth of the Town in Land; Is what is ofered to your Consideration upon your next anual meeting on February the sixth nex Coming

JOSEPH WILDER *Clerk*

1   at a meeting February the sixth 1720 '21 first made Choyce of Jabaz ffairbanks Moderator of Said Meeting

2   They Granted the Request of Capt Peter Joslin Refering to a hiway in Quasaponacan in the Remoueal of it from the medow side to where it might be moor Conveniant

3   they so far granted the Propozition of David Whetcomb and John Prescott that if there bounds Cannot be found they may Lay out said fourty acres as neer where it was before as may be & make a new Record of it; it being Read before the proprete as other Lands

4   Vpon the propozition of Josiah Wilder and Joseph atherton They made Choyce of Capt Ephriam Wilder Josiah White and Joseph Wilder to marke out said waies as far as to ye Town line

5   The Propozition of Josiah Wheelor was Read but he not appeaering it was defered

6   The Propozition of John Benit was voted & pased in the negative

7   upon the Propozition of Josiah White to pay Ebenezer Wilder in Land: Jabaz fairbank entered his desent; and then ye Question was put whether the Propriety will grant Ebenezer Wilder Seventy thre acres & a half of Land for Said Debt which he Clameth as due to his father for work don for the Town in fineshing a Minesters Hous: being fourteen pounds fourteen shillings & threepence: and it was Caried in ye Efermitive.

2   it was put whether he shall haue it Layed in two or in three peces; and the vote Caried in the Affermitive for two peces

8   they Receved a Report of a Committy to wit of Left John Houghton and Josiah Wheelor viz:

Here a blank was left for the record, which was never set down.

Lastly they ajorned the Meeting to the first Munday in March next Coming and from thence to ye Eight of Said Month and from that to the 24 of May in 1721   A Copy of what was further brought in to said meeting upon the ajornment   To the Proprietors of Lancaster   These to Give Notice that James Keyes and Jeremiah Holman proposs for a Convenant Hiway to where they Live   James Wilder for the Exchange of a small slip of Land for som moor Conveniant for a hiway   Thomas Wilder for the Remouall of the hiway that is betwixt his hous and the hous of Thomas Tookers sum what neerer the River.   Henry Willard for a Hiway to the Plumtrees may the 4 1721.

JOSEPH WILDER *Clark of the Propriety*

The following record is in the hand of Jonathan Houghton, son of the Town Clerk:

Wednesday y° 22d of March 1720/21, the Town meet at y° meeting House according to due warning given in order to choose Select men, a Town Clerk, & to chose Assessors if y° Town see cause, it appering that some persons voted in y° former meeting that were not duly Quallified to vote, & also to consider & act what may be necesary to be done about Swine going at Large.

1 the Town voted & Chose John Houghton Sr moderator.

2 the Town voted to Chose five Selectmen, & accordingly Chose John Houghton Sr Jabez fairbank Josiah White Capt Ephraim Wilder & Ensign James Wilder Selectmen for y° year ensuing.

3 the Town Chose John Houghton Sr Town Clerk

4 the Town voted to Choose Assessors, & accordingly Chose James Wilder John White & John Houghton Jun Assessors for y° year ensuing.

May the 24th 1721 upon ajornment from the 8 of March Last past

1 In answer to the Propozition of James Wilder The Propriety Grant him Leberty to Record a small slip of Land which he hath already Layed out and Red before The Propritey which Lyeth in y° Swan Swamp upon the Consideration that he Lay down the like Quantity to Enlarge the Hiway that Runes through the hed of his Intervail Lott neer y° River as be most accomadable for the Hiway this was put to vote and Caried in the Effermitive

2 Vpon the Revivall of Josiah Wheelors propozition they Granted a Committy to vew and Lay out a Hiway to Hog Swamp if they think fit and Convenian and mak Report to the Propriety at sum other meeting the Persons chosen were Cpt Ephriam Wilder John Wilder and Josiah White

3 They also voted that y° same Committy should vew the Hiway proposed for by James Keyes and others and make Report of that likewise

1722. The Return of one of said Hiwaies Lancaster June y° first & 26 1722. Where as we the subscribers namely John Wilder Josiah White and Ephriam Wilder are a Committy to vew and Lay out a hiway from Jonath Moors to Hogswamp medowes we haue bin upon the spot the dayes aboue dated and proseeded as followeth we began at said hog swamp medow and marked trees on the west side of said way to sd moorses; we Ran through the Land of Josiah Wheelor fourty Rods through the Land of Jonathan Moors three hundred and fourty Rods and through the Land of Jabaz fairbanks one hundred Rods and in the Land of John moors two Rods the other part of said Hiway Lyeth in Common Land the Committy JOHN WILDER JOSIAH WHITE EPHRIAM WILDER said ways was Exsept to be three Rods wide Exsept where it Cross y° medow of Jabez fairbank and there to be one Rod and half

A COPY OF THE NOTIFICATION FOR THE MEETING 1721/22

These May Serue to notifie the Proprietors of Lancaster that Capt Samuel Willard propounds for a hiway to pass in to the Contery Rode to Boston: Henry Willard propounds for a hiway in the plumtrees so Called Josiah White for a Hiway to ye new Sawmill upon the North River Gamaliel Beman for a hiway straight to where he now Lives Last by Justice Houghton Requested that he may haue som alowance made him for the second devision of Entervail of Danil Gains if he cannot haue it where it was Granted him by the Town aboue the Red Spring up the North River; is what is to be layed before you at your meeting February the 5 1721/22.

January the 19th 1721/22   JOSEPH WILDER *Clerk*

February the 5th 1721/22 att a meeting of the Proprietors att ye meeting Hous first Made Choyce of James Wilder Moderator for Said Meeting

2 In answer to the Propozition of Capt Samuell Willard The Propriety made Choyce of a Committy to vew said way and se where it may be most accomodable to Serve the publick and make Report to the proprietey in order to haue it alowed and then made Choyce of Hooker Osgood Ebenezer Wilder & Jonathan Houghton to be the Committy.

3 In answer to the propozition of Henry Willard they voted that Capt Wilder Josiah White and Joseph Wilder be a Committy to vew sd way and make Report to the propriety

4 they voted to chuse a Committy to vew the Hiway propounded for by Josiah White and make Report to the propriety & then Made Choyce of Jabaz Fairbank Capt Peter Joslin & Capt Ephriam Wilder to be the Committy:

5 Jeremiah Wilson personally appeered before the Propriety and declared that he freely delivered up to the Town or propriety a Small Slip of Land Round ye west Corner of a dich Called Broad Medow Dich between that and the fut of broad medow Hill so much as may be accomodable for a hiway in that place

6 Refering to the Request of John Houghton Esq; they made Choyce of James Wilder Jonas Houghton Ju & Ebenezer Wilder to mesuer the Entervaill Lot of Danill Gaines down Penecuck River to see if it be not alredy Layed out neer that towit his Second Devision of Intervaill and make Report to the Propriety, & Then they ajorned the Meeting to the 5 day of march next Coming to three of the Clock in the after noone:

                                        JOSEPH WILDER *Clerk*

March y fifth the propriety meet and adjorned to the twenteth of Said March. March ye twenteth 1722 The propriety being meet first Granted to Capt Samuell Willard a Hiway that Run through a part of Broad Medow for and in Consederation of a pece of Land Given up to ye Town by Jeremiah Wilson to be a hiway in Lew there of Round ye Corner of ye sd Broad Medow betwixt that and the hill

2   They Exsepted the Returnes of Severall Hiwaies of the Committys appointed to vew and Lay them out to wit of the Contery Rode to Groton brought in by Cpt Wilder Josiah White and Joseph Wilder as followeth February ye 9 1721/22 Then prossed on sd Service first began at ye north line of Lancaster Township and marked a small white oke tree, and from thence to a white oke neer ye Corner of Seth Walkers Land from thence to a stump by the side of sd Walkers fence from thence to ye Corner of Walkers northermost Lott from thence to ye Corner of Samuell Rogerses Land & so along upon ye hed of that Lott to ye Corner of ye Land of Henry Willard to a Chesnut tree from thence to a Red oke neer ye brow of ye hill and so to a Walnut in the Riseing of ye Hill and from thence to a black oke at ye bottom of Said Hill from thence to a Rock a gainst Henry Willards barn and so bareing ye breth of five Rods to ye Eastward of all ye afore sd marks and so bareing the same wedth though betwixt ye Walls of Josiah Willard as marked out and so along upon ye heds of the Lots of Hezakiah an Joseph Willard baring ye bredth of five Rods to ye est from there fences as they now stand till itt Coms to ye Corner of Joseph Willards Lott from thence made an angle Runing to a small White oke bush standing in Joseph Willards hedge from thence to a white oke tree from that to a heep of Stons upon Hezakiah Willards Land makeing an angle Runing a Cross the Lott of Jonathan Willard from a heep of Stons to a small black oke from thence to ye Corner of Cpt Willards wall sd way Lying five Rods wide to the East ward or Sow est of all ye aforesd marks & so through betwix ye wall of Capt Samuel Willard and John Willard bareing ye same wedth to ye South East Corner of Capt Willard wall & then with a straight line to a small white oke marked at a Rock where ye former Committy Left marking the way Lying to the Sow east of sd line and also marked a Rode from sd Rode down the north side of Jonathan Willard lott to ye hed of ye lott of Joseph atherton of three Rods Wide sd Return was Exsepted by a vote Exsepting at Capting Willards at his Request it was alowed to godown ner his hous he promasing to Leve the hiway there Wider by Consederable then five Rods

JOSEPH WILDER *Clerk*

The road here described is now wholly in the town of Harvard.

2 of a hiway to ye mill up ye North River which was as followeth. Lancaster February the 14 1721/2 Whereas We namely Peter Joslin Jabaz fairbank & Ephriam Wilder are appointed a Committy to Lay out a hiway to David Whetcombs Land upon the North River: We haue bin upon ye Spot and haue Layed out a hiway from the Hiway that Goeth to Benits farm a Cross to Whetcombs Land and haue marked the trees upon ye north side of said way ye way Lying through Larances Land takeing

from him one acre of Land sd way for ye most part being two Rods Wide but where it Joyns to Whetcoms Land it is five Rods Wide.

JOSEPH WILDER Clerk

The terminus of this road was at the site lately occupied by the American Shoeshank Company's factory. Here the Whitcomb family had a mill for many years.

3 a hiway petistioned for by Capt Willard a Report there of was made by Hooker Osgood Ebenezer Wilder and Jonathan Houghton who informed the propriety that they judged the sd way Should goo by David Whetcombs & so in to the bay Rode & that it should leve Groaton Rode at ye South side of Joseph Hutchinses lott and to Run along by ye sd Hutchinses lott till it Came over ye brook at Round medow Joseph Hutchins allso appeared and offered ye Propriety to Give so much Land as would be nesesary for ye Hiway in that place according to ye Report of ye Committy; but at ye Re[quest] of Thomas Houghton the way was Granted by his door & was to Lye South of his hous so far as that ye north side of ye way should be thre Rods from his door and said way was Exsepted and Confermed to be three Rods Wide exsept where it pases through ye Land of Jacob & Henry Houghton and there to be but two Rods Said Committy Reports that they began to marke at ye Land of Thomas Houghton and ran through it by his hous sixty seven Rods & a half and through Ephriam Houghtons Land sixty four Rods & through Edward Houghtons Land 100 Rods and through James athertons Land fourty six Rods and through Jacob Houghtons Land fourty five Rods and throu the Land of Jacob Houghton & Benjamin Athertons Land ninty eight Rods and then it Ran upon Common Land till it Croses the Rode that pases to barehill February ye 25 we began at barehill Rode and went through ye Land of Jacob Houghton Seventy Rods and through ye Land of Henry Houghton by his hous eighty two Rods and then we Ran in Common till we Come to the Land of Hezakiah Whitcombes in his Land we Ran on hundred and twelve Rods through the Land of David Whitcombs twenty Eight Rods and then we ran in Common Land and in Land of David Whitcomb & ye Hairs of John Whitcomb Decesed in which there was alowance made for a hiway in ye Laying out of said Land: and then we Ran through a small Corner of ye Land of Nathanil HapGood in to ye Bay Rode, then we began at the Bay Rode neer Joseph Sawyers and marked a hiway a Cross to ye afore sd Rode and it Coms in to ye aboue said Rode abought eighteen Rods from David Whitcombs barn and ye said David whetcomb is satisfied for ye Damage it doth to him if he haue the old Rode which was formerly Layd out behind his feeld all which was Confermed by a vote. sd Report was Signed   HOOKER OSGOOD EBENEZER WILDER JONATHAN HOUGHTON

Entered upon Record by JOSEPH WILDER <i>Clk</i>

note that yᵉ Hiway through David Whetcombs Land is to be but two Rods wide—then the meetin was ajorned to yᵉ third Wednesday in May next

The next record was written by Jonathan Houghton, son of the Town Clerk.

March yᵉ 5ᵗʰ 1721/2, the freeholders & other Inhabitants of Lancaster Duly Quallified, meet together it being their anuall meeting for Choice of Town officers &c:

1. The Town Chose Capt Ephraim Wilder moderator for said meeting.
2. The Town Chose William Sawyer Grand Juror for yᵉ year ensuing, then yᵉ Selectmen gaue yᵉ Town an account of what they had done as to Reconing with Mr Prentice, & then examined who were voters in choice of Town officers.
3. The Town Chose five Selectmen namely John Houghton Sr Capt Ephraim Wilder Jabez ffairbank Josiah White & James Wilder.
4. The Town Chose John Houghton Town Clerk for yᵉ year ensuing
5. The Town Chose thre Constabels namely John Johnson Bezeleel Sawyer & John Willard.
6. The Town Chose Henry Willard & Joseph Stone Tything men.
7. The Town Chose Samuel Rogers Sr Joseph Atherton William Divol Nathaniel Wilder & James Snow Servairs of Highways.
8. The Town Chose James Wilder Town Treasurer.
9. The Town Chose James Atherton & Amos Sawyer fence vewers.
10. The Town Chose John Prescott Benjamin Wilson Daniel Houghton and Ebenezer Harries Hawyerds
11. The Town Chose Thomas Carter Sealler of Leather.

The following memorandum from an old account book of the first Judge Joseph Wilder, lately presented to the public library by Benjamin F. Wyman, gives the name of the Grammar School teacher in Lancaster 1721–22, and the money value at which his services for the year were estimated.

Delivered and payed to Mr Edward Broughton March y 14 1721/22 for Keeping Scool six pounds fiue shillings.
Moore in August yᵉ sum of fiue shillings by Ebenezer Wilder const. o.. 5..0
on a note answered by Josiah Willard   3..18..6
on a note to Mr dickenson   o.. 2..6
on a note to Bezaleel Sawyer   o. 5.8

on a note to Elias Sawyer	0 . 8 . 0
Upon two Recepts to Jonas Houghton Constable	3 . 0 . 6

  Reconed with Mr Edward Broughton October y⁰ 25ᵗʰ 1722
Remains Dew to yᵉ said Mr Broughton 7—6—10 for his years Scooling.

 Or 21 pounds 12 shillings for the year's salary.

  May the sixteenth 1722 the propriety being meet in answer to the Propositon of Samuel Warner it was voted that a Committy be Chosen to vew the hiway propounded for and if they shall think it needfull To Lay out a Hiway betwix the Land of Jonas Houghton and Jonathan Sawyer as they shall think meet and make Report to yᵉ next meeting in order to its being exsepted

 2 they voted that the same Committy vew what Damage is don to aboue said Land of Jonas Houghton that was hutsons by a hiway Laid to Barehill medows and how much of yᵉ ajasant Land out to be alowed for a Recompence the Committy Chosen was Jabaz Fairbank Capt Samuell Willard & Jacob Houghton

 3 they then Granted Elias Sawyer five acres of Land upon a brook Called Kerlys Brook for to make up the Conveniancy of Henry Kerly & William

 4 The Return of a Committy apointed to mesure the Lot of Danil Gains we yᵉ Subscribers mesured the Lott of Danil Gains or that which was soposed to be it and find betwixt sum mark trees and Snows Entervaill Lott and betwixt the Little piece and sum Entervaill Land of Ebenezer Wilder and find it to be about sixteen acres.

       JAMES WILDER
       EBENEZER WILDER } *Committy*
       JONAS HOUGHTON Ju

 An account of a hiway Laid out from yᵉ Town line beyond Wacapacit and went through the Land of Hooker Osgood on hundred and fifty Rods and through the Land of Justice Houghton fifty Rods and then through Hooker Osgoods land ninty four Rods and then through the Land of Samuell Carter one hundred Rods. JABAZ FAIRBANK NATHANIL SAWYER SAMUELL CARTER *Committy* this Return was Exsepted and said Hiway Confermed: and an aquevelant Granted to the Persons aboue named to wit to Hooker Osgood two acres for one to Justice Houghton deto to Samuell Carter an acre and half in lew of one.

 This is the road from Leominster line to Wickapeket Brook at the Phelps Mill.

 February yᵉ 2ᵈ 1721 Laid out another hiway we began at the end of a hiway that Goeth up between the Lots of Nathanil Wilder and Oliver Wilder and Ran through Nathanil Wilders Land fifty four Rods and through the Land of Oliver Wilder eighty eight Rods and through Jonathan Wilders Land twenty six Rods and through Nathanil Hapgoods Land

Sixteen Rods and through Danill Ruggs Land fourty Rods and through Samuell Carters Land fourty Rods and then through another piece of Oliver Wilders Land on hundred & twenty three Rods to the Town line to a little Run of water neer Wakapacet Brook neer the old Cartway aboue John Kindals Said way Laid out three Rods wide by JABAZ FAIRBANK SAMUELL CARTER and NATHANIL SAWYER a Committy: the aboue said way was exsepted and Confermed by the propriety for a hiway as it is marked out.

This describes the westerly extension of the first road over George Hill. Oliver Wilder, afterward colonel, lived upon the north side of the highway on or near the site of the house now standing just above the George Hill schoolhouse. His brother Nathaniel lived on the southerly side of the highway.

The hiway to Whashacomb was accordingly marked out by said Commity and Ran throu the Land of Jonathan Moor sixty three Rod and through the Land of Thomas Sawyer ten scoor and seventeen Rods to ye town line. JABEZ FAIRBANK NATHANIL SAWYER S̶A̶W̶Y̶E̶R̶ SAMUEL CARTER Committy

February ye 4 1722/3 at a meeting of the proprietors first made Choyce of Capt Wilder Moderator and then Discharged Edmund and Ebenezer Harris Judgeing that they had fulfilled the obligation they ware under in Cleering and keepin the bering feeld well Subdued

2 a Committy made a Report to wit Jabaz Fairbank & Cpt Samuell Willard and Reported that the hiway Petistioned for by Samuell Warner &c be granted and that it ly along by the Side of the Land that was Hutsons two Rods Wide which Report was Confermed and said way Granted by a vote

3 Capt Wilder &c brought in a Report Conserning Sum hiwaies from hog swamp which waies was Exsepted and Granted to be three Rods in wedth Exsept where it Croses the medow by Jabaz Fairbanks In and there to be but one Rod and a half also of a hiway Jeremiah Holmans and Whitneys, which is to Run along through the Land of Josiah Wheelor seventy nine Rods through the Land of James Wilder Sixty two Rods throuh the Land of John Wilder on hundred and twelve Rods through James Butlers Land two Rods through the Land of Joseph Sawyer on hundred and fifty four Rods Said way to be three Rods wide Said way was alowed and Confermed by a vote to Lye as it is marked out by Said Committy Save at ye brook by Whitneys there to pass the brook where it is marked and then to Run down the brook neer the said brook till it Coms neer the Hous of Said Holman to where the way was formerly Layed out

3 The propriety made alowances to the Severall persons aboue said for what damage they had Recevd by said way as followeth to Jabaz Fairbanks at y⁰ Law or proportion of two acres and a half in the Lew of one, to John Wilder two acres for one, to James Wilder one acre and half for one, to Joseph Sawyer acres for acre, then the meeting was ajorned to y⁰ 18 of sd February.

A COPY OF NOTIFICATION FEBRUARY Y^E 4 1722/3

These may notifie the propriety of Lancaster that Jonath moor Requests that the Contery Rode or Hiway from Marlburough may Run by his door in to Hog swampt Rode. 2 Hezakiah Whetcomb for a hiway to the bay Rode from the hiway propounded for by Capt Willard Severall persons for alowance for damage for hiwaies Jos Wilds and Richard Wilds that the Last halfe of y⁰ 4 devision may be Granted

Febrewary the 18th 1722/3 the Propriety being Meet first they Granted the propozition of Jonathan Moor to wit that y⁰ Contery Rode to Marlburrough be Remoued from the north side of his orchard and to pass through betwixt his hous and his new Barn to y⁰ hiway that goeth to hog swamp and to be five Rods wide.

2 they voted upon the proposition of Hezakiah Whetcomb that y⁰ Committy appointed to vew the hiway proposed by Capt Willard to wit Mr Osgood Ebenezer Wilder and Jonathan Houghton vew y⁰ same and make Report to y⁰ propriety when they Report Conserning the other Hiway

3 they Granted to James Wilder three acres in Lew of on for what was taken of off his Land by a hiway to wacapacet: to Joseph Wilder & Edmund harris four acres in Lew of one and so proporsonablely

4 they voted that Mr Osgood &c mark out the hiway ask[ed] for by Capt Willard and take an account of what it takes from every man that it Runs through his Land and make Report to y⁰ next meeting

5 upon the proposition of Richard Wilds they voted that it be defered till y⁰ next meeting and then the meeting was ajorned to that day month

A COPY OF THE NOTIFIECATION TO Y^E PROPRIETIE OF LANCASTER

these may serue to notifie you that Josiah Wheelock desiers that the hiway [through] his Land to pine hill may be Remoued further north and that it may be but two Rods wide William Sawyer Desiers alowance for a hiway that goeth through his Land Jonas Houghton that James Keyes may be appointed to Lay out Land in y⁰ old Township it is also desiered that all persons who haue bin damnified by hiwaies going through there Land would bering in there accounts in order to there being alowed

therefor   Thomas Wilder desiers that a hiway may be Laid to Shuesbery and from that to his Entervaill   JOSEPH WILDER *Clerk*
   Lancaster March ye 4th 1722/3:

   March ye 18th 1723 at a meeting of ye proprietors and in the first place they voted that Edward hartwill haue a peece of Land that lyeth betwene his Land and walnnut Swampt Lot with the addition of one acre and half to Lay out as other undevided Land alowed him for alowance for a hiway that goeth through his Land to Wacapacet
   2   they exsepted a former Report made by Capt Houghton &c Refering to ye Remoueal of a hiway propounded for by Hezakiah Townsend by his hous.
   3   they voted that James Wilder Josiah White and Ebenezer Wilder Lay out a hiway to pine hill where shall be most Conveniant
   4.   they made Choyce of James Keyes to Lay out Land in that which was Called the old Township
   5   in answer to ye Request of Thomas Wilder they made Choyce of Left Houghton John Prest & Bazaliel Sawyer to vew the same and Report there on to ye Propriety and also mark it out if they think fit and most Conveniant
   6   they Granted the Last half of ye 4 devision to begin to Lay out the first of may next which will be in 1723
   7   the propriety Granted that Oliver Wilder haue the alowance of 3 acres for one for so much as is taken from him by a hiway to Wacapacet & 2 for one Ruges pece one acre and half for ye Rest and so for all others

   Aprill ye 29th 1723 the Proprietors of Lancaster being meet by vertue of a Warrant Given out by John Houghton Esquier for the Calling there of
   And first made Choyce of John Houghton Esquier for a Moderator and then voted that all Land Laid out Since Joseph Wilder was Chosen A proprietors Clerk and Recorded by the Town Clerk be Signed by the proprietors Clerk
   Secondly it was put to vote whethor they will Now prosced to the Choyce of a proprietors Clerk and it pased in ye Negative
   3   They voted that Noperson Layout any part of ye Last half of his forth Devision before he hath made out his Right there to the Sattisfaction of those that shall be Chosen a Commity to Seve in to that affair to see whether he hath ajust Right there and hath also procured a Sirtificate under there hands to Sign it to Such as are appointed to Lay out Lands in sd propriety
   4   They voted to Choos three men for the Service aforesaid
   5   They made Choyce of John Houghton Esqr Joseph Wilder and Jonathan Houghton to be the Committy for the Said Service

6   They voted that none of ye Land in the Last half of ye forth Devision be Laid out till after ye third Wednsday of may next,

Jonas Houghton ju then Made a motion in s^d meeting Requesting that the propriety would Rectifie the Land formerly Laid out to Mr [*name gone*] Sum part of it being Laid in to sum Land Laid out to Jeremiah Rogers and that sumthing may be don upon it at ye ajornment of ye meeting and then the meeting was ajorned to ye third wednsday of may being the 15 of may next at nine of ye Clock but before ye ajornment there was these alowances made as followeth for a Recompence for damage don them by hiwaies Runing through there Land   Thomas Houghton three acres for one Ephriam Houghton deto Edward Houghton deto James Atherton deto Jacob Houghton ju four acres for one Benjamin Atherton deto Jacob Houghton deto Henry Houghton deto Hezakiah Whetcomb three acres for one David Whetcomb Deto   it was also then voted that William Divoll should haue the Slip of Land Lying a Gainst his Land at ye Wallnut Swamp in Lew of the hiway which Crosses his Land there with ye alowance of half an acre for damage

May wednsday ye 15 of s^d month the propriety being meet ajorned the meeting to ye 3 wednsd in august and defered the devision till then

Wednsday the 21 of August the propriety meet and opened the meeting and ajorned the same to ye 3 wednsday in October and defered the Last half of ye 4 devision till then and from thence it was ajorned to 3 wednsday in November and that the Last half of the forth Devision was Continued till ye first of february following

The following financial statement of the selectmen for 1723 is from Judge Joseph Wilder's memorandum book.

Thomas Carter Town Treasurer for ye year 1723.

minester's Rates		Town Rates
34 – 12 – 7	Edward Hartwill Constable of ye Town	£40 – 9 – 0
23 – 13 – 3	Benjamin Bailey Constable	28 – 19 – 11
27 – 11 – 9	Samuell Warner	34 – 6 – 10
		103 – 15 – 9
	Where of he is ordered to pay to Jabez fairbank for Serving as Representative in 1723	20 – 12 – 0
	to ye Selectmen for makeing Rates in 1722	2 – 0 – 0
	to Mr Edward Broughton for Keeping Scool	{ 10 10 20
	to ye Selectmen for Glace	2 – 5
	to Edmund Harris for Sweeping ye meeting hous	1 – 15

to ye Selectmen for making Rates in 1723 towit to Joseph Wilder   1 – 4 – 6
    Josiah White   10 – 2
    John White   9 – 0
    Samuell Carter   10 – 0
    Ebenezer Wilder   12 – 4
to Nathan Hawood for two wind frames for ye meeting hous   3 – 0
to Edward Hartwill for to make up what his province List was
    Les than his warrant   15 – 0
to the Committy for ye bridge   30£ – 0 – 0
to John Prescot for plank   14 – 6

                        101 – 10 – 6
                        £2 – 5 – 3

    LANCASTER february 18th 1723/4 then Rekoned with Deacon Joseph Wilder Mr Samuell Carter: Mr Josiah White & Mr Ebenezer Wilder; Selectmen for the Town of Lancaster: & the Subscriber hath Received the wholl of his Sallery till July 1st 1723.   JOHN PRENTICE

    Sd Receipt entered as above being a true Copy May the 12th 1724.
                      p JOHN HOUGHTON *Town Clerk*

    LANCASTER March 2 1723/4   The Inhabitants of sd Lancaster met at ye Meeting House in sd Towne according to appointment & notice Given to be the Publick Anniversary Meeting for Choyce of Town officers &c:
    1   & first Chose Jonathan Moore Moderator for s^d Meeting: & then the Selectmen Gave Some account of what they had Done as to making of Rates: & particularly Had Reconed with Mr Prentice who is Cleered till ye first of July 1723 as by his Receipt as above entered
    2   & next voted that the Late Select men do Give in a faire account of theire Proceedings in the Towns affaires the Last yeare unto ye Next Selectmen that may be Chosen to Succeed as Selectmen in sd Town
    3   next voted to Choose 5 Selectmen & accordingly Chose Joseph Wilder; Josiah White; Jonathan Houghton; ebenezer Wilder & Samuell Carter Selectmen to serve for the year ensuing

The above record, left incomplete, is in the hand of John Houghton, as also is the next.

    1724.   Munday ye 11th of May 1724 The free Holders &c: of ye Town of Lancaster met at ye Meetinghouse in sd Town In order to Choose a Representative according to Due warning Given, & after the Reading of the Precept & ye Laws Relating to sd affaire, votes were called for & Given in & then John Houghton Senr was Chosen Representative for sd Town of Lancaster: to serve at ye Generall Court according as specified in sd Precept.

August 1724. The Selectmen of Lancaster are allowed to enter their caution against Robert Darby, Moses Chandler & his wife with three children, Barnard Twoells, Sarah Hubbard and Mary West being Inhabitants, they having been warned to depart the said Town as pr their caution on file.

[Middlesex Court Records.]

A COPY OF Y^E NOTIFICATION FOR Y^E MEETING FEBRUARY Y^E 3^d 1723/4

the warning being Taken away there Remains only a breef account of the things propounded for to wit Thomas Wilder propounded for a hiway from the Road by his hous to ye Hous that was Robert Houghtons ju decesed John Warner for a hiway from Caleb Sawyers to his Hous Jonathan Whitney and Jonathan Crouch for a hiway from where they Live to ye Hous of Danil Preest Decesed John Darbey for Som alowance for a hiway Taken Through ye Land he purchassed of John Willard. Josiah Willard also mosoned that Sum alowance be made him and Joseph Atherton for damage by a hiway into ye plumtrees

Lancaster February the 3^d 1723/4 the propriety meet and first made Choyce of John Houghton Esqr Moderator for Said meeting and then Granted a Committy for to vew two hiwayes propounded for, to wit one by John Warner and the other by Jonathan Whitney &c. and to mark out the same if they think them needfull and to Report to ye propriety the place of there Lying and also ye Quantity of Land they Take from any Land they may Run through and Likewise ye Quallity thereof

2 They made Choyce of Jacob Houghton Caleb Sawyer & Jonas Houghton to be ye Committy

3 they voted that ye Same Committy vew what Damage John Darbey Sustaned by a hiway that is Laid through ye Land he purchassed of John Willard & what he ought to be alowed therefor and also what Josiah Willard and Joseph Atherton ought to be alowed for the hiway Crossin their Entervaill in to ye plumtrees

4 they made Choyce of James Wilder Jonathan Houghton & Ebenezer Wilder to be a Committy to vew the hiway propounded for by Thomas Wilder and to marke out ye same & to Report to the propriety there Doings there in : and then the meeting was ajorned to ye third wednsday of may next to eight of ye Clock

Lancaster May ye 20 1724 upon ye ajornment from February the 3^d and first Receved a return of a Committy which was as followeth : We the Subscribers being appointed a Committey to mark out a hiway to where Robert Houghton Jr did formerly live we began to mark out the way at the turn of the old way beyond Thomas Wilders hous and marked along till we Came to Sum Land of Thomas Tookers where we Took a slip of the said Land into ye hiway and from thence we marked the hiway through Common Land till we Came to Land of Robert Houghton Decesed : and we are of opineon that there is a Little Corner of Land on the same side of the hiway south of the piece taken from said Tooker may be a Recompence to him for the damage dun him by ye hiway JAMES WILDER EBENEZER WILDER JONATHAN HOUGHTON this Return was Exsepted and the hiway Confermed and a small slip of Land Lying on the West Side of said way by the said Tookers Land Granted to said Tooker for alowance

2 They made Choyce of Benjamin Bellows Jonas Houghton and Thomas Tooker to be a Committy to vew the Hiway formerly propound[ed] for by Benjamin Houghton to See where it may be with most Conveniancy and make Report to the propriety at there next meeting

3 they made Choyce of Joseph Wheelock William Divoll and John Benit to be a Committy to vew the hiway propounded for by Edward Hartwill to se where it may be most Conveniant and make Report to the propriety at there next meeting

4 they Receved a Report of a Committy sent out on the propozition of John Warner John Darbey and Jonathan Whitney which was as followeth viz May the Eighteenth 1724 we the Subscribers marked Severall Waies viz one Hiway Begining at the Hiway neer to Caleb Sawyers barn and Ran as the markes directs to a white oak a Corner of John Warners Land: and do alow it to Run Twenty Rods along side of John Warners Land: but Samuell Warner appeered in said Meeting and made an offer that if the Town would Lay out the said Hiway along by his Hous and Gabriell Preists Hous through there Land that they to wit Gabriell Preist and Samuell Warner would Give the Land free and would be at half the Charge of Makeing and Keeping in Repare the way through there Land the Committey also Gave there voice that it might be as serveable to the publick

another Hiway is marked out begining neer to the westerly end of Caleb Sawyers Feeld at the Hiway and Runeth as the mark trees direct upon to barehill and along by Land that was Laid out to [Josiah] White and it Runs along by the Southerly end of the Land that [*leaf torn*] Danil Priest by the northerly side of a Corner Mark at the westerly end of a piece of Land of Nathanil HapGood and then it Runs by said Land the whol Lenth of it then it Runs eigty four Rods through Land of Samuell Warners to Jonathan Whitneys and Jonathan Crouches Land and ten Rods by said Crouches Land and we think said Warner ought to be alowed three acres in Lew of one or according to that proportion

We also mesored the Hiway in John Darbes Land and find it to Run in his Land on hundred and fifty Rods and we think he ought to be alowed thre acres for one JACOB HOUGHTON JONAS HOUGHTON *Committey* this return was exsepted the hiwayes alowed and ye alowances Granted by the propriety

5 they Granted a Committey to wit Joseph Sawyer James Keyes & Hezakiah [Town]send to vew the Hiwaies propounded for by Samuell Rugg . . . . . [*leaf torn*]

Lastly they Granted ye Request of Jonas Houghton in Remoual of a Hiway which Goeth to barehill Medows where it Runeth through the Land that was Danil Hutsons that it might Run along upon the South Edge of it by the Land of Joseph Fairbank

At a meeting of the [proprietors] February the 1st 1724/5 first made Choyce of John Houghton Esquier for a Moderator then Receved sum Reports of Committyes formerly Chosen Refering to Sum Hiwaies they are as followeth January ye 29th 1724/5 Wee the Subscribers being Choosen a Committey by the propriety of Lancaster to vew a hiway petistioned for by Benjamin Houghton upon the Day aboue said we went and vewed the Same and have marked it out viz through the Land of Ebenezer Wilder thirty Rods then through the Land of Jabaz Fairbank twenty nine Rods then a Long in the Land of Jabaz Fairbank & Thomas Sawyer to Run along half upon Each thirty four Rods and then wholly in the Land of Said Sawyer Twenty Eight Rods and then in said Fairbanks Land twelve Rods. BENJAMIN BELLOWS THOMAS TOOKER JONAS HOUGHTON *Committy* This Report was exsepted and the hiway Confermed accordingly by the propriety by a vote in said meeting

January ye 18th 1724/5 Marked out a hiway for the Conveniance of Samuell Rugg to Com to the Contery Road and it began at a white oak about ten Rods from the norwest angle of his Land which was Laid out for his Father on the northerly side and Runs northerly a Cross the Land of Jonathan Moors Seventy one Rods then it Run a Cross sum of the Land of John Moor twenty six Rods and Coms in to the bay Road at the edge of the plain neer a little Brook where the way has bin diged Easterly from the pond brook Called west pond brook JAMES KEYES JOSEPH SAWYER *Committy* this hiway was Confermed by a vote, and then the meeting was ajorned to the first Monday in March next

March ye 1 the propriety being meet ajorned ye meeting to ye 3 monday in May nex to ten of ye Clock

It has been usual to state that Josiah Flagg, whose excellent penmanship adorns the town books for thirty-four years, between 1800 and 1836, was without a rival in the length of his service as clerk for Lancaster. But the signature of John Houghton, later known as Justice Houghton, who succeeded Cyprian Steevens as clerk of the writs, is found attached to records of lands, petitions to the court, and other public documents, as town clerk, for nearly every year from 1685 to 1724, a period of forty years. Less than half a dozen town-meeting records in his distinct chirography have been preserved to our day, and in only three of these are elections of a clerk noted. In 1719, 1721 and 1722 not only was John Houghton, Esquire, chosen clerk, but moderator, selectman or assessor as well. He is the first named as schoolmaster in any records of the town. Joseph Willard, Esquire, states that he represented the town for fourteen years in the legislature, but omits the years 1690 and 1692 when John Houghton was undoubtedly one of the two deputies sent, and includes the year 1718 when Lancaster elected not John Houghton, Sen., but Lieutenant John, his son. We find the title Justice given him as early as 1718, though the date of his commission is put down in the civil list 1729. Perhaps Justice Houghton might have been appointed the first judge of the Worcester County Court of Common Pleas in 1731, instead of his younger neighbor, Joseph Wilder, but for his growing blindness. Although then eighty years of age, his mental and physical vigor were little impaired.

John Houghton was the son of John and Beatrix, who in 1653 set up their roof tree somewhere near Dean's, now Goodridge Brook. Not far away on the south side of the Narrow Lane, lived Jacob Farrar whose only daughter, Mary, must have been John's nearest playmate. February 22, 1672, when John was about twenty-one, and Mary twenty-three years of age, she became his wife. Their home, at least after the massacre of 1676, was on the Old Common as it is now called, though then and long after known as Bride Cake Plain. Their house stood on the south side of the highway opposite the grounds of the State Industrial School. After fifty-two years of married life, the wife died April 7, 1724, and January 27, 1725, John Houghton, at the age of seventy-five, married Hannah Wilder, aged seventy-two. The Boston Evening

Post for Monday, February 14, 1737, thus briefly records his death :

> LANCASTER, February 8th 1736-7.
> On the 3d Instant died here (after a few Day's Indisposition) *John Houghton*, Esq : in the 87th Year of his Age. He was a sensible, religious, peaceable and useful Man. He was serviceable (in several Capacities) for many Years among us. A constant and devout attender on all the Ordinances and Worship of God in his House. Tho' his Eyes were dim some Years before his Death, yet his Bodily Strength and Intellectual Powers remained with him to an uncommon Degree. He hath left behind him a sorrowful Widow in the 84th. Year of her Age, under bodily Blindness, and who hath been confined to her Bed for more than three Years past : Also a numerous Offspring. There are now living of his Children 7, of his Grandchildren 54, and of his Great Grand Children 73, in all 134.

Joseph Wilder, son of the second Thomas Wilder, born in 1683, was proprietors' clerk for forty years, from 1716 to 1757, and perhaps during some years previous, the records of which are missing. He also became town clerk in 1737, continuing in that office seven years. These offices he held by common consent, in spite of the fact that his penmanship is execrable, and almost illegible in the late years of his life, when he wrote with a palsied hand. He was deacon in the Lancaster church for forty-two years, and representative to general court in 1720, 1725 and 1726. Upon the organization of Worcester County in 1731, he was appointed judge and held the office of chief justice at his death. He was, however, very illiterate, excelling all his clerical predecessors and rivalling the most untaught of his successors, in the perversity of his spelling. Had his decisions as a judge been as versatile and independent of precedent, as was his orthography, trials before him would have had all the exciting uncertainty of the modern horse race. In punctuation he displayed greater consistency, ignoring it altogether, nor deigning like the eccentric pamphleteer of the next generation, to add to his work any postscript supply of points for eclectic distribution. He also bears, justly or unjustly, the ill name of having by his narrow minded opposition, prevented the locating in Lancaster of the county offices, this then being the foremost town in the new county. He is charged with having in his blind conservatism, presaged woes unnumbered to the rural paradise about him, should it become habituated to the society of lawyers and litigants.

There must have been great native force in him, as well as discretion and tact. Rev. Timothy Harrington in a sermon preserved in manuscript, headed *Post Funera Hon. Viri J. Wilder armigeri*, portrays his character in these flattering colors:

> God furnished him with a penetrating Judgment, strong Reason, and a tenacious Memory, and all, so far as we can judge, were consecrated to ye Honour of ye most high. God was pleased to advance him to numerous seats of trust and Im[portance] in ye Town County and Province, which he filled with Integrity and Honour. In his domestic character, a kind and faithful Husband a tender and Instructive and Exemplary Parent, a pleasant chearful and —— Christian, a friend to Truth and Virtue, A lover of God, man and his country, and a Benefactor to ye poor and ye Distressed. This, This is he whom God hath taken from us.

He died March 29, 1757, aged 74. His wife, who outlived him, was Lucy, sister of Reverend Andrew Gardner. One son, Colonel Caleb, followed him as clerk of the proprietors, and another, Colonel Joseph, succeeded him in the offices of town clerk, deacon and Judge of the Court of Common Pleas.

LOVEWELL'S WAR.

1722–1726.

MILITARY CORRESPONDENCE, JOURNALS AND MUSTER ROLLS.

In the Muster Roll of Sergeant Thomas Buckminster of Framingham, are the names of four Lancaster men, engaged during July and August, 1722, in some service not specified:

Henry Houghton, 1 week, 6 days.   John Beeman, 4 weeks, 5 days.
John Wilder, 4 weeks, 5 days.   Richard Wild.
[Massachusetts Archives, XCI, 32.]

In the Muster Roll of Sergeant Samuel Wright, serving from October 25th to November 25th, 1822, is found the name of Simon Stevens of Lancaster.
[Massachusetts Archives, XCI, 71.]

1723.   BOSTON Nov 20 1723.

Sir. I rec^d your Lett^r this morning of the 18th Instant & haue enquired at the Secry^s Office concerning the orders to Coll. Tyng & find by a great Neglect they were misplaced & never sent forward. Now you acquainting me that you can enlist very good Men to compleat the Number for yor Command, These are to direct you forthwith to do it & return me their Names; I doubt not but you will keep them to their Duty & take all Occasions if possible to perform some Signal Service.
                    Yo^{rs}
To Lt. Jabez Fairbank.   W^M DUMMER
[Massachusetts Archives, LXXII, 138.]

LANCASTER December ye 2th 1723

May it plese your Hon^{er} I have in observance of your Hon^{rs} order Inlisted fifteen able bodyed men fit for service & haue sent the List of them herewith to your Hon^r with ye List of those that ware in ye service before

and haue put them on duity: we haue made no decovery of ye Inemy as yet: the barer is one that is in the service & is Capable if your Hon^r Seas Case to demand; to give a full account of our management your
Humble

[*Superscribed*]   Servant JABEZ FAIRBANK
To ye Hon^le William Dumer Esq Left Governer & for His Majesties service, by Mr Edward Hartwell.

A List of the Names of ye Soldiers first enlisted in Lancaster Groaten & Dunstable.

Edward Hartwill
Aaron Willard
Benjamin Osgood
Benjamin Houghton jun
John Bennit
Samuell Sawyer
Jonathan Shipley
Joseph Blood

James Shattuck
Samuell Scripter
John Stephens
William Larrance
Jabaz Davice
Thomas Chamberlin
Ephriam Chandler
Benjamin Nicholds
John Barrit

The names of those Last in Listed
Joseph Blanchard
Ephriam Wheeler
David Osgood
Joseph Wheelock
Ezra Sawyer
Benjamin Harris
Phineas Parker
David Satell

Isaac Woods
Jacob Lakin
Thomas Lund
Isaac Farwell
Ebenezer Cumins
John Usher
Jonathan Combs

LANCASTER December the 2th 1723
JABEZ FAIRBANKS

[Massachusetts Archives, LXXII, 144, 145.]
Lancaster names are printed in italics.

LANCASTER, April 28 1724
May it please your Honour.

Sr. I have attended your order referring to the Placing of the men at each Town, and have also Sent your Honour the Journalls of all the long Scouts. The Scouts going from three Particular Towns, I am not able to give your Honour so particular an account of Every Days march as Possibly your Honour may expect. I endeavour to Improve the men Constantly to the most advantage according to the Best of my Judgment. If your Honour Please, I would now and then Send out A Scout at Considerable Distance from the Towns, and I think it would be very agreable to the minds of the People so to do. I stand ready to attend your Honours Orders & am your Honours Most Obedient Servant.

JABEZ FAIRBANK.

[Massachusetts Archives, XXXVIII, A, 65.]

GROTON May 28, 1724.

May it please your Honour.

I have Posted the men Committed to my care at the Towns of Lancaster Groton Dunstable & Turkey Hill according to your Honours Orders; and Improve them in the best manner I can for the protection of the People & Discovery of the Enemy and I think to General Satisfaction. I have ordered one man to Mr. Prescotts Garrison During his attendance on the Court. I beg Leave further to acquaint your Honour that ye people in these Towns apprehend themselves in Great Danger, and cannot (in my humble opinion) be in any measure safe with so small a number of men.   I am your Honours

Humble & most obedient Servt.

JABEZ FAIRBANK

[Massachusetts Archives, LXXII, 176.]

LANCASTER, July 1st 1724.

May it please your Honour.

I recieved your Letter the Last night in the evening, and not before tho I suppose I might have had it sooner had the bearer pleased, Your Honour is pleased in your Letter to give me my choice of A Lieutenants Post in Groton or Turkey Hills or A Serjeants at Lancaster. I am sensible that Serjeants Pay in Town would be as Profitable as to keep constantly abroad, but yet upon Some Considerations I choose to Abide in the Post I am, and to go to Groton. I return my thanks to your Honour for the choice you have given me. I would Inform your Honour that on Monday Last I sent A Scout to Rutland who Returned yesterday and gave me an Account that In the way they discovered the tracks of four or five Indians bearing towards Wochoosett whom they Judged had been gone 2 or 3 days. Yesterday Part of Groton men & Part of this Town went out for the week to range above the Towns to see what Discovery they could make, and I am myself this Day going out with what men I can Raise to see what I can discover. I desire the favour of your Honour, That the souldiers now under my Command in Lancaster and Groton might have the Liberty of abiding with me or of being Dismist. If it be your Honours Pleasure to let Edward Hartwell who hath been a Serjeant under me Abide still in that Post in this town I should take it as a favour. I stand ready to attend your Honours Orders & Commands and am S^r

Your Humble Servant

JABEZ FAIRBANK

[Massachusetts Archives, LII, 9.]

GROTON July 20th 1724.

May it please your Honour

I have attended your orders in posting the men at the Towns of Groton Lancaster & Turkey hill — precisely except at Turkey Hill there is but eleven men Capt. Stevens having not as yet sent so many as ordered

& I have Taken my post at Groton where I Improve the souldiers in the best manner I can agreeable to your orders, & I have ordered them to Lodge in Some of y⁰ most Exposed Garrisons as often as may be, but I find it impossible to Improve So Small a number of men So as to answer yᵉ Necessities of the people here; whose circumstances are so verry Difficult & Distressing that I am not able fully to Represent to your Honour; the poor people are many of them obliged to keep their own Garrisons and part of them Imployed as Guards while others are at their Labour whose whole Time would be full Little enough to be expended in Getting Bread for their families. My own Garrison at Lancaster is very much exposed & with Humble Submission I think Requires Protection as much as any in that Town, therefore I Humbly pray your Honour would be pleased to give me Leave to post a Souldier there Dureing my absence in the Service of the province. I beg your Honours Pardon for giving you this Trouble, and ask Leave to Subscribe mySelfe

Your most Obedient Humble Servᵗ

JABEZ FAIRBANKS.

[Massachusetts Archives, LII, 16.]

Lieutenant Jabez Fairbank was a grandson of John Prescott. His father, Jonas, and two brothers, Joshua and Jonathan, were slain in the early Indian wars. The stone over his grave in the old burying ground records that he died in 1758, aged about 84 years; the recorded date of his birth however is "8ᵗʰ 11ᵐᵒ· 1670." The following journals are not in the handwriting of Fairbank, nor are they all by one hand. A sergeant or clerk made up the report of each scout for the Lieutenant to sign, and hence the diversity in expression and spelling. The names of localities mentioned are of interest. Journals of the scouts by Lancaster soldiers only are here transcribed. Those from Dunstable and Groton were similar and equally numerous.

LANCASTER December the 6ᵗʰ 1723.

A Journal of yᵉ Scoutes sent out By Liueᵗ Jabez farbank first to quasoponican and to assoatetick hill and round the turkey Hills and another Scout up Wecapickit and to Wickapimsee and to Beehill and to the parke another scout sente to washacom pond and to stillwater and to Rutland and then to Lancaster again

January the 6ᵗʰ 1723¾ &c

Another Scout sente up Nashawa riuer to ye role stone Hill and to the Wachusets Hills and to rutland and to Shrubury and on the carts [*skirts*] of Wossester.

another Scoute sente throu the woods to rutland and from thence to Brookfield and then return^d

another Scoute sente throu the woods to groton and from thence to the Turkey Hills &c.

February 3th 1723¾. another Scoute sent to wanomihouck ponds &c called 30 miles from Lancaster and from thence to wachusets hills and from thence to Ocsechoxit hills & washacom ponds and then hom

another Scoute sent to Watatick hill called 20 miles from Lancaster and came hom By the Dimon hills

another Scoute sente to the Turkey hill to mashapoge pond to cateconimoug pond to unchecowalounk pond and came hom By Lancaster north riuer.

another Scoute sent to rocke hills and to quiticous hills and to the red stone and came hom By George Hill.

March 1 1724 another Scoute sente to the Turkey hills and so to rang the woods upon there front and to mullipurs riuer and to Squanicock riuer and to the Head of Sowhegon riuer and cross the woods to Lancaster.

another sent to menousnuck hills and up the stremes that run Into Nashawway riuer and then returned.

another Scoute to mashapouge hill and penequid entervails and to monipnet Brook and to the fall Brook and to Harris enterval and then hom.

April 1 1724. another Scoute Sent to gard the men at work at Turkey hills and to Scout abought them.

another Scoute Sente up to Wachusets Brook and to rang the woods upon the frount of Lancaster and to gard the people at there plow working in the woods.   Yours to sarve

JABEZ FARBANK

[Massachusetts Archives, XXXVIII, A, 49-50.]

LANCASTER February 5th 1723/4

A Journal of a Scout of ten men sent out by Liuet Jabez fairbanks 1, to Turkey Hills & from thence to ye Dimon Hills and to the Head of Mullipurs riuer and to the Head of Squanicook river and from thence to the Head of Sowhegon riuer, to the Watatick Hill and then steared to wards the grand wanadnock Hill, and from thence to Wanominock ponds and from thence to Wachusets Hills and to Oxsechoxets Hills and mostly to such places as the Indains are moste Likely to Hount In there coming to our Towns.

Sarvice don by we the Subscribers to witt.

     SER EDWARD HARTWELL EZRA SAWYER
     JOHN BENNIT   ISAAC FARNWORTH
     EPHRAIM WHEELER   ISAAC LACAIN
     JOSEPH WHEELOCK   MOSES WILLARD
     DAUID OSGOOD   JOHN EAMES
      Yours to command
              JABEZ FAIRBANKE
[Massachusetts Archives, XXXVIII, 53.]

            LANCASTER, April 28, 1724

 Jurnals of the Scouts Sent out By Lift ffarbank to Wachusets and from thence to Rutland and then return^d to Lancaster again to gard the fields.

 may 2. and another Scoute Sente to the Oxsechoxits hill and to garde the people abought there feilds.

 may 6 another Scoute Sente to Turkey Hills and from thence to mashapoge Hills and so down Lancaster north River and In to Lancaster to gard the feilds at Lancaster.

 may 10 another Scoute Sente up Nashaway River to Wachusets Ponds and then returned to Lancaster to garde ye feilds. another Scoute Sente to rutland and hom By wachusets hill.

 may 14 another Scoute sent on the west of Lancaster Town to rang the front on the Back side of the feilds.

 may the 28th another scoute of five men sente up Nashaway north River tow on one side and tow on the other side and so up said river abought ten miles to a hill called Rolestone hill and from thence to Lancaster again to gard men at there work in their feilds

 June the first day, a Scoute wente to Wachusets ponds and from thence to Crow hill and from thence to Back sid of the Rocke hill and from thence to Rocke Hill meadow and to Chesnut hill to wickepocket.

 June the 4th another Scoute sente to Turky hills and from thence to Bennits meadow and to Whites pond and to Lancaster to gard the feilds.
      Yours to Command.
              JABEZ FARBANK
[Massachusetts Archives, XXXVIII, A, 64.]

MUSTER ROLL OF THE COMPANY OF JABEZ FAIRBANKS, CAPTAIN, JUNE 18, 1724.

Lancaster.

Name		Service			l	s	d	
Jabez Fairbanks Lt.		31 weeks service			31	0	0	wages
Edward Hartwell Serjt.		31	do	do	20	13	4	
Aron Willard	Centle	8	days 2		4	2	10	
James Boughton	"	22	5		11	7	1	
Jno. Bennitt	"	14			7			
Aron Willard	"	16	6		8	8	6	
Eph^m Wheeler	"	20	6		10	8	6	
Isaac Farnworth	"	7	6		3	18	6	
Samuel Sawyer	"	31			15	10		
Ezra Sawyer	"	28	6		14	8	6	
Joseph Wheelock	"	28	6		14	8	6	
David Osgood	"	28	6		14	18	6	
Benj^a Hosgood	"	31			15	10		
Benj^a Houghton	"	31			15	10		
Benj^a Harris	"	28	4		14	5	8	

Groton.

Name				l	s	d
Phinias Parker Serj^t		7		4	13	4
Jon^a Shipley Sent^l		9	1	4	11	5
Jo^s Blood		31		15	10	
Ja^s Shaduch		31		15	10	
Samuel Screpter		31		15	10	
Wm Lawrance		31		15	10	
Josiah Bauden		21	6	10	18	6
Jacob Ames		28	6	14	8	6
Isaac Woods		28	6	14	8	6
Jason Williams		28	6	14	8	6
Nathl Lawrance		28	6	14	8	6
Jona Shepley serj^t		21	6	14	11	6

Name	Town			l	s	d
Jon^a Blanchard Serj^t	Dunstable	28	6	19	4	10
Jona Butterfield Sent^le	Chensford	28	2	14	2	10
Noah Johnson	Houbourne	28	2	14	2	10
Jno Barrett	Chelnsford	28	2	14	2	10
Thos Chamberlin	Groton	28	2	14	2	10
Jabez Davis	Haverhill	28	2	14	2	10
Benj^a Nichols	Redding	28	2	14	2	10
Eben Virgin	Chelnsford	28	2	14	2	10
Joseph Chamberlin	do	20	6	10	8	6
Jno Wright	Dracut	7	3	3	14	3

Benja Chamberlin	Chelnsford	3	6	1	18	6
Jonᵃ Hildreth	"	3	5	1	17	1
Jno Williams	Dracut	21	4	10	15	8
Mich¹ Gillson	Groton	6	5	3	7	1
Ephrᵐ Chaundler	A niver	16	3	8	4	3
Wᵐ. Cummings	Dunstable	11	6	5	18	6

$$519 \quad 17 \quad 2$$

For Bellitting The above men 979 Weeks & 2 Days
at 5 p Week

244. 16. 6

JABEZ FAIRBANK

[Massachusetts Archives, XCI, 124.]

LANCASTER March yᵉ 18, 1724/5.

May it please your Honour.

According to your Honours leave, & orders, the Inhabittants of this Town which entred their names have hitherto Scouted in their turns, till now Colon! Tyng has sent for all yᵉ Scout & standing Soldiers to appear next Wednesday with 50 Dayes provision at Dunstable, the most of our Inhabitants utterly refuse to go; though men listed in yᵉ scout; & several of them have listed under Capᵗⁿ White. I humbly beg your Honʳ will send me yʳ comands: who am yʳ Honʳˢ most Humble & most obedient Servᵗ to Comand.
EDWARD HARTWELL

[Massachusetts Archives, LXXII, 221.]

LANCASTER, March, 18ᵗʰ 1724/5

May it please your Honour.

Sʳ. We the subscribers having lately been Informed, that by an order from your Honour, Coll Tyng hath ordered, Capt Josiah Willard of Turkey Hill, to be at Dunstable with *all* the men under his command, in Groton, Lancaster, & Turkey Hill; with fifty Days provision ready to march from thence, the next Wednesday, must crave leave to Inform your Honour, that the men that are sent for from among us, are the most of them Inhabitants, Imployed in Scouting, those that are Inhabitants are frequently changed by Leave from your Honour, so that some that are Imployed are heads of familys. We would Intreat your Honour to Consider our Circumstances, and that the time when we may expect the enemy upon us, is at hand, and that we shall be greatly weakened, and exposed, if our men are now removed, besides the Great Damage which familys will sustain hereby. Moreover. A Considerable Number of our men, are but Just returned home, that have been out against the Enemy, with Capt Lovel, and we have reason to suppose that a Considerable Number of them will go voluntarily again with Mr White who we understand is designed to go out again in a short time. We would also add, that as we understand the point Coll Tyng designs to march on, we cannot Imagine that we shall be much guarded by him. We would therefore humbly & earnestly Intreat your Honour that all among us under pay might abide with us and not be

Removed. We would crave leave Just to Intimate to your Honour referring to Turkey Hill, that if all the men that are sent for; must go, the familys there will be in a manner wholly destitute of men. We return your Honour thanks for your Readiness to gratify our desires, and hope you will still do so. Who are, Your Honours most humble and most obedient Servants.
          JOHN HOUGHTON
          PETER JOSLEN
For the Honourable   EPHRAIM WILDER
 William Dummer Esqr Lieut. Governour in Boston.
      These.
       [Massachusetts Archives, LXXII, 220.]

March, 1724 *Lt. Gov. Dummer to Colonel Eleazer Tyng.*

 Sir, I here enclose Letters I have rec^d from Lancaster, Wch I have fully consider^d, and think it proper to limit you to sixty men for you$_r$ march at most, and that you leave the Rest to be a Security to y^e Towns especially Turkey Hills which is very much exposed, & let Lancaster & Groton likewise have their Proportion of men left; I think it proper likewise to restrain the Time of your being out to forty Days which you must not exceed unless upon a good Prospect of meeting wth the Enemy, and therefore take but 40 Days Provision; wch may be lengthen^d out If Occasion require. If you find it necessary, you may assure those that are Inhabitants & are ready & forward for this Service, That they shall be continued in Pay after the March is perform^d and that the others shall be dismiss^d. You must be sure to support your authority by a proper & resolute Management in this affair. I suspect Lt. Hartwell has been concern^d in raising this Discontent, among the People. You must therefore make strict Enquiry Whether it be so or not & let me know, & I shall deal with Him accordingly. You may take a skilful Pilot with you who will be entituled to ye Established Pay & if the Docter mentioned is willing to serve & trust to ye generosity of Genl Court for what He may bee allowed above Souldiers pay, It will be very well for you to take Him & therefore you sh encourage his Going. You have inclosed the Commiss you desir^d
      [Massachusetts Archives, LXXII. 222.]

May it please your Honour.

 According to your orders I have been at Lancaster and accordingly made enquiry into the Conduct of Lieut Hartwell and cannot find that he has been in the least measure to blame, but on the contrary did all that lay in his Power to promote & further the Designe your Honour Comanded us to go upon. Wee marched yesterday & Campt the last night at ye Mouth of Neesonkeeg brook. I am, Your Honours
     Most obed^t Humble Servt.
          ELEAZAR TYNG
Natacook, Ap: 1. 9 in ye morning.
P S Inclosed I send those papers according to your Honours ord^r
      [Massachusetts Archives, LXXII, 223.]

LANCASTER August ye 23 1725.

May it plese your Honer:

Your Hon^{rs} Haveing Given me the Subscriber the Inspection of the Soldiers at sd Lancaster under Command of Capt Josiah Willard and I haveing bult at Turkey Hils and my Enterest lying there, I am desined to Remoue theither ye nex weak if I may but obtain your Hon^{rs} Leave therefor hopeing that I shall there be in as Good a Capasaty to serve both my King and Contery, I Humbly Request your Hon^r would Signifie your pleasuer herein by ye barer:

Your Hon^{ers} most Humble Servent

by ye hand of Ensigne Oliver Wilder. EDWARD HARTWELL

[Massachusetts Archives LII, 249.]

Edward Hartwell removed from Lancaster and was for many years Lunenburg's most prominent citizen, serving as representative for the town after he was eighty years old. In 1750 he was appointed Judge of the Court of Common Pleas. Reverend Peter Whitney closes a sketch of his career thus: "and finally he died in the ninety seventh year of his age, as full of piety as of days."

LANCASTER May 9th 1725.

May it please your Honour.

Being returned home I thought myself oblidged to Inform your Honour that on the 5th of April last, I went from Lancaster to Dunstable and the 8th Day of April from thence up Marrimack with 30 men, two of which came back in A short time, one of them being taken sick, and ye other having scalt himself very badly. I marcht up Marrimack about 130 mile, and there discovered some signs of Indians, some old, which we Judged were made sometime this winter and one new track on the Bank of the River, wch we Judged had gone but a few days before I sent out scouts but could discover nothing further. We then turned off to ye Westward towards Coos, marched 10 miles the 24th of April Att evening one of our men viz Sam^{ll} Mossman of Sudbury being about Encamping, took hold of his Gun that stood among some Bushes drew it towards him with the muzzle towards him some twigg caught hold of the cock, the Gun went off, and shott him throgh, he died Imediately. We went across to Connecticutt River came down that to Northfield and from thence across the woods to Lancaster, we gott in yesterday. I have endeavoured faithfully to attend your Honours orders already recieved, and if your Honour has any further service for me I desire your Honour would let me know it. I have not as yet compleated my Journal, but hope to finish it in a short time that it may be Laid before your Honour. I am your Honours most obedient humble Servant

    On his Majesties Service   JOHN WHITE
For the Honourable William Dummer Esq.
    Leivt Governour &c. In Boston. These
          [Massachusetts Archives, LXXII, 230.]

 Sir, I have the Account of y^r March & Return by your Letter of the 9th Instant & Approve of your Proceedings, tho I am heartily grieved for the Death of the poor Man, & wonder that so many unhappy Accidents of this Kind have not been sufficient to warn our People of the Effects of such Indiscretion. The Season being now advanced for the Appearance of the Enemy, and it being more likely to meet with them now than before, I desire you would go out with the Same Number of Men & upon the same Establishm^t which will be allow^d you; I should be glad you could immediately proceed, & make up a Muster Roll for your two Marches upon your Return. For m^{ch} Time will otherwise be lost at this critical Juncture. However if you must first come to Town let there be no Delay; If any of your men are backward to go out again you must enlist others to make up your number. I shall not prescribe any Rout to you, you being best able to judge where the Enemy may be mett with: Carry out as much Provision as you can, That so you maynt be obliged to return very soon: Be very silent & watchful on your March & Ambushments. I heartily wish you Success, and am your Servt.

 Boston 11 May 1725.   W^M DUMMER
  Capt White
  Capt Welds
         [Massachusetts Archives, LXXII, 233.]

         DUNSTABLE July the 10: 1725.
May it Please your Honr:
 Old Christian Being this morning Being Taken with a violent Bleeding Caused our Companyes to stop and within a few hours he died & the other mohaucks are not willing to Leave him before he is Buried & our desine is to march ouer Merimack River and There to Take a True List of our mens Names, & shall march as Quick as Possible. Who Remain Still your Honours at Comand   JOHN WHITE
               SETH WYMAN
 [Massachusetts Archives, LII, 222.]

 1725. June 10. Answering a—"Memorial of Capt John White, Shewing that he has lately raised a Company of Volunteers, who have made Two Marches against the Indian Enemy, That the Memorialist, in raising the said Company of Volunteers has been at greater expence than what his Wages have amounted to, he having no more Allowances or. Pay than a Private Man of the said Volunteers is entitled to, praying that as what he did in raising the said Voluntiers was with a View and Design to serve the Interest of the Province, that he may have such Recompence and Satisfaction for his said Service as to the Wisdom and Bounty of this Court shall seem meet;"— twelve pounds were allowed by the General Court.

[Massachusetts Records.— Journal of General Court.]

Instructions to Captains Willard, White and Blanchard.

S^r. Having Commissionated you to Command a Company of Voluntiers against the Indian Enemy, you are hereby Directed to Exercise and maintain good Discipline and Government among your Officers and Soldiers and to Suppress and punish all Disorders, Vice, and Immorality and to Keep up the Worship of God in your said Company. You must march to Pigwacket, unless you shall upon mature Consideration Judge any other tour more effectual for the service, withall Convenient Dispatch Joining such Companys of Voluntiers in the County of Middlesex as shall be ready to proceed with you and from thence march to such places where by your Intelligence may Judge it probable to meet with the Indian Enemy. If you Judge it necessary to keep the whole Body together in order to attack any Tribe or Settlement of Indians I shall approve of your so doing, othwise that Two Companys or halfe your Body proceed Eastw^d & the other halfe to proceed from Pigwacket to Strike over to Amrescoggin & Kennebeck River, endeavouring to get higher up the said Rivers then the places of the Indians Settlements one party of which to Come down Amrescoggin River to Fort George & the other down Kennebeck River to Richmond, and if your provision should fall short so as that the whole cannot be sufficiently furnish^d for the march to Amrescoggin & Kennebeck Rivers, some of your Feeblest men must Come into Berwick, The remaining part of the Body to go off to the North Westward in Quest of the Indian Enemy said to be there taking with them the Mohawks for their Guides. Let your Marches be with all the Secrecy & Silence as well as Dispatch, you are Capable of. You must Kill, Take & Destroy to the utmost of your power all the Enemy Indians you can meet with in your March, & Search for their Corn, destroying all you can find. And give Intelligence from time to time of every thing of Importance that may happen.

[Massachusetts Archives, LXXII, 250.]

This seems to be a rough draft of a circular letter, there being in the original frequent interlineations, alterations, and erasures.

Orders to Capt White & Wyman Aug 7 1725.

Received an acct. from Coll. Wentworth of your returne to Cocheco. I am very sorry for the Sickness & the difficultys of a wet Season that has attended your march, & make no dout but you have done the uttmost practicable under these pressures & misfortunes, but since It has Pleased

God it should bee so & that we have lately concluded a cessation of armes wth the Penobscott Indians in order to bringing about a general peace, I would have [you] repair home & disband your Companyes & make out Muster Rolls forthwith.

[Massachusetts Archives, LII, 234.]

To the Hon[ble] William Dummer Esq[r]. Lieut. Governour and Com̃ander in Chief the hon[ble] the councill and Representatives for the Province of the Massachusetts Bay in New England in General Court Assembled at Boston the 23[d]. day of December Anno Dom 1727.

The Petition of Eunice White Relict widow of Capt. John White late of Lancaster deced. Humbly Sheweth. That Whereas your Pet[rs] sd husband in his life time in the years 1724 & 1725 as well as at other times performed sundry marches ag[t] the Indian Enemy and did other services for the good of his Country & was active and vigorous in the Defence thereof against those barbarous Salvages, not only hazarding his life but Expending good part of his substance therein, as is well known to many, Some few Instances whereof your Pet[r] would humbly ripresent to this Hon[ble] Court. Yo[r] Pet[rs] sd. husband altho he had divers times had the honour to bear command yet voluntarily Enlisted himself under the late Capt. Lovewell, and choose rather to go as an Under Officer at that time because he would do what in him lay to Encourage others to Enlist and marched with him at the time when they killed the Ten Indians, in which march they were out near Forty days, Then he performed a march to a place called Cohosse on Connecticut River thinking to meet with the Enemy there and came in at Fort Dummer, being out thirty four days, tho they missed of their desired Success; Then in about Eight days time he had a Company raised and went to Pigwacket to bury Capt. Lovewell which he performed in a very difficult season of the year. Then he went to Connecticut at his own cost and charge to get a Company of Mohege Indians in order to go down to St Francois to take an Indian fort there, but failing of his aim, he returned home and then enlisted a Company of Volunteers and marched designing for a Fort beyond Pigwacket, but was taken sick before he got there, returned home and dyed leaving your Pet[r] his bereaved widow with seven Children the Eldest about Fifteen years old and Four of them very young, & one she then went with who is now living; In all which Services your Petit[rs] said husband cheerfully underwent many hardships and difficulties for the good of his country, and was at considerable Cost and Charge, by Supplying those that Enlisted under him with necessaries which could not be readily obtained elsewhere, purely to make dispatch.

Now Forasmuch as the Sickness of which your Pet[rs] husband dyed was in all probability Occasioned by means of y[e] difficulties he underwent in the Publick Service, & that he never in his life time had an Opportunity of asking your Hon.". Favour for his past Services but was taken away in the Strength and vigour of his life, without receiving anything from the Publick more than 2^s 6^d p day for the three marches he performed as afores.^{d} and in regard your Pet^r. is left a disconsolate widow with several Fatherless Children to bring up who stand in daily need of relief and Support, your Pet^r finding it very difficult to provide for them, She therefore most humbly Implores your Hon^r.^{s} pity and Compassion to herself & Children, and that as you have been pleased in like cases to reward those that have served the Province, and the Representatives of those that have lost their lives in the Publick Service. So that she may Experience of the Bounty & Goodness of this Hono^{ble}. Court to her in her difficult Circumstances, and that you will be pleased to Grant her Two hundred and Fifty acres of the unappropriated Lands of the Province that she may dispose of the same for the Education and bringing up her afores.^{d} Children or that your Hon^r.^{s} would otherwise relieve her as in your Great Goodness & Compassion you shall see meet. And as in duty bound your Petit^r shall ever pray &c. EUNICE WHITE

In the House of Representatives December 28th. 1727. Read and in answer to this Petition, Resolved That the sum of One Hundred pounds be allowed and paid out of the publick Treasury to the petitioner the widdow Eunice White in Consideration of the good Services done this province by her late husband Capt. John White, and great expences for which he has had no Consideration, as particularly set forth in the petition and the better to enable the petitioner to support her Family and bring up her Children. Sent up for Concurrence W^M DUDLEY *Spr*

In council Dec. 28. 1727. Read & Concur^d. J. WILLARD *Secry*
       Consented to   W^M. DUMMER.
[Massachusetts Archives, LXXII. 325, et. seq.]

Captain John White was grandson of the pioneer bearing the same name. He was born September 29, 1684, son of Josiah and Mary White. An elder brother became prominent in Lancaster as Deacon Josiah White, and his brother Jonathan was slain by the Indians in 1707. Captain White was a blacksmith by trade, and well to do for his times; his inventory dated January 1725–6 summing 1220 pounds. In 1728 Reverend John Prentice records baptizing "the widdow Whites children": Eunice, John, Bette, Dorothy, Thomas, Lois, Mary, Nathanael.

DEC^A OF PERSONS W^N Y^E 10 INDIANS WERE KILLED.

Jno White	*Jona: Houghton*	Moses Chandler
Sam Tarbol	*James Houghton*	Joseph Wilson
Jer. Hunt	*Henry Willard*	Jona Parks
Eben. Wright	*Jacob Gates*	Joshua Webster
Jos. Read	*Joseph Whitcomb*	Samll: Johnson
Sam Moor	Samll Learned	Steph Murrill
Phin. Foster	*Robt Phelps*	Jacob Pearly
Fra: Dogett	Moses Graves	John Hazzen
S Hilton	Moses Hazzen	Eb: Brown
Jno. Pollard	John Levingston	Jon^a Ferren
Ben Walker	Jerem Pearley	Samll. Stickney
Jos. Wright	*Wm Hutchins*	Joshua Hutchins
Jno. Varnum	*Jacob Corey*	Benony Boynton
Robt Ford	*Oliver Pollard*	Eph Farnsworth
Ben Parker	Samll: Trull	Ruben Farnsworth
Sam Shattock	Ben^a Parker [*bis*]	Thos. Farmer
Jacob Ames	Wm: Spalden	Rich. Hall
Jno Stephens	Samll Fletcher	Neh. Robinson
Jos: Wheelock	Jno. Duncom	Jona. Parks [*bis*]
Sam Sawyer	*Jethro Ames*	Caleb Dolton
Ezra Sawyer	*John Sawyer*	62

At killing of them 10 Indians. Lovell & White.

[Massachusetts Archives LXXII, 368.]

The names of Lancaster men are printed in italics. The petitioners for the grant of Nichewaug, now Petersham, in 1733, asked it in consideration of "the Hardship & Difficult marches they vnderwent as volunters vnder the Comand of the Late Cap^te Lovell & Cap^te White after the Inden enemy and Into their Countrey." Most of the above names appear in the list of Proprietors of that Grant. The chief inducement to volunteer in a service so arduous, was the enactment of 1722, offering "volunteers without pay or subsistence, for the scalp of any male Indian of the age of twelve years or upwards the sum of 100 pounds." Women and children, scalped or unscalped, were paid for at half price.

In an appendix to an Address delivered in Bolton at the Centennial Celebration, July 4, 1876, by Reverend Richard

S. Edes, is printed part of a diary "found among the papers of the first clerks of the town." The copyist adds, "How old the book is, no one can tell." It is a journal of the scout of Captains Lovell and White "when the 10 Indians were killed," February, 1724; probably written by one of the Lancaster soldiers there present. The minutes of the first eight days have been torn off.

    9. We traveled 14 miles and camped at the norwest corner of winipisocket pond.

    10. We traveled 16 miles, and camped at the north side of Cusumpe pond.

    11. We traveled 6 miles N by E from Cusumpe and there camped—and sent out scouts, and some of our scouts thought they discovered smoke.

    12. We sent out scouts, and they discovered nothing.

    13. We lay still and sent out scouts, and to strengthen us to go farther we sent home 29 men.

    14. We traveled 10 miles toward Pigwackett, and then came upon a branch of the Saco river, and sent out scouts.

    15. We lay still and sent out scouts and discovered nothing.

    16. We traveled 6 miles and came upon an Indian wigwam—the Indians being gone we left 16 men with our packs and the rest pursued them till dark and stayed there all night.

    17. We followed their track till eight o'clock next day and then we came back to fetch our packs, traveled the remaining part of that day and the night ensuing six miles.

    18. We traveled 20 miles and camped at the great pond upon Sawco river.

    19. We traveled 22 miles and camped at a great pond.

    20. We traveled 5 miles and came to a wigwam where the Indians had been lately gone from, and then we pursued their track about 2 miles further and discovered their smoke and then tarried till about two o'clock at night and then came upon them and killed 10 Indians which was all there was.

    21. We traveled 6 miles.

    22. We lay still and kept scouts upon our back tracks to see if there would any pursue.

    23. We traveled 30 miles and Camped at Cocheco.

Another journal of this march has been printed in the New England Historical and Genealogical Register, VII, 62, differing very slightly from the above, q. v.

A tru jurnall of my travells began the 5th of April, 1725

We traueld to Groten 12 milds and thear stayed by reson of foul wether

6 day we traueld to dunstabel 12 milds and thear Lay that night

7 day we Lay stil by reson of foull wether

8 day we mustared and went ouer the riuer to the hous of John Taylors about 3 milds

9 day we marcht up the riuer about 8 milds and then campt one of our men being taken uerey sik for he kold trauel no ferther, his name was Thomas Simson, Our Doctor Joseph Whetcomb that night set his fut into a Ketel of biling broth that he cold trauel no ferther

10 day was foul wether and we sent 2 men in to dunstabel with the sik and Lam men and [they] returned that night to us again

11 day we traueled about 13 milds and then campt about 3 mild aboue amoskeeg falls.

12 day we traueled 11 milds and then campt at the mouth of penekoock riuer

13 day we traueled 7 milds and then campt at the iarish fort in penekook Enteruals that day it rayend uery hard all day.

14 day we traueld 10 milds and then Crost meremack riuer aboue the mouth of Contookock riuer and then Campt.

15 day we traueld 8 milds north west from Contockock to a litel stream that runs into meremack Riuer about 3 milds westard from meremack and then campt and sent out skouts

16 day we traueld 12 milds and Cam to a pond which was uery Long and we turned to the east sid of it and then campt, and then sent out skouts that day we lay about 3 milds westard of the mouth of Winepiseocket

17 day it raynd uere hard the fore part of the day and a litel before night it cleard up & we sent skouts but found northen

18 day we traueled 14 milds and that day we Crost 2 great streames that runs in to meremack, one of them comes out of a great pond which sum indens says it is 3 days jurney round it the Land is uerey full of great hils and mountains and uerey rockey abundance of sprus and hemlock and fur and sum bech and maple and we campt

19 day we traueld 11 milds and then campt at the Louar End of pemichewashet Lour Enteruals and sent out skouts.

20 day we lay stil by reson of foull wether and towards nit it Cleard up and we sent out skouts and found whear Cornol Tyng crost meremack

21 day we traueld 12 milds up pemichewashet Riuer and found old sines of indens and we sent out skouts that night and found one new track and we lay that night by the riuer and mad new camps. The Land that lys by this riuer is uere rich and good the upland uere full of hils and mountains, uery bad traueling

22 day we traueld 2 milds and then sent out skouts ouer the riuer and up a stream that runs into the riuer but found northen

23 day we traueld up the riuer about 14 milds and that day we Crost 3 streames that runs into the riuer this riuer coms sheafly from the north west & then we campt

24 day we traueld 10 milds westward and that day we found old signs of indens whear they had bin this spring and in the winter, and sent out skouts but cold find now indens This day Samll Moosman actidently kild himself with his own gun

25 day it rained uery hard and we lay stil that day til amost night it cleard up and we sent out skouts but found northen

26 day we traueld 18 milds and came upon Conetecut riuer and one of our men was taken uere sik that night we campt by the riuer

27 day we traueld down the riuer and found a bark cannow which was of great saruis to our sik man & to us; that day we traueld about 18 milds and then campt.

28 day we traueld 19 milds and then campt This Riuer runs cheafly upon a south westerly pint this day we crost seural litel streams that runs into Conetecut riuer.

29 day we traueld 20 milds and then campt.

30 day we traueld 17 milds and crost one litel riuer below the great falls and then campt

May the first we traueld 24 milds and came to the fort above north field and thare lay all night

2 day we traueld 10 milds and came to northfield and there stayed that night

3 day we lay still it Lookt uery lykly ferr foul wether and we lay thare that night

4 day we set out for Lancaster a cros the woods and traueld about 12 milds and then campt

5 day we traueld 15 milds and then campt

6 day we traueld 14 milds and comm to Lancaster about 4 a clock this day it raind uery hard all day.

[*Endorsed*]   Capt Whites Journal May 1725
[Massachusetts Archives XXXVIII, A, 97-98.]

A Journal of my March with a company of Voluntiers against the Indian Eenemy in July 1725.

July 6   muster'd at my house at Lancaster
7   march'd to Groton
8   march'd to Dunstable
9   Remain'd at Dunstable preparing for our march the next day
10.   Tarried at Dunstable till noon waiting for Capt. Wyman his Com-

pany not being quite Ready. Christian was taken with a violent Bleeding and Died about one Clock, we then went over the River the Canada Mohawk not being willing to Go, we left him behind.

11. We Went up the River about Two miles, & waited for Capt. Wyman.
12. We Travel'd about 7 miles & then Encamp'd.
13. we march about 3½ miles, Capt Wyman overtook us. We sent out scouts, We kill'd a Bear & sev^l Rattle Snakes.
14. March'd about 4 miles, & some of our men thinking they heard Guns up Piscataquag River, we sent out 40 men up the River and 20 more Eastw^d who Returned not that night.
15. our Scouts came in but made no Discovery, we Kill'd two Bairs & divers Rattle Snakes, which pester'd us very much in our march
16. One of Capt. Wymans Men being very sick, we travel'd but about 4 miles, but kept Scouts out Continually.
17. Excessive Rain occasion'd our laying still, but sent out Scouts who Killed a Black Moose.
18. We March'd about 7 miles, our Indian being taken very lame we lay still a while but his lameness continuing we sent him home, we encamp'd at Suncook
19. We March'd to Pennecook about eleven miles.
20. Lay still by Reason of a Bad Storm of Rain. Several of our men taken ill.
21. Four of Capt Wymans men were sent home with two sick men. We travel'd about 5 miles.
22. Several more of our men were taken very ill with a Bloody Flux, which we Suppose was occasion'd by Excessive Rains, & Immoderate Heats. It rain'd this day very hard that obliged us to lay still, Keeping our Scouts out.
23. men being very Sick & Weak we Travel'd 8 miles & Encamp'd
24. Our men Continuing very Ill we march'd but 7 miles.
25. It being good Travelling we march'd about 9 miles notwithstanding the weak Condition of the Company. Our Well men being obliged to carry the Sick mens packs.
26 Lay still by Reason of a Storm of Rain, our men continuing sick.
27. the Storm continuing, & our men growing worse we lay still all day.
28. We Travel'd about Eleven miles & Encamp'd
29 we March'd about Ten miles & come upon Cocheco path
30. We March'd to the Town of Cocheco 19 miles
31 Came to Oyster River
Aug: 1 Travel'd from thence to Exeter
2. March'd from Exeter to Kingstown
3. We March'd to Bradford.

4. Raind hard, we got to Billerica
5. I arrived at Lancaster and Dismiss'd my Company
Boston Aug 11 1725

[Massachusetts Archives XXXVIII, A, 107.]

LETTERS OF CAPTAIN SAMUEL WILLARD TO LIEUTENANT GOVERNOR WILLIAM DUMMER.

1725. Honoured Sir, after my duty presented to you these are to informe you that on Monday the nineteenth of this current July in the afternoon I marched from Rutland with fifty two able Bodyed men towards Watchusett with —— days Provision one of the men before we camped that night by an accident sprained his ankle who was oblidged to Return into Rutland and Capt. Wright was so Ingenious as spare one of his men for him   I have left four more good men with Capt. Wright and have four of his men in their stead the first night we Camped on the south side of Ware River, and the next day lay still by Reason of foul weather sent out scouts and tracked Indians   the next day we marched over the River where we camped west from Watchusett I desighn to march about twenty mile farther towards menagnick and ther to Scout about 3 or 4 days and then march to pemichawassett   We are all in good health write in the woods about six or seven mile of Watchusett and sent in by Rutland scout this twenty second day of July anno Domini 1725.

Writt in hast.   I Remain y^r to Command

SAM^{LL} WILLARD

[Massachusetts Archives, LIII. 383.]

July 25 1725

Honoured Sr.   these are to Informe you that this day being wide of Wattchusett and Menadnick upon our march towards Pemishewassett with fourty seven able bodyed men, four of our men being sick and not able to travel who I have sent into Lancaster with Joshua Parker a well man to take care of them   I doe not think to be into any town this five and thirty days unless we get some Indians   Yesterday I being upon the scout heard a Gun which I supposed to be an Indian gun have sent out scouts there several ways this day   there is fourty seven men besides the five who are come in

Yrs to sarve   SAM^{LL} WILLARD

S^r I desire that there may be preparation for canoes att Northfield If your honour designs any march to St. Francis this summer   Capt. Blanchard desiring the same we not thinking of it when in Boston

Yrs to serve   SAM^{LL} WILLARD

[Massachusetts Archives, LII, 230.]

LANCASTER August 16 1725

For ye Honnerable William Dummer Esq

   May it Plese your Honner Persuant to your Honners Instructions to me I marched from Rutland North or thereabouts tille we came to Wanadnack and from thence North East for pemissiwassett untill Sabbath day ye 8 of August Intending to have mete Capt Blancher there But By Reason of much foule weather and Extreme Bad Woods to travele in we Being preswead^d Capt Blancher was come from pemisiwassett thought it more searvisable to come Down at a Distance from ye river which we Did about 35 miles and then came to ye River and mete with Capt. Blancher at ye mouth of Contocook and so came Down ye River and arived well at Lancaster Thursday August ye 12 with most of our mean Some Being so weary with their march we Left them at Groton: if your Honner Have any farther Instructions I shall be Ready to sarve:

   Your Honners very Humble Sarvent   SAMUEL WILLARD

   I should Have sent to Informe your Honner Before But Capt Blanchard told me he shold send that we Both Came In together.

[Massachusetts Archives. LXXII. 257.]

   May it please your Honour Yesterday I arriv^d at Dunstable with a Company of very good, likely, effective men; I had been here sooner but my march was retarded by the sickness of my Lieut^t who remains so bad that he cannot go with me; to supply whose place, I would if your Honour see Cause desire a blank Comission might be sent me to be bestowed upon one whom the Company is desirous to choose among themselves. I have advised wth Col Tyng with regard to my March & taking the young Mohawk with [me] who is, I find willing enō upon the encouragement proposed to go. I would beg leave to represent to your Honour that the march will be long and hard, if He Pilots up where I design to go, & would desire that Capt Blanchard & his men may be ordered to go with me, so that if any of our men grow faint and weak, we may have still enō to prosecute our design, and may send such in either eastward or westward as we shall judge best, & those that go forward may be supported with their Provision. I humbly conceive this to be of great importance to the Province to serve which I design to us my utmost endeavour in this March, & in this Representation, which I have adventured to trouble you with I remaine   Your Honours most obedient Humble Servt

   Dunstable Sept 7 1725   SAMUEL WILLARD
]Massachusetts Archives, LII. 267.]

May it Please your Honr

   Yesterday my men marched they being sixty eight in Number and that the young mohauck assures us that he can Lead us to the Indians Head Quarters and Goes Cherfully a Long with us. & Capt Blanchard is

Imediately marching after me and we desire when come to Cusumpe pond or penesiwassett to send forty of our weakest hands back with a small matter of Provision in to the westerd or easterd and to proc^d with the Rest to the place where the mohauck tels us of if by Good Providence we have our healths Who Remain y.^r Hon.^rs

DUNSTABLE Sep^tr the 9th
1725
[Massachusetts Archives, LII. 270.]

Most obedient Servant
SAM^LL. WILLARD

Sept^br 19. 1725.

Honoured Sir after my Duty to you These Lines are to inform you that I am well, & all my men excepting Three one of which badly wounded himself with his Hatchett, which is Richard Burtt & Two others being ill not able to pform the Service, by name Sergt, Abial Chapin & Benj. Atherton, & I Thought it proper to send home Twelve men more under the Comand of Lei^t Combs, & I with Capt Blanchard do send one Party down Mirimack, & the other Party between Marimack & Conecticut into Turkey Hill, & if it is your Honours Pleasure to Keep them Scouting where you think it best they are at your service. And Capt Blanchard, & I, have taken all their Provisions, for to lengthen our Journey excepting enough to carry them home. We are now Near the Crotch of the River.

No more at Present but I Remain Your Humble Servt.

SAM^LL. WILLARD

[Massachusetts Archives, LII. 286.]

SACO October 14 1725

May it please your Honner pursuant to your Honners Instructions Capt Blanchard and I marched up Marrimack about one Hundard and fiefty milles from Dunstable till we Came to Head of it we saw some signes of a wigwarm where we supose some Indians had Been about six weeks since and from Marrimack in about 3 milles we came upon Saco River and Came Down sd River to Saco falls on wensday October 13 and in ye evening come to winter harber to Capt Jordens and tooke some stores of him for our subsistence, for we had not any Provision Laeft, for in the morning we Before we came to Saco falls we fineshed all our provisions so that we had not any Laeft and we are now coming Home as fast as we can we shall give your Honner more particurler acount in our Jornnall wh^ch is all in hast from your Honners Humble Sarvent

For the Honble Wm Dummer Esqr SAM^LL WILLARD
[Massachusetts Archives, LII. 302.]

Captain Samuel was grandson of Major Simon Willard. His father, Henry, who lived on the Still River farm, left him a considerable estate which he largely increased. Besides other lands he bought the "night pasture," the Edward Breck lot, and the homestead of his grandfather. He is reputed to have built and lived in the large house on the Breck lot, near the railroad crossing just north of the Lancaster station, wherein three generations of his descendants succeeded him. He commanded the Fourth Massachusetts regiment in the Louisburg expedition of 1745, his son Abijah being captain, and his son Levi ensign in the first company of the regiment. The slate over his grave in the old burying ground, records that the " Honourable Coll SAMUEL WILLARD Esq " died November 20, 1752, at the age of sixty-two.

A Journall of my March.

Thursday July 15   muster^d at Lancaster
Friday July 16   I marched from Lancaster to Rutland
Satturday 17   it was foul weather in ye forenoon
Sabbath 18   I fixed the men out with the stores
Monday 19   We marched toward Ware River and then Camped and sent out scouts & tracked some Indains & Haerd two Guns
tuesday 20   we lay still By Reason of foule weather
Wensday 21   we marched over Ware River & Camped for we saw it Like to Rain.
thursday 22.   we lay stille by Reason it Rained hard all day.
Friday 23   we marched about six milles & it Being very hot we camped about ye middle of ye afternoon by reason of several of our weeke men could not travele there packs Being so havy   I sent out three scouts & ordered them [to] travell five or six milles which they Did three severale ways
Satturday 24   we marched about seven miles northerly & sent out our scouts which haerd a gun but Discouered nothing elce
Sabbath day 25   four of our men not Being able to travele I sent them home who are by name Thomas Burt Robert Gray Jacob Moor & Jeremiah Belcher I also sent Joshua Parker Home with them we marched Northeast about three milles
Munday 26   Lay stille by Reason of rain we sent out scouts who scouted about 3 mille Round but Discouered nothing.
Tuesday 27   we could not travele By Reason of Rain But we sent out severale scouts & Discouered nothing
Wensday 28   Mr William Brintnall Being sick & Daniel How Lame I sent them Home we marched about 13 miles north and be Wast Round some pounds and Camped at ye South end of Nockeeg pound and sent out scouts 3 milles each way & Discouered nothing

Thursday 29 we marched North and be wast about nine milles and corsed severale Branches of Millers Riuer and Camped and sent out scouts which found where ye Indians had Lived Last year and made a Conoe at ye north End of a Long pond.

Friday 30. we marched North in ye fornoon & Came to a pound which Run into Contocook Riuer in ye afternoon we marched north wast in all about 12 milles & Camped at Peewunsenn pound and sent out scouts 4 milles and they found 2 wigwarms made last year they also found a paddle & some squash shells in one of them which we suppose they caried from Rutland

Satturday 31 we marched 12 milles and I with 14 men Campt on ye top of Wannadnuck Mountains & Discouered 26 pounds saw Pigwackett Lying one point from sd mountain & Cusagee mountain and Winnepeseockey Laying north east from sd Wannadnuck the same Day we found several old signes which ye Indains had made the Last yaer & where yy campt when they killed ye peaple at Rutland as we Imagine.

Sabbath August ye 1th we marched from ye wast side of Wenadnuck & corsed three stremes that Run into Contocook and then Campt and sent out Scouts and found two wigwarms made in June or July as we suppose and found sixteen of those spitts which they Rost there meat with all in sd wigwarms & one of our scouts went so far that thay could not Return y^t same night

Monday 2 we marched about seven milles & crosed a Grate Branche of Contocook River & sent out our Scouts up and Down the River each Scout traveled about 8 milles.

Tuesday 3 we marched N E about sixteen milles and campt and sent out scouts who found many old signes of Indians

Wensday 4 we lay stille By Reason of foule weather, we sent out our Scouts and they haerd a Gun

Thursday 5 we marched about 16 milles northerly and crosed two stremes that Run into Merimack & sent out our Scouts and Discouered nothing

Friday 6. we marched about 18 milles in the morning we found a mogerson tracke, and spent some time scouting after sd Tracke we campt near a Little pound.

Satturday 7 we traveled about 20 milles N E and crosed two Stremes that Run into Merimack

Sabbath 8 we Returned Homeward By Reason of our Indians Having no Provision and several of our English But Little we come to a Streme that Run into merimack we traveled about 24 milles South and By East.

Monday 9 we traveled about East tille we came to Merimack Being about 10 milles and mette with Capt. Blanchard coming from Pemisewassett and in afternoon came to ye Lower End of Pennicook, which is about sixteen milles & campt

Tusday 10 we Traveled 24 milles Down the [Merrimac] to Cohassett falls.
Wensday 11 We came 14 milles & came to Dunstable.
Thursday 12 Came 24 milles and came to Lancaster

SAM^{LL} WILLARD

[Massachusetts Archives, XXXVIII. A 109–10.]

A Journal of y^e March of Capt. Samuel Willard accompanied with Capt. Jos: Blanchard: In Pursuit of y_e Indian Rebells. Mustard at Lancaster friday Sepr. y^e 3^d:

Sepr 4 Saturday Leiut. Warner marched wth all sd Willards Company to Groton, except those of Lancaster.

Sabbath, 5th Lay still by Reason of Rain.

Mund: 6: Capt Willard & those of Lancaster Rid & overtook Lt: Warner & y^e rest at Dunstable.

Tuesday Wednesday & thursday, Lay still by reason of hard rains.

Friday 10. We marched over ye River about 7 mile & campt.

Saturday 11th We marched up ye River to Parkers Brook & campt.

Sabbath 12th We lay still by reason of Rain.

Munday 13th We marched up ye River to Neticoock & campt.

Tuesday 14th We marched up sd River to Cohassett falls & sent out scouts, & campt.

Wednesday 15. We marched to Ammoskeeg, sent out scouts and campt.

Thursday 16. We sent a scout consisting of 40 men over ye River wch marched on ye west side. Capt. Blancher went to Hannichoockset falls & campt, & Capt Willard went to Suncook about 3 miles further & campt.

Friday 17 we marched to Pennicoock Lower falls, & Capt Willard & Comp^a went over on ye West side of ye River, & marched to Pennicook upper falls, & campt. This day Capt Blancher saw some shoe tracks, & having gone up to Penicook old fort found where they campt, & supposed them to be scouts sent out from New Hampshire Governm^t & sd Capt. Campt a mile above ye fort.

Saturday 18. we marched about 3 mile above Contocock River & there Capt. Blancher came over to ye West side of ye River, sent out scouts and campt.

Sabbath 19. Y^e Captains agreed to send back a parcel of Men & took their Provisions vizt out of Capt Blanchers Comp^a 28 Men, out of Capt Willards Comp^a 15 men; in all 43 men under ye comand of Leiut. Comes; two of Capt. Willards men being sick, viz Abel Chapin had a spavⁿ & Benj^a. Atherton the Bloody Flux, & Richd Burck cut his leg with a hatchit wch Disenabled him for ye service, being also one of Capt. Willards men, and all included in ye said number of 43 men;

Monday 20 We marched to ye crotch of ye River wch is about 70 miles from Dunstable and crossed ye West Branch, sent out scouts, & campt.

Tuesday 21. We marched toward Pimiwachet, alias Pimissiwassett about 11 miles, and sent out Scouts, & campt.

Wed. 22 We marched about 9 mile & sent out scouts & campt; this day Barn^d Davis cut his foot with a stone.

Thursday 23. We sent out scouts to ye River & up by ye side 4 miles, and ye army by reason of Rain lay still.

Friday 24. Capt Willard sent back 11 of his men & of Capt Blanchers 8. which made 19., Some of wch. were sick, viz of Capt. Willards men Jona. Adams, Ebenez^r Polley of a flux, & Symon Atherton ye feaver & ague, & said Davis wch cut himself. The Capt^s. ordered them to take one Conoe from ye Crotch of ye River where we had left ye rest, & ord^{ed} ye rest shou^d be left for fear of any more sickness, after this marched about 6 mile & came to ye River, & sent out scouts, & campt.

Saturday 25 we marched about 6 mile & came to ye carrying place, where ye Indians carry their Conoes from Pemichiwasset to Sowhaig River & found that ye Indians had lately been there & Carried their conoes: Capt Willard took half a scout of his men & half of Capt. Blanchers being in all 24 & followed ye Indians & a little before we come to Cusumpy Pond we found where they brook one Conoe & coming to ye Pond cou^d follow them noe further; & in ye mean time Leiut. Warner with 24 men out of both Companies scouted up ye River, & returned about ye middle of ye afternoon, & ye army being all met marched about 2 mile up ye River & campt.

Sept 25 Saturday We also examined Jos : ye Mohak (taking Nessa Gawney for an Interpreter) which was the best way to goe to ye Fort he told of: and he said we must goe up to ye head of merimack because there was noe goeing over ye hills neer Cusumpy Ponds.

Sabb^a 26 We marched about 12 mile up ye River & sent out scouts & campt.

Mund. 27 We marched about 12 mile & crossed a stream which ran from ye Hills where Capt Lovel killed ye first Indian last winter & sent out Scouts & campt.

Tuesday 28 We marched about 12 mile up ye River & in about 3 mile found a large Wigwam where ye Indians had lately been, as we judged about 20 in number, and our Indians said there was Squaws as well as Sannups, we tracked some of them as we Suppose through Ossippy, and some up ye River, towards Night we crossed a stream of some considerable bigness & sent out scouts & campt.

Wednes. 29 We marched up ye River, about 14 mile, & come this day to ye foot of a great mountain on ye West side of ye River, where ye stream was small, we tracked Indians all this day which we suppose ware gone directly to Canada. the mountains being steep & rocky we could not track them further. This morning we see where they had been about at week before (we supposed), built a Conoe, & judged them to be them which we tracked from Pimichiwasset to Cusumpy Pond, & then campt.

Thurs⁴. 30 In yᵉ morning sent a scout of 20 men about 4 or 5 mile up yᵉ River who made noe further discovery. after that we left yᵉ River & steared East about 3 mile up a very steep mountain, & campt by reason of Rain; having this morning examined Jos : (yᵉ Mohauck) and he said he did not know them woods, and did not think that the hed of merimack had been so fur up, & couᵈ tell nothing without he found Sawco River.

Friday octoᵣ 1 : We marched up yᵉ same hill about 6 mile, and being on yᵉ top of yᵉ hill cou Discover no where nigh us anything but steep mountains, & marched down yᵉ hill about five mile, & we generally judged said 5 mile to be 2 mile on a perpendicular, then campt by a small brook wᶜʰ ran out of yᵉ mountain.

Saturday 2 We lay still by reason of rain, but sent out some scouts who discovered Meremack ran from yᵉ So Eᵗ round said mountain.

Sabbath 3 We marched S. E. up said River about 6 mile & came to yᵉ head of it, & then steared N. E. about three mile over a steep hill & then came to yᵉ head of Sawco River, and then marched down said River about 11 miles East & we judged that River all yᵗ way had fall 5 foot in 30 & mountains on each side thereof, Sent Scouts down yᵉ River & campt.

Mund : 4 This Morning Examinᵈ sd. Mohack, & said he couᵈ tell nothing till he came lower down yᵉ River. We marched down said River abour 5 mile & sent out Scouts, & campt by reason of rain.

Tuesday 5 This morning we came on some Entervalls & plain land, & found where Indians have been in yᵉ Spring, having found yᵉ hoops whereupon they Dried their Bear Skins, & we judged might be about 8 or 10 in number. this Day we judged we marched about 24 mile & sent out Scouts, & camped.

Wednesᵈ. 6. we marched down yᵉ River about 20 mile to yᵉ place where Capt. Lovel first came upon Sawco River 2 days before his fight at yᵉ mouth of a stream which he followed from Pigwacket hill, Sent out Scouts, & Campt. We discovered a River yᵗ come from yᵉ N. W. into Sawco River.

Thursd. 7 : We Exᵈ. said Jo. yᵉ Mohauck. whether that was not yᵉ stream, whereupon the fort was, who said he couᵈ not tell whether it was that, or one lower. Captᵗ Willard & Blancher, took said Jo. with 30 of yᵉ ablest men & scouted up said N. W. branch about 10 mile, & found it to be a still stream fit for canoes with plenty of Entervals & old planting land of yᵉ Indians, & couᵈ not learn anything encouraging from said Jo. & at night returned to yᵉ army. Perceiving Provisions to be short, thought it advisable to stear homewards.

16

Friday 8 of Octob.: we marched about 6 mile down y" River, & Having Campt by reason of Rain, sent scouts down y" River.

Saturday 9. we marched down y" River to Pigwacket old fort about 16 miles, & Capt. Willard sent Leiut. Warner out with Leut. Wilder & 40 men from both Companies Into y" Neck of y" River & Ordered them to meet y" Army where Capt. Lovil was killed. after meeting we marched to y" lower end of Sawco pond, & sent out scouts, & Campt by y" Rivers side, in all about 24 miles.

Sabb:a 10. We marched about 26 mile & sent out scouts & campt, & discovered Ossippy River about a mile below us.

Mun. 11, We waded this morning sd River marched about 20 mile down y" River, & sent out Scouts & campt.

Tuesday 12 We waded this morning over another River & marched down Sawco River about 28 mile & came to Salmon falls, sent out Scouts & campt below y" falls.

Wednes: 13 We marched about 13 miles & came into Sawco falls, having no subsistance, we marched down to Winter harbour 7 miles & took some provisions from Capt. Jordan & lodged there.

Thursd: 14. It rained in y" forenoon & in y" afternoon marched to Cape Porpus & there lodged, being about 7 miles

Frid: 15 We came to Wels about 9 miles & lodged there, and there parted w:th Capt. Blancher, who went by Kingstown & Nutfield.

Saturd 16. We came to Kittiry about 18 mile & lodged there.

Sabb: 17 We travill:d to Hampton falls & lodged there about 20 mile.

Mund. 18 Came to Andavor being about 23 mile

Tuesday 19. Capt. Willard Rid & got home that night, and y" rest of the men got home, some Wednesday, some thursday & some Friday being about 40 mile. So that from Lancaster In Capt. Willards March accordin to his best Judgment & agreed with by y" Comp:s being in all 503 mile. p BENJA. GOODRIDGE *Clerk*.

[Massachusetts Archives, XXXVIII, A, 119-21.]

LANCASTER MEN IN JOSEPH BLANCHARDS MUSTER ROLL AUGUST TO OCTOBER 1725.

Oliver Wilder Lieut
Samuel Sawyer Sergt
Joseph Whitcomb
Stephen Houghton
Ezra Sawyer
Thomas Littel John
Jona Osgood

John Wheelock
Joseph Wilson
John Divoll
William Stevens
Jonathan Bayley
Henry Sawyer

[Massachusetts Archives, XCI, 173-7.]

LANCASTER MEN IN THE MUSTER ROLL OF CAPTAIN SAMUEL WILLARD AUGUST TO NOVEMBER 1725.

Sam Willard Capt
Eleazar Warner Lt of Groton
Eleazar Robins 2ᵈ Lt   do.
Henry Willard Ens:
Benjᵃ. Goodridge Clerk
Ephraim Wheeler
Moses Chandler

Joshua Phelps
Barnabas Tuel
Benjᵃ Atherton
Simon Atherton
Ebenʳ. Polley
Richard Wiles

[Massachusetts Archives, XCI, 175.]

MUSTER ROLL OF CAPTAIN JOSIAH WILLARD'S COMPANY JUNE 3 TO NOVEMBER 10, 1725.

Josiah Willard Captain
Edward Hartwell Lieut
Jonathan Shepley Ens.
Aaron Willard Sergt.
Philip Goodridge Sergt.
John Dean Sergt.
John Holden Corp
Isaac Farnsworth Corp
Benjamin Corey Centinel
James Jewall
Samuel Davis
John Shepard son to Danl Shepard
Richard Rice
Saml Farnsworth son to Saml Farnsworth
Benja Harris
Samuel Stow
Uriah Holt
Thomas Ross
Daniel Power
John Goodridge
Joseph Page
Jona Willard
Won   Ind. servt to Joseph Mainer
Benja Rugg
Jonas Fairbanks
John Haywood
Daniel Albert

David Osgood
Jona Pierson
Edw. Pratt
Jeremiah Belcher
Saml Hardy
Roᵗ Gray
Thomas Bruce
Jer. D. Belcher
Joseph Woods
Robᵗ Gray [*bis*]
Hezekiah Fletcher
Cyprian Stevens
Jona Lilley
Jona Temple
Jona Richardson
Walter Malone
Joseph Bennet
Benja Manning
William Qurrin servᵗ
John Shepley
Isaac Parker
Jona Hubbard
Joseph Lakin
Phineas Parker
Ebenʳ Blood
Jona Borden
John Lakin
Isaac Woods

Richard Wiles
Richard Gore
Richard Wiles [*bis*]
Josiah Witherby
Andrew Watkins
Henry Houghton
John Wilder
John Wilder Junr son of Thomas Wilder
Simon Atherton son of James Atherton
Thomas Fairbanks son of Jabez Fairbanks

Nathl Nutting
Phineas Burt
Stephen Boynton
Eben^r Jafts
Jno. Grout
Daniel Collins
Robt Mears
Josiah Corey
Jona Fisk
Lawrence Lacey
John Nutting
Daniel Kelsey
Timothy Barron

Names supposed to be of Lancaster are printed in italics. Residences are not given in the roll. Captain Josiah was brother of Captain Samuel Willard. He removed to Turkey Hills and became colonel in the French and Indian war.

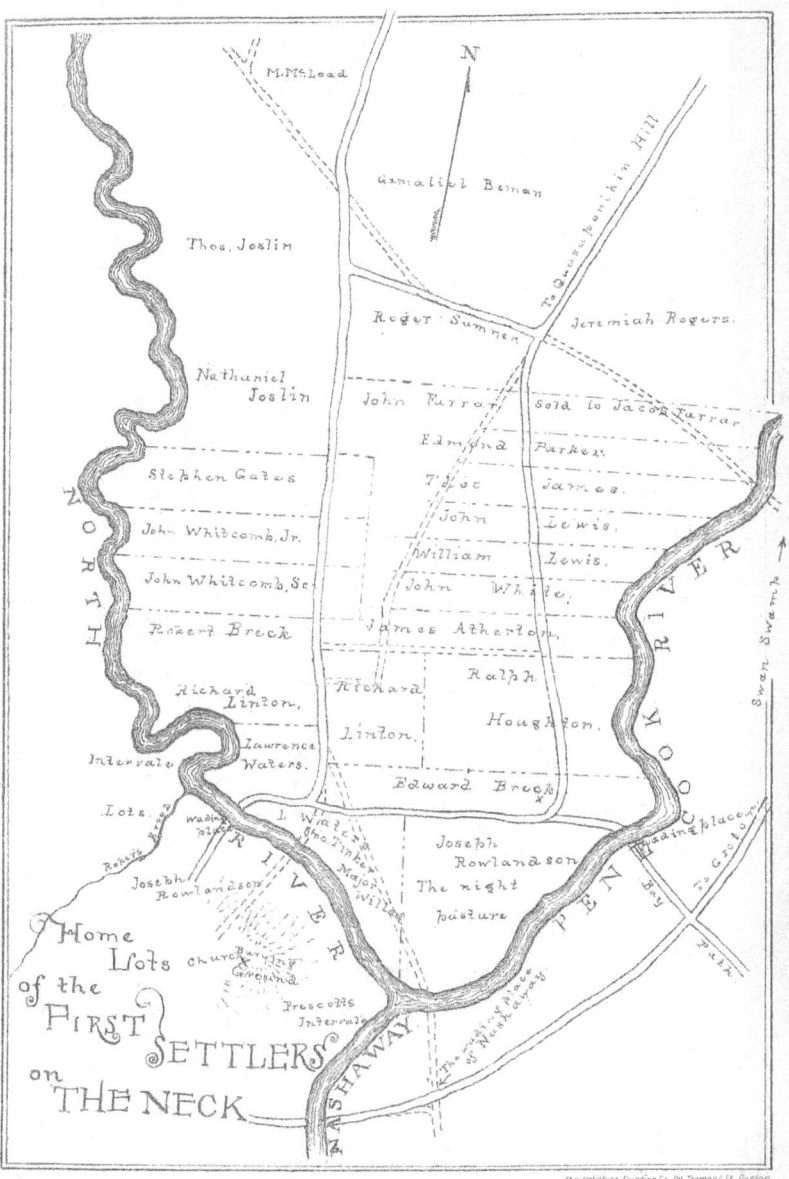

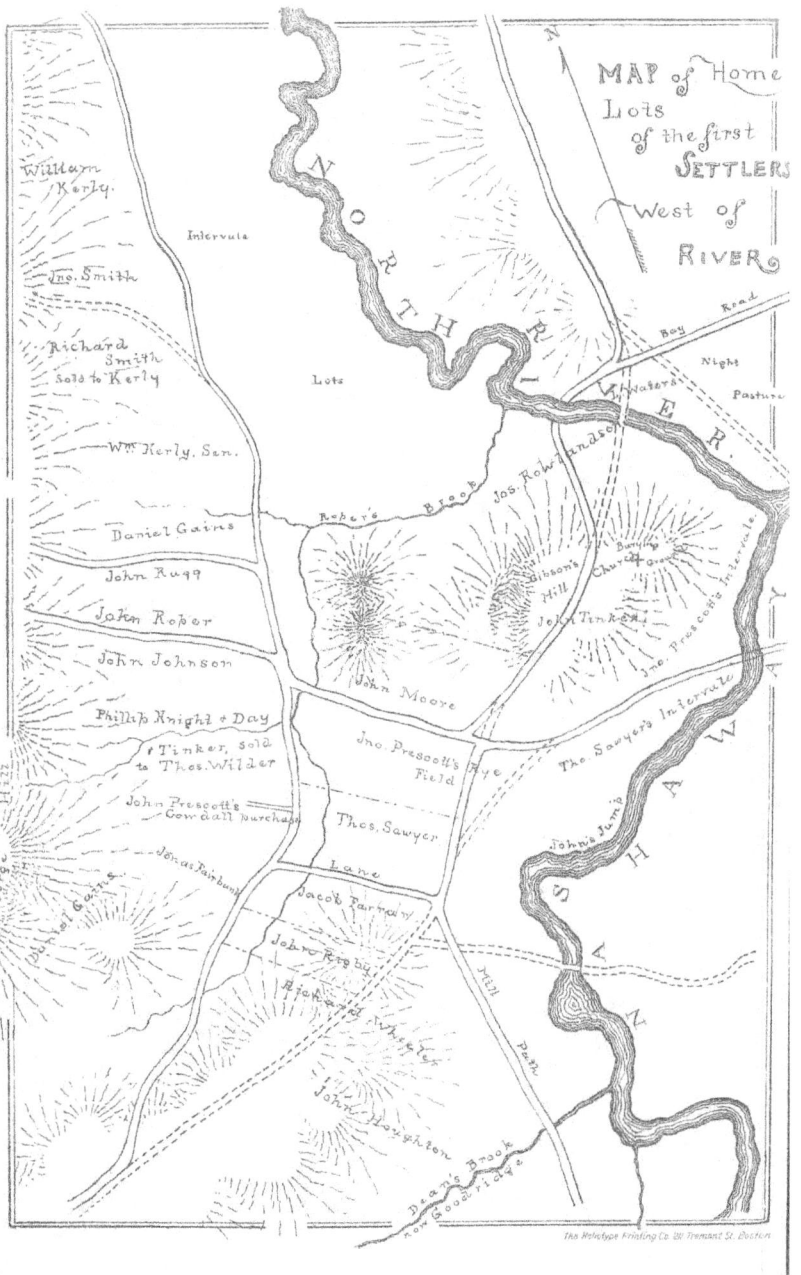

THE BOOK OF LANDS.

ALL reports extant of the meetings of the proprietary before A. D. 1725, have been given in full on previous pages. The first allotments, special grants, and successive divisions of commons, were registered in the Book of Lands. These valuable records are continuous from April, 1656, — when Ralph Houghton was instructed by the Arbitrators to begin them, — to the laying out of the last of the common land in 1835. The title to all the real estate of Lancaster, Clinton, Bolton, Berlin, and much of that in Harvard, Boylston and Sterling, is founded upon these records. The original proprietors of the Nashaway plantation, with the single exception of John Prescott, had before the organization of 1653, abandoned, sold, or by inaction lost their rights in the company. Of the fifty-five who signed the covenant before 1660, fifteen failed to fulfill its requirements, and their corporate rights thereby lapsed, while four names were added, making forty-four members of the Proprietary. This number was soon reduced to forty by purchases. Among these forty men and their successors Lancaster's original territory, less a few special grants, was distributed. The first allotments each comprised twenty acres of upland styled the "house lot," and twenty acres of intervale. The special grants were by way of inducement to persons desired as inhabitants, as rewards for particular services, as a "conveniency," or as allowance for highways, barren land, &c. The divisions of common lands were made from time to time, to the number of seven, each proprietor's share of the acreage distributed being proportionate to his original estate. Due regard was always paid to differences in value arising from situation and quality of soil, a well known field being fixed upon as a guide for estimation in the last respect. Very generally the danger of prejudice in the distribution was eliminated by giving the final determination to lot.

After the selection of the site whereon to plant the hearthstone, the pioneers naturally sought the lands that could most easily be made to yield food for man and cattle. Daniel Neal, writing about A. D. 1700, of "The Present State of New England," tells us " The first Planters found the Grass in the Vallies above an ell in Height; and consequently pretty rank for want of cutting, but their cattle eat it and thrive very well with it." The broad and fertile intervales of the Nashaway doubtless formed a chief inducement to the settlement here at so early a date. The rank growth of natural grasses upon these comparatively treeless tracts furnished abundant fodder for the winter supply to the cattle, a matter of the greatest importance in those days, when starvation often threatened the planter's stock if the deep snows belated the spring-time. The land of the earlier divisions consisted, for this reason, of intervale and meadow only, this latter designation being used in its older meaning, grass land. The swamps and wooded uplands obtained value as population increased.

Transfers of land find no place in these records save as casually mentioned in descriptions, and — notwithstanding the law of October 19, 1652, defining the only legal conveyance of real property to be by written deed and registry— until several years after the settlement of Lancaster, we find very few instances where the alienation of land was made matter of record. John Cowdall's sale of the Symonds & King trucking house site to John Prescott, in 1647, is found in the Suffolk Registry, but neither Lawrence Waters' transfer to John Hall, Hall's to Richard Smith, Smith's to John Tinker, Philip Knight's to Tinker, nor Tinker's to

Major Simon Willard and Thomas Wilder, can be found anywhere recorded. Very generally the pioneers made their wills, and from these, and the settlement of estates, we obtain many facts useful in ascertaining the outlines of home lots. The two maps inserted herewith are the outcome of a diligent study of the Book of Lands, the Middlesex Probate Files, and the Registry of Deeds. In them will be found the results of an honest endeavor to correctly locate the homes of the earliest proprietors. While the editor makes no pretence that the property lines are laid down with the accuracy of a survey, he is not conscious of having evolved one of them from any self-satisfying sapience of his own respecting the fitness of things, nor of having placed one merely to suit dubious tradition. Facts of record have fixed every starting point, and these will be as clearly set forth as economy of space will admit, in the proper places.

It should be borne in mind that the early surveyors made very generous allowance for swag of chain, inequality of ground, *et cætera*, and that the conventional term "more or less," in old deeds rarely meant less. Swampy, rocky or undesirable "slips" and "angles" of land were sometimes left between two lots in a range as common, or were given to abutters without measurement. As for example: the half home lot of Daniel Gains (who came after the first allotments had been made), "a peice of Land that was left by the Lott of John Rugg and Goodman Kerly;" and the swamp between the lands of Thomas Joslin and his son Nathaniel, "the one half thereof belonging to Nathaniel Joslin by the town's Gift, and the other to his father."

The plan of the present publication includes only the location of "first allotments." The original Book of Lands cannot be found, and the following extracts from the transcript made by Caleb Wilder about 1763, prove that he neither copied closely nor improved upon Ralph Houghton's orthography. He knew of no mark of punctuation but the colon.

THE ESTATES OF THE FIRST INHABITANCE OF LANCASTER

as thay are Entered in the old Book of Enteries by which the Lands in Lancaster are all diuided Exept the first Lotts of upland and first Lotts of Enteruail which was twenty acres Each Lott and the Rest of the Lands both upland [and] Enteruail was Diuided acording to thair Estates to witt four acres of meadow in Each deuision to a 100 pounds of Estate and acordingly for a Grater or Lesser Estate as entered below and ten acres in the second deuision of enteruail to euery 100 pounds of Estate and acordingly for a Grater or Less Estate and one pound of Estate draws one acre in euery deuision of upland Exept the first and fifth deuision and it is now the Seuenth deuision.

	l	s	d		l	s	d
John Prescutt	366	15	0	Thomas Sawyer	110	0	0
William Carley Sen	270	00	0	Edward Brick	202	11	0
Ralph Houghton	264	04	0	William Carley Juner	186	00	0
Edmond Parker	98	00	0	John Moors	110	00	0
Thomas James	36	00	0	William Lewis	285	09	0
John Johnson	30	00	0	John farrah	107	00	0
John Smith	58	19	0	Roger Sumner	232	00	0
James Atherton	69	5	0	Jonas fairbanks	172	00	0
Robert Brick	10	0	0	Jacob farrah	275	17	0
John Rugg	83	10	0	Richard Smith	313	13	10
John Lewis	18	10	0	Thomas Joslin	210	00	0
Henery Carley	78	4	0	Thomas Wilder	340	00	0
Richard Linton	90	0	0	Stephen Gates	314	00	0
John Whitcomb Jun	29	0	0	John Whitcomb	241	00	0
Mordicai Mackload	50	0	0	Larrance Waters	277	00	0
John Rigbe	50	0	0	John Houghton	250	00	0
James Butler	59	0	0	Jeremiah Rogers	310	00	0
Daniel Gains	50	0	0	Gamaliel Beman	210	00	0
John White	380	06	2	John Tinker	200	00	0
Phillip Knight	100	00	0	Joseph Rowlandson	200	00	0
John Roper	100	00	0	Nathaniel Joslin	155	00	0
Richard Wheeler	300	00	0				

THE NAMES OF THOSE THAT HAD 30 ACRE LOTTS GRANTED THEM BY THE TOWN AFTER THE SETTELMENT OF THE TOWN.

    John Bush   John Priest
    Samuel Bennitt   Caleb Sawyer
    James Frost   Jeremiah Willson

William Hutson	Josiah Wheeler
John Hinds	John Warner
Jonathan Moore	John Willard
John Moors	

The reason of these special grants is not found in records. With a single exception they were laid out in the limits of Harvard and Bolton.

THE LANDS OF EDWARD BRICKE IN THE FIRST DEUISION.

House Lott. His house Lott upon which he builded his house Lyeth on the east Side the neke in that Range of Lotts it being the first Lott thare as it is Recorded in his Grant and it buts Eastardly upon penecooke Riuer and westward it buts upon a highway that goes to quasaponikin enteruail and Southardly it is bounded by Sum Land that was Left for a hiway and Sence is Laid out for a Cuntrie highway by Concord men and it is bounded northardly by the Lott of Richard Linton now in the possion of Ralph Houghton and it is Laid out for twenty acres be it more or Less.

enteruail Lott. more he hath this enteruail Lott Lying on the east side penicooke Riuer Lying at the north east end of Swans Swamp buting easterdly upon the meadow Lott of John Moore and partly upon the upland and westward it buts upon penecooke Riuer and it is bounded Southardly by a highway that goes through the Swans Swamp to the Commons and northardly it is bounded by the Lott of his son Robert Bricke and it Lyeth for twenty acres be it more or Less.

Edward Breck came from Ashton, England. He was in Dorchester, 1636, was made freeman, 1639, and in 1645 received a land grant on Smelt Brook conditioned upon his erection of a mill there. He became prominent in Dorchester, being a selectman for several years both before and after his brief residence in Lancaster, which was perhaps shortened by the death of his wife in 1653. He died in 1662. His house here was upon the east end of his lot, which extended along the north side of the existing street, twenty rods in width, from the wading place in the main river to the corner now occupied by Dr. J. L. S. Thompson. This land and house came by purchase into possession of John Glazier, who came here from Woburn soon after the settlement, and died October, 1688. It remained in the ownership of the Glazier family until 1727, when

George Glazier sold it to Captain Samuel Willard, who is credited with having built the old mansion on this lot, now standing near the railroad crossing.

THE LANDS OF ROBERT BRICK.

house Lott. his house Lott Lyeth on the west side the neck and on the East side the nort Riuer buting easterly upon a highway that Goes betwen the two Ranges of Lotts and it buts westerly upon the north Riuer and Southardly it is bounded by Sum Land of Richard Linton whearon he hath builded his house and northardly it is bounded by the house Lott of John Whitcomb Sener and It Lyeth for twenty acors be it more or Less.

Enteruail Lott. more he hath an enteruail Lott Lying on the east side of penicook Riuer butting easterly upon the meadow Lott of John Moore and westerly upon Penecook Riuer and It is bounded Southarly by the Lott of his father Edward Brick and northarly it is bounded by the Lott of Ralph Houghton to Gether with a small quantity of Land the Grant whareof is to be seen in the old town Book Lying betwen his proper Lott and the Lott of Ralph Houghton all Lying to him for his full due acording to his first Grant in the enteruail be it more or Less.

Recorded by me RALPH HOUGHTON *Clerk* ye 2^d of January 1666

Robert Breck, the son of Edward, married Sarah Hawkins in 1653, settled in Boston, and became a merchant — never occupying his lot in Lancaster, which was opposite the public buildings.

THE LANDS OF RALPH HOUGHTON.

his pp lott. The pp house Lott of Ralph Houghton is the third Lott in that Rang of upland Lotts Lying on the neck on the west side of penicook Riuer being bounded south by Richard Lintons Lott an north by the Lott where he bought of John Prescutt buting easterly upon Penicook Riuer and west upon that Rang of Lotts that Lyeth on the west side of the neck whare Goodman Whitcomb Liueth

a Lott he Bought of John Prescutt. his house Lott which he bought of John Prescutt being the fourth Lott in the same Rang of Lotts bounded south by his own pp Lott and north by the Lott of James Atherton buting Easterly upon Penicook Riuer and west upon another Rang of Lotts that Lyes on the west side of the neck acording to the Record of Grants in the old town Book which Lotts being Eight Score Rods in Length and twenty Rods wide: but now upon Exchange he stands possesied of the East end of Richard Lintons Lott which is the second Lott in that Rang of Lotts and Lyes on the north side of Edward Bricks Lott which is the first Lott upon which he hath planted his house: in Lew whereof Richard Linton hath his twenty acres at the west end of his own and the two Lotts of Ralph Houghton as appears by a deed of Exchange betwext them Both the Lotts of the said Ralph Houghton being and Lying for twenty acres be thay more or Less thay being two home Lotts.

his Enteruail Giuen him by the town. His enteruaile Lott which was Giuen him by the town lying on the East side of penicook Riuer being the third Lott in that Rang of Lotts wherein Edward Bricks Lott is the first Lying bounded by the Lott ot Robert Brick (so called in the old town Book) on the south side and north by the Lott of Ralph Houghton which he bought of John Prescutt buting east on the Still Riuer and west upon Penicook Riuer and Lyeth for twenty acres be it more or less.

his enteruail he bought of John Prescutt. and his enteruail which he bought of John Prescutt Lyes bounded south by his own pp Lott which was Giuen him by the town and bounded north by James Athertons Lott buting Easterly upon the Still Riuer and west upon Penecook Riuer which is by Estemation and also by his deed of sale from John Prescutt fifty acres: . . . . .

Ralph Houghton was one of the four who first signed the Lancaster covenant, in 1652, coming here, it is said, from Watertown. He was then about twenty-nine years of age. Being the best penman of the pioneers, he was made clerk of records, and held that position until the massacre. He was admitted a freeman in 1668, and elected deputy in 1673 and 1689. The date of his death is not found, but must have been after 1692, as in that year he, with wife Jane, transferred the northern half of his house lot to his son Joseph. His children were Ralph; James; Mary, 11, 4, 1653; John, 28, 2, 1655; Joseph, 1, 5, 1657; Experience, 1, 8, 1659; Sarah, 17, 12, 1661; Abigail, 15, 5, 1664; Hannah, October 16, 1667. All but Ralph and James were born in Lancaster. John and Hannah died October, 1679, in Charlestown. Joseph Houghton sold his half of the homestead to John Glazier, and he sold it to Simon Stevens.

THE LANDS OF RICHARD LINTON

his house Lott. The house Lott of Richard Linton Containing more or Less twenty acres is scittuate Lying and being on the neck of Land : and by exchange and barter betwen him and Ralph Houghton, is Layed out betwen themselues at the west end of the Lott or Lotts of the said Ralph Houghton being the bredth of his two Lotts and is bounded East by the said Lotts South by the Lott of Edward Brick north by James Atharton his Lott and west by the Lott of John Whitcomb Sener. Also more or Less Six acres on which his Dwelling house now Standeth Giuen him by the town and arbitrators Consent bounded south and west by the Ground of Lawarance Waters north by Robert Bricks Lott so named In the town Book and the highway easterly scittuate Lying and being near to his house Lott aforesaid being part upland and part swamp neere to the form of a triangle.

enteruail Lott The enteruaile Lott of Richard Linton containing—— acres more or Less Lyeth at the Sonth end of quosapanakin in the maner and form of a triangle bounded by the north Riuer towards the north the enteruail of John Whitcomb towards the North and Southward by his own meadow Ground

In September, 1645, Richard Linton deeded his house and lot in Watertown to Robert Sanderson. About that date, or perhaps earlier, he and his son-in-law, Lawrence Waters, began life with their families upon the Nashaway, having been induced by the first proprietors to undertake the task of preparing the way for further settlement. He died March 30, 1665, and by his will it would seem that his wife Elizabeth outlived him. His house stood upon the west side of the present street, somewhere between the residences of Miss Levantia Bradley and Henry M. Latham, but he owned the land along the opposite side of the way for sixty rods, including the ground upon which the public buildings stand. His daughter, Anne Waters, received ten acres of this in trust for his grandson, Joseph Waters. The other lands he left to another grandson, George Bennett, who being slain in the massacre August 22, 1675, Samuel Bennet, his son, succeeded to possession.

THE LANDS OF JAMES ATHERTON.

House Lott His upland Lott for a house Lott Lyeth on the east side the neck buting easterdly on penicook Riuer and westerly it buts upon another Rang of Lotts that Lyeth on the west side the neck and it is bounded Southerly by the Lott of Ralph Houghton and northardly by the Lott of John White Lying for twenty acres be it more or Less.

Enteruail Lott More he hath an enteruaile Lott Lying on the east side of penicook Riuer buting easterdly upon sum part of the Hosokie meadow and westardly upon penicook Riuer and Southardly it is bounded by the Lott of Ralph Houghton and at the west end of it by the high way that Runs sloping threw the Lott that goes to the meadows and northardly it is bounded by the Lott of John White and it Lyeth for twenty acres be it more or Less.

James Atherton came here from Dorchester with wife Hannah. He is thought to have been a brother of Major General Humphrey Atherton. In Lancaster children were born to him as follows: James, 1654; Joshua, 1656; Hannah, 1657; Mary, 1660; Elizabeth, 1666; Deborah, 1669; Joseph, 1672. In 1697, being then of Milton, he conveyed his land in Lancaster to his eldest son James, Jr. In 1703 the eastern part of the home lot is found in possession of Joseph Wheelock, he having purchased it from Isaac Temple of Marlborough. The western portion had been bought by William Divoll. James and James, Jr., were then resident near Bare Hill, and Joshua near Still River in Harvard. James, the father, died at Sherborn in 1707, aged 84 years. The highway from the brick store east to the neck road probably lies on the south side of the Atherton lot.

JOHN WHITE'S LANDS.

No record of John White's first allotment is found in the Book of Lands, though this is probably an omission of the copyist. We know, however, that the house lot joined Atherton's, and that his house stood upon the east end of it. Direct descendants have resided upon the land until modern days, and perhaps the first settler's home was on or quite near the site of Edward Houghton's residence. Goodman White, however, owned the land across the highway, bounding upon the river. He came here from Salem, where he was admitted an inhabitant in 1639, and had an estate in what is now Wenham, upon which his eldest son, Thomas, remained. He brought with him to Lancaster his wife Joanna, a son Josiah, Elizabeth, who married Henry Kerley November 2, 1654, Mary, wife of the Reverend Joseph Rowlandson, and Hannah, who married John Divoll in 1663. He had also married daughters Joanna and Sarah. His wife died in 1654. Hannah, the youngest daughter, we learn from his will, was " a nurse to him in his old age," and the Lancaster estate was bequeathed to her and her brother Josiah. John White died in the spring of 1673, his will being signed March 10, and offered for probate May 28th of that year. His son Josiah died November 11, 1714. The famous Indian fighter, Captain John White, was son of Josiah.

THE LANDS OF WILLIAM LEWIS

house Lott. his upland Lott for a house Lott Lying in that Rang of Lotts on the west side penicook Riuer on the neck and it is bounded southwardly by the Lott of John White and northardly it is bounded by the Lott of John Leweis his son and Easterdly it buts upon the said penicook Riuer and westardly it buts upon an other Range of Lotts that was Laid on the west side the neck a high way Running Cross the Lott near the east end of it to quasaponikin hill and it Lyeth for twenty acres be it more or Less

his enteruail Lott. More he hath his enteruail Lott Lying on the east side penecook Riuer and it Lyeth bounded southardly by the Lott of John White northardly by the Lott of John Leweis and it buts easterdly upon part of the hasokie meadow and westardly it buts upon penicook Riuer a high way Runing through it to the meadows and other Lands below it which is allowed for in meashuring the Lott Laid out for twenty acres be it more or Less.

William Lewis was of Roxbury, where he was made freeman in 1642. His children were John, born in England, 1635; Christopher, 1636; Lydia, born in Roxbury, 1639; Josiah, 1641; Isaac, 1644; Mary, 1646; and Hannah, 1649. He deeded to his son Christopher the eastern half of his home lot, April 19, 1662. He died 1671, 10th month, 3d day, leaving by will his house and land to his wife Anne and son Isaac. Mary became the wife of Josiah White. Lydia married Mordecai MacLoud.

THE LANDS OF JOHN LEWEIS

House Lott. his upland Lott for a house Lott Lyeth in that Rang of Lotts on the east side the neck buting Easterdly upon penicook Riuer and westardly it buts upon a Rang of Lotts that Lyeth on the west side the neck and it is bounded southardly by the Lott of William Leweis his father and northardly it is bounded by the Lott of Thomas James a high way of 5 Rods Runing Crosse it near the east end of it to quasaponikin hill and It Lyeth for twenty acors be it more or Less.

Interuail Lott. more he hath his enteruail Lott Lying on the east side of penicook Riuer bounding Southardly by the Lott of William Leweis his father and northardly it is bounded by the Lott of Thomas James and it buts easterdly upon sum part of the hosokie meadow taking in sum swamppy land their for his Conueniencie in the 2 deuision and also for allowance for the highway that Runs Sloping through his Lott. and westardly it buts upon penecook Riuer and it is Laid out to him for twenty acres be it more or Less.

John Lewis, son of William, had by wife Hannah children born in Lancaster, as follows: Barrachia, 1663; Rebeccah, 1665; Patience, 1668; John, 1671; William, 1673. At the massacre he removed to Dorchester, where were born Hannah, 1678; Thankful, 1680; and Judith. He built a house in Dorchester in 1679, and was living there in 1687, whence it may be inferred that he did not return to Lancaster. Josiah White obtained the Lewis lands.

THE LANDS OF THOMAS JAMES

his House Lott. the house Lott of Thomas James Containing twenty acors is the ninth Lott Lying on the neck of Land on the west side of penicook Riuer buting east upon the Riuer and west upon another Rang of Lotts that Lyeth on the west side of the neck bounding south by the Lott of John Leweis and north by the Lott of Edmon parker being eight Score Rods in Length and twenty Rods wide and Lyes for twenty acres be it more or Less a high way of fiue Rods wide Runing ouer Crosse it to quosaponikin hill near about the midel of the Lott.

his enteruail His enteruail is also the ninth Lott Lying on the east side of penicook Riuer being Eight Score Rods in Length and twenty

Rods wide and Lyeth for twenty acres be it more or Less buting east upon a highway that goes to the plumtrees and to the meadows and enteruails and buting west on penicook Riuer bounded South by the Lott of John Leweis and north by the Lott of Edmund Parker.

Thomas James had a wife Elizabeth, and a son John born in Charlestown, 18..11..1632. He left his property in Lancaster to his cousins, the Lewises, and Christopher Lewis sold the east end of the house lot, between the river and the highway, to Josiah White, in 1705. Thomas James died March 15, 1660.

EDMUND PARKER'S LANDS.

The copyist of the Book of Lands has omitted Edmund Parker's estate from the records. His house lot was between that of Thomas James and John Farrar's, and of the same extent as theirs. Edmund Parker came here from Roxbury with wife Elizabeth [Howe], and children Elizabeth, born 1649, and Abraham, born 1652. There were born to him here Mary and Esther, 1654, and Deborah, 1655. The wife died June 9, 1657. Ralph Houghton has left us a very unflattering account of the family, which can be found in previous pages. They disappear from Lancaster at the massacre, returning to Roxbury. In Parker's will, dated Roxbury, April 13, 1692, he mentions all the children above named, and makes his "trusty & well beloved Friends John Moore and Thomas Wilder Liuet, both of Nashaway whole and sole executors." He probably died early in 1694, as his inventory is dated May 28th of that year. By the will Josiah White was to have the eastern part of the home lot at appraisal. The executors were to sell the rest.

THE LANDS OF JACOB FARRAH THAT HE BOUGHT OF JOHN FARRAH

his house Lott. and he hath also a house Lott which he had from his brother John farrah Giuen by him and Confirmed and Rattified by the town which Lott Lyeth on the Neck on the west side of penicook Riuer buting east upon the said Riuer and west upon another Rang of Lotts that Lyes on the west side of the neck bounded South by the Lott of Edmon parker and north by the Lott of Roger Sumner at the west end and by the Common at the east end and by sid Land of Jeremiah Rogers which Lott being Eight Scoore Rods Long and twenty Rods wide and Lyeth for twenty acres be it more or Less

The Farrar brothers were from Lancashire. John, after a brief stay here, went to Woburn, where he was admitted an inhabitant in 1656, and there died "very old," in 1690. John Houghton and wife Mary [Farrar] transferred the above house lot to George Glazier in March, 1706.

THE LANDS OF ROGER SUMNER.

his house Lott. The house Lott of Roger Sumner Lyeth on the neck bounded South by the Lott of Jacob farrer north by a high way betwen it and the house Lott of Gamaliel Beman eastward by the high way that Goes to quosaponikin hill and west by [a] parcel of upland Giuen to his father in Law Thomas Joslin the said house Lott being laid out for twenty acres be it more or Less.

his enteruail Lott his enteruail Lott Lyeth at quosaponikin contains more or Less twenty acres Southardly bounded by the Lott of Nathaniel Joslin northardly by Gamaliel Beman westerdly by the North Riuer easterly on the high way Runing betwen it and the meadow.

Deacon Roger Sumner, the son of William, born in England, came here from Dorchester, where he had been made freeman in 1657. He was a member of the church, and August 26, 1660, was dismissed in order that he might assist in organizing a church at Lancaster. His wife was Mary, daughter of Thomas Joslin. Their children were Abigail, 1657; Samuel, 1659; Waitstill, 1661; Mary, 1665; Jaazoniah, 1668; Rebecca, 1671; William, 1673; Ebenezer, 1678. Deacon Sumner left Lancaster at the time of the massacre, returning to Dorchester. He died in Milton, May 26, 1698, aged sixty-six years. The house lot above described extended along the south side of the highway that leads west from Lane's Crossing. The land rights of Roger Sumner were purchased of his sons William and Samuel by the brothers Edmund and Ebenezer

17

Harris, who came to Lancaster from Sudbury about 1708.

THE LANDS OF JEREMIAH ROGERS

House Lott. his house Lott Lying on the neck on the east Side thare of near to a Brook that we pass ouer to go to quasaponikin hill their being ten acors or thare abouts Lying bounded Southardly by the Lott of Jacob farrah and northardly by sum Common Land which since was Laid out to him for Second deuision and westerdly it is bounded by the highway that goes to quosaponikin hill and easterdly it is bounded by a Swamp that Lyeth betwen the Stated Common and it and he hath ten acres more or their abouts Lying at the South end of a peice of Land called Pine hill bounded northardly by the said pine hill and Southardly it is bounded partly by the house Lott of Jacob farrar and partly by sum enteruail Land of his own and easterdly it buts partly upon Penecook Riuer and partly upon his own enteruail Land and westerdly it buts upon the stated Common called timber plain both the aforsaid percells of Land is Laid out unto the said Jeremiah Rogers for 20 acres be it more or Less.

enteruail. His Lott of enteruail as it was Granted by the town and Laid out in two pieces one peice whereof Lyeth near to a peice of Land called pine hill bounded northward by sum part of his own house Lott that Lyeth betwen it and the said pine hill and southardly it is bounded by sum enteruail Land of Jacob farrars that Lyeth at the end of his home Lott and easterdly it buts upon penicook Riuer ouer against an Inden ware Called Jameses ware and westerdly it buts upon sum part of his own house Lott there being six acors or there abouts and another part thareof Lying in the outermust side of the Sound Land at quosaponikin enteruail and Lyeth bounded Southerly by the Lott of Gamaliel Beman and northardly by a high pine hill and it buts westardly upon the North Riuer and Easterly upon a high way that Leads into the enteruail swamp that is Laid out for second deuision this benig fourteen acres or thare abouts both which parcels of enteruail are Laid out to the said Jeremiah Rogers for twenty acres be it more or Less.

Jeremiah Rogers was from Dorchester. At the massacre he returned thither, and there died September 26, 1676, leaving a widow, Abiah, who, with two daughters, Abigail and Bathsheba, died of small-pox in March, 1678. His children were Margaret, 1653; Ichabod, 1659; Hittabel, 1662; Jehosaphat, 1663; Abiah, 1664; Bathsheba, 1667: Israel, 1671; Susanna, 1673; also Jeremiah, Abigail and Sarah, the dates of whose births are not found. The Rogers house lot is cut in twain by the old turnpike, and included the upper brick yard of Samuel R. Damon, the Anthony Lane homestead, and the lands of Emory H. White. May 12, 1710, Jeremiah Rogers of Salem, wheelwright, and Jehosaphat Rogers of Topsfield, tailor, sold their father's lands to Edward Phelps, weaver, from Andover. Rogers had sold, in 1663, one hundred acres of his outlying land to Henry Kimball, a blacksmith of Boston.

THE LANDS OF GAMALIEL BEMAN

House Lott His house Lott being near unto Quosaponikin Brook bounded by Sum Common Land that sence was Laid out to himself for second deuision on the north side of it and South it is bounded by a highway that Lyeth betwen the Lott of Roger Sumner and it buts easterdly upon a high way that Goes to quosaponikin hill the southeast corner of it and at the northeast Corner it buts upon Sum Land Laid out to nathaniel Joslin and Roger Sumner for second deuision and it buts westardly upon Sum Comon Land Laid out to himself for second deuision Lying for twenty acors be it more or Less.

his enteruail Lott. His enteruaile Lott Lyeth at quosaponikin Interuail buting west upon the North Riuer and east upon sum swampy brushey Ground that Lyeth between sum meadow of Stephen Gates and this Lott a highway Runing at the eand of it bounded Southardly by the Lot of Roger Sumner and north by the Lott of Jeremiah Rogers and Lyeth for twenty acres be it more or Less.

Gamaliel Beaman came from England in the Elizabeth and Ann, A. D. 1635, and settled in Dorchester. In 1659, being then thirty-six years old, he came to Lancaster, bringing a large family. At the time of the massacre he returned to Dorchester and there died March 23, 1678. An indication of their poverty at this date is the fact that the tax-rates of Gamaliel, Sen., Gamaliel Jr., John and Thomas Beaman are set down in the Dorchester Records as "Desperate Debts." The Beamans were among the first to return to Lancaster upon its re-settlement. John and Gamaliel set up new houses on their father's lands at Wataquadock. John, Jr., lived upon the old homestead on the neck. The children of Gamaliel, Sen., and Sarah (Clark) Beaman were John, 1649; Joseph, 1651; Gamaliel, 1653;

Thomas, 1654; Mary, 1656; Sarah, 1658 — all born before the family came from Dorchester; and Noah, 1661; Thankful, 1663; Mehitabel, 1667, born in Lancaster. John Beaman's headstone in the old burial ground records that he died 1740, aged ninety years. His son Gamaliel, born in 1684, was the first settler in Woonksechocksett, now Sterling. Thankful married Nathaniel Wilson who, in 1694, sold to William Sheafe Gamaliel Beaman's "house and lot in Lancaster."

THE LANDS OF LAWRENCE WATERS

his house Lott. The house Lott of Lawrence Waters part whareof Lies in that feild he hath enclosed by his house their being six acors and half and nine acors of enteruail in that feild butting south upon the high way that Lyes between the Carting place in the north Riuer and it bounds north upon the Lott or orchard of Richard Linton and upon the Lott of Robert Brick and bounded east by a highway that Goes to quasaponikin meadows and west and south west by the North Riuer upon which he hath planted his house garden and orchard both which persels of upland and Enteruail being parte of his house Lott and enteruail Lott more he hath a part of his upland Lott Lying on the east side of the Swans Swamp being about thirteen acres and half or thare abouts: bounded South by a brook and north by a hill at the side of the pine plain and west by the Swans Swamp and buting east upon a Littel Corner of a plaine:

his enteruail Lott More he hath eleuen acres of enteruaile Lying on the east side of Penicook Riuer butting east upon the high way that Goes to the Plumtrees and west upon the Riuer it Lyes bounded South by sum common enteruail Reserued for a lott and north by sum enteruail that was sum time Laid out for a Lott to Goodman Wilder: all which parcels of upland and enteruail Lying for his upland Lott and enteruail Lott and Lying for fourtie acres be thay more or Less.

Lawrence Waters, a carpenter of Watertown, was one of three sent up, in 1645, by the grantees of the Nashaway Plantation, to make suitable preparation for their own coming. By his wife Ann Linton he had six children born in Watertown: Lawrence, Feb. 14, 1635; Sarah, Dec. 7, 1636; Mary, Jan. 27, 1638; Rebecca, February, 1640; Daniel, Feb. 6, 1642; Stephen, Jan. 24, 1643; and the following born in Lancaster: Adam, 1645 (?); Joseph,

April 29, 1647; Jacob and Rachel, March 1, 1649; Samuel, Feb. 14, 1651; Joanna, March 26, 1653; Ephraim, Jan. 27, 1655. The proprietors assigned him a lot upon which he built a house, probably the second building erected by white men in Lancaster, (the trucking house on George Hill being the first). This house was situated in the grounds now owned by Caleb T. Symmes, Esq. Waters, before 1650, had sold his home to John Hall, and it became the property successively of Richard Smith, John Tinker, Major Simon Willard, Cyprian Stevens, and Simon Stevens. Waters removed but a few rods, building on the lot above described, the chief portion of which is now the homestead of S. J. S. Vose, Esq. He became a freeman in 1663. After the massacre of 1676, we find him with his wife, and Samuel with his wife and two children, seeking shelter in Charlestown, where Stephen became responsible to the authorities for them. Lawrence Waters was then blind. He died December 9th, 1687, in Charlestown, aged about eighty-five years, outliving his wife seven years. Joseph Waters came back in 1679, and occupied part of his father's and grandfather's lands. In the distribution of the estate of Lieutenant Nathaniel Wilder, in 1709, there was given to Oliver, the youngest son, "upland and Interval where Lawrence Waters formerly Dwelt about fifteen acres," and the inventory shows that it had been bought of John Skeath, the husband of Waters' oldest daughter, Sarah. In 1714, Simon Stevens, whose wife was Mary, daughter of Lieutenant Nathaniel Wilder, sold to Hooker Osgood "Lawrence Waters' lot on the Neck bounded southerly and easterly by yᵉ Highway, west and south west by the River." Adam Waters, perhaps the first born of English parents in Lancaster, in 1663 bought John Smith's lot upon George Hill. He died 1670, at Charlestown.

THE LANDS OF MASTER JOHN TINKER

Upland Lott bought of Richard Smith. His house Lott which he bought of Richard Smith is a Lott that Lyeth by it Self and Lyes bounded

South by the North Riuer and buts east upon a peice of Enteruail Called the night pauster and west upon the high way that Goes from the Bridge by goodman Waterses to quasaponikin meadows and it is bounded north by the Countie highway that goes allong from Goodman Waterses to Penicook Riuer it being first a home Lott Giuen by those that first had to do with the place to Goodman Waters and he built a house upon it and sold it to Goodman hall whose wife sold it to Richard Smith the said Goodman hall being in England and sending for his wife which Lott Lay for twenty acres but upon exact mesur acording to Libertie Granted by a town order Recorded in the old town book it was found to be but Seuenteen acres which is made up with and by a peice of Land Lying on the east side of the North Riuer bounded east by a hill of upland and west by the North Riuer butting south upon the Lott of Thomas Joslin and north also upon sum enteruail of thomas Joslin. . . . .

his enteruail Lott he bought of Richard Smith. and the enteruail Lott he bought of Richard Smith lyeth on the east side of penicook Riuer at the meeting of the Riuers butting west upon the Riuer and east upon the upland on the east side of the still Riuer and bounded south by John Ruggs Lott and north by John Rigbes Lott, which Lott was Laid out to Richard Smith for twenty acres. . . . . .

his own house Lott at Gibson hill. His own upland Lott Giuen him by the town is known by the name of Gibson hill which is twenty acors of upland be it more or Less bounded by a streat or highway west that goes betwixt two Ranges of Lotts and butting east upon the Commons bounded south by the house Lott of John Moors and north by the meadow that is Master Rowlandsons.

his enteruail. His enteruail Lott ten acors of it Lying on the west side of the North Riuer butting east upon the Riuer and west upon Sum Common upland that Lyes by or near to the house of William Kerley Jun bounded southardly by the Lott [of] goodman Prescutt that was Giuen him for bulding a Corn mill and north by the Lott of John Johnson: and ten acors of which Lies on the West Side of the Still Riuer buting east upon the Riuer and west upon the Lotts of John Leweis and thomas James bounded South by a high way that Goes to the meadows and to the ponds and north by a Swamp or Swampy Ground in which thare Lies a peice of meadow of James Athertons and in which Lott of enteruail there Lies a Spung of meadow Lotted out to Goodman Smith and James Atherton.

John Tinker was of Windsor, Connecticut, in 1643, whence he came to Boston, where we find him living in a hired house, 1651. In 1652 he appeared before the Middlesex Court as attorney for the defendant, in the case of " Hermon Garret & John Shawe *vs.* John Hall, for taking

away part of theire night pasture fence," and won for his
clients. In 1654, Tinker was made freeman, and the next
year joined the petitioners for "Groaten a new plantacon . .
formerly knowne by the name of Petapawag," and in the
grant was appointed one of the selectmen. For a year or
two thereafter he seems to be wavering in his choice of
residence between Lancaster and Groton, until perhaps the
town's gift of Gibson Hill decided him. He was at this time
and afterwards an Indian trader, buying beaver, otter and
other furs, then abundant in the region about, from the
native hunters. What manner of exchange he paid for
them other than peage or wampum and "trucking cloth,"
we may imagine, for the Court records show that in 1655
he was fined ten shillings "for selling now & then a gill of
strong waters to ye Indians," contrary to the law of 1654,
which imposed a fine of twenty shillings for each pint so
sold by persons not specially licensed. The original duly
witnessed notes of hand exist which show that prominent
men of the Nashaway tribe became so deeply indebted to
him as to mortgage the prospective gains of two hunting seasons for payment. In 1658 he was licensed as trader "of
Nashaway & Groaten for ye year," paying eight pounds for
the privilege. The "Mr." prefixed to his name assures us
that he was either a graduate of some university, or had
occupied high social rank in England. Only he and Reverend Joseph Rowlandson, in Lancaster, were dignified
with this title before the coming of Major Simon Willard.

Master Tinker was probably yet a young man when in
September, 1657, the commissioners appointed to order the
affairs of Lancaster placed his name first in the list of five
men chosen to manage the prudentials of the town. His
wife Alice was then twenty-seven years old, and of his two
children, Mary and John, the oldest was four years of age.
The town had given him twenty acres in a central and desirable position, known as Gibson's Hill. He purchased of
Richard Smith the original house and lot of Lawrence

Waters, and of Philip Knight the house and lot next to Prescott's home on the slope of George Hill. Two sons were born to him, Amos and Samuel, and he was prosperous, and honored of his neighbors; but through failure of health, or because the field proved too limited for his abundant ability and ambition, the town was soon to lose his valuable services. In the Court files of Middlesex is this undated letter, probably of the winter 1658:

To the honor^d County Court at Charlstowne.

Right Wor'll be pleased to understand that the Lord hath visited me of late with 3 fitts of sikness one after another uppon my jornies to and fro, sinc which I have bin very tender & have not atained my perfect helth to travell this sharpe winter season, wherefore intreat though I am one of the Grand iury that I may be excused for this preasent and I shalbe redy at the pleasure of this honrd Court to doe the best service I can for ye County and shall thankfully abide with my duty presented

Yo'r devoted humble servant   JNO. TINKER

Before the year 1659 he had removed to Pequid, now New London, and was there winning respect and distinction. The next year he was deputy to the general court, and became assistant. The court licensed him to distill and retail liquors, and gave him complete monopoly of the trade in the township. Being on the road to wealth and fame, he died in October, 1662. The public esteem for him is shown by the fact that the expenses of his illness and funeral were paid from the State treasury. Major Simon Willard obtained possession of his Lancaster property, above described.

THE LANDS OF JOHN WHITCOMB SENER

home Lott. his house Lott Giuen and Granted by the town Lyeth on the west side [of the] neck being twenty acors bounded [south] by the Lott of Robert Brick and north by the Lott of his son John Whitcomb buting east upon the Lotts that Ly upon the east side the neck and butting west upon his enteruail a high way Runing Cross it to quasaponikin enteruail.

Enteruail Lott. Aand his enteruail Lott part of it Lying on the east side the North Riuer thare being by Estimation about fifteen acors and a half bounded west by the North Riuer and east by his upland Lott butting South upon the Lott of Robert Brick that was Granted him by the town and butting north upon the enteruail Lott of his son John Whitcomb : nine acors of enteruail at quasaponikin betwen his son John Whitcomb and him either of them hauing an Equall pportion that is either four acors and half but it was not diuided between them when it was Laid out the whole being bounded southardly by a high way that Goes between the meadow Lott of Ralph Houghton and it and it is bounded north by a Lott of Stephen Gates and westardly by the North Riuer and south west by a Lott of Richard Linton this four acres and half makes up the other fifteen and half his full Lott of twenty acors acording to the town Grant but acording to Liberty Granted by a town order the fifteen acres and half exactly meashuered it was found to be but fourteen acres and half and so it is an acre wanting which is Laid out together with his second deuision of enteruail.

John "Whetcomb"— as the name is always spelled in our earliest records — was of Dorchester in the year 1635, but removed to Scituate in 1644, and to Lancaster in 1652. He died September 24, 1662, leaving a wife Frances, who survived until 1671. His children were John, Jonathan, Job, Josiah, Robert, Catherine, Abigail and Mary, all born before the coming of the family to Lancaster. John Whitcomb died intestate, and the widow and children mutually agreed upon a division of the property, which was approved by the Court. By the inventory it is shown that the chief products of the farm in 1662 were corn, tobacco and flax. The present post-office and bank building are probably upon the Whitcomb lands. Both the father's and son's house lots extended across the street eastward, meeting the other range of lots upon the neck.

THE LANDS OF JOHN WHITCOMB JUNER

his house Lott his house Lott being twenty acors Lying on the west side the neck Lying Bounded South by his father his Lott and north by the Lott of Stephen Gates butting west upon his own enteruail Lott and east upon the end of the Lotts of the Inhabitance that Liue on the east side the neck It being by Estimation twenty acres be it more or Less

enteruail Lott His enteruail Lott lying on the east side the north Riuer part of it their being about fifteen acors and a half bounded south by his fathers enteruail and north by the Lott of Stephen Gates butting easterly upon his own upland Lott and westerly upon the north Riuer and four acors and half Lying at quasaponikin enteruail Lying in Common with 4 acres and half of his fathers . . . . .

In the division of the estate of John Whitcomb, senior, his home lot was assigned to John and Jonathan jointly, and the house lot which had been John's was allotted to the youngest sons, Job and Josiah. Job did not return at the re-settlement of the town, but followed the Reverend Joseph Rowlandson to Wethersfield. Robert settled in Scituate. John and Jonathan, April 7, 1683, were conveying hay across the Penecook upon two canoes, when by the boats sinking the former was drowned. He left a widow Mary and two daughters, Ruth and Sarah. Ruth married William Divoll. Jonathan Whitcomb died in 1690, and his widow, Hannah, was killed by the Indians two years later. Their children were Hannah, 1668; Jonathan, 1669; Hannah, 2d, 1671; Abigail, 1674; Elizabeth; Mary; Katherine; Ruth; John, 1684. Jonathan inherited the home estate, and in 1696, with his cousins William Divoll and Sarah Whitcomb, entered into a mutual agreement whereby the whole Whitcomb estate was divided by east and west lines, upon both sides of the highway, into three equal divisions, each about twenty-two rods in width. Josiah Whitcomb married Rebecca Waters and set up his home in the southeast part of what is now Bolton. His children were Josiah, 1665; David, 1668; Rebecca, 1671; Johanna, 1673; Mary; Damaris; Abigail; Hezekiah, 1681; Deborah, 1683. He died April 12, 1718.

The original lot of John Whitcomb, junior, assigned in the agreement mentioned above to Job and Josiah, was by them sold to John Moore, senior. He dying in 1703, Benjamin Bellows, his administrator, sold it to Josiah White, who, July, 1708, transferred it to John Bowers, describing it as "bounded Northerly by Peter Joslin, southerly by William Divoll, west by the River, easterly by another range of Lotts, a highway crossing said Land near the

Dwelling house, also all other housing, fencing, *fortifications*, orchard garden &c." A very old headstone in the first burial ground is inscribed "JOHN BOWARS," and upon its footstone is "D : 1718." John was the grandson of Benanuel Bowers, born 1686, and married Elizabeth Stevens of Lancaster, November 17, 1707. His children were Elizabeth, John, Mary and Nathaniel. The inventory of his estate amounts to 436 pounds 11 shillings, and from one item in it we derive the estimated value in 1718 of a chattel somewhat rare in Lancaster : "one bought servant 19£".

THE LANDS OF STEPHEN GATES.

his house Lott. The house Lott of Stephen Gates : is on the neck Lying north to the house Lott of John Whitcomb Juner bounded by the saaid Lott of John Whitcomb south by the house Lott of Nathaniel Joslin north by a Rang of Lotts Easterly which Lyeth on the west side of Penicook Riuer and westward by a peice of enteruail of his own nigh adioyning to the North Riuer the said house Lott being Laid out for twenty acors more or Less :

enteruail Lott. His enteruail Lott Containing more or Less twenty acors partly Lyeth in one peice at quasaponikin thirteen acors more or Less bounded southardly [by a piece] of enteruail of John Whitcombs northardly [by the lot] of Mordica Maclode west by the North River [and east] by sum meadow of Edward Brick and [seven acres] more or Less lyeth betwen his house loott and the North Riuer bounded in Like maner by Nathaniel Joslins Lott north and John Whitcombs south his house Lott [east and] said Riuer west. . . . .

He hath his Second deuision of upland Lying to the ——- of hog swamp meadow a considerable part of a pond Lying within the sd Land & bounded on all the sides of it by Common undiuided Land a Rock called the Sleeping Rock is on the outside of it near the norwest corner the place whare it Lyes by the Indians was called Kequassagansit and is Laid out to the estate of the sd Stephen Gates for three hundred & fourteen acres. . . .

Stephen Gates came to Hingham from England in the Diligent, A. D. 1638, with wife Ann and two children. From Hingham he removed to Cambridge, and thence to Lancaster in 1654. He was made freeman and chosen constable in 1656. He had sons Stephen, Simon and Thomas, and daughters Elizabeth and Mary. The Gates blood seems to have been of decidedly tropical nature.

The daughter Mary very boldly contradicted the minister in the public assembly. Stephen Gates quarreled with his neighbors, the Whitcombs, was deprived of his constable's staff, and moved away from Lancaster after less than three years' residence. He died at Cambridge, 1662, and his sons attempted, without success, to break his will, alleging that their father "was not of disposing mind." By this will Stephen, the eldest son, received the house and lot in Lancaster. Direct descendants in the male line continued to hold land here, ending with Captain Thomas Gates, who led the Lancaster troop to Cambridge at the Lexington alarm. In 1718 Peter Joslin was in possession of the Gates homestead. Mary Gates married John Maynard of Sudbury.

THE LANDS OF THOMAS JOSLIN

House Lott 20 acors. The house Lott of Thomas Joslin is Scituate Lying and being upon the neck of Land on the east side of the North Riuer bounded by the North Riuer west and Runing easterly in Length untill it come within twenty Rods of the Length of the Lott of Stephen Gates and is bounded by Commons or ways east the Lott of his son Nathaniel Joslin South and the Lands in common [towards] quassaponikin meadows on the north by estamation more or les fourty acres Giuen him by Consent of the town

A Swamp Lying betwen or west [of the lots] of him and his son Nathaniel Joslin the one half thareof to him and [the other half to] his said son by Consent of the town.

his enteruail Lott The enteruail Lott of Thomas Joslin one part thare of Lyeth on the west side of the North Riuer bounded by the said Riuer easterly [and running] northward untill the Riuer and the upland do cut off that percell of enteruail [bounded] south by the enteruail of his son [and] west by the Commons Containing more or Less thirteen acres but scince being more exactly meashured [by those] appointed is found to be but ten acres and twenty Rods: more he hath seuen acors Lying on the North Riuer in one Slip along by the Riuer bounded at the head up the Riuer north [by the] meeting of the Riuer and upland east by the upland south by the Land [of Nathaniel Joslin.]

The Joslin family came from London in the Increase, A. D. 1635, landing in Hingham. Thomas was then forty-three years old, and his wife Rebecca the same age. They brought with them Nathaniel, aged eight years; Rebecca, eighteen; Dorothy, eleven; Elizabeth, six; and Mary, one year. Another son, Abraham, a sailor, came to Lancaster some years later than the father, who was here in 1654. Mary became the wife of Roger Sumner, and Rebecca married —— Nichols. Thomas Joslin died Jan. 3, 1660, and his widow married William Kerley, senior, 16..3..1664, being his third wife. The lands above described extended from the river eastward along the south side of the North Village street.

THE LANDS OF NATHANIEL JOSLIN

his house Lott The house Lott of Nathaniel Joslin is Scituate Lying and being upon the neck of Land on the East Side of the North Riuer being bounded upon said Riuer west and so Runing east in Length untill it Reach within twenty Rods of the Length of the Lott of Stephen Gates and is bounded east by the Commons: South by the Lott of Stephen Gates and north by the Lott of his father Thomas Joslin by Estemation more or Less [fourty] acors

his Swamp Also a certain Swamp Runing betwixt the Lands of him and his father is the one half thareof belonging to Nathaniel Joslin by the towns Gift and the other to his father

his enteruail The enteruail Lott of Nathaniel Joslin [one part] thereof Lyeth on the west side of [the North] Riuer bounded by the said Riuer easterly [by the Commons] west the enteruail of his father thomas Joslin north & of John Smiths South by Estamation Thirteen acors more or Less:

Nathaniel Joslin was born in England about 1627, coming to Hingham with his father in the Increase from London in 1635. He married Sarah, daughter of Thomas King of Marlborough, and had sons Nathaniel, born 1658, and Peter, born 1665; and daughters Sarah, 1660; Dorothy, 1662; Elizabeth, 1667; Rebecca, 1672; and Martha. He was made freeman in 1673. After the massacre he remained in Marlborough, and there died April 8, 1694. His son Peter received the Lancaster home lots, and seems to have added the Gates house lot to his inheritance.

THE LANDS OF MORDICAI MUKLOAD

His home Lott being tenn acors as it was Laid out be it more or lesse, Lyeth in a pine plain near to quasaponikin gate, butting westward vpon the path that goes to quasaponikin interuaile and easterly vpon a little foot path that goes to the medowes at quasaponikin, bounded northward by the skirts of the hill adioyning to the medow. Leauing a Convenient highway acording to the order of the towne fiue Rode wide on that side his Lott, And it is bounded sutherly by the Comons near vnto a swampe sum pte of it Laid out for a half home Lott be it more or lesse tenn acors.

His interuaile Lott being tenn acors be it more or Lesse Lyeth at quasaponikin, buting westward vpon the North Riuer and easterly vpon sum ground Left for a highway, betweene the medowes and the interuailes, bounded sutherly by the Lott of Steeven gats and northerly by the Lott of Nathaniell Josllin.

His medow Lott in the first deuision being two acors or their abouts be it more or Less, Lyeth at Wataquadocke, at the plac wher trauilers pas ouer to malbrow, A cuntrie highway of six Rode wide Lying Cross it, bounded sutherly by the broke and northerly by the vpland, buting westward vpon sum medow Laid out to Jerimiah Rogers, And easterly it is cut of by the vpland coming to the brooke, which medow was first giuen him by the towne, being he had noe estat on the towne booke to draw medow by in deuision. Recorded this 6: 10: mon: 1664 By me Ralph Houghton.

This record is a transcript of the original in Ralph Houghton's hand, which is found bound in with the earliest town records. Mordecai MacLoud signed his mark to the covenant March, 1658. He brought a brother John with him, who was killed in the Rowlandson garrison Feb. 10, 1676. Mordecai MacLoud married Lydia, daughter of William Lewis, 31..11..1670, and had two children: Hannah, born 16..9..1671, and another. The whole family were slaughtered by the Indians Aug. 22, 1675. Their home was at the North Village, near the cemetery.

THE LANDS OF MAJOR SIMON WILLARD

the Rights of John Tinker which is 200^{lb} *and Richard Smith is* 313^{lb} 13^s 10^d

This is a discription of the Second deuision Lands of Mr John Tinker & Richard Smith which by purchas Major Simon Willard Came to be possessor of both before aney second deuision Lands were Laid out therefore thay ware both Laid out together to him as followeth upon the acount of thair estates:

196 *acers* 2 *deuision* first he hath a peice of upland Laid out to him Sumtimes Called by the name of Still Riuer farm bounded Southwest by the enteruail & South or Southeast by sum second deuision Land of Ralph Houghton & easterly it buts partly upon sum meadow of Goodman Wilder and the most part upon Common upland and westerly it buts upon the highway to the plumtrees enteruail and northerly it is bounded by sum second deuision Land Laid out to William Lewis and part by sum other Land Laid out to the estate aforementioned and this peice of Land is Laid out for one hundred ninty six acres be it more or Less highways to Groten to pond meadows & brook meadow allowed for in meashur :

100 *acres* 2 *deuision* Mo·e thare is another peice of upland Laid out to the estate aforesaid known by the name of winter plain which buts northerly upon Common Land Sum part pine Land & partly oak Land & Southerly it buts upo Sum other Land Laid out upon the same acount and easterly it is bounded by hills of Rockey Land which is Common and westerly it is bounded by Common pine Land sum part of it and sum part oake Land Lying betwen the s^d Land & plumtree meadows and is Laid out for one hundred acres be it more or Less :—

32 *acres* 2 *deuision* More there is another peice Laid out on the same acount at the South end of the sd winter plain and is bounded northerly by the sd winter plain for the most part and westerly it is bounded [by] sum Land of William Lewis and easterly it buts upon Common Land & southerly it is bounded by that called the Still Riuer farm and is Laid out for 32 acres be it more or Less a highway to Groten allowed for in meashur :

80 *acres* 2 *deuision* More thare is another peice of upland Laid out upon the Same acount Lying between the aforementioned Lands and Mahamachekamaks hill bounded easterly by Land Laid out to the estate of Edward Brick and westerly by sum hilly stoney Land and it buts northerly and Southerly upon Common Land and is Laid out for eighty acres be it more or Less : a highway Runing throw it at the South end of it allowed for in meashure :—

4 *acres* 2 *deuision* More thare is fower acres of upland Laid out near to the Brook meadow in Common with sum Land Laid out to John Bush which was Giuen him by the town :—

100 *acres* 2 *deuision* More there is another peice of upland Laid out upon the side of Bare hill upon the acount of the aforementioned estate Laid out by order of Goodman Hutson who purchased it of Majer Willard tho the bounds of it are not yet known it Lyeth for one hundred acres all the aforementioned percells of upland are in full the perprotion of upland due to the two estates afore named

Major Simon Willard, son of Richard of Horsemonden, Kent, England, born 1605, came to New England in 1634 with wife Mary Sharpe and daughter Mary, and settled in

Concord. Having been appointed, May, 1657, one of three commissioners to order the affairs of Lancaster, he was persuaded by offers of land grants to take up his residence here, which he did in 1658. He acquired most of John Tinker's rights, and at first resided upon the Waters lot, probably a few rods south of the house of Caleb Symmes, Esq. About 1672 he removed to his Nonacoicus farm, a five hundred acre grant, now included in the town of Ayer. Cyprian Stevens, who married his daughter Mary, 22..11.. 1671, occupied the homestead thenceforward. The Major's sons, Simon and Henry, lived upon the Still River farm. He had before coming to Lancaster attained the highest military grade then recognized, that of Sergeant-Major, and was annually elected Assistant from 1654 to his death, which took place suddenly at Charlestown, April 24, 1676. He had for his second wife Eliza Dunster, who lived but a short time, when he married her sister Mary. Seventeen children were born to him — Josiah; Elizabeth; Mary; Dorothy; Samuel, 1640; Sarah, 1642; Abovehope, 1646; Simon, 1649; Mary 2d, 1653; Henry, 1655; John, 1656; Daniel, 1658; Joseph, 1661; Benjamin, 1665; Hannah, 1666; Jonathan, 1669; and a second Elizabeth. In 1727 Simon Stevens, son of Cyprian, sold the Major Willard homestead, together with the night pasture, to Captain Samuel, son of Henry, the fourth son of Major Simon Willard. Until the Revolution it remained in the possession of his children.

THE LANDS OF JOHN PRESCOTT

A grant of persons in the Infancy of the Plantacion wee whose Names are subscribed doe Agree that John Prescott Shall haue these perticuler pcells wch are Allotted to him, 50 Acors of Entervale more or less allso a litle Corner of Entervale, lying beyound the mill Lott from 2 oakes wch stands by the Riuer and a pine tree marked vppon the Skirts of the vppland, and a Swamp wch hee hath taken in Lew of twelve acors of wett meddow; and 12 acors of wett meddow, 6 of them Lying towards the Lower end of the Still Riuer on this side the great meddow, and the other

6 Lying high vppon the Still Riuer, 4 acors of it on the further side and 2 acors on this side.
EDWARD BREK
WILLIAM KERLY
NATHANIEL HADLOCK
JOHN JOHNSON
JAMES ATHERTON
SAMUEL REANER

I Steephen Day coming vpp to Nashaway & hearing of some disturbance betweene Goodman Prescot & Lawrenc Waters do acknowledg that I laid out in the year 1650: vnto Goodm̄ Prescot 4 acors of wet meddow on the south side & 2 acors on this side on the still riuer where the bridg is, wch 2 acors on this side Lawrenc Waters hath mowed, and at the end of 4 acors of meddow of goodm̄ Prescots Mr Dayes meddows lies in reversion towards that which belongs to him. In witness wherof I haue set to my hand
   This is a true Coppie   STEEPHEN DAY

The house lott of John Prescott vpon which his house stands, being the first lott in that Range of Lotts according to the Record of Grants, in the old Towne book, lying bounded, south by the com̄on, and north by a lott of Steven Dayes, vpon which Philip Knight built a house butting Easterly vpon the highway, that runes between the two ranges of lotts, and west vpon the Com̄on, being twenty acres be it more or less, being eight score rod long and twenty rod wide.

And also a lott lying on the East side of the highway, a little brooke runeing cross the west end of it, which lott is knowne by the name of Ry feild, lying bounded south by a lott of Thomas Sawyers and north by a highway, that runes betwixt the lott of Jno. Moore and it, and it butts easterly vpon the Com̄on that lyeth betwixt his intervale and it, and westerly vpon the high way that lyes betwixt the Ranges of lotts, and lyes as a streete being twenty acres, be it more or less, being fourescore rod long, and forty rod wide.

And his intervale lott lying in a peece of intervale on the west side Nashaway riuer, part whereof lyes between the wading place which is named in the Court grant for the center of the Towne, and the meeting of the riuers lying bounded easterly by the riuer, and west by a hill of vpland within fence, which the Towne gave to him, and his heyres for ever, for his privilege in fencing in his lott, and bounded south by the highway that runes betwixt the lott of Thomas Sawyer and it and north by the burying place hill, and north river, and another part of it lying at the vpper end of that peece of intervale, bounded south and east by Nashaway riuer and north by Thomas Sawyers lott, and west by a hill of vpland both of which parcells being by estimation fifty acres be it more or less, which appears to be his due, by the Records of grants in the old Towne booke, but vpon exact measure according to liberty granted by a Towne order, recorded in the old Towne booke, there wanted six acres, which is made vp in and with a peece of intervale which lyes on the south side of Nashaway riuer over against a peece of intervale of Thomas Sawyers and John Ruges meadow, lying bounded southerly by some vpland granted to him for the building of a sawmill and north by the riuer and east by some intervale that falls within the sawmill lands, and west the vpland meets the riuer, and cuts it off at the riuer all wch parcels of intervale make vp fifty acres be they more or less.

And his meadow lying some part at the Birch meadow there being six acres, bounded east by the still riuer, and south by an intervale swamp, and west by some intervale and a peice of meadow of Thomas James, and north by a peice of meadow that was layd out to Thomas Rowlandson, and six acres at the Still riuer bridge as it is called, bridge meadow, four acres of which lyes on the east side of the still riuer, butting south on the highway that goes to the meadowes, and so to the Ponds, and butting north vpon a peice of meadow of James Atherton, and two acres lying on the west side of the still riuer, bounded east by the still riuer and west by some bushy land, laid out to Mr John Tinker, butting south by the high way that goes to the ponds, and north by a little brooke that runes into the still riuer, all lying for twelve acres be it more or less.

And a swamp Lying on the north side of John Gibsons Hill, betwixt the Hill and the north intervales which he hath taken and accepted for twelue acres of meadows lying bounded easterly by a lott of meadow of Mr Joseph Rowlandsons and southerly by the skirts of Gibsons Hill, and westerly by the Com̃on, and highway, that runes between the house of William Kerley Junr and it, and north & north west by a peice of intervale laid out to Mr John Tinker and north east by the intervale belonging to the mill, wch Swamp lyes for twelue acres of meadow be it more or less.

upland to his Corne Mill. And his vpland belonging to his mill ten acres of which takes its beginning at a little round hill, fourty rod aboue the mill and so runes on both sides the brooke to the riuer, bounded south by some land giuen him for the building a saw mill, and northerly by a peice of pine Land that is com̃on, butting east by the riuer, and west by the little round hill by the mill where his stake stands, and forty acres part whereof lying on the south side of that ten acres, and lying in a corner, and compassed about south and east by the riuer, and bounded west by a pine plain giuen him for the building of a saw mill, and a peice of intervale compassed about by a ledge of Iron Stone Rockes on the north and north west sides and bounded south by Nashaway riuer, all which parcells of Land ly for fifty acres be they more or less wch was giuen him for encouragement to build a corne mill as appeared by a covenant copied out & truly recorded 3^d 10mo. 1659 by me   RALPH HOUGHTON.

The descriptions of Prescott's lands as above given are transcribed from volume III of the Middlesex Registry, being much more complete than the later copies in the Book of Lands. The records of Prescott's special grants from the General Court, and his sale of a twenty acre house lot upon the Neck to Ralph Houghton, have been set down in previous pages. The title to the homestead where he lived until his removal to the vicinity of his mills, was derived from Symonds & King through John Cowdall, a Boston trader, by deed duly recorded in the Suffolk Registry, a copy also being recorded in volume III of the Middlesex Registry.

A Coppie of a deed from John Cowdall

Bee it Knowne by these presents that I John Cowdall of Boston, for good & valluable consideration, by mee in hand receiued, haue giuen, granted, bargained & sold and by these presents do giue grant, bargain, & sell vnto John Prescott late of Watertown my house at Nashaway, and twenty acres of land therevnto belonging and adjoyneing, bounded with John Prescotts owne lott on the east, Steeven Day on the North, and George Adams south, as also twelue acres of wett meadow belonging to it, and fifty acres of Intervale bounded with Penycooke riuer west, and still riuer east, vpon which parcell of land Richard Linton, and Lawrance Waters haue planted corne, together with all appurtenances, conueniences and priueledges, comunes, pastures, mindalls &c belonging & apperteyneing to the said lands to haue and to hold the said house & Lands with all other the appurtenances & priuelidges to him and his heyres for euer, witnes my hand & seale this 5th of the 8mo. 1647.

JOHN COWDALL

Sealed and delivrd In the presence of { WALTER ASPINWALL
RICHARD BAILY

Recorded 5..8..1647   WALTER ASPINWALL *Recorder*

James Wisers deed of Washacum lands

Know all men by these p^{r}sents that I James Wiser of Washakim in the countie of midlesex, Indian, in New England, for good consideratione and mouinge therevnto, but especially for & in consideratione of fouer pounds teen shillings allredy rec^d by me haue giuen grantted bargined sold alinated & confirmed & do by these psents giue grant bargine sell alinate & confirme vnto John Prescott of Lancaster some nintie accers of vnimproued land be it more or lesse lyinge vpon a plaine & twentie accers be it more or lesse beinge a corne feilld lyinge vpon a hill weastward of this plaine bounded by a pond a littill remote easterly frome the plaine: Washakim fort beinge aboutt fiefteene rods frome the neerest pt of this plaine & the hill whear on the Indian field is, weasterly of this plaine, only Adagunapeke & his Aunt & his sister reserue one accer a yere, the hill beinge called by the name of moantuhcake, this land joynes to the farme that the Country gaue John Prescott which allso is bounded by a hill to the south runinge downe to his meadow belonginge to his farme & the countryes land ellsewhear aboutt it, the sayde bargined Pmisses withall and singular ther puiledges & apertananses to be to the sayde John Prescott & his heyers for euer to haue & to hold for his or their pposes & Uesies without any lawfull lett molestatione or disturbance from by or vnder me or any my heyers executors or asignes or any other pson or psons what soeuer fermely bindinge my sellfe my heyers executors & asignes heervnto, & we whose names arre vnder written, Pummannommon & Pompoweagon do afirme and testifie that the aforesayde James Wiser hath full power & right to alinate thes lands & in wittnesse heerto I ye aforesayde James Wiser do putt to my hand and sealle.

The 3 acc^{rs} of brok vpland expressed heerin that is reserued lyes at the northerly end of the feilld. datted this 22^d of the first mo. 1669/70

the marke ⊘ JAMES WISER

Read signed & sealled & deliuered in the presence of
  ye marke of (M) MARY WILLARD
     SIMON WILLARD Jr.
 the marke of C PUMMANNOMMON
 the marke of C; POMPOWEAGON

[From Shattuck Manuscripts in possession of the New England Historic Genealogical Society.]

 See page 91 of this volume.

John Prescott died in December, 1681, possessed of about 700 acres of land, having moreover given lands and a mill at Nonaicoicus to his son Jonas. Three hundred acres of this estate lay about the Washacum Ponds, including the Sterling camp-grounds; he owned nearly all the lands upon which the manufactories and most densely peopled streets of Clinton are located, and one hundred acres in South Lancaster, stretching from the summit of George Hill to the meeting of the rivers. But the sworn inventory of his estate amounted to only 330 pounds 8 shillings. After the completion of his corn mill, he took up his residence near it, and the site of his garrison house has been heretofore noted as near the southeast corner of High and Water streets, in Clinton. The location of his earlier home is important, because from it as a starting point, all the home lots west of the rivers were laid out. Luckily we are left neither to conjecture nor tradition regarding its position. The site of the Symonds and King trucking house, bought of Cowdall, was sold to Nathaniel Wilder for twenty pounds by Jonathan Prescott, in 1697, and is thus described:

> Twenty acres . . . . being in the south end of ye Town where John Prescott Senr and John Prescott Junr some time Lived, being the first Lott in number in that Range of Lotts butting westerly vpon the stated common near Georges Hill, and easterly vpon a highway y^t goeth between the two Ranges of Lotts and southerly it is bounded partly by ye Lott of Jonas ffairbanke and part by a halfe Lott of Daniel Gaines now in ye possession of said Jonathan Prescott, And northerly it is bounded by the Lott of ye said Nathaniel Wilder.

In the settlement of Lieutenant Nathaniel Wilder's estate his son Ephraim received "all the house Lott that formerly belonged to the Prescotts," except one acre, which was set apart for the widow. The direct descendants of Captain Ephraim Wilder have resided upon the property until within the memory of some now living. William Toombs bought it, and the estate is by our older residents often called the Toombs place. This land has lately come into possession of H. A. Marshall.

Reference to the record of Daniel Gains' grant will show that he had "ten acors lying on the top of George Hill . . . and northardly it is bounded by the house lott of John Prescott, and it buts easterly upon the Lott of Jonas Fairbanks." The description of Jonas Fairbank's home lot reads: "it buteth west upon a hill called George Hill and it is bounded . . . . . north by the Lott of John Prescott." Fairbank's lot, now included in the farm of Jonas Goss, extended forty rods along the highway, and from east to west was eighty rods long; that of Prescott, his father-in-law, being half as wide and twice as long, extending to or beyond the crest of the hill.

The Rye-field, with Roper's "Brooke runeing cross the west end of it" as of old, is mostly included in the lands of G. F. Chandler, John A. Rice, W. H. Graham, and Rufus Eager, the road to George Hill forming its northern boundary. May 1, 1698, Jonathan Prescott, in a deed of gift to his son Samuel, transferred "my house Lott known by the name of the Rye ffield . . . . . conteyning one Dwelling house and barne." June 1, 1708, Samuel Prescott, having removed to Concord, sold to Reverend John Prentice all his "houseing, lands, and meadows," including the Rye-field fully described and stated to be "the lott where ye said Samuel Prescott formerly Lived,"— also the intervale "bounded easterly by Nashua River for the most part and Northerly by the burying place . . . . . and North East it butts on the meeting of the Rivers". This intervale now belongs to the Thayer estate, and the existing ditch that separates it from the old burying ground and other uplands was first dug by John Prescott, and is mentioned as early as 1659. A few acres of Prescott's intervale were located a little higher up the south branch of the Nashaway, near the place long familiarly known as the *Old Rock*, but formerly, probably, called *John's Jump*, as that suggestive name is frequently found in old land records attached to some place in that immediate vicinity.

John Prescott, the founder of Lancaster, was the youngest son of Ralph and Ellen of Shevington, Lancashire, England, born about 1604, and married to Mary Platts, Jan. 21, 1629. He is supposed to have been a Cromwellian soldier, and to have left England to avoid religious persecution. He first sailed to Barbadoes in 1638, and thence to Boston in 1640. Soon thereafter he became the holder of one hundred and twenty-six acres of land in Watertown,

and in 1643 we find him prominent among the associates of
the Nashaway Company. His invincible energy, manual
skill, and fertility of resource pushed the enterprise to final
success, in spite of dangers and discouragements which
soon drove all his copartners from the undertaking. Such
as the town became, it was his building. For nearly forty
years he was its very heart and soul, and after the massacre he came back to die at his post, enjoining in his will,
that the worn out mortal part of him should be committed
"to the cõmon burying place here in Lancaster." Over his
grave stands a rude fragment of slate rock, and few are the
eyes that can readily read the characters rudely cut upon
it: "JOHN PRESCOTT DESASED." The footstone with the
date has crumbled away.

John Prescott's children were eight in number: 1. Mary,
baptized at Sowerby, England (Halifax Parish), Feb. 24,
1630; married Thomas Sawyer in 1648. 2. Martha, baptized at Halifax Parish, March 11, 1632; married John
Rugg in 1655. 3. John, baptized at Halifax Parish, April
1, 1635; married Sarah Hayward, 1668; he lived with his
father and succeeded him at the mills. 4. Sarah, baptized
at Halifax Parish in 1637; married Richard Wheeler in
1658. 5. Hannah, probably born in Barbadoes in 1639;
she became the second wife of John Rugg, May 4, 1660,
her Sister Martha, with her twin babes, having died in
1656. 6. Lydia, born in Watertown, August 15, 1641;
married Jonas Fairbank, May 28, 1658. 7. Jonathan, born
probably in Lancaster about 1646; he removed to Concord
after the massacre and became a man of note there, dying
Dec. 5, 1721. 8. Jonas, born June, 1648, in Lancaster;
married Mary Loker of Sudbury, 1672, and was a prominent citizen of Groton. John Prescott's grandchildren
numbered fifty.

THE LANDS OF PHILIP KNIGHT

his house Lott his house Lott being twenty acres Lying on the west
side of Nashway Riuer and the south end of the town being the second

Lott from Goodman Prescuts in that Range of Lotts buting east upon a
Streat or highway that Runs betwen two Ranges of Lotts in that end of
the town bounded south by the Lott of Goodman Prescutt and north by a
Lott of John Johnsons buting west upon the stated Common upon which
Lott Goodman Knight sum time erected a house and Liued thare being
160 Rods in Length and twenty Rods wide Lying for twenty acors be it
more or Less —

his enteruail Lott His enteruail Lott Lying on the east Side of Penicook Riuer In a common feild in the uper end of that enteruail buting
west upon penicook Riuer and east upon the Still Riuer bounded south
by a Lott of John Rigbees and north by sum Land of John Ruggs which
was Laid out to him to make up his enteruail Lott this Lott was Laid
out to Goodman Knight for twenty acors . . . . .

Philip Knight did not sign the covenant. He was probably that Philip who was admitted an inhabitant at Charlestown in 1637, and had wife Margery, and children Jonathan, Philip, Elizabeth, Rebecca, and Mary. He died in 1668, the inventory of his estate being found in the Essex Registry. Knight sold all his rights here, and there is no evidence found to show that when the family name was brought to Lancaster again, after an absence of one hundred years, it was borne by a direct descendant of Philip Knight. The Knight lot was first sold to John Tinker, and purchased of him by Thomas Wilder, who probably established his residence there at his first coming, in 1659. It remained in the hands of his direct descendants until the present century.

THE LANDS OF JOHN JOHNSON.

The first land grants to John Johnson, by an omission of the copyist, have no page in the Book of Lands. This proprietor signed the covenant in 1654, was alloted the twenty acres next north from the Knight lot, and built and lived there. May 20, 1667, John Johnson and wife Mary, of Cambridge, deeded to John Roper, carpenter. "all my Home Lott whereon I sometime lived . . . . bounded south by a house lott of Thomas Wilder and northerly by a highway that runes up into the woods, and it butts East

upon a high way or street that lyes between two ranges of
lotts and west upon a stated comon, with fruit trees, buildings, fences &c". In 1670, John Roper deeded to Archelaus Courser, a "potter" from Boston, who had married his
daughter Rachel, sixteen acres of the John Johnson lot,
and after the death of Archelaus, his son, John Courser,
sold it to Nathaniel Wilder. In 1729 the second Nathaniel
Wilder transferred to his brother Oliver, "Land on which
I formerly dwelt, & is the Lott that was granted to John
Johnson and part of the Lott that was Phillip Knights and
afterwards Thomas Wilders." Johnson came to Lancaster
from Watertown. His wife was Mary, daughter of Thomas
King of Marlborough. His house lott, twenty rods in
width, bordered the southern side of the highway over
George Hill by the school-house.

THE LANDS OF JOHN ROPER

his house Lott   his house Lott is the fourth Lott from John Prescuts in that Rang of Lotts that Lyeth west of the Street or highway that Lyeth betwen two Ranges of Lotts in the south end of the town buting east upon that highway and west upon the stated Common bounded south by the countie high way that Goeth in to the woods, and so whare need shall Require and bounded north on the Lott of John Rugg upon which Lott Goodman Johnson the taylor who sum time Liued at Sudbury bult a house and Liued thare for sum space of time which Lott was sumtime in the possesion [of] Master day of Cambridge it being a hundred and Sixty Rods Long and twenty Rods wide and Lyeth for twenty acors be it more or Less.

his enteruail Lott   His enteruail Lyeth in the north enteruail about the middel of it buting east upon the North Riuer and west upon the upland bounded South by the Lott of John Johnson and north by the Lott of John Moore which Lott is Laid out and Lyeth for twenty acors be it more or Less.

"Goodman Johnson the taylor," was Solomon of Sudbury
and Marlborough. He exchanged, in 1652, "forty acres of
land lying at Nashaway plantation with one Dwelling house
uppon it," for a grant of three hundred acres of Stephen
Day's. Day was one of the first proprietors, and an ener-

getic promoter of the interests of the plantation; but his energy so often outran his discretion that he was constantly in debt. He signed the covenant, but never came to Lancaster to live. His land rights either went to satisfy creditors, or as in this case, lapsed by non-improvement. The town assigned the Solomon Johnson lot to Roper. John Roper was of Norfolk County, England, coming to America when twenty-six years old, in 1639, with wife Alice and two children, Alice and Elizabeth. He for some time lived in Dedham where were born to him Rachel, 1639; Hannah, 1642; Ephraim, 1644; and Benjamin, 1647. He was a carpenter by trade, and a man respected of his neighbors and of good standing in the church, for he was chosen one of the selectmen in 1664. He was killed by the Indians in 1676. Roper's Brook perpetuates his name. In a deed from John Moore to Daniel Hudson, A. D. 1682, the right is reserved "for the occupiers of John Roper's house for ever free liberty to fetch water from the Brook." The George Hill school-house now stands on the southeast corner of the Roper lot. Ephraim Roper succeeded his father in possession of it, and had a garrison house here, which was destroyed and its inmates slaughtered or carried captive in 1697. Nathaniel Wilder, who was administrator of Ephraim Roper's estate, is found in possession of the lot later, and in 1722 the second Nathaniel sold it to Oliver, whose descendants occupied it until the death of Joel Wilder, 2d. James Keyes bought a portion of Roper's town right and had lands laid out near the Marlborough line in 1723.

THE LAND OF JOHN RUGG

House Lott His house Lott Lyeth in the South End of the town in A Rang of Lotts on the West Side of a Street or highway that Runs betwen two Ranges of Lotts being the fifth Lott in that Range bounded Southerly by the Lott of John Roper and Northerly by the Lott of Daniel Gains and It buts Easterly upon the said Street or highway afore[sd] and Westerly it buts upon the stated Common and Lyeth for twenty acres be it more or Less.

Enteruail Lott More he hath his Enteruail Lott in the first deuision Lying on the East side of Nashaway Riuer butting westerly upon the Riuer and Easterly upon the upland and It is bounded Southerly by the Lott of Jacob farrah Sener and Northerly it is bounded by a Lott which was sum time the Lott of Richard Smith now in the possession of Majer Willard and was Laid out for twenty acres . . . . . .

John Rugg had for his first wife Martha Prescott, who died, with her twin babes, in 1656. His second wife was Hannah Prescott, by whom he had children : John, 1662 ; Mercy, 1664; Thomas, 1666; Joseph, 1668 ; Hannah, 1670 ; Rebecca, 1673 ; Daniel, 1678 ; Jonathan, 1681. He was made freeman in 1669. John Rugg's will was proved in February, 1697, and his widow was slain by the Indians the same year, together with her son Joseph, with his wife and three children. The Rugg house lot had been assigned to Henry Kerley in the first allotment, but he refused it, and built on church lands not far from the Rowlandson garrison.

THE LAND OF DANIEL GAINS

his house Lott his house Lott part of [it] Lyeth in a peice of Land that was Left by the Lott of John Rugg and Goodman Kerley where now the Said Daniel hath built an house there being ten acors or thare abouts be it more or less bounded Southardly by John Ruggs Lott and northardly by the Lott of old Goodman Kerley and it buts easterly by the Street or hyway that Runs betwen two Ranges of Lotts and it buts westerly by the stated Common and more he hath ten acors Lying on the top of George Hill be it more or Less bounded Southardly upon the Common and northardly it is bounded by the house Lott of John Prescutt and it buts easterly upon the Lott of Jonas fairbanks and westerly it buts upon the Stated Common both the said peaces of upland Lyeth for his full house Lott of twenty acors be thay more or Less—

his enteruail Lott His enteruail Lott Lyeth on the east side of penicook Riuer and is bounded southardly by the Lott of Jonas fairbanks and northardly it is bounded by sum Enteruail of Lawrence Waters and it buts Easterly upon the enteruail Swamp and west it buts upon the said penicook Riuer A high way runing Cros the Lott to the meadows and to the plumtrees and Lyeth for his full Lott of twenty acors be it more or Less.

Daniel Gaines was a late comer, appearing here in 1660. There is no evidence that he had wife or children, but a brother, "Samuel Gaynes," was appointed administrator of his estate. He was slain in the massacre of the Rowlandson garrison. John Prescott bought the ten acres on the top of George Hill.

THE LANDS OF WILLIAM KERLEY SENER

house Lotts, his own 20 *acors* the house Lott of William Kerley Sener is the Sixth Lott from John Prescutts house Lott northward contains more or Less twenty acors—

his purchased house Lott 20 *acors of Richard Smith* The house Lott of Richard Smith first Granted to the said Richard and afterwards purchased of him by the said William Kerley and now in his possession is the Seuenth Lott from John Prescutts aboue said Containing more or Less twenty acors: These two house Lotts Containing as aforesaid more or Less: fourty acors ioyning the one to the other are Scittuat Lying and being in that Rang of Lotts on the west side of the North Riuer bounded by the Street highway or Common Eastward the woods or Commons westward the house Lott of John Smith northward and the house Lott of Henery Kerley Southward in bredth and Length acording to the order of the town in the Book of Records for that Range

enteruail lotts his own 20 *acors and Richard Smiths* 20 *acors* The enteruail Lott of William Kerley Contains twenty acors more or Less is scituate Lying and being in the north enteruail west of the North Riuer also twenty acors more or Less Granted to Richard Smith and purchesed by the said William Kerley next adioyning to the said twenty acors Southward this fourty acors of enteruail of and belonging to the said William Kerley is bounded by the North Riuer eastward the Commons or common Land westward the enteruail Lott of John Smith north and the enteruail Lott of William Kerley Juner Southward—

William Kerley, "husbandman," from Ashmore, England, came over in "the good Shipp the Confidence of London," April, 1638. We find the family in Hingham first, but of Sudbury in 1641. In 1647 he became freeman. His first wife, Ann, died in Lancaster, 1658. The next year he married Bridget Rowlandson, mother of the minister. She dying, 1662, he took for his third wife Rebecca, widow of Thomas Joslin, A. D. 1664. He died July 14, 1670. It would seem that he had been a soldier, for in the inventory of his personal effects were "Iron cloathes" and a "cutlash." William Kerley was appointed one of the first prudential managers of the town, and seems to have been a very strong willed if not influential member of the board. The Kerley lots are now the homesteads of F. D. Taylor and H. B. Stratton. A deed dated April 30, 1688, from Henry Kerley, then of Marlborough, to Samuel Carter of Woburn, "clerk," transfers "the 6th house lott & three quarters of the 7th house lott," in all thirty-five acres.

Richard Smith's deed of his dwelling-house and twenty acre house lot to William Kerley, senior, is dated June 4, 1658. Smith was of Sudbury, son of John. His first wife, Mary, and her infant, died 27..3^{m}..1654, and August 10 of the same year he married the widow Joanna Quarlls, by whom he had in Lancaster, John, 1655, and Francis, 1657. He appears in 1656 among the proprietors of Groton, but perhaps did not become resident there, although he disappears from Lancaster.

LANDS OF MR SAMUEL CARTER

40 acors of Land Granted to Mr Samuel Carter Mr Samuel Carter hath fourty acres of Land Laid out to him which was a proper Gift of the town Lying at the east end of sum Second deuision Land of John farrahs now in the possession of Mr. Thomas Swift buting west upon s^{d} Swifts Land and easterly upon Swampie Low Land and Southardly it is bounded upon Second deuision Land of William Kerley Sener and northardly by Common plain Land.

Thomas Swift seems to have been a transient resident, perhaps from Milton. He was a non-resident proprietor in 1684, and disappears from the records thereafter. Samuel Carter, a teacher and clergyman, was the son of the Reverend Thomas Carter of Woburn, born 1640, graduated from Harvard College in 1660, died as minister of Groton, 1693. He sometimes preached in Lancaster, between 1681 and 1688. By wife Eunice Brooks he had four sons and four daughters: Mary, 1673; Samuel, 1678; John, 1681; Thomas, 1682; Nathaniel, 1685; Eunice, 1687; Abigail,

1690. None of these births are found in Lancaster Records. The widow Eunice married John Kendall of Woburn, who, with his brother Samuel, were the progenitors of numerous descendants bearing the name Kendall in Lancaster, Leominster and Sterling. John Kendall received a forty acre grant from the town, January 26, 1714, "on the easterly side of Wecapeket Brook." John, Samuel and Thomas Carter occupied the paternal estate purchased of William Kerley's heirs, and there the two last named had large families, which so multiplied the number bearing the family name that it was soon rivalled only by the Willards and Wilders in the Lancaster census.

THE LANDS OF JOHN SMITH

house Lott The upland Lott of John Smith being the Eighth Lott In that Range of Lotts that Lyes on the west Side of the North Riuer and on the west side of the Street or hyway that Lyes betwen the Ranges of Lotts on the South end of the town being by estamation twenty acors being eight score Rods in Length and twenty Rods wide buting East upon the highway or Street that Runs betwen the Ranges of Lotts and west upon the Commons bounded south by the Lott of William Kerley Sener which he bought of Richard Smith and north by the Lott of William Kerley Juner lying for twenty acors be it more or Less.

enteruail Lott His enteruail Lott being twenty acors Lying on the west side of the North Riuer bounded east by the Riuer and west by the Common upland and South by the Lott of William Kerley Sener which he bought of Richard Smith and north by a Littel Run of water or Brook Ranging acording as the Brook Runs it being his due and his Lott Giuen and Granted him by the town. . . . .

John Smith was father to Richard before named, and to Ann, the wife of John Moore. He came from Sudbury with wife Mary, who died 27..10^m. 1659. In 1660 he gave the intervale lot above described to John and Ann Moore, and March 18, 1663, he deeded to Adam Waters "all my dwelling house in aforsaid Lanchaster wherein I lately lived," with the house lot described above. Adam Waters died A. D. 1670, and his brothers, Stephen Waters and John Skeath, sold the Smith lot to Thomas Ross, a weaver from Woburn. On the 5th of 2d month, 1669, John Smith transfers all his then estate to John Moore, with this condition: "Now in my old age I being old and infirme, & not able to improve land, nor to maintayne myself by my labours nor to pay publique charges for my land, therefore in consideration of my foresaid son John Moore & his wife are to keepe mee duringe my naturall life." .... He died July 16, 1669. His will mentions children — John, Richard, Ann and Alice.

LANDS OF WILLIAM KERLEY JUNER

house Lott his house Lott which is acording to his Grant in the old town book the ninth Lott from John Prescutts Lying and being on the west side of the highway that Goes to the north enteruail and to Wallnutt Swamp and it buts Easterly upon that highway and westerly upon the Stated Common and it is bounded Southardly by the Lott of John Smith and north by sum second deuision Land of William Kerley Sener and It Lyeth for twenty acors be it more or Less—

enteruail Lott More he hath his enteruail Lott Lying and being in the north enteruail and according to his Grant appears to be the fourth Lott thare and it buts easterly upon the North Riuer and westerly upon Common [land] and is bounded Southerly by the Lott of John More and northardly it is bounded by the Land [of] William Kerley Sener and it Lyeth for twenty acors be it more or Less

William Kerley, junior, came from Sudbury, signing the Nashaway covenant in 1653. He was made a freeman in 1666, having removed to Marlborough, where he became ensign. He died January 4, 1684. No children are named in his will, although by first wife, Jane, he had three daughters: Mary, 1667; Sarah, 1668; and Hannah, 1670. A second wife, Anna, daughter of Thomas King, survived him. He sold his Lancaster lands to Abraham Joslin, Jr., who perished with his wife and child in the massacre of 1676. In 1693-4, Henry Kerley and the Joslin heirs transferred the "House lot of Wm Kerley" to Thomas Harris, a butcher from Boston, who had married the widow Rebecca Crocker, or "Croakham," Abraham Joslin's sister. Thomas

Harris in 1682 had bought the lands of John Ball, who was killed in the massacre. Ball's lands are not described in the Book of Lands, although he was one of the first inhabitants. Harris died 1698. Abraham Joslin also sold fifty acres to Nathaniel Robinson, with a proprietor's right. Nathaniel Hapgood possessed lands at Bare Hill and elsewhere, laid out to the right of William Kerley, junior.

THE LANDS OF JOHN MORE

his house Lott The house Lott of John More Lyeth on the west side of the North Riuer and on the east side of the highway or Street that Runs betwen the two Ranges of Lotts that are Laid out in the South end of the town being called the first Lott from the Lott of John Prescutts in the Records of Grants in the old town book and it Lyes bounded South by a highway that Runs betwen the Lott of John prescutt Called the Ry field and it and bounded north by Gipson hill and buting east upon the Common and west upon the Street or highway Runing betwen the two Ranges of Lotts his Lott being four score Rods in Length and fourty Rods wide Lying for twenty acors be it more or Less—

his enteruail Lott His enteruail Lott Lying in the north enteruail being Called the fifth Lott In the Records of Grants in the old town Book and it Lyes bounded north by the Lott of William Kerley Juner and south by the Lott of John Roper buting east upon the North Riuer and west upon the upland being twenty Rods wide and Eight Score Rods in Length it Lying for twenty acors be it more or Less.

By a deed dated March 25, 1682, "John Moore of Sudbury sometime of Lancaster" transferred to Daniel Hudson "All his House lot in the sd Lancaster upon wh. he the said John More built a House & for some time Lived, Lying betweene Gibsons Hill, & John Prescot his Rye field, & is bounded southerly by a Highway" . . . . . reserving "¼ acre in some place neer the highway, as also Liberty for the occupiers of John Ropers house for ever free liberty to fetch water from the Brook that runs on the Lot near the west end." Daniel Hudson being slain by the Indians, September 11, 1697, his son Nathaniel possessed the Moore lot, but removing to Billerica, sold it to John Buss of Concord, a tailor, for 400 pounds, June 1, 1709. March 25,

1719, John and Hazadiah Moore transfer to John Buss the reserved one-fourth acre above named, describing it as "on the north side of a Highway w^h lies between it and a Lott now belonging to the Reverend Mr John Prentice . . . . . . Something in a square form, in south east corner of sd lott, bounded south by sd Highway, east by land that was called stated Common, North & west by part of sd lott." Samuel Locke became the next owner, purchasing of the second John Buss in 1742.

Two John Moores signed the Lancaster covenant — one in 1653, the other a year later. But one, however, shared in the first allotments, if we may trust the Book of Lands. John Moore of Sudbury, in his will proved in 1674, leaves to his son John of Lancaster, "five shillings and no more, for I have given him his portion formerly." This John married in Sudbury, November 16, 1654, Ann, daughter of John Smith. Their children born in Lancaster were Mary, 1655; Elizabeth, 1657; Lidia, 1660; John, 1662; Joseph, 1664; Ann, 1666; Jonathan, 1669; and Maria. The same date, 10..1^m 1670–1, marks the birth of Maria and the death of the mother, Ann. John Moore became Ensign, and died in 1702, leaving a widow Mary. He removed from his first home and built upon Wataquadock about 1665, for in that year, in an exchange of lands with Ralph Houghton, he mentions "my new dwelling house at Wataquadoke." John Moore, junior, was delegate to General Court from Lancaster, in 1689. His sons John and Jonathan lived to ripe old age upon the paternal acres, south of Wataquadock.

THE LANDS OF THOMAS SAWYER

house Lott his house Lott Lyeth on the east side of the Street or highway that Runs betwen the two Ranges of Lotts on the south end of the town bounded west by the Street or highway and east by the Common that Lies betwen the enteruail and it bounded south by the Lott of Jacob farrah and north by the Lott of John Prescutt called the Rie field this lott being Eightie Rods in Length and fourty Rods wide and Lyeth for twenty acors be it more or Less *his enteruail Lott*   His enterual Lott Lyes in a peace of enteruail that Lies on the west side of Nashaway Riuer bounded northward by the highway that Goes to Wataquadok and south by sum part of the enteruail Lott of John prescutts and east and south east by the Riuer and west it buts with an angle upon the Common or pine hill acording to the Records of Grants in the old town book it was first Laid out for twenty acors but upon trial by exact meashur it was found to want five acors which the town Granted to be made up twenty and it was Confirmed by the Committee and is made up with and by a peice of enteruail that Lies up Nashaway Riuer. . . . .

Thomas Sawyer was a blacksmith, of Rowley, 1643. He came to Lancaster in 1647, and married Mary Prescott, by whom he had children : Thomas, 1649; Ephraim, 1651 ; Mary, 1653; Joshua, 1655; James, 1657 ; Caleb, 1659; John, 1661 ; Elizabeth, 1663; Nathaniel, 1670. Over his grave in the old yard the headstone records that he died Sept. 12, 1706, aged about ninety years. Thomas, junior, who seems to have inherited a share of his grandfather John Prescott's energy and capacity, established the second saw-mill in Lancaster before 1700, upon Deans, now Goodridge, Brook, at the dam near the Deer's Horns school-house. Upon the Sawyer house lot now stand the church and several dwellings of the Seventh Day Adventist Society. The venerable Mrs. Sally (Sawyer) Case, a direct descendant of Thomas Sawyer, lives very near the original house site. An ancient dwelling, with stone chimneys, was torn away, just in the rear of the present house, when it was built in 1812. June 18, 1701, Sawyer transferred half of this house lot to his youngest son, Nathaniel, it being described as the " south side of the Lott bounded north by rest of lott & south by a narrow Lane or way lying betwixt it and the lot of Jacob ffarer & it butts east & west on highways." June 14, 1706, he transfers the above described intervale to Nathaniel, stating its southern bound to be upon "some intervale land in the possession of Thomas Sawyer, Jun. & known by y[e] name of Johns Jump about 15 acres." At the same date he gives eight acres of the northern half of his house lot to his oldest son, Thomas, "he having sold 2 acres before" to him. This last is the farm lately owned by L. G. Cilley.

THE LANDS OF JACOB FARRAH

house Lott   The house Lott of Jacob farrah upon which his house stands Lying South from the North Riuer and west from Nashaway Riuer in a Rang of Lotts on the east side of the Street or highway that Lyes betwen two Ranges of Lotts buting west upon that Street or highway and east upon the Common that Lies towards Johns Jump a place so called bounding north by the Lott of thomas Sawyer and South by the Commons where thare was a Lott sum time Laid out to John Rigbe a Littel Brook Runing cros the west end of it near to the end, and a highway of a Rod wide Lying betwen the Lott of Thomas Sawyer and it which Lott being fower score Rods in Length and fourty Rods wide ondly upon his Request for a Conuenient place to build a house the Square of his Lott was altered and the South west corner Runs out twenty Rods further and the South east corner so much in which Lott Lyeth for twenty acors be it more or Less.

his enteruail Lott   The enteruail Lott of Jacob farrah Lyeth on the east side of Nashaway Riuer by which Riuer it is wholley Bounded on the west side and on the east side at the east end it is bounded by sum meadow called the frog holes and so downward by the pine plain buting South by a Swamp called pins Swamp and north by John [Ruggs] Lott one highway Going threw it two ways the bay [road] and another highway Goes down the enteruail to the meadows both of them being two Rods and half wide either of them so much of which Lott is his own Lott of enteruail Granted him by the town and was laid out to him for twenty acors . . . . .

The "highway of a rod wide" above stated as the north bound of Farrar's land is the east and west street, known as the Narrow Lane, on which the Seventh Day Adventist meeting-house stands. Near an unfailing spring beside Roper's Brook there was visible, many years ago, a depression marking a half filled cellar; and various relics of a residence were there frequently ploughed up, but no one could remember even a tradition of a house standing there, or of its ownership. Possibly this may have been the location of the Farrar home, though the extension of the southwest corner would rather indicate a site on the high ground opposite of Jonas Goss barn. The Farrar entervale was just east of the Atherton bridge.

Jacob Farrar came to Lancaster with an older brother John, in 1653, from Woburn. John returned thither, transferring his land allotments to Jacob, who prepared a home for his family left behind him in Lancashire, England. His wife Ann with four children — Jacob, John, Henry and Mary — joined him in 1658, bringing 168 pounds 7 shillings additional estate. Two of the sons, Jacob and Henry, were slain by the Indians in 1675 and 1676, the former leaving a wife Mary (Hayward) and four sons — Jacob, George, John and Henry. John, another son, died Nov. 3, 1669, leaving two children, Mary and John, and wife Mary (Hillard). In his inventory is the item, "Timber prepared for a house." After the massacre, Jacob Farrar, with his wife and daughter Mary, who had married John Houghton, junior, in 1672, fled to his relatives in Woburn, where he died Aug. 14, 1677. The name Farrar very seldom appears thereafter in Lancaster. The widow Ann married John Sears of Woburn in 1680. In the old burial ground is a venerable headstone inscribed, "ANNA SERS," which, perhaps, marks her grave. John Houghton purchased all the Farrar lands, A. D. 1700.

THE LANDS OF RICHARD WHEELER

house Lott first he hath his house Lott whereon he built near unto danes Brook bounded southerly by the Lott of John Houghton and partly by the Common and northardly by the Stated Common and easterly and westerly it buts upon the Stated Common Lying for twenty acors be it more or less together with sum small additions one adioyning to it and another Lying near Johns Jump —

Enteruail Lott More he hath twenty acors of enteruail laid being his enteruail Lott in the first deuision Lying on the east side of Nashaway Riuer lying in two peices bounded westwardly by the Riuer and easterly by the upland and buts Southerly upon sum enteruail of thomas Sawyer and northardly upon the upland and Riuer meeting —

Wheeler's home lot must have been partly included in the estate of the late Sally Flagg. One portion of his in-

tervale is mentioned more than once in early records as
Abram's Hole. Old residents sometimes used this name,
applying it to a deep place in the river, near the Scar now
called Emerson's Bank. It seems to be, however, a chance
survival of the disused provincial English term *holl,* meaning a small area of ground sunken below its surroundings.
Abram's Hole is a depressed and hill-girt meadow seen
across the river east from the north extremity of High
street, in Clinton. Richard Wheeler came here from Medfield. He married John Prescott's daughter Sarah, Aug.
2, 1658, and had children born in Lancaster: Jacob, 1663;
Zebediah, 1664; Sarah, 1666; Elizabeth, 1669; Samuel,
1671. He was made a freeman in 1669, and was killed by
the Indians in 1676. His widow married Joseph Rice of
Marlborough. Samuel went as a soldier in the Canada
expedition, and died 1691. David and Hezekiah Whitcomb came into possession of Wheeler's rights.

THE LANDS OF JOHN HOUGHTON

his house Lott his house Lott where upon he hath built and planted Lyeth on the north side of Deans Brook bounded Southerly by the said Brook and northerly by the Lott of Richard Wheeler and easterly it buts upon the mill path and westerly it buts upon sum Land of his own that is part of his second deuision and it Lyeth for twenty acors be it more or Less.

his enteruail Lott His enteruail Lott [is] on the east side of Penicook Riuer and is bounded westerly and norwest by the said Riuer and it is bounded easterly by the enteruail Swamp a highway of two Rods and half Runs through it to Go to the meadows and to Groten and that part of it that Lyeth on the east side the path buts southerly by sum Land of James butler and northerly it buts upon a high way that Goes into Goodman Wateres Littel Round Meadow that Way Lying betwen it and sum Land of John More now in the possession of Jeremiah Rogers and the other part of it that Lyeth on the west side the path is bounded southerly by sum enteruail Land of Goodman Wateres Runing with a Corner up into the bent of the Riuer and it buts northardly with an angle upon Goodman White his feild so called both percels of enteruail Lyeth for his Lott and for twenty acors be it more or Less.

John Houghton came from England in the Abigail, 1635,

being then a mere boy. A rude slate stone in the old yard records his death April 29, 1684. His wife's name was Beatrix. Although he signed the covenant in 1653, it is doubtful if he came here to reside for several years, as the records of his children's births are not found as of Lancaster until that of Beatrix, in 1665. In his will he mentions his "seven children." They were John, born about 1650; Robert, 1658; Jonas; Mary; Beatrix, 1665; Benjamin, 1668; Sarah, 1672. During the desertion of the town the family sought refuge in Charlestown. At the re-settlement the sons established new homes east of the river, upon Bridecake Plain, now known as the Old Common. The intrusion of so fanciful a baptismal name as Beatrix among the otherwise rigidly scriptural designations of the family, denotes, perhaps, an imaginative tendency in some member of it, and this found freer scope in the naming of real estate acquired. Thus we find in John Houghton's various parcels of land, "Rosemary meadow," "Horse swamp," "Houghton's park," "Cranberry meadow," "The meadow of the three fountains," "Job's corner conveniency," and "Tobacco pipe meadow." The daughter Beatrix married John Pope, Sept. 20, 1683. The oldest son, John, became the most prominent citizen of Lancaster in his day, for many years serving in various town offices, and as representative, and justice.

THE LANDS OF JONAS FAIRBANKE

his house Lott The house Lott of Jonas fairbanke Lyeth on the west Side the Street or highway that Lyeth betwen two Ranges of Lotts in the South end of the town buting east upon that highway or Street and it buteth west upon a hill Called George hill and it is bounded South by the Common and north by the Lott of John Prescutt this Lott being eighty Rods In Length and fourty Rods wide Lyeth for twenty acors be it more or Less —

his enteruail Lott His enteruail Lott Lyeth on the east side of Penicook Riuer below the Common feild bounded south by the Lott of Jacob farrah which came to him by the acount of his brother John farrah and north it is bounded by a Lott which is since Granted to Daniel Gains it buts East upon a peice of Swampie brushie enteruail the highway Crosing that end of it and it buts west upon Penicook Riuer which Lott is Laid out to him for twenty acors be it more or Less —

Jonas Fairbank came from the same English township as the Prescotts, being the son of Jonathan Fairbank, who settled in Dedham. His marriage to Lydia, daughter of John Prescott, 28..3mo. 1658, is the first recorded in Lancaster. He had seven children: Mary, 1659; Joshua, 1661; Grace, 1663; Jonathan, 1666; Hazadiah, 1668; Jabez, 1670; Jonas, 1673. He, with his son Joshua, were killed by the Indians, Feb. 10, 1676, and his widow married Elias Barron of Watertown, afterwards of Groton and Lancaster. Fairbank's home was upon the farm now owned by Jonas Goss. By later allotments he acquired lands southward, including much of the farm now belonging to George A. Parker. Certain items in his inventory indicate that he was a carpenter by trade. His house lot had originally belonged to George Adams, whose right fell to the town through his inaction and absence. Of Fairbank's sons, Jonathan was killed by the Indians in 1697; Jonas removed to Watertown; Jabez retained the paternal estate, attained prominence in town affairs, and as a lieutenant, gained some reputation in the Indian war. In the year 1700 he had lands laid out to him, "on both sides of danes Brook aboue Thomas Sawyers Sawmill." This site became the home of the Fairbanks, and so remained for a hundred years or more. George W. Howard now owns their homestead.

THE LANDS OF JOHN RIGBE

house Lott The house Lott of John Rigbe Lyeth on the East Side the highway or Street that Lyeth between two Ranges of Lotts in the South end of the town buting west upon that high way and east upon the high way that Goes to the South meadow bounded south by the Common which he hath now taken ten acors of it for part of his Second deuision and bounded north by the house Lott of Jacob farrah where he now dwelleth, this Lott is Laid out for ten acors and is Eighty Rods Long and twenty Rods wide and Lyeth for half a home Lott be it more or Less — .

His enteruail Lott His enteruail Lott Lyeth on the east side penicook Riuer a Littel below whare the North Riuer and Nashaway Riuer meeteth buting west upon the Riuer and east partly upon the upland and part upon the Still Riuer the Still Riuer Runing down through part of it bounded South by the Lott of Richard Smith now in the possession of Maior Simon Willard and bounded north by the Lott of Phillip Knight now in the possession of thomas Wilder this Lott being Laid out to him for ten acors be it more or Less —

The marriage of John Rigby and Elizabeth ———, in Lancaster, August 30, 1662, is duly recorded. Rigby was probably of Dorchester, son of John. He survived the massacre of 1676, but thenceforward disappears from Lancaster records. The family name clings to an old highway between Clinton and the Deer's Horns district, and a little brook long bore the same name, for reasons not discovered. In 1715, James Wilder sold to Jabez Fairbank lands once Rigby's. His first house lot is perhaps mostly included in the estate of the late Stedman Nourse. Near Roper's Brook thereon is a hollow marking an old cellar, close to which, fifty years ago, were the decaying trunks of two huge apple trees — perhaps relics of the Rigby home.

THE CHURCH LANDS RECORDED

the enteruail for as much as in the begining of this plantation of Lancaster the men apoynted by the General Court to Sett forward and to order and dispose of the affairs of this plantation and amongst the Rest of thair fundimentall orders which are upon Record in the old town book and also to be found in the Book of orders thare is an act Stating of thirty acres of upland and fourty acres of enteruail but upon seueral Considerations the town not well waying that former act haue nesesitated disposing of the Greatest part of the enteruail Land so as that thare is none left for the use aforesaid but a little peice by master Rowlandsons house about four acres which Lyeth bounded northardly by the Brook and part by master Rowlandsons fence and Southerly by the pine hill that is Laid out for Church Land and easterly it buts upon a hill of upland of master Rowlandsons and westerly it buts upon the meadow at Gipson hill :—

the upland the thirty acres of upland is Laid out Southerly from the enteruail and is bounded northerly by the said enteruail and by sum Land of master Rowlandson and Southerly by the Stated Common one Corner mark being a pine tree by the enteruail hill Gate and another in a Little Swamp and easterly it is bounded by Goodman Prescutts and Goodman Sawyers fence and westerly it is bounded by the Stated Common and is laid out for thirty acors be it more or Less by Jacob farrah and Ralph Houghton :—

the meadow The meadow Laid out by the four men apoynted and Impowered to Lay out the first deuision of meadows on the east side of the hemp Swamp and Lyeth bounded easterly by sum pine Land of Ralph Houghton and westerly by sum brushie enteruail Land of Edward Brick and thomas Joslin and Ralph Houghton which is there for Conueniancie and it buts northerly upon a swamp of the said Ralph Houghtons and southerly upon a pine hill.

Recorded this 15: March 1669/70: by me RALPH HOUGHTON

THE LANDS OF THOMAS WILDER

his house Lott his house Lott p^{to} wherof is situate Lying and being within a Certain tract of Land Stated by the town for a Common it being allowed by the town at the same time the Common was Stated Lying near to the Walnutt Swamp and Red Spring upon the Riuer a Littel below both buting east upon the North Riuer and west upon the Common and also bounded South and north by the Common there being Seuenteen acors Laid out to him: and three acors Lying bounded east by his enteruail at the Walnutt Swamp whare he hath fenced and brok up Land and west by the Stated Common buting north upon the North Riuer and Runs with a Sharpe angle coming to nothing at the south end and Runing into the Line of his enteruail both of which percels of Land are Laid out to him for twenty acors be thay more or Less—

his enteruail Lott His enteruail Lott Lying at the Walnutt Swamp the Gratest part of it bounded easterly by the North Riuer and westerly by his three acors of upland and partly by the Stated Common butting northardly upon the North Riuer and Southardly upon his Seuenteen acors of upland part of his house Lott a highway Crosing the enteruail from the neck to the Commons at the usual place where the herd useth to pass ouer the North Riuer the highway being fiue Rods wide there being sixteen acors and fourty Rods the Rest by which it is made up twenty acors Lyeth below upon the Riuer begining where his Seuenteen acors of upland ends and so foloweth the Riuer to an elbo or bend in the Riuer and a Great pine tree on the Common on the upland a Litle before Goodman Joslins enteruail coms in bounded easterly by the Riuer and west by the Stated Common buting north upon his Seuenteen acors of upland and Southarly upon that bent in the Riuer and Great pine tree both of which percels of enteruail is Laid out to the said Goodman Wilder for twenty acors be they more or Less.

Thomas Wilder, or, as he signed himself, "Wyellder," never resided upon the above house lot, but bought of John Tinker a house and land half a mile south, next to John Prescott's Cowdall purchase, then known as the Knight lot. This remained the home of the Wilders for more than one hundred and fifty years. Wilder was about forty years of age when he came here from Charlestown, in 1659. He had been admitted to the church there in 1640, and was made freeman in 1641. Upon his arrival in Lancaster he was at once installed in the position of selectman, vacated by John Tinker's removal. He died October 23, 1667. The inventory of his estate sums 405 pounds 18 shillings. There are named in his will, his wife Ann, and children Mary, Thomas, John, Elizabeth, Nathaniel, and Ebenezer. None of these were born in Lancaster. Thomas and John, at the re-settlement of the town established their homes on Bridecake Plain, now known as the Old Common, living on the north side of the highway. Nathaniel retained the old homestead, and was there an inn-keeper for nearly twenty-five years. During the war of the Revolution, twenty-two soldiers bearing the family name Wilder served for Lancaster, then including Sterling. In the year 1798 there were seventeen landholders in town named Wilder, exceeding the number of Willards, the next most frequent patronymic, by four. Thomas Wilder's daughter Mary married Daniel Allen, a cooper in Charlestown, and upon a gift of forty acres of land from her father, they came to Lancaster, bringing children born in Charlestown and Watertown, but after some years' residence here, returned to Watertown. Their son Ebenezer returned to Lancaster, and his son Ebenezer was a man of note here in revolutionary times. The Allen homestead is in the borders of Clinton, and now occupied by E. A. Currier. Benjamin Allen, who had children born in Lancaster before the massacre, was probably a brother of Daniel. In 1716, Thomas Tucker had lands under Thomas Wilder's rights, near Clamshell Pond.

THE LANDS OF MASTER JOSEPH ROWLANDSON

his enteruail Lott and Land in Lew of a house Lott He hath twenty Six acres of enteruail and also Thirteen acres of upland the enteruail Giuen him in Lew of an enteruail Lott and the upland in Lew of a house Lott by the town and it Lyeth togather all in one peice as it was Laid out by Jacob farrah and Ralph Houghton in the night pasture within that fence that was formerly sett up by the Copartners bounded northardly by the sd night pasture fence part of the fence being standing when the Land was Laid out, Southardly by the North Riuer easterly by penicook Riuer and westerly by the Lott of Richard Smith then in Possession of Master John Tinker and northeast by the town highway in the night pasture the whole Lyeth for thirty nine acors be it more or Less. Recorded this : 15 : 1 : mon : 1669   By me RALPH HOUGHTON

Sufficient has been said of the origin of the name "night pasture," in former pages. This land is now divided among many owners, and cut in twain by a highway. The larger portion is in the farm of Charles L. Wilder. In 1687, Joseph Rowlandson, the son of the minister, sold it to Philip Goss, merchant, of Boston, who died in 1698. John, the son of Philip Goss, sold it to Simon Stevens, and he, May 5, 1727, transferred it to Captain Samuel Willard, together with the Major Simon Willard homestead adjoining it on the west. The minister's residence was never upon this land, but for his convenience was located quite near the meeting-house, which stood on the highest ground in the middle cemetery. The Rowlandson property in that place is not described in the Book of Lands, but its bounds have been discovered elsewhere. Joseph Rowlandson, junior, probably came back to Lancaster and rebuilt, for January 20, 1687, calling himself of Lancaster, he deeds to Philip Goss :—

his Dwelling house in Lancaster and orchard and all ye Land about the house as it lyeth boundèd Easterly by a street or highway and westerly partly by a brook and partly by some ministeriall meadowish Land and it, and butts southerly upon a little Hill by the Meeting House, & northerly upon some Comon Land according as it is already fenced . . And also other peice of Land known by ye name of burying place ffield, bounded Northerly by the North Riuer, and southerly by Jonathan Prescotts Land, and it buts Westerly upon the said street or highway and Easterly it buts upon the Land of Jonathan Prescott taking in both upland and Intervale a high way lying through it to the burying place, and also a peice of Intervale known by the name of Kerley Intervale . . . . and also a house Lott of Twenty acres . . . . upon which George Newby liues [*near Walnut Swamp*] . . . . and his meadow Lott in the first Division lying neer Gibsons Hill . . . .

Nov. 22, 1710, Philip and Judith Goss of Brookfield deeded the homestead to Hooker Osgood, a saddler, from Andover:

being the place where Mr Joseph Rowlandson formerly liued one part thereof lying on the east side of the highway on which peice the Barn standeth, It is by estimation about ten acres of upland and Intervale . . . . bounded west by the highway northerly by the North Riuer and comes to a point neer the meeting of the Riuers, and bounded southerly partly by ye burying place and partly by some Land now in possession of Mr John Prentice . . . . Reseruing liberty of conuienient passage for the Inhabitants of Lancaster to the burying place, also one Barn & fencing standing on ye Land, also about six acres more or less lying on ye west side of sd highway on which land ye Dwelling house formerly stood [*it was burned by Indians*, 1704] together with all orcharding & fencing on sd land, and is bounded easterly by the highway towards the Bridge and westerly by a Brook and partly by ministers medow and butts southardly on a peice of ministry Land and northerly it comes neer to the Riuer by the Bridge . . . .

Thomas Rowlandson, the father of the minister, must have come from Ipswich to Lancaster very soon after his son's settlement, with wife Bridget, but his name does not appear among the grants of lands. He died here, Nov. 17, 1657, and his widow married William Kerley, senior, 31..3^m. 1659. A curious item in the inventory of his estate, which summed 113$^£$. 9^s. 9^d., is: "Old shop tools Damnified by salt water, being Left at Charlstown by the Sea Shores, a Long season, accounted at 3$^£$."

Joseph Rowlandson, born in England, was sole graduate at Harvard College in 1652, began to preach at Lancaster, 1654, and was ordained in 1660. He married Mary, daughter of John White, and had children: Mary, 15..11..1657, died 20..11..1660; Joseph, 7..1..1661; Mary, 12..6..1665; Sarah, 15 Sept., 1669. He went to Wethersfield, April, 1677, as colleague of Reverend Gershom Bulkeley, and died suddenly, Nov. 3, 1678. The son Joseph died in Wethersfield, in 1713.

THE LANDS OF JAMES BUTLER

his house Lott and enteruail first he hath a tract of Land being for the most part pine Land Laid out to him to the southward of the Cold Spring which is Laid out to him for 134 acors be it more or less so much being his due acording to order and Grant of the town to him 20 acres whereof is for a house Lott and 40 acres in Lew of an enteruail Lott, 60 acors for his second deuision of upland and 14 acors in Lew of his second deuision of enteruail and it Lyeth all together and it buts easterly upon a Rokey bushey hill of Common upland and westerly it buts upon a pine plain the South west corner marke standing near to a brook taking in the Brook and southerly it is bounded by hillie pine Land for the most part and northardly it is bounded by pine Land and sum Rocky Called Ratel Snake hill the northeast Corner is near to sum Land of Edmon Parker

James Butler, in 1664, received from Rebecca Joslin, widow of Thomas, certain land east of Still River. The above lands, recorded 1666, are upon the east slope of Wataquadock, and there his son James lived after the massacre, the elder James Butler dying March 19, 1681, and his widow, Mary, marrying John Hinds.

THE LANDS OF JOHN HINDS

John hinds hath his thirtie acre lott Granted by the town Lying one the east side of the Nashaway Riuer in seueral places one peice Lying to the Southeast of Ratlesnake hill . . . . More he hath a peice Laid out at the head of the Little Brook that Runs threw James Butlers Land near his house place . . . . .

John Hinds, and Mary, widow of James Butler, were married Feb. 9, 1681–2. Hinds came from Woburn. By a former wife he had a son James, and perhaps others. By Mary, in Lancaster, he had John, 1683; Jacob, Hopestill, Enoch, Hannah, Deborah, and Experience. He removed to Brookfield, but his son John remained on the homestead, southeast of Wataquadock.

THE LANDS OF JOHN WARNER AND JOHN PRIEST

their 2 : 30: *acre Lotts* Part whereof is Laid out acording to town Grant on the eastward side of Bare hill easterly it is bounded by sum Common undiuided upland baring towards Goodman Moors meadow and westerly by the assent of bare hill for the most part and south and north by Common undeuided upland and Lyeth for 24 acres be it more or Less: more thay haue another peice Laid out for 36 acres be it more or Less on which thay haue built bounded northerly by sum Land of Nathaniel Wallis [*Wales*] and on all other sides by common undiuided upland and is Laid out to them for their two thirty acre Lotts . . . . .

John Warner was from Woburn, where, by wife Sarah, he had children: John, 1684; Sarah, 1686. A headstone in the Old Common Cemetery records the death of Rebekah Warner, daughter of John and Sarah, March 30, 1718, aged 20. Samuel and Ebenezer Warner, taken into the church 1713–16, were sons of John.

John Priest was also from Woburn, where were born his children: Elizabeth, 1679; John, 1681; Daniel, 1686. The homes of Warner and Priest were upon the eastern slope of Bare Hill in Harvard, where John Priest commanded a garrison in 1704.

THE LANDS OF WILLIAM HUDSON

30 *acres Granted by the town* 6 *acres for killing wolues* William Hudson hath his thirty acre Lott Granted by the Town Laid out on the north side a Range of Lotts in the south end of the town next to the Stated Common twenty acres be it more or Less bounded southerly by a Lott whear George Newbey Liues and northerly by the Stated Common and it buts easterly upon a highway that Leades to the Lotts in the north enteruail and to Walnutt Swamp and westerly upon the Stated Common And also Sixteen acres be it more or Less ten acres whearof is part of his thirty acre Lott and six acres due to him by a town agreament for killing of wolues the whol sixteen acres Laid out in a plain that Lyeth west or South west from Walnutt Swamp . . . . .

[Recorded 1687.]

William, son of Daniel Hudson, was born June 12, 1664, in Lancaster. In 1690 he was prosecuted for bastardy, made a brilliant but unavailing written defence, and fled, so far as the records show, never to return. His neighbor,

George Newby, about the same date was convicted of being a libertine, probably a thief, and certainly — what was perhaps esteemed more unpardonable in those days — a slanderer of the minister, and a despiser of the catechism. He, too, disappears. They lived on George Hill, perhaps not far from the Divoll place. Newby lived upon land belonging to Joseph Rowlandson.

LANDS OF JOHN BUSH

30 *acre Grant* Twenty acres of upland formerly Granted John Bush by the town is Laid out near Makamachekamucks hill . . . . John Bush hath more ten acres of Land Giuen him by the town Laid out in three seueral places 5 acres whareof Lyeth on the east side the plumtree meadows on both sides a little brook Called Bemans Brook . . . . one acre whearof is allowed for a highway through his Land to Joshua Athertons House two acres more or Less Lying on both sides a Little Brook Called Kerleys Brook . . . . fower acres more or Less Lying on the north west side of Bare hill . . . .

[Recorded 1684 and 1694.]

Besides the town grant, Bush had lands given him by Major Willard, which his son John sold to Samuel Willard and Benjamin Bellows, with the above grant, in 1710. John Bush, senior, died Sept. 1, 1688, leaving a widow, Hannah (who married ——— Rutter) and two children, John and Sarah.

THE LANDS OF JAMES FROST

30 *acres his first Lott* A discription of a 30 acre Lott formerly Laid out to Nathaniel Wales by uertue of a town Grant but now in the possession of James frost as appears by a Later Grant of the town to him the sd frost and also with the Consent of Nath.ll Hutson who had formerly had a Grant of sd Lott by the town but sence Resigned it up to the town again Laid out to sd frost the most part of it on the east side of bare hill bounded easterly by the Land of John Warner & Southerly by Common Rockey Land and northerly by Common undiuided Land on the sd bare hill and westerly by common Land baring towards the meadow path and is Laid out for 25 acres : and another peice of Swampy meadowish Land . . . . Laid out for thirty acres be thay more or Less togather with 30 pounds Right and estate on the town Book :—

[Recorded 1694.]

Nathaniel Wales was of Milton. James Frost was, perhaps, of Billerica. As neither of these grantees appear again in land records, they probably abandoned their claims.

THE LANDS OF JOSIAH WHEELER

The Lands of Josiah Wheeler Granted him by the town being his 30 acre Lott and other deuision : there is Laid out to the sd Josiah Wheeler twenty three acres of his first Lott Lying whear he first built not far from the hog swamp his house Standing near the middle of sd Land . . . . and buts on Marlbrough path the east Line part of it Runs ouer a Rockey hill and takes in a Long pine Swamp at that side and a little aboue the house the Line turns with a short Crook and so Runs up to Marlbrough path this peice 23 acres more he hath seuen acres Laid out upon the brook that Runs from hog Swamp meadows to Spectacle meadow near whare sd Brook Coms out of the hog Swamp meadows and Lyeth mostly on the north side of the Brook . . . . both peices is Laid out for his first thirty acres Granted him by the Town Read the 5th : of february 1699/ 10 in order to be Recorded :—

In the church records, 1710, "Josiah Wheeler and his wife from Concord church," were admitted members of the Lancaster church. Nahum Ward purchased ten pounds town right of Josiah Wheeler, on Wataquadock, about 1718.

THE LANDS OF JEREMIAH WILLSON

30 acre Lott Granted by the town Jeremiah Willson hath his 30 acre Lott Granted by the town Laid out in three places on the east side Nashaway Riuer one peice Lying near the Cold Spring by the Countrey Road bounded north by the Countrey high way and South by the Common Land and west by Sum Land of Gamaliel Beman adioyning to it and east by Sum Common Land Left for a Cart way to James Butlers Land whare his house stood and the said peice of Land is Laid out for six acres and half be it more or Less :— More he hath a peice Laid out on the hill aboue that bounded east by sum Land of Roger Sumner and west by Common Land and South by Common Rockey Land and north by Sum Common Land that Lyeth betwixt it and the Countrie highway and Lyeth for fourteen acres be it more or Less . . . . More he hath a a peice of Land Laid out on the top of Wataquadoke hill on the north side the Countrie highway to Marlbrough buting South on the sd way and north on sum Land of Nathaniel Joslin Joyning to his southwest Corner marke and east and west it is bounded by plain Common Land and is Laid out for nine acres and half be it more or Less: and was Laid out by John Houghton all the sd three peices of Land are Laid out for his full due for his thirty acre Lott be it more or Less :—

[Recorded 1690.]

Jeremiah Wilson was the son of Benjamin of Charlestown. The stone over his grave in the Old Common burial ground tells us that he died March 22, 1743, aged 77 years. He was an active church member at the coming of Reverend John Prentice, and had sons Benjamin and Nathaniel.

THE LANDS OF JOHN MOORE

A discription of Sum Land Laid out for John Moore being part of the Lott Granted for him by the town and Land belonging to it he hath one peice Laid out near the Cartway that Lyeth Round Wataquatock hill in an ash swamp . . . . . 3 acres be it more or Less : . . . . . one peice of Land Laid out to John Moore part of his 30 acre Lott in a plain . . . . six acres be it more or Less: and also he hath about three quarters of an acre Laid adioyning to thair former Land by their house at the place whare a yong orchard is planted . . . . . More Laid out for sd John Moore about 50 acres of Land being part of the Lott and Lands in deuisions belonging that was Granted for him by the town and Lyeth on the east side of the way to Marlbrough part of it was formerly Laid out by Insine John Moore and Lyeth in one Intire peice and bounded westerly partly by sd Road and partly by a Spruce Swamp . . . .

[Recorded 1708-9 and 1714-15.]

THE 30 ACRE LOTT GRANTED TO JOSEPH MOORE

A discription of the thirty acre Lott Granted for Joseph Moore and since his Death sd Lott is acounted to his brother Jonathan Moore & is Laid out to him as followeth . . . . . part of said Lott is Laid out near to hog Swamp . . . . laid out for two acres be it more or less :—more he hath another peice Laid near to it being a long slip of meadowish Ground . . . . two acres be it more or less :—more he hath a peice of upland laid out towards the Great hill by hog swamp meadow adjoyning to his former Land . . . . . twelue acres be it more or Less :—more he hath a Long Slip Lying betwen that and his house in the edge of a swamp bounded west by his former Land . . . . fiue acres be it more or Less : . . . . . ten acres formerly marked out by Insine John Moore . . . . nine acres of the said ten is Laid out to the said Jonathan Moore to make up his first 30 acors and one acre on the acount of the 30 pound Right Granted with sd Lott : . . . . . .

[Recorded 1708-9.]

20

John, Joseph and Jonathan Moore were sons of Ensign John and Ann (Smith) Moore. In the oldest Bolton burial place, east of Wataquadock, the headstones above the graves of John and Jonathan state that the former died in 1740, aged 79 years, and the latter in 1741, aged 74 years. They had a garrison east of Wataquadock in 1704.

THE LANDS OF CALEB SAWYER

A discription of Sum Land Laid out for Caleb Sawyer January 14: 1716/17 He hath fifty six acres and a half of Land Laid out in one intire peice on the easterly side of Bare hill whear the sd Caleb Sawyer now Liueth and is bounded southerly for a Considerable part of that Line upon a highway . . . . . and hath a highway of fiue Rods wide Lying through sd Land allowed for in meashur sd way being near 90 Rods in Length in sd Land . . . . . twenty six acres and half is part of his 30 acre Lott in the first deuision Granted him by the town and was Laid out to him formerly by Ralph Houghton and is now encompased and Included within the Lines aboue priscribed the whole Laid out for fifty six acres and half more or Less: the other part of his first deuision of his 30 acre Lott Lyeth on the easterly side of Bare hill towards the northerly end it being a peice of meadow Ground called the horse meadow . . . . .

Caleb Sawyer was the fifth son of Thomas Sawyer, and grandson of John Prescott, born 1659.

SAMUEL BENNETS LAND

Samuel Bennits 30 acre Lott Granted him by the town now Sheafs A discription of the thirty acre Lott Granted to Samuel Bennit and since Exchanged by him for the thirty acre Lott formerly Granted by the town to John Willard the said Lott Granted to Samuel Bennit being now in the possession of William Sheaf of Charlstown Laid out one the west side of bare hill a Little distant from Joshua Athertons meadow and is bounded on all sides by common undiuided Land It being Eighty Rods Long and Sixty Rods wide: the discription whearof was Read before the town the fifth day of february: 1693/4 in order to be recorded . . . .

Samuel Bennett was the son of George, who was the grandson of Richard Linton. George Bennett was slain in Monoco's raid, Aug. 22, 1675, and left widow Lydia and children — John, born 1659; Mary, 1661; Samuel, 1665; George, 1669; Lydia, 1674. Samuel owned Linton's lands in the centre of Lancaster. Samuel Bennett's saw-mill, "up the north river," is mentioned as early as 1717. He died 1742, aged seventy-seven years. Bennett sold his John Willard lot to Joseph Waters, and it was by him transferred to Isaac Hunt.

JOHN WILLARDS LAND

John Willards Lott 30 *acres all Laid out hear* This day being the first of february 1691/2 the town Confirmed the Same to Benjmin Willard John Willards Lott now in the possession of Benimin Willard is Laid out in seueral peices one part whareof Lyeth betwen the Lands of Henery Willard and Zebadiah Wheelers Land bounded westerly by Henery Willards Land & easterly by Henery Willards & Zebadiah Wheelers Land and southerly by sum of his own Land Lying partly in a triangle: and he hath another peice on the south side of Zebadiah Wheelers Land and westerly it buts upon Henery Willards Land & easterly it buts upon or near the Great pond meadow . . . . more he hath ten acres Lying near the Brook meadow . . . . which makes up his compliment of thirty acres Granted him by the town: Recorded this first february: 1691/2

p JOHN HOUGHTON *Recorder*

If this land grant were proof of residence, Lancaster could perhaps claim one victim, at least, to the hideous persecutions for witchcraft. What relationship this John Willard bore to Benjamin and Henry, whose lands bordered upon this grant, has not been discovered. But the date of the record and the transfer to Benjamin, favor the opinion that this was the John Willard who had lived at Groton and suffered death at Salem after his attempted escape and capture at Lancaster. Robert Calef, in "More Wonders of the Invisible World," tells us:

John Willard had been imployed to fetch in several that were accused; but taking dissatisfaction from his being sent to fetch up some that he had better thoughts of, he declined the Service, and presently after he himself was accused of the same Crime and that with such vehemency, that they sent after him to apprehend him: he had made his Escape as far as *Nashawag*, about 40 Miles from *Salem:* yet tis said those Accusers did then presently tell the exact time, saying now *Willard* is taken.

He was tried for witchcraft, convicted upon the absurd statements of his accusers, and hung Aug. 19, 1692. A full account of his trial is given in "Groton in the Witchcraft Times," by the Honorable Samuel A. Green.

THE LAND OF CAPT BORDMAN

<blockquote>
Laid out for Capt Bordman one hundred Acres of Land being Granted by the town to his Grandfather Stephen Day near Waschacomb one peice of sixty acres thareof Lyeth upon a hill called waschacomb hill upon the north side thareof . . . . the other fourty acres Lyeth under a Great hill aboue a meadow called prescutts meadow . . . . Laid out february the 4th : 1718
</blockquote>

William Boardman, the grandson of Steven Day, and administrator of his estate, received the above grant as some recognition by the town of the services of one, who, more than any other of the first proprietors, save John Prescott, aided in establishing the settlement and forwarding its interests. Steven Day of Cambridge, England, reached America in 1638, being, though a locksmith by trade, brought over as a printer by the Reverend Jesse Glover. Glover died during the passage, but Day, early in 1639, set up for the widow the first printing press in America north of Mexico, and during that year printed "the Freemans Oath" and an almanac, and the next year, "the Book of Psalms." In 1641 the General Court took notice of his enterprise, as follows:

<blockquote>
Stephen Day, being the first that set upon printing, is granted 300 acres where it may bee convenient wthout preiudice to any town—

[Massachusetts Records.]
</blockquote>

But Day is soon found in financial difficulties. In 1643 the court released him from jail upon his giving "100$^£$ bond for his appearance when he is called for," and in 1644 he is again under duress, sending from prison a petition for relief, complaining of the harsh dealing of creditors. In 1647 he had been deposed from the management of the Cambridge press, his son Matthew, first steward of Harvard College, receiving his place. Matthew died in 1649, and Day became a journeyman printer at the press he had set up, under Samuel Green, where he remained until his death, in 1667. He never lived in Lancaster, though often here. He owned two house lots, that next Prescott's Cowdall purchase on the north, which he sold to Phi lip Knight, and the lot afterwards assigned to John Roper, which Day obtained of Solomon Johnson, exchanging for it his three hundred acre grant, above mentioned. His land rights here were all vacated finally by his inability to improve them.

In Massachusetts Archives, xxx, 134–5, is the following petition of Steven Day, giving his own estimate of his labors in behalf of Lancaster in its infancy:

To the Honoured Generall Court now sitting at Boston:

The humble Petition of Steven Day: In most humble wise sheweth; That whereas yor Petition^r was one of the first vndertakers for the Plantation now called Lancaster, & for the furtherance of the Planting thereof at great expences of time & estate with both English & Indians, for the gaining of a placid entertainment with the one, & helping on the other, as is well known to the Inhabitants of that place, as allso in part to my neighbors who were eye witnesses of my continued burthen, either by being absent from my ffamily, which was then more considerable than (through Gods Providence to me) now it is: or by entertaining both English & Indians at my own house from day to day for some yeares together: yet so it hath hapned, that although many others haue increased their estates & comforts, by acquiring to themselues great Accomodations (by reason of divine Providence obstructing my personall residence there) I haue failed of such personall Accomodations in that place: And after all my Labo^r & expence of time, strength & estate, although through Gods blessing on my endeavo^{rs} I haue a Town & a Church of God there setled, to behold as the birth of my Labo$^{r.}$ which I esteem a greater Reward from God, then my own particular advancement: yet cannot rejoyce in any Lands therein acquired to me or mine. Now so it is, that the Sagamore of that Plantation [*Matthew*] (his ingenuity somewhat exceeding others of the barbarous Natives,) remembring my former kindnesses, hath by Deed of Gift giuen & granted vnto me & my heires for ever, all his Right in a certain Tract of Planting Land, by him there for a long time possessed:

My humble request therefore is for this favo^r. That a Comittee of meet persons appointed by this honoured Court may be impowered to bound out the said Land vnto me, according to the intent of the Law determining the Indians Right: with such an addition of Meadow as may happen to fall within the Planting Lands: And that the same may be Legally setled on me & mine by the Authority of this honoured Court.

And yor Petion^r shall ever pray &c.

Endorsements 1 The Committee haueing pused this Peticon: do Judge meet that 2 or 3 meet persons be impowered to veiw & bound to ye Peticioner, what shall appear to be granted him by the Indians according to ye true intent of ye law setling the Indians right, and y^t some small accomodacion of meadow be added thereto not exceeding 40 acc^{rs}—

THOMAS DANFORTH
EDWARD COLLINS
HENRY BARTHOLOMEW

21 – 3 – 1667

2. The deputyes doe not approue of the returne of the comittee in answer to this petition, but doe Judge meete to graunt the pet^r libertie to procure of the sd Indians by sale or otherwise to the quantitie of one hundred & fifty Acors of vpland, & this Court doth also graunt to the pet^r twenty Acors of meaddow where he can find it free from former graunts & all wth refference to the Consent of o^r Honored Magists. hereto.

24 – 3 – 1667— Consented to by ye magist^s

WILLIAM TORREY *Cleric*

Stephen Day died before the close of the year 1667.

The papers from the case of "Administrator of Steven Days Estate, vs John Roper," found in Middlesex Court Files, give some facts in our local history not set down in town records:

To the Marshall General or his Deputy or to the Constable of Lancaster or his Deputy—

You are hereby required in his Majesties name to attach the goods or in want thereof the person of John Roper Senr of Lancaster and take bond of him to the value of two hundred and fifty pounds with sufficient surety or suretyes for his appearance att the next County Court holden att Cambridge upon the first day of October next, There and then to answer the complaint of William Bordman of Cambridge in an action of the case for denying of the said Bordman full and true possession of house and Lands that is att present in the possession of said Roper in the town of Lancaster which sometime was in the hands of Solomon Johnson Senr now of Marlborough and after that in the hand of Mr Stephen Day of Cambridge which house and lands with the appurtenances and priveledges

thereto belonging doth by due and true right belong unto the said William
Bordman with all due Damages about the same and hereof you are to
make a true return under yor hand and not to fayle. Dated this 26 of
July 1667   By the Court. SAMUEL GREEN
[*Endorsed.*]

  I have attached the possessions of John Ropper and taken security,
by the consent of the Plaintiff, his own Bond.

             EDWARD MITCHELL *Marshall*

 Verdict. In the case depending betweene William Bordman & John
Roper we find for the defendent. Costs of Court.

Accompanying above is a copy of the town's grant of
1653, and this certificate :

  This may certify any man vnto whom these p^{r}sents may com. that
about 9 years ago Mr Day of Cambridge laying claim to a lot somtime
in the possession of Goodman Johnson of Marlborough, the Town was
willing he should possess prouided he would subscribe to the orders of the
Town which he readily consented to, and subscribed his hand to our Town
book, wherin was this Act of the Town vpon Record. That euery one
bound themselues to build, plant land and inhabit within one whole year
after this acceptance of their lots or els to loose all their charges and Lots
and pay 5^{lb} to the Town, and herevnto Mr Day subscribed his hand the
15th 1st month 1653. But he neuer came to inhabit, nor do anything about
building or breaking Land vnto this day nor bear any publick charg, but
about 6 or 7 years ago goodman Roper who somtime liued at Charlestown, desired to com to liue among vs, and had a liking to that Lot being
Mr Day had forfeited it by his not keeping covenant wth ye Town. Yet
notwithstanding the Town had so much respect to Mr. Day that they
allowed him that goodman Roper should pay to Mr Day what buildings,
fencing &c might be worth which both Mr Day and goodman Roper consented vnto. They made choise of vs whose hands are subscribed to
jvdg betwixt them what it may be worth that is to say the building and
fencing as aforsaid, and it was judged that goodman Roper should pay 15^s
to Mr Day.

  Lancaster this 9 : 8 month : 1662. Witnesses
                JOHN PRESCOTT
                RALPH HOUGHTON
  Sworne in Court 1 : 8th : 1667 by y^e ptys subscribed as attests
               THOMAS DANFORTH *Re*

  The lott in question was that upon the east end of which the George Hill school-
house now stands.

BIRTHS, MARRIAGES, AND DEATHS

IN

LANCASTER FAMILIES,

1645–1700.

A YELLOW and torn leaf from original records, in the hand-writing of Ralph Houghton, was, in 1826, discovered by Josiah Flagg, town clerk, among the papers of Captain Hezekiah Gates, and has been carefully preserved. It contains the dates and names of fifty births in Lancaster previous to 1666. The returns of the two earliest clerks of the writs, Ralph Houghton and Cyprian Stevens, seem, however, to have been regularly made to the Middlesex Court, and as found in the Middlesex Registry, have been printed in the New England Historical and Genealogical Register, XVI, 352–9, and XVII, 70. Ten years had elapsed, however, from the founding of the first homes on the Nashaway, before Ralph Houghton was made clerk of the writs and began his returns; and for dates previous to 1656 he must have relied upon family memorials and individual recollections. Errors and omissions for that period therefore doubtless exist. If records were kept between 1686 and 1700, no trace of them has been found. The first book of such records in the town archives contains a disorderly mass of material, its dates covering the eighteenth century. Of its three hundred and sixty pages one-third are devoted to "marriage intentions." The death roll is especially scant, having but three dates earlier than 1718. The birth records are at first by families, and in some cases may be complete from 1700. The book bears evidence of having been begun by John Houghton, but probably not before 1718, if so soon, the earlier births being gathered from family records. The following chronologically arranged lists embrace those of the Middlesex Registry, and such other births, marriages and deaths in Lancaster families to A. D. 1700, as have been ascertained from various sources. When copied from an *original* record the orthography of the recorder has been retained.

BIRTHS.

The first birth noted by Ralph Houghton is that of Joseph Waters in 1647. It is quite possible that earlier births than this were unrecorded, for in previous pages it has been shown that the Prescott and Waters families were here in 1645 and 1646, and to each a son was added during those years, the place and exact date of whose birth have not been discovered. In a deposition Nov. 6, 1683, Jonathan Prescott is called "about thirty-eight," and in another of 1670,"twenty-three years old." The list of the Waters family, on a preceding page, shows so remarkable a regularity of periodic increase as almost to prove that a child was born here in 1645, or brought into the wilderness at an exceeding tender age. Perhaps Adam Waters was the first white child born in Lancaster, and Jonathan Prescott the second.

A. D.	Month.	Day.	Name.	Parents.
1645?	—	—	Adam Waters.	Lawrence and Ann (*Linton*). [*not recorded*].
1646?	—	—	Jonathan Prescott.	John and Mary (*Platts*). [*not recorded*].
1647	2	29	Joseph Waters.	Lawrence and Ann.
1648	—	—	Jonas Prescott.	John and Mary. [*not recorded*].
1649	1	1	{ Jacob Waters. { Rachell Waters.	Lawrence and Ann.
1649	5	2	Thomas Sawyer.	Thomas and Marie *(Prescott).*
1650	11	16	Ephraim Sawyer.	Thomas and Marie.

A. D.	Month.	Day.	Name.	Parents.
1651	3	26	Daniel Hudson.	Daniel and Joanna.
1651	11	14	Samuell Waters.	Lawrence and Ann.
1652	11	4	Marie Sawyer.	Thomas and Marie.
1653	1	26	Johanna Waters.	Lawrence and Ann.
1653	4	11	Marie Houghton.	Ralph and Jane.
1653	7	7	Marie Hudson.	Daniel and Joanna.
1654	3	23	—— Smith.	Richard and Marie.
1654	3	13	James Atherton.	James and Hanna.
1654	8	28	Marsa Parker. / Ester Parker.	Edmund and Elizabeth *(Howe)*.
1655	1	13	Joshua Sawyer.	Thomas and Marie.
1655	2	28	John Houghton.	Ralph and Jane.
1655	9	4	Marie More.	John and Ann *(Smith)*.
1655	11	6	Debora Parker.	Edmund and Elizabeth.
1655	11	17	*Twins* Rugg.	John and Martha *(Prescott)*.
1655	11	20	John Smith.	Richard and Johanna *(Quarlls)*.
1655	11	27	Ephram Waters.	Lawrence and Ann.
1656	3	13	Joshua Atherton.	James and Hanna.
1656	11	1	Sarah Hudson.	Daniel and Johanna.
1657	1	22	James Sawyer.	Thomas and Marie.
1657	5	1	Joseph Houghton.	Ralph and Jane.
1657	5	15	—— Josllin.	Nathaniell and Sara *(King)*.
1657	6	26	Frances Smith.	Richard and Johanna.
1657	9	27	Elizabeth Moore.	John and Ann.
1657	11	—	Henrie Kerley.	Henrie and Elizabeth *(White)*.
1657	11	10	Hanna Atherton.	James and Hanna.
1657	11	15	Marie Rowlandson.	Joseph and Marie *(White)*.
1657	11	26	Marie Davis.	Samuell and Marie *(Waters)*.
1658	4	21	Nathaniell Josllin.	Nathaniell and Sara.
1658	11	11	Elizabeth Hudson.	Daniel and Johanna.
1658	11	22	William Kerley.	Henrie and Elizabeth.
1659	2	20	Caleb Sawyer.	Thomas and Marie.
1659	4	20	Marie Fairbanke.	Jonas and Lidia *(Prescott)*.
1659	5	31	John Bennit.	George and Lidia *(Kibbie)*.
1659	8	1	Experience Houghton.	Ralph and Jane.
1659	11	9	Icabod Rogers.	Jerimiah and Bia.
1660	2	6	Lidia More.	John and Ann.
1660	5	15	Sara Josllin.	Nathaniell and Sara.
1660	11	4	Joseph Willard.	Simon and Marie *(Dunster)*.
1660	11	6	Johanna Hudson.	Daniel and Johanna.
1660	11	17	Marie Atherton.	James and Hanna.
1661	1	7	Joseph Rowlandson.	Joseph and Marie.
1661	2	3	Noah Beman.	Gamaliell and Sara *(Clark)*.
1661	2	6	Josua Fairbanke.	Jonas and Lidia.

A. D.	Month.	Day.	Name.	Parents.
1661	2	6	John Sawyer.	Thomas and Marie.
1661	6	19	Mary Bennitt.	George and Lidia.
1661	10	20	Waitestill Sumner.	Roger and Mary *(Joslin)*.
1661	12	17	Sarah Houghton.	Ralph and Jane.
1662	1	4	Dorathy Josllin.	Nathaniel and Sarah.
1662	1	10	John Hudson.	Daniel and Joanna.
1662	2	7	John More.	John and Ann.
1662	4	4	John Rugg.	John and Hannah *(Prescott)*.
1662	8	1	Hittabel Rogers.	Jeremiah and Abiah.
1662	10	8	Rachell Courser.	Arklous and Rachell *(Roper)*.
1663	2	18	Thankefull Beaman.	Gamaliell and Sarah.
1663	5	2	John Rigby.	John and Elizabeth.
1663	5	8	Hannah Kerley.	Henry and Elizabeth.
1663	5	26	Joseph Josllin.	Abram and Beatrix.
1663	5	31	Barrachia Lewis.	John and Hannah.
1663	8	4	Jehosephat Rogers.	Jeremiah and Bia.
1663	9	15	Grace Fairbanke.	Jonas and Lydia.
1663	9	25	Jacob Wheeler.	Richard and Sarah *(Prescott)*.
1663	11	5	Elizabeth Sawyer.	Thomas and Mary.
1664	2	17	Samuell Allin.	Daniell and Marie *(Wilder)*.
1664	4	12	William Hudson.	Daniel and Joanna.
1664	5	11	Mercy Rugg.	John and Hannah.
1664	5	15	Abigail Houghton.	Ralph and Jane.
1664	6	3	Simon Courser.	Archelaus and Rachel.
1664	7	28	John Divoll.	John and Hannah *(White)*.
1664	8	20	Joseph Moore.	John and Ann.
1664	11	2	Zebediah Wheeler.	Richard and Sarah.
1665	?	?	Benjamin Willard.	Simon and Mary.
1665	5	17	Steeven Gates.	Steeven and Sarah *(Woodward)*.
1665	July	22	Samuell Benit.	George and Lidia.
1665	6	5	Mary Sumner.	Roger and Mary.
1665	6	8	Rebecca Lewis.	John and Hannah.
1665	6	12	Mary Rowlandson.	Joseph and Mary.
1665	9	12	Josiah Whetcomb.	Josiah and Rebecca *(Waters)*.
1665	10	3	Beatrix Houghton.	John and Beatrix.
1665	12	22	Peter Joslin.	Nathaniel and Sarah.
1666	5	6	Abiah Rogers.	Jeremiah and Abiah.
1666	5	13	Bethia Lewis.	John and Hannah.
1666	5	17	Ann Moore.	John and Ann.
1666	—	—	Deborah Sawyer.	Thomas and Mary.
1666	7	15	Thomas Rugg.	John and Hannah.
1666	8	6	Hannah Willard.	Simon and Mary.
1666	8	6	Elizabeth Atherton.	James and Hannah.
1666	8	7	Jonathan Fairbank	Jonas and Lidia.

A. D.	Month.	Day.	Name.	Parents.
1666	8	14	Mary Kerley.	Henry and Elizabeth.
1666	10	14	Marie Joslin.	Abram and Beatrix.
1666	11	7	Elnathan Allen.	Daniel and Mary.
1666	11	7	Josiah Whetcomb.	Josiah and Rebecca.
1666	12	1	Sarah Wheeler.	Richard and Sarah.
1667	Jany	6	Bathsheba Rogers.	Jeremiah and Abiah.
1667	April	28	John Wedge.	Thomas and Deborah.
1667	May	26	Mehittable Beaman.	Gamaliel and Sarah.
1667	June	7	Elizabeth Joslin.	Nathaniel and Sarah.
1667	June	12	Hannah Divoll.	John and Hannah.
1667	Aug.	3	Simon Courser.	Archelaus and Rachel.
1667	Sept.	7	Abigail Hudson.	Daniel and Joanna.
1667	Oct.	16	Hannah Houghton.	Ralph and Jane.
1668	Jan.	1	Anne Hudson.	Daniel and Joanna.
1668	Jan.	21	Patience Lewis.	John and Hannnh.
1668	Feb.	20	David Whitcomb.	Josiah and Rebecca.
1668	Feb.	28	Hazadiah Fairbank.	Jonas and Lidia.
1668	March	26	George Bennett.	George and Lidia.
1668	April	11	Jaazoniah Sumner.	Roger and Mary.
1668	May	12	Mary Wedge.	Thomas and Deborah.
1668	May	25	Benjamin Houghton.	John and Beatrix.
1668	June	18	Mary Farrar.	John and Mary (*Hillard*).
1668	Sept.	17	Hannah Whetcomb.	Jonathan and Hannah.
1668	Dec.	15	Joseph Rugg.	John and Hannah.
1669	Feb.	2	Mary Prescott.	John and Sarah (*Hayward*).
1669	Feb.	20	Thomas Allen.	Daniel and Mary.
1669	Feb.	26	Jonathan Whitcomb.	Jonathan and Hannah.
1669	March	28	Joseph Kerley.	Henry and Elizabeth.
1669	March	29	Jacob Farrar.	Jacob and Hannah (*Hayward*).
1669	May	19	Jonathan Moore.	John and Ann.
1669	May	24	Elizabeth Wheeler.	Richard and Sarah.
1669	June	1	Deborah Atherton.	James and Hannah.
1669	Sept.	15	Sarah Rowlandson.	Joseph and Mary.
1669	Sept.	27	Josiah Divoll.	John and Hannah.
1669	Nov.	28	John Farrah.	John and Mary.
1669	Dec.	14	Jonathan Willard	Simon and Mary.
1670	1	30	Joshua Wedge·	Thomas and Deborah.
1670	3	11	Mary Courser.	Archelaus and Rachel.
1670	5	17	—— Lincorne.	William and Elizabeth.
1670	6	16	George Farrah.	Jacob and Hannah.
1670	9	24	Jonathan Kettle.	John and Elizabeth (*Ward*).
1670	9	24	Nathaniel Sawyer.	Thomas and Mary.
1670	11	2	Hannah Rugg.	John and Hannah.
1670	11	8	Jabez Fairbank.	Jonas and Lidia.

MASSACHUSETTS. 1643-1725.

A. D.	Month.	Day.	Name.	Parents.
1671	1	10	Maria Moore.	John and Ann.
1671	2	29	Samuel Wheeler.	Richard and Sarah.
1671	3	2	*Twins* Prescott.	Jonathan and Dorothy.
1671	3	15	Nathaniel Hudson.	Daniel and Joanna.
1671	4	20	John Lewis.	John and Hannah.
1671	6	29	Hannah Whetcomb.	Jonathan and Hannah.
1671	7	10	{ Benjamin Allen. { Hannah Allen.	Benjamin and Hannah.
1671	8	9	Rebecca Sumner.	Roger and Mary
1671	9	12	Rebecca Whetcomb.	Josiah and Rebecca.
1671	9	16	Hannah McLoud.	Mordecai and Lidia (*Lewis*).
1671	9	26	Israel Rogers.	Jeremiah and Abiah.
1671	10	27	Mary Whetcomb.	Job and Mary.
1671	11	30	Mary Sawyer.	Thomas Jr. and Sarah.
1672	1	5	William Bennett.	George and Lidia.
1672	2	8	William Divoll	John and Hannah.
1672	2	10	Jonathan Prescott.	Jonathan and Dorothy.
1672	2	18	Joseph Atherton.	James and Hannah.
1672	3	14	Rebecca Joslin.	Nathaniel and Sarah.
1672	4	10	Martha Kerley.	Henry and Elizabeth.
1672	4	27	Ruth Whitcomb.	John and Mary.
1672	5	30	Sarah Houghton.	John and Beatrix.
1672	6	6	John Farrar.	Jacob and Hannah.
1672	6	26	William Lincorne.	William and Elizabeth.
1672	9	22	Mary Steevens.	Cyprian and Mary (*Willard*.)
1672	9	24	John Prescott.	John and Sarah.
1672	11	26	Priscilla Roper.	Ephriam and Priscilla.
1672	12	13	John Houghton.	John Jr. and Mary (*Farrar*).
1673	1	12	Abigail Allen.	Benjamin and Mary.
1673	1	23	Samuel Waters	Samuel and Mary (*Hudson*).
1673	3	6	Jonas Fairbank.	Jonas and Lidia.
1673	3	16	Rebecca Rugg.	John and Hannah
1673	5	11	John Wilder.	John and Hannah.
1673	6	10	Martha Sawyer.	Thomas and Mary.
1673	11	2	Susanna Rogers.	Jeremiah and Abiah.
1673	11	2	William Lewis.	John and Hannah.
1673	11	26	William Sumner.	Roger and Mary.
1673	12	26	Elizabeth Lincorne.	William and Elizabeth.
1674	1	8	Johanna Whitcomb.	Josiah and Rebecca.
1674	2	17	Jacob Houghton.	John Jr. and Mary.
1674	3	5	Abigail Whitcomb.	Jonathan and Hannah.
1674	3	9	Beatrix Joslin.	Abraham Jr. and Ann.
1674	6	7	Lidia Bennett.	George and Lidia.
1674	?	?	Sarah Whitcomb.	John and Mary.

Born in Lancaster Families during Exile after the Massacre.

A. D.	Month.	Day.	Name.	Parents.
1675	—	—	Nathaniel Wilder.	Nathaniel and Mary (*Sawyer*).
1676	1	2	Thomas Wilder.	John and Hannah, in Charlestown.
1677	August	13	Simon Stevens.	Cyprian and Mary, in Boston.
1677	April	16	Ephraim Wilder.	Nathaniel and Mary, in Sudbury.
1678	9	15	David Rugg.	John and Hannah, in Concord.
1678	9	27	Elizabeth Prescott.	John Jr. and Sarah, in Concord.
1679	2	5	Priscilla Roper.	Ephraim and Hannah (*Goble*), in Concord.
1679	Oct.	31	Hannah Wilder.	John and Hannah.
1679	2	12	Mary Wilder.	Nathaniel and Mary, in Sudbury.
1680	10	12	Jonathan Rugg.	John and Hannah, in Concord.
1680	Feb.	14	Elizabeth Wilder.	Nathaniel and Mary, in Sudbury.
1680	—	—	James Wilder.	Thomas and Mary (*Houghton*).
1681	1	7	Ruth Roper.	Ephraim and Hannah, in Concord
1681	—	—	Elizabeth Steevens.	Cyprian and Mary.
1681	—	—	James Wilder.	John and Hannah, in Charlestown.
1682/3	—	—	Joseph Steevens.	Cyprian and Mary.

Births in Lancaster after the Re-settlement.

A. D.	Month.	Day.	Name.	Parents.
1679	August	11	Elizabeth Waters.	Joseph and Elizabeth.
1680	Oct.	21	Sarah White.	Josiah and Mary (*Lewis*).
1681	Sept.	16	Hezekiah Whitcomb.	Josiah and Rebecca.
1681	Jan.	25	Sarah Beman.	John and Priscilla.
1682	April	2	Joseph Waters.	Joseph and Elizabeth.
1682	April	20	Jonathan Wilder.	Nathaniel and Mary.
1682	July	2	Jonas Houghton.	Jonas and Mary (*Burbeen*).
1682	July	6	Ebenezer Prescott.	John and Sarah.
1682	Sept.	15	Josiah White.	Josiah and Mary.
1683	Jan.	17	Martha Waters.	Joseph and Elizabeth.
1683	Jan.	19	John Hinds.	John and Mary (*Butler*).
1683	Jan.	24	John Houghton.	Jonas and Mary.
1683	March	3	Abigail Wheeler.	Abraham and Tabitha.
1683	June	23	Ebenezer Wilder.	John and Hannah.
1683	July	5	Joseph Wilder.	Thomas and Mary.
1683	Nov.	2	Hannah Houghton.	Robert and Esther.
1683	Dec.	26	Deborah Whitcomb.	Josiah and Rebecca.
1684	Feb.	27	James Atherton.	James and Abigail (*Waters*).

MASSACHUSETTS. 1643-1725. 319

A. D.	Month.	Day.	Name.	Parents.
1684	Feb.	29	Gamaliel Beman.	John and Priscilla.
1684	May	8	Anna Houghton.	John and Mary.
1684	May	12	John Whitcomb.	Jonathan and Hannah.
1684	Sept.	29	John White.	Josiah and Mary.
1684	Nov.	22	Isaac Wheeler. / Experience Wheeler	Isaac and Experience..
1685	Jan.	22	Sarah Wilder.	Thomas and Mary.
1685	Feb.	20	Jonathan Houghton.	John and Mary.
1685	April	20	Jonathan Wilder.	Nathaniel and Mary.
1685	Sept.	3	Beatrix Houghton.	Robert and Esther.
1686	July	24	John Wheeler.	Isaac and Experience.
1686	Dec.	8	Peter Joslin.	Peter and Sarah.
1786	—	—	Dorothy Wilder.	Nathaniel and Mary.
1687	March	30	Edward Sawyer.	John and Mary (*Ball*).

After this date the records of Lancaster births, in Middlesex Registry, abruptly cease. The following have been gathered from various sources supposed trustworthy:

A. D.	Month.	Day.	Name.	Parents.
1686	—	—	Hezekiah Willard.	Henry and Mary.
1687	—	—	Elizabeth Wilder.	Thomas and Mary.
1688	March	13	Abigail Whitcomb.	Josiah and Rebecca.
1688	—	—	Nathaniel Wilder.	Nathaniel and Mary.
1688	—	—	Joseph Willard.	Henry and Mary.
1689	March	27	Thankful White.	Josiah and Mary.
1689	April	18	Abigail Houghton.	Robert and Esther.
1689	—	—	Anna Wilder.	Thomas and Mary.
1690	Jan.	27	Elizabeth Phelps.	Edward and Ruth.
1690	May	31	Samuel Willard.	Henry and Dorcas.
1690	—	—	Anna Wilder.	John and Hannah.
1691	—	—	Mary Wilder.	Thomas and Mary.
1691	—	—	Mary Goss.	Philip and Mary.
1692	—	—	James Willard.	Henry and Dorcas.
1693	March	26	Hooker Osgood.	Hooker and Dorothy.
1693	June	20	Amos Sawyer.	Nathaniel and Mary.
1693	—	—	John Goss.	Philip and Mary.
1693	—	—	Josiah Willard.	Henry and Dorcas.
1694	March	28	Hannah Whitcomb.	Josiah and Mary.
1694	—	—	Oliver Wilder.	Nathaniel and Mary.
1695	May	11	Mary Wheelock.	Joseph and Elizabeth.
1695	—	—	Jonathan Willard.	Henry and Dorcas.
1700	June	6	Josiah Wilder.	John and Sarah.

MARRIAGES.

Under date May 26, 1658, the following order is found in Massachusetts Records:

> Itt is ordered that Mr John Tincker shall & is heerby impowred to marry George Bennett & Lyddia Kibby & . . . . . . who are published according to lawe.

Before this authority was conferred upon Master Tinker, Lancaster couples wishing to be joined in wedlock were compelled to seek a magistrate elsewhere. In 1660, Major Simon Willard became a permanent resident in Lancaster, and by virtue of his office as Assistant, solemnized marriages.

A. D.	Month.	Day.	Names.
1648			Thomas Sawyer and Mary Prescott.
1654			John Rugg and Martha Prescott.
1654	6	2	Richard Smith and widow Joanna Quarlls, in Boston
1654	November	2	Henry Kerley and Elizabeth White, in Sudbury.
1654	November	16	John Moore and Ann Smith, in Sudbury.
1656			Joseph Rowlandson and Mary White.
1656			Nathaniel Joslin and Sarah King of Marlborough.
1656			Roger Sumner and Mary Joslin.
1656			Samuel Davis and Mary Waters.
1658	April	5	John Maynard and Mary Gates, in Sudbury.
1658	3	28	Jonas Fairbanke and Lidia Prescott, in Lancaster.
1658	4	13	George Bennett and Lidia Kibby.
1658	6	2	Richard Wheeler and Sarah Prescott.
1659	3	31	William Kerley Sen. and Brichett Rowlandson.
1660	May	4	John Rugg and Hannah Prescott.
1661	?	?	Archelaus Courser and Rachel Roper. [*Not in Lancaster Records.*]
1662	August	30	John Rigby and Elizabeth ——.
1663	10	23	John Deuall [*Divoll*] and Hannah White.
1664	3	16	William Kerley Sen. and Rebeccah Joslin, widow.
1664	11	4	Josiah Whetcombe and Rebeccah Waters.
1667	June	30	John Farrar and Mary ——.
1667	November	25	Jonathan Whetcombe and Hannah ——.
1668	June	25	Thomas Wilder and Mary Houghton.
1668	November	11	Jacob Farrah Jr. and Hannah Hayward.

A. D.	Month	Day	Names.
1668	November	11	John Prescott, Jr., and Sarah ——.
1669	May	19	Job Whitcombe and Mary ——.
1669	June	22	Reuben Luxford and Margaret ——.
1669	September	14	Henry Maze and Ales ——.
1670	6	3	Jonathan Prescott and Dorothy ——.
1670	8	11	Thomas Sawyer, Jr., and Sarah ——.
1670	11	13	Mordecai Mackload and Lidea Lewis.
1671	1	16	John Whitcomb and Mary ——.
1671	9	16	Benjamin Bosworth and widow Beatrice Joslin.
1671	11	22	Cyprian Steevens and Mary Willard.
1671	11	22	John Houghton, Jr., and Mary Farrar.
1672	1	21	Samuel Waters and Mary Hudson.
1672	5	17	John Wilder and Hannah ——.
1672	9	14	Jonas Prescott and Mary Loker.
1672	9	21	Thomas Sawyer, Jr., and Hannah ——.
1672	9	29	Abram Joscelyn and Ann ——.
1672	10	11	Jeremiah Rogers, Jr., and Dorcas ——.
1673	11	24	Nathaniel Wilder and Mary Sawyer.
1674	February		Daniel Hudson, Jr., and Mary Maynard of Sudbury.
1676/7	2	18	Henry Kerley and Elizabeth How at Charlestown.
1677	November	20	Ephraim Roper and widow Hannah Goble of Concord.
1678	February	4	James Sawyer and Mary Marble.
1678			Joshua Sawyer and Sarah Potter, in Woburn.
1679	5	3	George Hewes and widow Lydia Bennett, at Concord
1681	February	15	Jonas Houghton and Mary Berbeane of Woburn.
1681/2	February	9	John Hinds and widow Mary Butler.
1683	September	20	John Pope and Beatrix Houghton.
1683			Nathaniel Wilson and Thankful Beaman.
1684	June	6	James Atherton and Abigail Hudson.
1688			Jonathan Fairbank and Mary Hayward.
1690	March	29	Philip Goss and Mary Prescott, in Concord.
1693	October	31	Joseph Houghton and Jane Vose of Milton.
1695			William Divoll and Ruth Whitcomb.
1698	January	1	John Moore and Hazadiah Fairbank, in Concord.
1698	July	21	Henry Willard and Abigail Temple, in Concord.
1698	November	20	John Houghton, Jr., and widow Mary Goss, in Concord.
1698	October	31	John Willard and Mary Hayward, in Concord.
1699	August	30	Philip Goss and Judith Hayward, in Concord.
1700	January	2	Henry Houghton and Abigail Barron, in Watertown.
1700	May	31	David Whitcomb and Mary Fairbank.
1700	December	17	George Glazier and Sarah Barrett, in Chelmsford.

DEATHS.

A. D.	Month.	Day.	
1643	September		Henry Symonds, one of first proprietors, in Boston.
1644	December	3	Thomas King, the purchaser of Nashaway, in Watertown.
1649	1	31	Rachel Waters, daughter of Lawrence and Ann, aged one month.
1653	—	—	Nathaniel Hadlocke, one of first prudential managers, in Watertown.
1654	2	21	Joanna Waters, daughter of Lawrence and Ann, aged one year.
1654	3	18	Joane White, wife of John White.
1654	3	27	Mary Smith, wife of Richard, with her infant.
1654	October	—	Sholan alias Showanon, Sagamore of the Nashawäs
1655	11	18	An infant of John and Martha Rugg, aged one day.
1655	11	24	Martha Rugg, wife of John, and another infant.
1657	5	16	A child of Nathaniel and Sarah Joslin, aged one day.
1657	9	6	Elizabeth Parker, wife of Edmund.
1657	9	17	Thomas Rowlandson, father of Reverend Joseph.
1658	1	12	Ann Kerley, wife of William, Senior.
1659	4	17	Ephraim Waters, son of Lawrence and Ann, aged three and one-half years.
1659	10	27	Mary Smith, wife of John.
1660	1	13	Thomas James.
1660	11	3	Thomas Joslin.
1660	11	20	Mary Rowlandson, daughter of Reverend Joseph, aged three years.
1660	11	20	Hittabel Rogers, daughter of Jeremiah and Bia, aged three years.
1662	4	14	Brichett Kerley, second wife of William, Senior.
1662	4	15	Henry Renie, servant of Roger Sumner.
1662	7	24	John Whitcomb, Senior.
1662	September	—	Stephen Gates, at Cambridge. [*Inventory* 29 7*mo*.]
1662	October	—	John Tinker, at New London, Connecticut.
1662	November	2	Edward Breck, in Dorchester.
1662	November	7	Hittabel Rogers, daughter Jeremiah and Abiah.
1663	10	20	Isaac Wright.
1663	December	23	Hope [*Abovehope*] Willard, daughter of Major Simon, aged seventeen years.
1663	12	21	Jacob Wheeler, son of Richard and Sarah.
1665	1	30	Richard Linton.
1665	6	10	Elizabeth Atherton, daughter of James and Hannah.
1665	7	20	Rebeccah Lewis, daughter of John and Hannah.

MASSACHUSETTS. 1643–1725. 323

A. D.	Month.	Day.	
1665	9	12	Josiah Whitcomb, son of Josiah and Rebecca, aged one day.
1666	5	17	Deborah Sawyer, daughter of Thomas and Mary, an infant.
1667	June	8	Nathaniel Joslin, son of Nathaniel and Sarah.
1667	October	23	Thomas Wilder, Senior.
1668	January	—	Stephen Day, a first proprietor, at Cambridge, [*Inventory January* 27.]
1668	November	3	John Farrar, son of Jacob, Senior.
1668	December	19	Hannah Whetcomb, daughter of Jonathan and Hannah.
1668	—	—	Philip Knight, at Salem.
1669	April	3	Isabell Walker.
1669	June	15	Simon Courser, son of Archelaus and Rachel.
1669	July	16	John Smith.
1670	July	14	William Kerley, Senior.
1670	July	17	A child of William and Elizabeth Lincorne.
1670	September	—	Adam Waters, at Charlestown. [*Inventory* 23, 7*mo*.]
1670	9	4	Mary Atherton, daughter of James and Hannah.
1671	1	10	Ann Moore, wife of John.
1671	3	2	A child of Jonathan and Dorothy Prescott.
1671	3	4	Jonathan Prescott, son of Jonathan and Dorothy.
1671	3	17	Frances Whitcomb, widow of John, Senior.
1671	10	3	William Lewis.
1672	1	2	Sarah Sawyer, wife of Thomas, Junior.
1672	1	14	William Bennett, son of George and Lydia.
1672	8	26	Benjamin Adams, son of George.
1673	April	—	John White. [*Will proved May* 23*d*.]
1673	8	2	John Farrar, son of John and Mary.
1674	—	—	Dorothy Prescott, wife of Jonathan.

The Massacre of August 22, 1675.

George Bennett.
William Flagg.
Jacob Farrar, Junior.
Mordecai MacLoud.
Lydia MacLoud, wife of Mordecai.
Hannah MacLoud, aged about three years, daughter of Mordecai.
An infant child of Mordecai and Hannah MacLoud.
Joseph Wheeler.

The Massacre of February 10, 1676.

Jonas Fairbank.
Joshua Fairbank, son of Jonas, aged fifteen years.
Richard Wheeler.
Ephraim Sawyer, son of Thomas, aged twenty-five years.
Henry Farrar, son of Jacob, Senior.
John Ball.
Elizabeth Ball, wife of John.
An infant child of John and Elizabeth Ball.
Ensign John Divoll.
John Divoll, Jr., aged twelve, died in captivity.
Josiah Divoll, son of John, aged seven years.
Hannah Divoll, daughter of John, aged about nine years, died in captivity.
Abraham Joslin, Jr., aged twenty-six years.
Ann Joslin, wife of Abraham, killed in captivity.
Beatrice, daughter of Abraham and Ann Joslin, aged two years, killed in captivity.
Daniel Gains.
Thomas Rowlandson, aged nineteen years, nephew of Reverend Joseph.
John Kettle, aged about thirty-seven.
Joseph Kettle(?) son of John, aged about ten years.
John Kettle, son of John, aged about sixteen years.
Elizabeth Kerley, wife of Captain Henry.
Henry Kerley(?) son of Captain Henry, aged eighteen years.
William Kerley, son of Captain Henry, aged seventeen years.
Joseph Kerley, son of Captain Henry, aged seven years.
Priscilla Roper, wife of Ephraim.
Priscilla Roper, daughter of Ephraim, aged about three years.
Sarah Rowlandson, daughter of Reverend Joseph, died of wound, February 18.
John McLoud, brother of Mordecai.
George Harrington, a soldier, killed February —?
John Roper, killed March 26.

Died during Abandonment of Town.

A. D.	Month.	Day.	
1676	April	24	Major Simon Willard, at Charlestown.
1676	September	26	Jeremiah Rogers, at Dorchester.
1676	September	26	Sam, alias Uskattuhgun, sagamore of Nashaway, hanged at Boston.
1676	September	26	Monoco, alias one-eyed John, Nipnet Sachem at Lancaster, hanged at Boston.

MASSACHUSETTS. 1643-1725.

A. D.	Month.	Day.	
1677	August	14	Jacob Farrar, Senior, at Woburn.
1677	November	4	Mary Hudson, wife of Daniel, at Concord.
1678	1	6	Abigail Rogers, daughter of Jeremiah, at Dorchester.
1678	1	10	Bathsheba Rogers, daughter of Jeremiah, at Dorchester.
1678	1	10	Abiah Rogers, widow of Jeremiah, at Dorchester.
1678	1	23	Gamaliel Beaman, Senior, at Dorchester.
1678	4	20	Samuel Rugg, son of John and Hannah, at Concord.
1678	7	20	Benjamin Allen, at Charlestown.
1678	November	23	Reverend Joseph Rowlandson, at Wethersfield, Conn
1679.	—	—	Nathaniel Wilder, child of Nathaniel and Mary, in Sudbury.
1679	—	—	Archelaus Courser, in Boston.
1679	October	8	Hannah Houghton, daughter of Ralph, at Charlestown, aged twelve years.
1679	October	10	John Houghton, son of Ralph, at Charlestown, aged twenty years.
1680	February	6	Ann Waters, wife of Lawrence, at Charlestown.
1681	March	19	James Butler, at Billerica.

After Re-settlement of Town.

1681	December	—	John Prescott, [*the Founder of Lancaster,*] aged about seventy-seven years.
1682	February	—	William Whittborn. [*Inventory February* 23.]
1683	April	7	John Whitcomb, drowned.
1684	January	4	William Kerley, Jr., at Marlborough.
1684	April	29	John Houghton, Senior.
1687	December	9	Lawrence Waters, at Charlestown.
1688	September	1	John Bush.
1688	October	—	John Glazier, Senior. [*Inventory October* 29.]
1691	February	—	Jonathan Whitcomb. [*Inventory February* 25.]
1691	March	—	Samuel Wheeler, a soldier, son of Richard. [*Inventory April* 7.]

The Massacre of July 18, 1692.

Sarah Joslin, wife of Peter.
Peter Joslin, Jr., aged six years. [*Killed in captivity.*]
Three children of Peter Joslin.
Hannah Whitcomb, widow of Jonathan.

1693	October	—	Reverend Samuel Carter, in Groton. [*Administration granted October* 30.]

A. D.	Month.	Day.	
1693	—	—	Ralph Houghton. (?)
1694	April	8	Nathaniel Joslin, in Marlborough.
1694	March	7	Daniel Allen, in Watertown.
1694	May	—	Edmund Parker, at Roxbury. [*Inventory May* 28.]
1695	November	—	Abraham Wheeler, killed by Indians. [*Inventory November* 6.]
1696	October	10	George Adams, in Cambridge.
1697	January	—	John Rugg. [*Inventory January* 19.]
1697	May	19	Alice and Fannie, twin children of Reverend John Whiting, aged two years, ten months.

The Massacre of September 11, 1697.

Reverend John Whiting.
Daniel Hudson.
Joanna Hudson, wife of Daniel.
Joanna Hudson, daughter of Daniel, aged thirty-seven years.
Elizabeth Hudson, daughter of Daniel, aged forty years.
Two children of Nathaniel and Rebecca Hudson.
Ephraim Roper.
Hannah Roper, wife of Ephraim.
Elizabeth Roper, daughter of Ephraim, aged fourteen years.
John Scate, *or Skeath*.
The wife of John Scate.
Joseph Rugg, aged about twenty-nine years.
The wife of Joseph Rugg.
Three children of Joseph Rugg.
Hannah Prescott Rugg, widow of John.
Jonathan Fairbank, aged thirty-one years.
Grace Fairbank, daughter of Jonathan.
Jonas Fairbank, son of Jonathan.

1697	November	4	Eunice, daughter of Reverend John Whiting.
1698	May	26	Deacon Roger Sumner, at Milton.
1698	May	—	Philip Goss. [*Administration granted May* 26.]
1702	September	—	Ensign John Moore. [*Inventory September* 23.]
1703	—	—	John Moore, Senior. [*Nuncupative will sworn to November* 26.
1704	July	31	Lieutenant Nathaniel Wilder, killed by Indians, aged fifty-four years.
1704	—	—	John Priest, Senior.
1706	September	12	Thomas Sawyer, Senior.
1707	—	—	James Atherton, in Sherburn, aged eighty-six years.
1714	January	—	Captain Henry Kerley, at Marlborough. [*Will proved January* 7.]

APPENDIX.

ACKNOWLEDGMENT.

To the several members of the Committee of Publication — especially to the Reverend George M. Bartol, chairman, — and to the Honorable Samuel A. Green, the thanks of the editor, due for valuable suggestions and assistance, are hereby cordially tendered. Various courtesies received from the accomplished custodians of the Massachusetts Archives, the Massachusetts State Library, the Boston Public Library, and the Libraries of the Boston Athenæum, the Massachusetts Historical Society, and the New England Historic Genealogical Society, are gratefully acknowledged.

THE FIRST INNKEEPERS OF LANCASTER.

There is no evidence that any house here, previous to the destruction of the town in 1676, was devoted to the accommodation of travellers, or the sale of drink. Whenever Reverend John Eliot, General Daniel Gookin, and other gentlemen of the Bay towns, were called hither by official duty or private business, they doubtless found all doors hospitably open to them. Humbler travellers were but few, and those chiefly visiting friends and relatives. The licensed fur traders kept a small variety of goods suitable for barter with the native hunters, including spirituous liquors, and at first naturally monopolized all trade in such articles. Thus the list of debtors in the inventory of Thomas King's estate, besides "the Indyans," includes many of his English neighbors. By an act of 1681, but one innkeeper was permitted in each of the smaller towns, and license was granted by the county courts annually, on a certificate of approval from the town's selectmen, of which the following are examples, from Middlesex Court Files:

LANCASTER ye 31st of March 1690

These may certifie ye hon^rd Court: or any concerned that Nathanaell Wilder of Lancaster hath ye approbation and consent of ye Selectmen of sd. Lancaster for ye Retaleing of strong Drinks and keeping Ordinary in ye s^d Lancaster.   by order of ye Selectmen

JOHN HOUGHTON *Town Clerk*

To the Hon^rable his Majties Justices for ye County of Middl^x.

May it please your Hon^{rs}. That Whereas John White of ye Towne of Lancaster in said County of Middlesex yeoman is Desiring to obtain a Licence for Retailing Rum & other strong Drink in said Towne of Lancaster & accordingly applyed himselfe to ye Selectmen of said Town for their approbation, who are Willing it may be Granted him in case yor Hon^{rs} se meet

Dated LAN^R: July ye 4: 1717.

JOHN HOUGHTON
NATHANIEL SAWYER } *Selectmen*
PETER JOSLIN

To the Hon^rable his Majties Justices for ye County of Middlesex.

May it please your Hon^{rs} that at ye Request of Jonathan Houghton of Lancaster in said County of Middlesex Yeoman applying himselfe to ye selectmen of said Towne for their approbation for his Receiving a licence for an Inholder in said Towne, we accordingly approve of ye same & Desire Licence may be granted him

Selectmen { PETER JOSLIN   JAMES WILDER
            { NATHANIEL SAWYER JOSEPH WILDER

Dated July ye 5: 1717.

To the Hon^rable Justices for ye County of Middlesex.

These may certifie that whereas Mr David Whetcomb of Lancaster hath applyed himselfe to us the subscribers for our approbation for his selling strong Drink by Retale we accordingly Request that your Hon^{rs} would please to grant the same.

Dated LAN^R: July 7: 1717/18.

JOHN HOUGHTON
PETER JOSLIN } *Selectmen*
JONAS HOUGHTON

Nathaniel Wilder was the first licensed " for Retailing of wine, Beere, Ale, Cyder, Rum &c" in Lancaster. His home was a garrisoned house on the southeast slope of George Hill, in close proximity to the site of the Symonds & King trucking house — a fact perhaps suggestive, as tending to show that the chief line of travel had not materially changed during forty years, and that the centre of population in Lancaster was yet west of the rivers. He remained the sole innholder until his death in 1704, and his widow Mary [Sawyer], granddaughter of John Prescott, continued the business.

July 10 1705 Widow Mary Wilder Admitted to renew her License as Inholder for yᵉ Town of Lancaster here Recognized as yᵉ Law demands . . . .

Simon Willard of Lancaster Licensed to be an Inholder in sd Town having entered into Recognizance persuant to Law.

[Middlesex Court Records.]

LIST OF LICENSED INNHOLDERS AND RETAILERS OF LIQUORS, 1685–1730, DERIVED FROM THE RECORDS OF THE MIDDLESEX COURT OF SESSIONS.

1685 to 1704.	Nathaniel Wilder.
1705.	Widow Mary Wilder, Benjamin Bellows and Simon Willard.
1706–7.	Widow Mary Wilder.
1708.	John Houghton, Jr.
1709–10.	John Houghton, Sen.
1711.	John Houghton and Benjamin Bellows.
1712–13.	John Houghton.
1714.	John Houghton, and "John Fay living near Marlborough."
1715.	John Houghton.
1716.	Hooker Osgood and John Houghton.
1717.	John Houghton, Hooker Osgood, and John White.
1718–19.	Jonathan Houghton, David Whitcomb, and Samuel Willard.
1720.	Samuel Willard and David Whitcomb.
1721 to '24.	Samuel Willard aud Thomas Carter.
1725.	Thomas Carter.
1726.	Samuel Willard, Thomas Carter, and Oliver Wilder.
1727 to '29.	Samuel Willard, Thomas Carter, John Wright, and Oliver Wilder.
1730.	Capt. Samuel Willard, Jonathan Houghton, Thomas Carter, John Wright, and Oliver Wilder.

The location of these tavern-keepers can be determined approximately only.

Benjamin Bellows, having married Dorcas, widow of Henry Willard, lived on the Willard estate at Still River. A locality upon the intervale near, yet retains the name "Bellows Hole."

Justice John Houghton lived upon Bridecake Plain, opposite the State Industrial School grounds. His sons John and Jonathan resided in the same neighborhood. A letter from the pen of the veteran town clerk gives us a glimpse of Lancaster and its tavern in 1715:

To Capt Samuel Phipps of Charlstowne.

Worthy Sr. After my Humble Service & Due Respects Presented to ye Hon'r'able Justices of ye County of Middlesex, together with yourselfe, these are to acquaint you that I am under such Indisposition of Body that I could not attend this Last Session of ye General Assembly, nor can I as yet Possibly (with comfort) come to pay my excise nor to Renew my Licence, but I have sent ye money for ye last years excise by Joseph Brabrook the Bearer hereof, which I hope will be to acceptance & in case yo'^{r} Hon'^{rs} shall see cause that my Licence may be continued I hope you will abate neer one halfe of ye excise for Doubtless I have paid very Deare considering what I have Drawne Compared with other Townes. I had but one Hogshead of Rum ye last yeare & that wanted about 12 Gallons of being full when I bought it : & it wants severall Gallons of being out now besides about 10 or 12 Gallons Lent out, & were it not that I am concerned with writing of Deeds & Bonds & other Publique Concerns of ye Town affaires, which Occasion Persons often to come to my House, in order to signing & Issuing such things, I should not be willing to be concerned with a Licence ; for what Drinks I sell I do it as cheap as at Boston & besides ye first cost I pay twenty shillings pr. Hogshead for carrying it up, besides the Hazard ; & as for Cyder there is none to be had, nor like to be this yeare at any price, fruit is so scarce, & for wine I never sold 5 Gallons in all ye yeares I have had a licence. So that my Draught being so Little (there being no Road or throughfare for travilers through our towne) I hope your Hon^{rs} will consider ye Premisses & do therein as in your Wisdom & Justice it shall seem meet, which will oblidge

Your Humble Servant

Dat. Lan^R: July ye 27th 1715.   John Houghton

[Middlesex Court Files.]

Hooker Osgood, a saddler from Andover, bought the Rowlandson lands west of the river, Nov. 22, 1710, of Philip Goss, and in 1714 purchased the lot whereon Lawrence Waters had his home, now the homestead of S. J. S. Vose.

Captain John White was the noted Indian-fighter, associated with Captain Lovewell. He lived upon the east side of the neck.

David Whitcomb's lands were in the southeastern part of Bolton.

Captain Samuel Willard in 1627 purchased the lands bordering the highway from the Sprague bridge to the Penecook wading place, in all seventy-six acres, including the Major Simon Willard home lot, the Edward Breck lot, and the Night Pasture. The Willard mansion near the railroad crossing is supposed to have been built by him.

Thomas Carter lived upon George Hill, his father, Samuel, having in 1688 purchased the Kerley lands, now in possession of F. D. Taylor and H. B. Stratton.

Colonel Oliver Wilder bought of his brother Nathaniel, in 1722, the Roper lot, and probably lived near, if not in, the present house on the hill just above the George Hill school-house.

The complaint in Justice Houghton's letter of the small local demand for strong drink must not be taken as a measure of the bibulous propensities of our ancestors. The frequent mention of beer and malt vessels in early inventories, and of orchards in wills, indicate that the home manufacture and consumption of fermented beverages was considerable. It may be reasonable to conclude from the above letter, that in olden time as now, the apple crop usually failed in the "odd years." The orchards of Lancaster were very early famous, and cider became a product of commercial importance. When in 1734 Captain Jonas Houghton, the Lancaster surveyor, was employed by the proprietors of Nichewaug to reconstruct the road from

Lancaster along the north side of Wachusett, the contract test for acceptance of this highway was that it should be "so feasible .... as to carry comfortably, with four oxen, four barrels of cider at once."

In an old memorandum book of Judge Joseph Wilder's is "an acompt of Cyder made in the ye 1728," for his neighbors:

		Barrels
for the	Reuerend Mr John Prentice	61
,,	Capt. Samuel Willard	12½
,,	Benjamin Wilson	52
,,	Thomas Wilder	22½
,,	Jos Wilder	17
,,	William Divol	5
,,	John Divol	15
,,	Jonas Houghton	6
,,	Jos Wheelock	21
,,	Joshua Houghton	63
,,	Ebenz Wilder	47½
,,	James Houghton	5
,,	Chas Sawyer	9½
,,	Richard Wild	9
,,	Jonathan Houghton	16
,,	Ebenezer Prescot	31
,,	Daniel Rugg	20½
,,	James Wilder	39
,,	William Houghton	113
,,	William Sawyer	23
,,	James Butler	17½
,,	Wedow Rugg	7½
,,	Phillip Larkin	2½
		616

THE REPRESENTATIVES OF LANCASTER.

Under the colonial charter, towns might legally choose a non-resident to serve them as deputy, and Lancaster did this in 1671 and 1672, electing Mr. Thomas Brattle, who at that date was one of the selectmen of Boston. Towns having not more than thirty freemen were privileged to be represented in general court or not, as they chose, and as each was required to pay the charges of its own deputies, the weaker settlements commonly sent no delegates, unless some local exigency made it necessary. In attempting to complete an accurate list of representatives, a curious difficulty is very early met with. In sixteen years, between 1689 and 1725, the name John Houghton appears recorded in the manuscript records of the general court as deputy from Lancaster. In two only of these (1721 and 1724) is a distinguishing title, "Esq.," added. The credit of this long service has heretofore been given, without question, solely to Justice Houghton. There are for this period the minutes of only two of the town's representative elections; those of May, 1718, and May, 1724. These, however, are enough to prove that Lieutenant John Houghton is entitled to receive some part of the honor attributed to his father, Justice John Houghton. The representative elected in 1719 was "John Houghton Jr," and it might with some reason be inferred that the delegate of same name in 1715, 1716, 1717 and 1719 was the same person, though diligent search has not been rewarded with any clue to aid decision. Instances of the elected refusing to accept the office were not rare during the first half of the eighteenth century, and it was quite usual for the town to advance twenty pounds to enable their deputy to meet the requirements of his official dignity, until his stipend from the Commonwealth should become due.

The dates given are those of the election, which was in the month of May until 1831, since when it has been in November. In the years not given the town was not represented.

1671 Thomas Brattle, of Boston.
1672 Thomas Brattle, of Boston.
1673 Ralph Houghton.
1689 Ralph Houghton.
    [*Courts of May 8 and 22.*]
    John Moore, Jr.
    [*June 5 and Nov. 5.*]
    John Moore, Sen.
    [*December session.*]

1690 John Moore, Sen.
    [*February session.*]
    John Houghton.
    [*December session.*]
1692 John Moore, Sen.
    John Houghton.
1693 John Houghton.
1697 John Houghton.
1705 John Houghton

1706 John Houghton.
1707 Thomas Sawyer.
1708 John Houghton.
1710 Josiah Whitcomb.
1711 John Houghton.
1712 John Houghton.
1714 Jabez Fairbank.
1715 John Houghton.
1716 John Houghton.
1717 John Houghton.
1718 John Houghton, Jr.
1719 John Houghton (Jr.?)
1720 Joseph Wilder.
1721 John Houghton, Esquire.
.Jabez Fairbank.
1722 Jabez Fairbank.
1723 Jabez Fairbank.
1724 John Houghton, Esquire.
1725 Deacon Joseph Wilder.
1726 Deacon Joseph Wilder.
1727 Captain Samuel Willard.
1728 Deacon Josiah White.
1729 Deacon Josiah White.
1730 Deacon Josiah White.
1731 Deacon Josiah White.
[*Elected and declined.*]
James Wilder.
1732 Jonathan Houghton.
1733 James Keyes.
1734 Captain Ephraim Wilder.
1735 Captain Ephraim Wilder.
1736 Captain Ephraim Wilder.
1737 Captain Ephraim Wilder.
[*Elected and declined.*]
Deacon Josiah White.
[*Elected and declined.*]
Jabez Fairbank.
1738 Jabez Fairbank.
1739 Ebenezer Wilder.
1740 Colonel Samuel Willard.
1741 Captain William Richardson.
1742 Colonel Samuel Willard.
1743 Colonel Samuel Willard.
1745 Captain Ephraim Wilder.

1745 Captain Ephraim Wilder.
[*Elected and declined.*]
Deacon Josiah White.
[*Elected and declined.*]
Captain William Richardson.
1746 Joseph Wilder, Jr.
1747 Joseph Wilder, Jr.
1748 Joseph Wilder, Jr.
[*Elected and declined.*]
1749 Colonel Samuel Willard.
1750 Captain William Richardson.
1751 Joseph Wilder, Jr.
1752 Joseph Wilder, Jr.
1753 Joseph Wilder, Jr.
1754 Captain William Richardson.
1755 David Wilder.
1756 Captain William Richardson.
1757 David Wilder.
1758 William Richardson, Esquire.
1759 William Richardson, Esquire.
1760 William Richardson, Esquire.
1761 William Richardson, Esquire.
1762 David Wilder.
1763 David Wilder.
1764 David Wilder.
1765 David Wilder.
1766 Asa Whitcomb.
1767 David Wilder.
1768 Asa Whitcomb.
1769 Asa Whitcomb.
1770 Asa Whitcomb.
1771 Asa Whitcomb.
1772 Asa Whitcomb.
1773 Asa Whitcomb.
1774 Captain Asa Whitcomb.
1775 Ebenezer Allen.
Hezekiah Gates.
1776 William Dunsmoor.
1777 William Dunsmoor.
1778 William Dunsmoor.
Samuel Thurston.
1779 Joseph Reed, Esquire.

Under the present constitution; the representation being based upon one hundred and fifty ratable polls, and three hundred and seventy ratable polls giving a town two representatives.

1780 Captain William Putnam.
1781 William Dunsmoor.
1782 John Sprague.
1783 John Sprague.
1784 John Sprague.
1785 John Sprague.
1786 Captain Ephraim Carter, Jr.
1787 Michael Newhall.
1788 Michael Newhall.
1789 Michael Newhall.
1790 Captain Ephraim Carter, Jr.
1791 Captain Ephraim Carter, Jr.
1792 Captain Ephraim Carter, Jr.
1793 John Whiting, Jr., Esquire.
1794 "Hon. John Sprague, Esq."
1795 John Sprague.
1796 John Sprague.
1797 John Sprague.
1798 John Sprague.
1799 John Sprague.
1800 Samuel Ward.
[*John Sprague having declined.*]
1801 Samuel Ward.
1802 William Stedman.
1803 Jonathan Wilder.
1804 Jonathan Wilder.
1805 Jonathan Wilder.
1806 Jonathan Wilder, Esquire.
  Eli Stearns.
  [*Elected unanimously.*]
1807 Eli Stearns.
1808 Eli Stearns.
  [*Elected unanimously.*]
  Jonas Lane, Esquire, *do.*
1809 Eli Stearns. *do.*
  Jonas Lane, Esquire. *do.*
1810 Eli Stearns.
  Colonel Jonas Lane.
1811 Colonel Jonas Lane.
  Major Jacob Fisher.
1812 Colonel Jonas Lane.

1812 Major Jacob Fisher.
1813 Jacob Fisher, Esquire.
  Captain William Cleveland.
1814 Captain William Cleveland.
  Captain John Thurston.
  [*Elected unanimously.*]
1815 Captain William Cleveland.
  [*Elected unanimously.*]
  Captain John Thurston.
  [*Elected unanimously.*]
1816 Captain John Thurston.
  Captain Edward Goodwin.
1817 Captain John Thurston.
  Captain Benjamin Wyman.
1818 Captain John Thurston.
  [*Elected and declined.*]
  Captain Benjamin Wyman.
  Major Solomon Carter.
1819 Benjamin Wyman, Esquire.
1821 Jacob Fisher, Esquire.
1823 Jacob Fisher, Esquire.
1826 Captain John Thurston.
1827 Joseph Willard, Esquire.
  Davis Whitman, Esquire.
1828 Joseph Willard, Esquire.
  (*Elected unanimously.*)
1829 Solon Whiting, Esquire.
1830 Solon Whiting, Esquire.

Constitutional Amendment X ratified, changing beginning of political year from last Wednesday in May to first Wednesday of January, and the elections to November.

1831 Davis Whitman, Esquire.
1832 John G. Thurston.
  [*Elected unanimously.*]
  Ferdinand Andrews.
1833 Doctor George Baker.
  Levi Lewis.
1834 Anthony Lane.
  [*Elected and declined.*]
  James G. Carter.
  Deacon Joel Wilder.
1835 James G. Carter.

1835 Deacon Joel Wilder.
1836 James G. Carter.
    [*Elected unanimously.*]

Constitutional Amendment XII adopted. Representation based on three hundred ratable polls.

1837 Silas Thurston, Jr.
1838 Silas Thurston, Jr.
    John G. Thurston.
1839 Silas Thurston, Jr.
    John Thurston.

Constitutional Amendment XIII adopted. Representation based upon twelve hundred inhabitants.

1840 John Thurston.
1841 Jacob Fisher, Jr.
1842 John M. Washburn.
1843 John M. Washburn.
1844 Jacob Fisher.
1845 Joel Wilder, 2d.
1846 Joel Wilder, 2d.
1847 Ezra Sawyer.
1848 Ezra Sawyer.
1850 Anthony Lane.
1851 Anthony Lane.

1852 John G. Thurston.
1853 John G. Thurston.
1854 Francis F. Hussey.
1855 John G. Thurston.
1856 James Childs.

Constitutional Amendment XXI adopted, 1857, Lancaster and Clinton forming 8th Worcester District.

1858 John M. Washburn.
1860 Dr. J. L. S. Thompson.
1862 Dr. J. L. S. Thompson.

The 8th Worcester District, 1865, formed of Lancaster, Bolton and Harvard.

1868 Jacob Fisher.
1869 George A. Parker.
1870 George A. Parker.
1871 George A. Parker.

The 5th Worcester District, 1875, formed of Lancaster, Bolton, Harvard, Sterling, Berlin, Lunenburg and Clinton, with two representatives.

1878 Samuel R. Damon.
1882 Henry S. Nourse.

DELEGATES.

To the Provincial Congresses of 1774 *and* 1775 :—WILLIAM DUNSMOOR, ASA WHITCOMB.

To the Convention that formed the State Constitution at Cambridge, September, 1779:—WILLIAM DUNSMOOR, EPHRAIM WILDER, WILLIAM PUTNAM.

To the Convention that ratified the Constitution of the United States :—JOHN SPRAGUE.

To the Convention for the Revision of the State Constitution in 1820:—DAVIS WHITMAN, MAJOR JACOB FISHER.

SENATORS.

JOHN SPRAGUE, 1785 to 1786.   JAMES G. CARTER, 1837 to 1839.
MOSES SMITH, 1814 to 1816.   JOHN G. THURSTON, 1845.
                  FRANCIS B. FAY, 1868.

EXECUTIVE COUNCILLORS.

MAJOR SIMON WILLARD, Assistant, 1654 to 1676.
CAPTAIN EPHRAIM WILDER, elected 1735, but declined.
JOSEPH WILDER, 1735 to 1752.
WILLIAM STEDMAN, 1803 and 1807.
ABIJAH WILLARD was appointed Councillor by writ of Mandamus, 1775.

REPRESENTATIVES TO CONGRESS.

WILLIAM STEDMAN, 1803 to 1810.

General John Whiting, as candidate of the Jeffersonian party, was Stedman's opponent. James G. Carter was an unsuccessful candidate in 1847.

PRENTISS MELLEN, born in Lancaster, 1764, was U. S. Senator 1818 —1820.

COUNTY OFFICERS.

SHERIFFS.

WILLIAM GREENLEAF, 1778 to 1788.
JOHN SPRAGUE, 1788 to 1792.

CLERK OF COUNTY COURTS.

WILLIAM STEDMAN, 1810 and 1812 to 1816.

COUNTY TREASURER.

JONATHAN HOUGHTON, 1731 to 1733.

ASSISTANT JUSTICES WORCESTER COURT OF SESSIONS.

JOHN WHITING, March 1, 1808 to April 20, 1809.
TIMOTHY WHITING, November 14, 1811.

JUDGE OF PROBATE.

JOSEPH WILDER, 1739 to 1757.

JUDGES OF THE COURT OF COMMON PLEAS.

JOSEPH WILDER, June 30, 1731 to March 29, 1757, Chief Justice.
COLONEL SAMUEL WILLARD, January 27, 1743, to November, 1752.
JOSEPH WILDER, JR., January 21, 1762, to 1773.
JOHN SPRAGUE, 1798 to 1800, Chief Justice.

22

JUSTICES OF THE PEACE.

JOHN TINKER was given special authority to marry, May 26, 1658.

MAJOR SIMON WILLARD, by virtue of his office as Assistant, performed the various duties of a Magistrate, 1654–1676.

JOHN HOUGHTON, called Justice before 1718, reappointed (?) 1729.

JOSEPH WILDER, SENIOR, 1727 and 1731.

BENJAMIN WILLARD, 1731.
COLONEL SAMUEL WILLARD, 1732.
COLONEL JAMES WILDER, 1737.
SAMUEL WILLARD, JR., 1743.
COLONEL OLIVER WILDER, 1744.
COLONEL JOSEPH WILDER, JR., 1747
WILLIAM RICHARDSON, 1753.
COLONEL JOHN WHITCOMB, 1754.
COLONEL JOSEPH REED, (?)
DAVID OSGOOD, 1762.
COLONEL ABIJAH WILLARD, 1762.
THOMAS WILDER, 1762.
JOSHUA WILLARD, 1762.
ABEL WILLARD, 1769.
LEVI WILLARD, 1772.
SAMUEL WILDER, 1772.
EZRA HOUGHTON, 1774.
DR. WILLIAM DUNSMOOR, —?
JOHN SPRAGUE, 1783.

DR. JOSIAH WILDER, 1788.
DR. ISRAEL ATHERTON, 1789.
TIMOTHY WHITING, JR., 1789.
WILLIAM STEDMAN, 1790.
SAMUEL WARD, 1799.
JOSIAH FLAGG, 1803.
BENJAMIN WYMAN, 1803.
JOSEPH WALES, 1806.
MERRICK RICE, 1808.
MOSES SMITH, JR., 1809.
PAUL WILLARD, 1811.
MAJOR JACOB FISHER, 1812.
EBENEZER TORREY, 1814.
EDWARD GOODWIN, 1816.
JOHN STUART, 1821.
JONAS LANE, 1822.
LEVI LEWIS, 1823.
JOSEPH WILLARD, 1825.
WILLIAM WILLARD, 1825.

SOLON WHITING.

CORONERS.

JAMES WILDER, 1731.
OLIVER WILDER, 1738.

JOSEPH WILDER, JR., 1744.
DAVID WILDER, 1747.

WILLIAM RICHARDSON, 1762.

THE CLERKS OF LANCASTER.

The first pages of Lancaster's oldest records are by the hand of Master John Tinker, who as scribe for the first prudential managers, copied some earlier records from "the old book"; but by whom that lost volume was kept is unknown.

RALPH HOUGHTON, clerk of the writs 1656 to 1682.
CYPRIAN STEEVENS, clerk of the writs 1682 to 1686(?).

JOHN HOUGHTON, (son of first John,) 1686 to 1725,—40 *years*.
JONATHAN HOUGHTON, 1726 to 1728 and 1730 to 1736.—*Died in office*.
JOSEPH OSGOOD, 1729.
JUDGE JOSEPH WILDER, SR., 1737 to 1743.
JOSEPH WILDER, JR., 1744 to 1752.
ABIJAH WILLARD, 1753 and 1754.
COLONEL SAMUEL WILLARD, 1755.
WILLIAM RICHARDSON, October 8, 1755, "*in room of Samuel Willard absent on his majesties service*."
LEVI WILLARD, 1756 to 1760 and 1761 to 1769.
ABEL WILLARD, 1760, "*in place of Levi Willard going out of town*."
DANIEL ROBBINS, 1770, 1772, 1773, 1775 and 1776.
CAPTAIN SAMUEL WARD, 1771, 1774 and 1782 to 1787.
COLONEL WILLIAM GREENLEAF, 1777, 1779, 1781.
NATHANIEL BEAMAN, September, 1777 to May 1778.
CYRUS FAIRBANK, May, 1778.
DR. JOSIAH LEAVITT, 1780 to May, 1781.
COLONEL EDMUND HEARD, 1788 to 1790.
JOSEPH WALES, 1791 to 1794.
WILLIAM STEDMAN, 1795 to 1800.
JOSIAH FLAGG, 1801 to 1835, except 1828,—34 *years*.
MAJOR JACOB FISHER, 1828.
JOSEPH W. HUNTINGTON, 1836 and 1837.
JOHN G. THURSTON, 1838 to 1853.
MATTHEW F. WOODS, 1853. *Died in office*.
FRANCIS F. HUSSEY, 1853 to 1855.
WILLIAM A. KILBOURN, 1874.
DR. J. L. S. THOMPSON, 1856 to present time, except 1874.

PROPRIETARY CLERKS.

RALPH HOUGHTON and JOHN HOUGHTON, probably to 1716.
JOSEPH WILDER, 1716 to 1757. *Died in office*.
CALEB WILDER, 1757 to 1776. *Died in office*.
LUKE WILDER, 1777 to 1779. *Died in office*.
JOSIAH WILDER, 1780 to 1788. *Died in office*.
DEACON CYRUS FAIRBANK, 1788 to 1800. *Died in office*.
BENJAMIN WYMAN, 1801 to 1826. *Died in office*.
MAJOR JACOB FISHER, 1832. *Died in office*.
SOLON WHITING.

THE MINISTERS OF LANCASTER.

FIRST CHURCH.

NATHANIEL NORCROSS, son of Jeremiah of Watertown; born in England; graduate of Cambridge University, 1637; chosen minister of the Nashaway Plantation, 1644, but returned to England, 1646.

JOSEPH ROWLANDSON, son of Thomas of Ipswich; born in England, 1631 or 1632; graduate of Harvard College, 1652; began preaching in Lancaster, 1654; ordained, 1660. April, 1677 he was settled as colleague of Reverend Gershom Bulkeley at Wethersfield, Ct., and there died, November 24, 1678.

> The first meeting-house, built probably in 1654, was near the parsonage, and crowned the highest part of the grounds now called the "middle cemetery."

SAMUEL CARTER, eldest son of Reverend Thomas Carter of Woburn; born August 8, 1640; graduate of Harvard College, 1660; bought land and resided on George Hill, 1688 or earlier, and supplied the Lancaster pulpit temporarily between 1680 and 1688. He removed to Groton, and died there, 1693.

EDWARD OAKES, son of Urian, graduate of Harvard College, 1679, preached temporarily in Lancaster; afterwards in New London, Ct.

JOHN DENISON, son of John of Ipswich, graduated at Harvard College, 1684, occupied the Lancaster pulpit for a time. He was settled as colleague with Rev. William Hubbard at Ipswich, and died 1689.

WILLIAM WOODROP, a non-conforming clergyman driven from his church in England, 1662, preached in Lancaster, and Cotton Mather recorded him in the *Magnalia* as minister here. He returned to England July 12, 1687.

> The first meeting-house was "burned by the enemy," after the abandonment of the town in 1676. The second was built upon the same site about 1684.

JOHN WHITING, son of Reverend Samuel of Billerica, born 1664; graduate of Harvard College, 1685; began preaching in Lancaster, February, 1688; was ordained December 3, 1690, and slain by Indians, September 11, 1697.

MR. JONES was invited to settle in Lancaster, but some obstacle arose to prevent ordination. This was probably John, son of William Jones of New Haven, born October 4, 1667; graduate of Harvard College, 1690; drowned January 28, 1719, in New Haven harbor.

JOHN ROBINSON, son of Samuel of Dorchester, graduate of Harvard College, 1695, for a time filled the Lancaster pulpit. He was settled at Duxbury, 1702, and died, 1745.

SAMUEL WHITMAN, graduate of Harvard College, 1696, preached here a while; was afterwards teacher and minister at Salem, and died, 1751.

ANDREW GARDNER, son of Captain Andrew, born in Brookline. 1674; graduate of Harvard College, 1696; began preaching in Lancaster May, 1701, and was soon to be ordained when accidentally killed by Samuel Prescott, October 26, 1704.

July 31, 1704, the second meeting-house was burned in an assault by the French and Indians. The third was built on the Old Common, opposite the burial ground, 1706.

JOHN PRENTICE, son of Thomas, born at Newton, 1682; graduated at Harvard College, 1700; began preaching at Lancaster, 1705; was ordained March 29, 1708, and died January 6, 1748.

In 1742-3 two meeting-houses were built; that of the first precinct on Schoolhouse Hill, nearly in front of the residence of Solon Wilder; that of the second, or Woonksechocksett precinct, "near Ridge Hill."

COTTON BROWN, son of Reverend John of Haverhill, graduate of Harvard College, 1743, was invited to settle in Lancaster February 28, 1748, but became pastor of the Brookline church October 6, 1748, and died April 13, 1751.

BENJAMIN STEVENS, son of Reverend Joseph of Charlestown, born 1720, graduate of Harvard College, 1740, preached here as a candidate. He settled at Kittery; became S. T. D., 1785; died May 18, 1791.

WILLIAM LAWRENCE, graduate of Harvard College, 1743, was also a candidate for the Lancaster pulpit. He died, 1780.

STEPHEN FROST, graduate of Harvard College, 1739, was master of the Lancaster Grammar School, 1740-1744, and preached temporarily, but was never ordained; died, 1749.

TIMOTHY HARRINGTON, born in Waltham, February 10, 1716; graduate of Harvard College, 1737; pastor in Swansey, N. H.; was installed at Lancaster November 6, 1748; died December 18, 1795.

ALDEN BRADFORD, born in Duxbury, 1765, graduate of Harvard College, 1786, temporarily supplied the pulpit in 1791; settled at Wiscasset, Me. LL. D., 1837; S. H. S.; secretary of state, 1812-1824, etc.; died, 1843.

THADDEUS MASON HARRIS, son of William, born at Charlestown, July 7, 1768, resident of Chocksett during the Revolution, graduate of Harvard College, 1787, supplied the pulpit for some time, 1791-2. S. T. D., A. A. S., etc.; died, 1842.

DANIEL CLARK SANDERS, graduate of Harvard College, 1788, preached as a candidate. S. T. D.. 1809; President of Burlington College; died, 1850.

JOSEPH DAVIS, son of Simon of Concord; born, 1720; graduate of Harvard College, 1740: pastor in Holden, 1744-1774, preached temporarily in Lancaster. He died March 4, 1799.

NATHANIEL THAYER, son of Reverend Ebenezer, born in Hampton, N. H., July 11, 1769, graduate of Harvard College, 1789, was ordained colleague pastor in Lancaster, October 9, 1793; S. T. D., 1817; died June 23, 1840.

The corner stone of the brick church was laid July 9, 1816, and the building dedicated January 1, 1817.

EDMUND HAMILTON SEARS, born in Sandisfield April 6, 1810, graduate of Union College, 1834, of Harvard Divinity School, 1837, pastor in Wayland, 1837-40; was installed at Lancaster, December 23, 1840, and resigned because of ill health, April, 1847; S. T. D., 1871, S. H. S.; died at Weston, January 16, 1876.

GEORGE MURILLO BARTOL, born in Freeport, Maine, September 18, 1820; graduate of Brown University, 1842, and of Harvard Divinity School, 1845; was ordained August 4, 1847.

SECOND PRECINCT CHURCH.
Set off with Sterling, 1781.

The first service in the meeting-house at Chocksett was held November 28, 1742. There had been "neighborhood meetings" several years earlier. Reverend John Prentice records a baptism there, May, 1738, by Reverend Job Cushing of Shrewsbury, he having "changed with Mr. Brown." This was probably Josiah Brown, graduate of Harvard College, 1736, a son-in-law of Mr. Prentice,— as also was Mr. Cushing.

JOHN MELLEN, born in Hopkinton, March 14, 1722, graduate of Harvard College, 1741, was pastor from December 19, 1744, to December 14, 1778. February 11, 1784, he was installed at Hanover, Mass., and died in Reading, July 4, 1807.

REUBEN HOLCOMBE, graduate of Yale College, 1774. was ordained June 2, 1779, continued pastor in Sterling until 1815, and died, 1826.

FIRST UNIVERSALIST CHURCH.
Organized April 3, 1838.

RUFUS S. POPE, born in Stoughton, April 2, 1809; studied theology with Sylvanus Cobb, D. D., 1833; settled in Milford, Sterling and Hyannis, dying at the place last named, June 5, 1882; preached in Lancaster as occasion offered, 1838.

JAMES S. PALMER, born in Brooklyn, Pennsylvania, January 24, 1815, preached six months, beginning May, 1839; now of Mansfield, Penn.

Lucius Robinson Paige, born in Hardwick, March 8, 1802, supplied the pulpit during 1840, meetings being held in the Academy and town hall. S. T. D., 1861. Author of a Commentary on the New Testament, etc., etc.

John Harriman, preached in Lancaster, 1841–3.

Benjamin Whittemore, born in Lancaster, May 3, 1801, son of Nathaniel; educated at Lancaster and Lawrence Academies; studied theology with Hosea Ballou. He was pastor here, 1843 to 1854; S. T. D., 1867; died April 26, 1881, in Boston.

A meeting-house was built in South Lancaster, and dedicated April 26, 1848. Services were discontinued, 1855, and the meeting-house was sold to the state for the Girls' Industrial School, 1858.

FIRST EVANGELICAL CONGREGATIONAL CHURCH.

This society was organized February 22, 1839, at the house of Reverend Asa Packard. The meeting-house was dedicated December 1, 1841; enlarged, 1868.

Charles Packard, son of Reverend Hezekiah; born at Chelmsford, April 12, 1801; graduated at Bowdoin College, 1817; ordained at Lancaster, January 1, 1840; resigned to accept pastorate of Second Congregational church in Cambridgeport, 1854; died at Biddeford, Maine, February 17, 1864.

Franklin Bradley Doe, born in Highgate, Vermont, December 5, 1827; graduate of Amherst College, 1851, and of the Bangor Theological Seminary, 1854; ordained in Lancaster, October 19, 1854; resigned to accept pastorate in Appleton, Wisconsin, September 24, 1858. Superintendent of the American Home Missionary Society for the Southwest.

John Edwards Todd, graduate of Yale, 1855, was invited to become pastor over the church, May 3, 1859, but declined. Pastor of Church of the Redeemer, New Haven, and D. D.

Sylvanus Cobb Kendall, graduate of Amherst College, 1849, and of Andover Theological Seminary, 1852; was invited to settle, December 13, 1859, but declined.

Amos Edward Lawrence, born at Geneseo, N. Y., June 25, 1812; graduated at Yale College, 1840, and the New York Union Theological Seminary, 1843; installed at Lancaster, October 10, 1860; resigned, March 6, 1864.

George Roswell Leavitt, born in Lowell, June 7, 1838; graduated at Williams College, 1860, and at Andover Theological Seminary, 1863; ordained in Lancaster, March 29, 1865; resigned in 1870 to accept pastorate of Stearns Chapel in Cambridgeport.

ABIJAH PERKINS MARVIN, born in Lyme, Ct., February 1, 1813; graduated at Trinity College in 1839, and Yale Theological Seminary, 1842; pastor at Winchendon, 1844-1866. In 1870 began preaching at Lancaster; installed May 1, 1872; asked dismission September 12, 1875.

HENRY CLINTON FAY, graduate of Amherst College, 1854, temporarily supplied the pulpit, 1876.

MARCUS AMES was acting pastor one year, beginning April, 1877.

WILLIAM DELOSS LOVE, JR., born in New Haven, Ct., November 29, 1851; graduated at Hamilton College, 1873, and at Andover Theological Seminary, 1878; ordained at Lancaster, September 18, 1878; asked dismission July, 1881.

DARIUS AUGUSTINE NEWTON, born October 1, 1855, at Westborough; graduate of Amherst College, 1879, and of Andover Theological Seminary, 1882; ordained September 21, 1882.

SECOND EVANGELICAL CHURCH.

This Society was organized November 14, 1844, in the village of Lancaster called Clintonville, which was set off as the town of Clinton, March, 1850.

JOSEPH MYRON RENSSELAER EATON, born October 14, 1814, in Fitchburg; graduated at Amherst College, 1841, and at Andover Theological Seminary, 1844; ordained January 9, 1845; dismissed April 11, 1847.

W. H. CORNING, ordained December 8, 1847; dismissed October 2, 1851. . . . . . .

FIRST BAPTIST SOCIETY.

This church was organized in 1847, in that part of Lancaster which became Clinton, A. D. 1850.

CHARLES MANNING BOWERS, born in Boston, January 10, 1814; graduated at Brown University, 1838, and Newton Theological School, 1840. D. D., 1871. Pastor of church from its organization.

ROMAN CATHOLIC CHURCH.

The Chapel was consecrated July 12, 1873.

FATHER RICHARD J. PATTERSON, born in Ireland, 1836, graduated at the College of the Holy Cross, Worcester, 1863, and Grand Seminary, Montreal; ordained priest December 22, 1866.

NEW JERUSALEM CHURCH.

This Society was formally organized January 29, 1876. Neighborhood meetings were held, however, as early as 1830, and, with several intervals of discontinuance, until the organization. From 1865 the Sunday meetings were in an ante-room of the town hall, and at certain seasons the pulpit was supplied by one of the three following clergymen :

JAMES REED, pastor of the Boston Society; born in Boston, June 8, 1834; graduate of Harvard College, 1855.

ABIEL SILVER, pastor of Boston Highlands society; born in Hopkinton, New Hampshire, April 3, 1795; accidentally drowned in Boston, March 27, 1881.

JOSEPH PETTEE, presiding minister of the Massachusetts Association; born in Salisbury, Connecticut, March 14, 1809; graduate of Yale College, 1833.

RICHARD WARD was called as pastor in April, 1880, and installed December 1, 1881; born in Sanbornton,—now Franklin,— New Hampshire, May 8, 1819.

The chapel was built in 1881, and dedicated December 1 of that year.

SEVENTH DAY ADVENTIST CHURCH.
Organized 1864.

STEPHEN NELSON HASKELL, born in Oakham, Mass., April 22, 1834; ordained Elder, August 1870.

DORES ALONZO ROBINSON, born in Brighton, New Brunswick, January 5, 1848; ordained Elder, August 28, 1876.

The meeting-house was dedicated May 5, 1878.

POSTMASTERS.

The establishment of the first post-office in Lancaster dates from April 1, 1795. The second was granted March 3, 1853, and called *South Lancaster*, the post-office department objecting to *New Boston*, the old name of the village. The following is an official list of the postmasters, with their dates of appointment :—

JOSEPH WALES, April 1, 1795.
TIMOTHY WHITING, July 25, 1803.
NATHANIEL RAND, March 14, 1825.
JOSEPH W. HUNTINGTON, December 19, 1832.
NATHANIEL RAND, December 27, 1844.
HUMPHREY BARRETT, September 5, 1849.
NATHANIEL RAND, September 6, 1853.

{ CHRISTOPHER A. RAND, August 31, 1854.
{ CHRISTOPHER A. POLLARD, July 25, 1855.
DANFORTH LAWRENCE, December 24, 1856.
HUMPHREY BARRETT, August 1, 1861.
SOLON WILDER, March 6, 1884.

SOUTH LANCASTER.

WILDER S. THURSTON, March 3, 1853.
EDWARD J. CROSSMAN, September 19, 1853.
STEVENS H. TURNER, November 28, 1853.
ANDREW J. BANCROFT, February 7, 1857.
CARTER WILDER, December 31, 1861.
AARON WILDER, September 22, 1863.
DANIEL M. HOWARD, February 9, 1866.
THOMAS E. BURDETT, April 14, 1873.
LOUIS J. BURDETT, January 18, 1875.
WILLIAM G. WILDER, December 8, 1875.
HENRY F. HOSMER, March 7, 1881.

GEOGRAPHICAL POSITION OF LANCASTER.

The United States Coast and Geodetic Survey station nearest to Lancaster is that upon Wachusett Mountain. By the Massachusetts Trigonometrical Survey, the spire of the Brick Church in Lancaster was determined to be eleven and sixteen hundredths miles distant from that station, and $2'..00,91''$ south, and $12'..49,71''$ east of it. From these data the United States Coast Survey locates "Lancaster Church" in $42°..27'..19,98''$ north latitude, and $71°..40'..24,27''$ longitude west of Greenwich.

The elevation above the sea level of the floor of the porch to the Brick Church is three hundred and eight and one-half feet, as obtained by extension of the levels of the Worcester and Nashua Railroad.

INDEX.

ABRAM'S HOLL, or Hole, 293.
Absentee proprietors, 17, 123.
Accommodations to encourage settlers, 29, 51, 127.
Act of Incorporation, 25.
Adagunapeke, 275.
Adams, Frances, 186.
    George, 83, 122, 177, 186, 275, 295, 323, 326.
    John, 83, 94, 177, 178, 186.
    Jonathan, 240.
Additional Grant, 8, 138, 174, 177, 179, 192, 194.
Admission of inhabitants restricted, 22, 28, 41, 52, 69.
Albert, Daniel, 243.
Allen, Benjamin, 122, 298, 317, 325.
    Daniel, 76, 298, 315, 316, 326.
    Ebenezer, 298, 334.
Allotments of land, 22, 29, 33, 245.
Allowances in land, 44, 83, 178, 179, 190, 205, 206, 245.
Allowance, Surveyors', 66, 193, 247.
Almanac, first American, 308.
Ames, Jacob, 221, 229.
    Jethro, 229.
    Reverend Marcus, 344.
Ammunition, town's supply, 79.
Amoskeag, *Ammoskeeg*, *Namaske*, [*Manchester, N. H.*] 16, 231, 239.
Andover, *Aniver*, *Andavor*, 222, 242, 259, 300, 331.
Andrews, Ferdinand, 335.
Androscoggin river, *Amrescoggin*, 226.
Appendix, 327.
Apple orchards, 55, 85, 260, 305, 331.
Aquiticus, John, 139.
Arbitration, 28.
Arbitrators' awards, 43.
Area of original township, 66, see map, 8.
Armor, 284.
Asiatick hill, *Assoatetick*, 218.
Assessments, manner of, 51.
Athenæum, Boston, 327.
Atherton, *Aderton*, Benjamin, 201, 207, 236, 239, 243.
    General Humphrey, 38, 252.
    Doctor Israel, 182, 338.
    James, 30, 32, 39, 40, 41, 44, 46, 48, 61, 71, 143, 248, 250, 251, 252, 253, 273, 274, 314, 315, 316, 317, 322, 323, 326.

Atherton, James, Jr., 143, 180, 184, 202, 207, 253, 314, 318, 321.
    Joseph, 127, 196, 197, 200, 202, 209.
    Joshua, 143, 190, 253, 306, 314.
    Simon, 240, 243.
Attack upon Lancaster, 1675, 98.
    1676, 100.
    1692, 130.
    1697, 132.
    1704, 146.
Autographs of early settlers, facsimile, 24.
Aunsocamug, Mary, 139.
Ayer, 272.

BAKER, Doctor George, 335.
Ball, John, 105, 288, 324.
Ballou, Hosea, 343.
Bancroft, Andrew J., 346.
Baptist church, 344.
Barbadoes, 278, 279.
Bare hill, 71, 76, 145, 177, 180, 182, 191, 195, 201, 203, 211, 253, 271, 288, 302, 303, 306.
Barnes, John, 177.
    Matthew, 15.
Barrett, Ensign Humphrey, 128.
    Humphrey, 345, 346.
    John, 216, 221.
    Sarah, 321.
Barron, *Barnes*, Abigail, 321,
    Elias, 295.
    Timothy, 244.
Bartholomew, Henry, 310.
Bartol, Reverend George Murillo, 4, 327, 342.
Bay Path or Road, 46, 71, 188, 201, 205, 211.
Bayley, *Bailey*, *Baily*, Benjamin, 177, 207.
    Jonathan, 242.
Bear, 233, 241.
Beasts, Wild, 21, 124, 233, 263.
Beer, 153, 329, 331.
Belcher, Jeremiah, 237, 243.
    Jeremiah D., 243.
Bellows, Benjamin, 141, 143, 156, 184, 189, 210, 211, 266, 303, 329, 330.
Bellows Falls, 232.
Bellows Holl or Hole, 330.
Beman, *Beaman*, *Bemand*, Ebenezer, 178.
    Gamaliel, 31, 71, 84, 90, 248, 257, 258, 259, 304, 314, 325.

INDEX.

Beman, Gamaliel, Jr., 144, 145, 259,
    John, 122, 144, 259, 319.
    John, Jr., 144, 156, 173, 215, 259.
    Nathaniel, 339.
    Thomas, 259.
Bennett, *Bennit*, George, 60, 99, 252, 306, 314, 315, 316, 317, 320, 323.
    John, 178, 196, 197, 210, 216, 220, 221, 306, 314.
    Joseph, 243.
    Samuel, 141, 144, 152, 156, 173, 177, 184, 248, 252, 306, 307, 315,
Berlin, 8, 142, 245, 336,
Berwick, 226.
Bigelow, *Biglow, Biglo*, John, 155.
Billerica, *Billeriky*, 48, 85, 109, 126, 234, 288, 304, 325, 340.
Billeting soldiers, 168.
Billings, William, 31.
Bills of Credit, 185.
Births in early Lancaster families, List of, 312, *et seq*.
Bitfield, Samuel, 15.
Blanchard, *Blancher*, Jonathan, 221.
    Captain Joseph, 216, 226, 234, 235, 238, 239, 240, 241, 242.
Blood, Ebenezer, 243.
    Joseph, 216, 221.
Bog ore, 49.
Bolton, 42, 142, 145, 192, 229, 245, 266, 306, 336.
Bond, Corporal William, 120.
Boocore, Monsieur, 146.
Book of Estrays, 6.
    of Lands, 6, 83, 245, 247, 275.
    of Psalms, 308.
    of Roads, 6.
    the old, 5, 31, 37, 248, 250, 273, 288, 338.
Booker, John, 177.
Books. 134.
Borden, *Bauden*, Jonathan, 243.
    Josiah, 221.
Bordman, *Boardman*, William, 308, 310, 311.
Boston, 10, 20, 21, 73, 84, 145, 154, 250, 281, 299, 322, 324, 325, 332, 333.
Boston Athenæum, 327.
Boston Evening Post, quoted, 213.
Boston News Letter, quoted, 146, 149, 165.
Boston Public Library, 114, 327.
Bosworth, Benjamin, 321.
Boughton, James, 221.
Bounds of Lancaster, original, map, 8, 25 65.
Bounds of Additional Grant, map, 8, 174, 192 to 194.
Bounty upon Scalps, 106, 229.
Bounty upon wild beasts, 124.
Bowers, Reverend Charles M., 344.
    Jerahmel, 144.
    John, 173, 267.
Bowman, Mr. [*Francis?*], 35.
Boylston, map, 8, 59, 245.
Boynton, Benony, 229.
    Stephen, 244.
Brabrook, John, 154.

Brabrook, Joseph, 330.
Bradford, 233.
    Reverend Alden, 341.
Bradstreet's, Simon, Journal quoted, 119.
Braintree, 149.
Brand-marks of Lancaster, 16, 80.
Brattle, Thomas, 332, 333.
Breck. *Brek, Brick*, Edward, 22, 25, 30, 33, 35, 39, 40, 41, 44, 45, 61, 71, 177, 236, 248, 249, 250, 251, 252, 267, 271, 273, 297, 322, 331.
    Robert, 30, 36, 39, 40, 248, 249, 250, 251, 252, 260, 264, 265.
Bridecake Plain, 157, 212, 294, 298, 330.
Bridges, 59, 64, 81, 86, 96, 100, 101, 103, 177, 180, 181, 183, 185, 192, 195, 273, 274, 300.
Brigham, Jonathan, 167.
    Samuel, 166.
Brinsmead, [*Reverend William*], 126.
Brintnall, William, 237.
Brookfield, 11, 17, 219, 300, 301.
Brook, Bare Hill, 182.
    Beman's, 303.
    Canoe, 184.
    Dean's, *Danes*, 82, 155, 212, 290, 293, 295.
    Fall, 219.
    Four-mile, 195.
    Goodridge, 82, 155, 212, 290.
    Kerley's, 203, 303.
    Mill, 32.
    Monipnet, 219.
    Neesonkeeg, 223.
    Parker's, 239.
    Plumtrees, 54.
    Quasaponikin, *Ponikin*, 78. 184, 259.
    Rigby, 196.
    Roper's, 61, 273, 278.
    Wachusett, 219.
    Wataquodock, 188.
    West-pond, 211.
    Wickapeket, 189, 190, 195, 196, 203, 204, 205, 206, 218, 220, 286.
    Wickapimsee, 218.
Brooks, Eunice, 123, 285.
Broughton, Edward, 202, 207.
Brown, *Browne*, Boaz, 128.
    Reverend Cotton, 341.
    Ebenezer, 229.
    Josiah, 342.
    Captain Thomas, 133, 136, 138, 144, 156, 160, 161.
Bruce, Thomas, 243.
Buckminster, Thomas, 215.
Bulkeley, Reverend Gershom, 119, 301, 340.
    Peter, 122.
Burbeen *Berbeane*, Mary, 318, 321.
Burdett, Louis J., 346.
    Thomas E., 346.
Burning woods, 81.
Burt, *Burck*, Phineas, 244.
    Richard, 236, 239.
    Thomas, 237.
Burying Ground, Bolton, 306.

INDEX.

Burying Ground, Old Common, 164, 305, 341.
    the old, 55, 183, 204, 273, 278, 279, 299, 300.
Bush, John, 248, 271, 303, 325.
Buss, John, 288, 289.
Butler, James, 72, 77, 79, 144, 182, 204, 248, 293, 301, 304, 325, 332.
Butterfield, Jonathan, 221.
By-Laws of Lancaster, 171.

CALEF, Robert, quoted, 307.
Calicott, Richard, 117.
Cambridge, 12, 17, 18, 19, 73, 101, 110, 111, 126, 267, 268, 280, 281, 308, 310, 311, 322, 323, 326, 340.
Canada expedition of Sir Wm. Phips, 127, 293.
Canoe, *Cannoo*, Brook, 184.
Cape Porpus, 242.
Captives, Lists of, 105, 131, 133, 136.
    Ransom of, 109, 131, 136.
Captivity, Mrs. Rowlandson's Narrative of, 98, 102.
Carts and cartways, 22, 59, 107, 108, 204, 261, 305.
Carter, Ephraim, 196.
    Captain Ephraim, Jr., 335.
    James Gordon, 335, 336, 337.
    John, 144, 152, 154, 285, 286.
    Reverend Samuel, 24, 123, 196, 285, 286, 325, 340.
    Samuel, Jr., 141, 144, 152, 182, 183, 195, 196, 202, 203, 204, 208, 285, 286.
    Major Solomon, 335.
    Thomas, 187, 188, 207, 285, 329, 331.
Carter's Mills, 67.
Case, Mrs. Sally (*Sawyer*), 145, 290.
Casting lots, 42, 71, 186, 246.
Catechism, Slighting the, 129, 303.
Cateconimoug Pond, 219.
Cattle running at large, 21, 171.
Centre of the town, 67, 273.
Cellars, ancient, 291, 296.
Chamberlain, Benjamin, 222.
    Joseph, 221.
    Thomas, 216, 221.
Chambly River, 155.
Champney, *Chamne*, Daniel, 113.
Chandler, Ephraim, 216, 222.
    George Frederick, 278.
    John, 15, 16.
    Moses, 209, 229, 243.
Chapin, Abiel, 236, 239.
Charlestown, 32, 109, 251, 256, 261, 272, 280, 294, 298, 300, 305, 306, 311, 321, 323, 324, 325, 341.
Chelmsford, 48, 98, 109, 130, 221, 222, 321, 343.
Chestnut Hill, 220.
Chesquonopog Pond, 70.
Child, Doctor Robert, 11, 14, 23.
Childs, James, 336.
Chimneys, ancient, 57, 290.
Chocksett, *Choxet, see Woonksechocksett.*

Christian, a Mohawk, 225, 233.
Church, David, 177.
Church, Covenant of, 169.
    Lands of, 27, 29, 45, 156, 182, 283, 296.
    Members of in 1708, 170.
    Records of, 6, 169.
Churches of Lancaster, list of, 340, *et seq.*
Cider, 153, 154, 329, 331, 332.
Cilley, L. G., 291.
Clamshell Pond, 298.
Clap, Roger, 73.
Clapboards, 57.
Clarke, Hugh, information of, 107.
    Thomas, 38.
Clergymen of Lancaster, list of, 340, *et seq.*
Clerks of the writs, 48, 53, 77, 84, 212, 251, 312.
    proprietors', list of, 339.
    town, list of, 338.
Cleveland, Captain William, 335.
Clinton, 82, 145, 180, 245, 276, 277, 293, 298, 336.
Clothes, iron, 284.
Cobb, Sylvanus, D. D., 342.
Cobbitt, Reverend Thomas, quoted, 114, 116.
Cocheco, [*Dover, N. H.,*] 116, 226, 230, 233.
Coffin, *Coffyn*, Lieutenant Peter, 115.
Cohassett Falls, [*Goff's Falls, N. H.,*] 239.
Cold Spring, 145, 301, 304.
Collins, Daniel, 244.
    Edward, 310.
Combs, *Comes*, Jonathan, 216, 236, 239.
Committee to order town affairs, appointed, 50.
Committee, the, withdraw, 78.
    of Publication, 3, 4, 327.
Commons, 6, 20, 41, 53, 82, 83, 171, 178, 180, 181.
Concord highway, 45, 128, 249.
Concord, 21, 48, 49, 101, 107, 109, 110, 114, 119, 127, 154, 272, 278, 279, 288, 304, 321, 325, 342.
Connecticut, new way to, 16, 73, 91.
Connecticut River, 227, 232, 236.
Constables, 22, 24, 26, 48, 84, 124, 128, 181, 187, 202, 207.
Contocook, *Contockock*, River, 231, 235, 238, 239.
Contract, Prescott's corn-mill, 32.
    Prescott's saw-mill, 72.
Controversies, settled by arbitration, 28.
Conway, alias Peter Tatatiquinea, 111.
Converse, Captain James, 156, 162.
    Josiah, 165.
Cook, Alice, 126.
Coos, *Cohosse*, 224, 227.
Corey, Benjamin, 243.
    Jacob, 229.
    Josiah, 244.
Corning, Reverend William H., 344.
Coroners, list of, 338.
Coroner's inquest, 121, 150.
Corwin, George, 91.
Coulter, William J., 2.

INDEX.

Councillors, 337.
County officers, 337.
Courser, *Corser*, Archelaus, *Arculeas*, 122, 281, 315, 316, 320, 333, 325.
    John, 281.
Covenant of Church, 169.
    of first planters, 27.
    of proprietors of new grant, 173.
Cow-pen, 21.
Cowdall, *Caudall*, John, 10, 13, 75, 79, 246, 275, 277, 298, 309.
Crocker, *Croakham*, Rebecca, 287.
Crosly, Robert, 85.
Crossman, Edward J., 346.
Crouch, Jonathan, 209, 210.
Crow Hill, 220.
Cumbery intervales, 184.
Cummings, *Cumins*, Ebenezer, 216.
    William, 222.
Cushing, Reverend Job, 342.
Cusumpe Pond, 230, 236, 240, 241.
Cutler, James, 10, 15.
Cutshamequin, *Kutchamaquin*, 10, 11.

DAHANNATA, *Tahanto*, 138, 173, 179, 193.
Damon, Samuel R., 259, 336.
Danforth, Thomas, 33, 50, 52, 59, 60, 68, 73, 78, 90, 94, 103, 310.
Darbey, *Darby*, John, 209, 210.
    Robert, 209.
Davenport's farm, 174, 194.
Davie, Humphrey, 91.
Davis, *Davies*, *Davice*, Barnard, 240.
    Jabez, 216, 221.
    Sergeant John, 15, 16.
    Reverend Joseph, 342.
    Samuel, 149, 314, 320.
    Samuel, Jr., 149.
    Samuel, 243.
    Simon, 342.
Day, Matthew, 308, 309.
    Stephen, 11, 12, 13, 15, 17, 18, 19, 24, 30, 79, 83, 273, 275, 281, 308, 309, 310, 311, 323.
Deacons, 107, 176, 213.
Dean, John, 243.
    Samuel, 30.
Dean's, *Dane's*, Brook, 82, 155, 212, 290, 293, 295.
Deaths, list of, 322, *et seq.*
Dedham, 283.
Deed of John Cowdall to John Prescott, 246, 275.
    Philip Goss to Hooker Osgood, 300.
    John Johnson to John Roper, 280.
    Henry Kerley to Samuel Carter, 285.
    John Moore to John Buss, 289.
    John Moore to Daniel Hudson, 288.
    Jonathan to Samuel Prescott, 278.
    Samuel Prescott to Rev. John Prentice, 182, 278.

Deed of Joseph Rowlandson to Philip Goss, 299.
    Sholan to Nashaway Planters, 22, 25.
    George Tahanto to Lancaster, 138.
    Alice Whiting to town of Lancaster, 138.
    Nathaniel to Oliver Wilder, 281.
    Major Simon Willard to Cyprian Steevens, 85.
    James Wiser to John Prescott, 275.
Deer's Horns, 145, 155, 290.
Deer Island, 109, 110.
Delegates to General Court, etc., list of, 332, *et seq.*
Denison, Reverend John, 340.
Diamond, *Dimon*, Hills, 219.
Diary of John Marshall, 132, 149.
    Samuel Sewail, 109, 117, 126, 132, 155.
Ditch, broad meadow, 199.
    Glaziers, 189.
    Prescott's, 29, 41, 278.
Divisions of common land, 29, 39, 41, 54, 65, 69, 76, 79, 179, 181, 183, 184, 186, 206, 207, 245, 248.
Divoll, *Divole*, *Divens*, *Divall*, *Divell*, *Drew*, Hannah, 104, 114, 115, 315, 316, 317, 320, 324.
    John, 243, 315. 332.
    Ensign John, 89, 94, 104, 122, 254, 315, 316, 317, 320, 324.
    Manasseh, 57.
    William, 105, 141, 144, 156, 176, 189, 202, 207, 210, 253, 266, 317, 321, 332.
Doe, Reverend Franklin B., 343.
Doget, Francis, 229.
Dolton, Caleb, 229.
Doors and windows in early houses, 58.
Dorchester church records quoted, 74.
Dorchester, 85, 249, 253, 255, 257, 258, 259, 260, 265, 296, 322, 324, 325, 340.
Dracut, 221, 222.
Drake, Samuel G., "Biography and History of Indians," quoted, 111, 115.
Draper, James, 30.
Drew, Mrs., [*Divoll*,] 104.
Dugway, 183.
Dummer, William, Lieut. Gov., Letters of, 215, 223, 225, 226.
Duncan, *Duncom*, John, 229.
Dunsmoor, Doctor William, 334, 335, 336, 338.
Dunstable, 85, 168, 216, 217, 218, 221, 222, 224, 225, 231, 232, 235, 239, 240.
Dunster, Eliza and Mary, 272, 314.
Dustin, *Dustan*, Hannah, 132.
Duxbury, 340, 341.
Dwelley, Richard, 31.

EAGER, Rufus, 278.
Eames, John, 220.
Eames, Thomas, 103.
Eaton, Reverend J. M. R., 344.

INDEX.

Education, 95, 172, 175.
Elevation of Lancaster above the sea, 346.
Eliot, Reverend John, 16, 17, 38, 327.
Emerson's Bank, 180, 293.
Equality in first division of land, 29.
Estabrooks, Reverend Joseph, 126.
Estates of first settlers, 39, 52, 248.
Excommunicants refused as inhabitants, 28.
Exeter, 233.
Expedition to Canada, 1690, 127, 293.
  against Loisburg, 1745, 236.

FACSIMILE signatures of early settlers, 24.
Fairbank, *Fairbanks*, Cyrus, 339.
  Lieutenant Jabez, 144, 145, 152, 168, 173, 176, 179, 182, 183, 184, 190, 195, 196, 197, 198, 199, 200, 202, 203, 204, 207, 211, 215, 216, 217, 218, 219, 220, 221, 222, 244, 295, 296, 316, 334.
  Jonas, 24, 31, 39, 40, 71, 82, 83, 106, 122, 135, 157, 218, 248, 277, 279, 283, 294, 314, 315, 316, 320, 324.
  Jonas, Jr., 243' 295, 317.
  Jonathan, 127, 133, 135, 218, 295, 315, 321, 326.
  Joseph, 211.
  Joshua, 106, 157, 218, 295, 314, 324.
  Mary, 133, 136.
  Thomas, 244.
Farm for country's use, 65.
Farmer, Thomas, 229.
Farnsworth, Ephraim, 229.
  Isaac, 220, 221, 243.
  John, 174, 192, 193.
  Reuben, 229.
  Samuel, 243.
Farrar, *Farer, Farrah*, Henry, 106, 292, 324.
  Jacob, 24, 31, 32, 39, 40, 41, 54, 61, 64, 71, 108, 212, 248, 256, 258, 283, 289, 290, 291, 292, 294, 295, 297, 299, 325.
  Jacob, Jr., 64, 99, 166, 292, 316, 317, 320, 323.
  John, 31, 39, 40, 41, 43, 71, 248, 256, 257, 292, 294.
  John, Jr., 292, 316, 320, 323.
  Ensign John, 166.
Farwell, Isaac, 216.
Fay, Colonel Francis B., 145, 336.
  Reverend Henry C., 344.
  John, 329.
Fence, the night pasture, 20, 299.
Fencing allotments, 29.
Ferren, Jonathan, 229.
Fever and ague, 240.
Fines and forfeitures, 28, 50, 51, 52, 60, 68, 70, 74, 81, 89, 118.
First allotments of land, 29, 33, *maps*, 244.
Fish-weir, *warre, wear*, 60, 258.
Fisher, Major Jacob, 335, 336, 338, 339.
  Jacob, Jr., 336.

Fisher, John, 11.
Fisk, Jonathan, 244.
Flagg, Josiah, 211, 312, 338, 339.
  Sally, 292.
  William, 99, 323.
Flag of truce, 110.
Flankers, 58, 148, 149.
Flax, 265.
Fletcher, Charles T., 4.
  Hezekiah, 243.
  Samuel, 229.
Fort, Dummer, 227, 232.
  George, 226.
  Iarish, 231.
  Penecook, 239.
  Washacum, 276.
Fortifications, 102, 149.
Ford, Robert, 229.
Foster, Captain Hopestill, 87.
  Phineas, 229.
Founell, John, 32. .
Framingham, 215.
Freeman's oath, the, 308.
Freemen, 25, 38, 48, 249, 251, 254, 257, 261, 263, 267, 269, 284, 287, 298.
French and Indian war, 140, *et seq*.
Frog-holes, 82, 291.
Frost, James, 248, 303, 304.
  Nicholas, 84.
  Stephen, 341.
Fryville, 145.
Fullam, Francis, 177, 179, 185.
Funeral charges, 154.
Fur traders, 9, 263, 327.

GAINES, *Gains, Gaynes*, Daniel, 24, 31, 72, 104, 122, 176, 177, 199, 203, 247, 248, 277, 283, 294, 324.
Gaines, Samuel, 284.
Gardner, Reverend Andrew, 137, 144, 145, 148, 150, 182, 214, 341.
  Mary, 24, 153, 165.
  Peter, 113.
Garrett, Harmon, 12, 13, 20, 23, 26.
Garrison, Fairbank's, 218.
  Gardner's, 58, 145, 148.
  Joslin's, 145.
  Moore's, 145.
  Prescott's, 145, 277.
  Priest's, 145, 302.
  Roper's, 135.
  Rowlandson's, 86, 101, 102, 104, 134, 152, 270, 283, 284.
  Sawyer's, 58, 108.
  Steevens', 101, 108.
  Whitcomb's, 145.
  Nathaniel Wilder's, 146.
  Thomas Wilder's, 145.
  Major Willard's, 108.
Garrisons, building, etc., 131.
  lists of, 143, 173.
Gates in highways, 53, 176, 177, 270, 297.
Gates tavern, the, 58.
Gates, Hezekiah, 312, 334.
  Jacob, 229.
  Mary, 46, 267, 268, 320.
  Simon, 122, 177, 184, 267.

INDEX.

Gates, Steven, 30, 39, 40, 42, 47, 48, 52, 57, 63, 72, 177, 184, 248, 259, 265, 267, 268, 269, 270, 315, 323.
    Thomas, 122, 267, 268.
Geographic position of Lancaster, 346.
George Hill, 82, 135, 141, 145, 186, 219, 261, 264, 276, 277, 282, 294, 303, 329, 331, 340.
Gibbs, Captain [*Benjamin,*] 107.
Gibson's Hill, 41, 134, 262, 263, 274, 288, 296, 300.
Gifts of land, 29, 51, 247, 251, 252, 262, 268, 269, 270, 273, 285.
Gillson, Michael, 222.
Glazier, *Glasser*, George, 141, 144, 187, 188, 196, 250, 257, 321.
    John, 141, 144, 168, 249, 251, 325.
    Joseph, 141, 144, 156.
    Mary, 134, 136.
Glover, Reverend Jesse, 308.
Gloves, 154.
Goble, Daniel, 117.
    Hannah, 321.
    Stephen, 117, 135.
Goodenough, *Goodnow*, Lieutenant Edmund, 38.
Goodridge, Benjamin, 242.
    John, 243.
    Philip, 243.
Goodridge, *Gutteridge*, Brook, 82, 155, 212, 290.
Goodwin, Captain Edward, 335, 338.
Gookin, General Daniel, 11, 85, 92, 97, 98, 101, 103, 109, 110, 327.
Gore, Richard, 244.
Goss, John, 177, 179, 180, 187.
    Jonas, 277, 292, 295.
    Philip, 85, 152, 299, 300, 319, 326, 331.
    Philip, Jr., 152, 156, 321.
Graham, William H., 278.
Grain, prices of, set by court, 55.
Grammar school, 175, 176.
Grant, additional, 138, 174, 177, 179, 192.
    original, 22, 23, 25, 26.
Grants, thirty-acre, 248.
Grass of intervales, 246.
Graves, Moses, 229.
Gray, Robert, 237, 243.
Green, Samuel, 309, 311.
    Honorable Samuel Abbott, 91, 96, 308, 327.
Greenleaf, William, 337, 339.
Groton, *Groaten, Groten*, 21, 42, 62, 80, 96, 100, 109, 114, 119, 123, 125. 130, 147, 149, 166, 168, 192, 196, 200, 201, 216, 217, 218, 219, 221, 222, 223, 231, 232, 235, 239, 243, 263, 271, 279, 285, 293, 295, 307, 308, 325, 340.
Ground-nut, [*Apios tuberosa*] 33.
Grout, John, 244.
Guild, John, 139.
Gunrashit, Sagamore, 111.

HADLOCKE, Nathaniel, 22, 25, 27, 322.
Haines, Lieutenant [*Josiah*], 120.
Hall, Elizabeth, 17, 18, 19.

Hall, John, 17, 19, 20, 246. 261, 262.
    Richard, 229.
Hampton Falls, 242.
Hannichoockset, [*Hooksett, N. H.*], 239.
Hapgood, Nathaniel, 184, 201, 203, 210, 288.
Hardy, Samuel, 243.
Harriman, Reverend John, 343.
Harrington, George, 106, 324.
    Reverend Timothy, 10, 12, 21, 123, 126, 134, 137, 146, 164, 166 ,214, 341.
Harris, *Harress*, Benjamin, 216, 221, 243.
    Ebenezer, 178, 183, 189, 202, 204, 258.
    Edmund, 178, 183, 185, 189, 204, 205, 207, 258.
    John, 144, 156, 190.
    Reverend Thaddeus Mason, 341.
    Thomas. 122, 287, 288.
Hartwell, Edward, 189, 206, 207, 208, 210, 216, 217, 220, 221, 222, 223, 224, 243.
Harwood, *Hawood*, Nathaniel, 128, 208.
Harvard, 8, 62, 142, 145, 245, 253, 302. 336.
Haskell, Elder Stephen N.. 345.
Haverhill, 221, 341.
Hayward, *Haywood*, Hannah, 316, 320.
    John, 243.
    Judith, 321.
    Mary, 292, 321.
    Sarah, 279, 316.
Haywards, 188, 202.
Hazzen, John, 229.
    Moses, 229.
Heard, Colonel Edmund, 339.
Henchman, *Hinchman, Hincksman*, Capt. Daniel, 118.
    Captain Thomas, 110, 129.
Herds and herdsmen, 21, 50.
Hewes, *Hues, Huse*, George, 121, 144, 145, 152, 156, 321.
    Robert, 181.
Highways, laid out, 45, 50, 51, 53, 60, 61, 62, 64, 77, 79, 80, 96, 176, 177, 178, 179, 180, 182, 183, 184, 188, 189, 190, 191, 195, 196, 197, 198, 199, 200, 201, 202, 203, 204, 205, 209, 210, 211.
    making and maintaining, 68, 81.
    marking and recording, 53, 54.
Hildreth, Jonathan, 222.
Hill, John, 12, 13, 15, 16.
    Joseph, 38.
    Assoatetick, 218.
    Bare, 71, 145, 177, 180, 182, 191, 195, 201, 203, 211, 271, 288, 302, 303, 306.
    Bee, 218.
    Broad-meadow, 188, 199.
    Chestnut, 220.
    Diamond, *Dimon*, 219.
    Crow, 220.
    George, 82, 135, 141, 145, 146, 186, 219. 264, 276, 277, 282, 283, 294, 303, 329, 331, 340.

INDEX. 353

Hill, John Gibson's, 41, 134, 274, 288, 296, 300.
Hurtleberry, 117.
Long, 71, 83.
Makamachekamucks, *Mahanekusts,* 97, 271, 303.
Massapaug, *Mashapouge,* 219.
Moantahcake, 276.
Monadnock, *Menocnuck, Menadnick, Menagnick, Wanadnock, Wannadnuck, Wenadnuck,* 219, 234, 235, 238.
Monoosuc, *Monosuk, Menousnuck, Manosok, Monosek,* 174, 193, 194, 219.
Piqwacket, 241.
Pine, 180, 190, 205, 206, 258.
Ponikin,   } *Quasopanagon,Qua-*
Quasaponikin, } *saponacin, Quasaponacan, Quascacanaquen, Quassaponikin, Quasoponican,* 42, 61, 78, 79, 179, 184, 196, 197, 218, 254, 255, 258, 259.
Quiticus, *Quiticous,* 219.
Rattlesnake, 301.
Redstone, 219.
Ridge, 341.
Rocky, 219, 220.
Rollstone, *Rolestone,* 219, 220.
Rolly, *Rooty,* 188, 191.
School-house, 340.
Turkey, 194, 217, 218, 219, 220, 222, 236.
Vaughan's, *Vahan's, Van's,* 192, 195.
Wachusett, *Watchusett, Wachusets, Wochoosett,* 10, 11, 85, 112, 130, 138, 139, 217, 219, 220, 234.
Washacum, *Whashacom, Waschacomb,* 186, 308.
Wataquadock, *Wataquadoke, Wataquodoc, Wataquadocke, Wattoquotlock, Wadaquodock, Waterquaduc, Wattoquoddoc,* 42, 45, 60, 71, 132, 141, 145, 188, 195, 270, 289, 290, 301, 304.
Watatick, 219.
Wickapeket, *Wakapaket, Wacapacit, Wakapacet, Wacapacet, Wickepocket, Wecapickit,* 189, 190, 195, 196, 203, 204, 205, 206, 218, 220.
Woonksechocksett, *Wonksacoxet, Ocsechoxit, Oxsechoxits,* 195, 219, 220.
Hillard, Mary, 292, 316.
Hilton, S., 229.
Hingham, 267, 268, 269, 284.
Hinckley, Thomas, letter of, 103.
Hinds, John, 143, 188, 249, 301, 318, 321.
Hoar, Daniel, 117.
   John, 111, 112, 114.
Hog Swamp, 196, 198, 204, 205, 304, 305.
Holcombe, Reverend Reuben, 342.
Holden, John, 243,
Holl, 293.
Holman, Jeremiah, 197, 204.
Holt, Uriah, 243.

Home lots of planters, 28, 33, 85, maps, 244, 245.
Hopkins, Mr. [*Edward?*], 73.
Horses and cattle, brand mark of, 16, 80.
Hosmer, Henry F., 346.
Houghton, *Haughton, Howton,* Benjamin, 294, 316.
   Benjamin, Jr., 276, 221.
   Daniel, 188, 202.
   Edward, 145, 201, 207.
   Ephraim, 201, 207.
   Ezra, 338.
   Henry, 143, 173, 201, 207, 215, 243, 321.
   Jacob, 143, 171, 172, 180, 187, 190, 191, 201, 203, 207, 209, 210, 317.
   James, 122, 143, 229, 332.
   John, 30, 71, 76, 80, 82, 108, 118, 177, 248, 293, 315, 316, 317, 325, 339.
   John, Jr., Esquire, 24, 108, 122, 125, 126, 127, 128, 131, 136, 139, 144, 151, 158, 160, 161, 163, 164, 171, 172, 175, 176, 178, 179, 180, 183, 184, 185, 186, 187, 198, 202, 203, 206, 209, 211, 212, 222, 257, 292, 294, 305, 307, 313, 317, 321, 328, 329, 330, 331, 333, 334, 339.
   John, 3d, Lieutenant, 144, 152, 153, 178, 184, 185, 195, 197, 206, 212, 317, 321, 329, 334.
   Jonas, 144, 151, 152, 153, 178, 179, 180, 184, 189, 190, 191, 195, 198, 203, 205, 207, 209, 210, 211, 294, 318, 321, 328, 331.
   Jonas, Jr., 187, 188, 199, 203, 332.
   Jonathan, 176, 187, 198, 199, 201, 205, 208, 209, 210, 229, 319, 328, 329, 332, 334, 337, 339.
   Joseph, 144, 251, 314, 321.
   Joshua, 332.
   Ralph, 6, 22, 24, 25, 31, 32, 35, 39, 40, 41, 42, 45, 48, 50, 54, 61, 65, 70, 71, 75, 77, 78, 79, 83, 89, 92, 99, 107, 118, 121, 126, 245, 247, 248, 249, 250, 251, 252, 253, 256, 265, 270, 271, 274, 275, 289, 297, 299, 311, 312, 313, 314, 315, 316, 325, 326, 333, 338, 339.
   Robert, 144, 164, 177, 179, 209, 210, 294, 318, 319.
   Robert, Jr., 209.
   Stephen, 242.
   Thomas, 201, 207.
   William, 332.
Houses, early, 57.
   log, 57.
Howard, George W., 295.
   Daniel M., 346.
Howe, *How,* Abraham, 146.

23

Howe, *How*, Daniel, 177, 237.
   Elizabeth, 131, 321.
   Captain Thomas, 147, 165, 181.
Hubbard, Reverend William, History of quoted, 58, 100, 102, 340.
   Jonathan, 243.
   Sarah, 209.
Hudson, 8, 145.
Hudson, *Hutson*, Daniel, 57, 78, 122, 133, 134, 189, 211, 271, 283, 288, 302, 314, 326.
   Daniel, Jr., 314, 321, 325.
   Elizabeth, 133, 135, 314, 326.
   Joanna, 133, 135, 314, 326.
   Nathaniel, 133, 141, 288, 303, 317, 326.
   William, 128, 249, 302, 314.
Humphrey, Deacon Charles, 182.
Hunt, Isaac, 177, 307.
   Jeremiah, 229.
Huntington, Joseph W., 339, 343.
Hussey, Francis F., 336, 339.
Hutchinson papers, quoted, 111.
Hutchins, Benjamin, 146.
   Joseph, 143, 168, 180, 190, 201.
   Joshua, 229.
   William, 229.

INCORPORATION, Act of, 25.
   Indian Fight, the, 165.
Indian land purchased, 9, 22, 26, 138, 173.
   traders, 9, 263.
   sagamores, 16, 38, 91.
   wear, 60, 258.
Indians, attacks by, 98, 102, 130, 132, 146, 165.
   Albanian, 130.
   Christian or Praying, 98, 99, 100, 110, 113.
   Connecticut, 130.
   Maquas, 97, 130.
   Mohawk, *Mohege*, 100, 225, 226, 227, 235, 240, 246.
   Narraganset, 103.
   Nashaway, 16, 17, 38, 91, 97, 102, 263.
   Natick, 85, 100, 102.
   Nipnet or Nipmuck, 98, 102.
   Quabaug, 103.
   Seneca, 130.
Innkeepers, early, 327, *et seq.*
Inquest, coroner's, 121, 150.
Intervales, 29, 245, 246.
Intruders fined, 52, 89.
Invitation to Master Rowlandson, 55.
   Major Willard, 64.
Ipswich, 300, 340.
Iron-stone ledge, 72, 274.
Iron works, 48, 49.
Iron clothes, [*armor*,] 284.

JAMES, Daniel, 94.
   Thomas, 30, 32, 36, 39, 40, 41, 71, 255, 256, 274, 322.
James' ware, 258.
James Printer, 111, 112.
James Wiser, alias Quanapaug, 91, 100, 139, 275.
Jefts, *Jafts*, Ebenezer, 244.
Jenkes, Joseph, 12, 13.
Jethro, Peter, 111, 117.
Jewell, *Jewall*, James, 243.
Job Kattenanit, 100, 103.
Job's corner conveniency, 294.
John, one eyed, alias Monoco, 98, 100, 107, 112, 117.
John's Jump, 80, 121, 278, 290, 291.
Johnson, Captain Edward, 33, 45, 50, 52, 60, 78, 90.
   John, 30, 34, 39, 40, 41, 44, 60, 71, 77, 248, 273, 280, 281.
   John, 2d, 141, 144, 156, 202.
   Noah, 221.
   Samuel, 229.
   Solomon, 281, 282, 309, 310, 311.
Jones, Reverend John, 137, 340.
   Samuel, 174, 192, 193.
Jordan, Captain, 236, 242.
Joslin, *Joslyn, Joslin, Joscelyn,* Abraham, 83, 86, 269, 315, 316.
   Abraham, Jr., 104, 287, 288, 317, 321, 324.
   Nathaniel, 31, 39, 44, 71, 247, 248, 257, 259, 267, 268, 269, 270, 304, 314, 315, 317, 320, 322, 323, 326.
   Peter, 130, 141, 144, 145, 156, 162, 173, 175, 176, 182, 184, 185, 186, 187, 196, 197, 199, 200, 222, 266, 268, 269, 315, 319, 325, 328.
   Thomas, 31, 39, 61, 71, 247, 248, 257, 262, 268, 269, 284, 322.
Journal, Bradstreet's, quoted, 119.
   Reverend John Pike's, quoted, 146, 148.
Journals, military, of Lieutenant Jabez Fairbank, 216–221.
   of Captain John White, 230–233.
   of Captain Samuel Willard, 234–240.
Judges, C. C. P., Lancaster. 212, 213, 224, 337.
Jurors, 68, 187, 202.
Justices of the Peace, list of, 338.

KATTENANIT, Job, 100, 101.
   Kearsage, *Cusagee*, Mountain, 238.
Kelsey, Daniel, 244.
Kendall, *Kindal*, John, 204, 286.
   Samuel, 286.
   Reverend Sylvanus C., 343.
Kennebeck River, 226.
Kequassagansit, 164, 267.
Kerley, *Kerly, Carley*, Elizabeth, 104, 105, 324.
   Henry, 24, 30, 34, 37, 39, 40, 41, 45, 47, 55, 72, 76, 77, 82, 87, 94, 105, 124, 177, 188, 196, 203, 248, 254, 283, 284, 285, 287, 314, 315, 316, 317, 320, 321, 324, 326.
   William, 22, 24, 25, 30, 32, 33, 34, 35, 37, 39, 40, 41, 42, 44, 47, 48, 50, 55, 64, 71, 195, 203, 247, 248, 269, 273, 283, 284, 285, 286, 287, 300, 320, 322, 323, 331.

INDEX. 355

Kerley, William, Jr., 24, 30, 32, 34, 35. 37,
    39, 40, 41, 42, 47, 72, 88, 248, 274,
    284, 285, 286, 287, 288, 325.
Kettle, *Kettel*, *Ketle*, John, 105, 107, 111,
    316, 324.
    Mrs. Elizabeth, 105, 111, 114, 316.
Keyes, James, 143, 177, 197, 198, 205, 206,
    211, 282, 334.
    John, 144, 156, 187.
    Thomas, 131.
Kibbie, *Kibby*, *Cibie*, Edward, 30, 38.
    Lydia, 30, 47, 48, 314, 320.
Kilbourn, William A., 339.
Killed by Indians, list of persons, 99, 104,
    130, 133, 146, 323, 324, 325, 326.
Kimball, Henry, 90, 122, 259.
King, Thomas, 10, 34, 322, 327.
    Thomas of Marlborough, 269, 281,
    287.
King Philip's War, 98.
King William's War, 125.
Kingstown, 233, 242.
Kittery, 242, 341.
Knight, Philip, 20, 39, 52, 71, 246, 248, 264,
    273, 279, 280, 281, 296, 309, 323.
Knop, James, 97.
Kutquen, 111.

LACEY, Lawrence, 244.
    Lakin, *Lacain*, *Larkin*, Isaac, 220.
    Jacob, 216.
    John, 243.
    Joseph, 243.
    Philip, 332.
Lancaster, act of incorporation of, 23, 25.
    geographical position of, 346.
    maps of, 8, 244, 245.
    military company of, 74, 86, 125,
    268.
    records, condition of, 5, 312.
Lands, book of, 6, 83, 245.
    church, 27, 29, 45, 156, 182, 283,
    296.
    common, 6, 53, 82, 83, 171, 178,
    180, 181.
    divisions of, 29, 39, 41, 54, 65, 69,
    76, 77, 79, 176, 181, 183, 184,
    186, 245, 248.
    first allotments of, 29, 33, 245, *et seq.*
    intervale, 29, 245.
    meadow, 29, 39, 41, 69, 70, 83.
    special grants of, 51, 54, 55, 56, 70,
    74, 79, 80, 82, 83, 91, 245, 248,
    272, 302, 310.
    standard of quality, 186, 246.
    waste, 247.
Lane, narrow, 64, 212, 290, 291.
Lane, Anthony, 259, 335, 336.
    John, 144.
    Colonel Jonas, 335, 338.
Latham, Henry M., 252.
Latitude and Longitude of Lancaster, 346.
Lawrence, *Larrance*, Reverend Amos E.,
    343.
    Danforth, 346.
    William, 216, 221, 341.
Laws, read in town-meeting, 187.

Laws regarding land conveyance, 246.
    regarding wild beasts, 124.
    respecting trainings, 56.
    about selling strong drink to Indians, 263.
    about innkeepers, 328.
    about education, 176.
Learned, Samuel, 229.
Leavitt, Reverend George R., 343.
    Doctor Josiah, 339.
Lecture-day, 74.
Leominster, 286.
Lewis, *Lewes*, *Leweis*, Christopher, 122,
    254, 256.
    John, 24, 30, 32, 36, 37, 39, 40, 41,
    71, 82, 122, 248, 254, 255, 322.
    Levi, 335, 338.
    William, 30, 36, 37, 39, 40, 41, 48,
    61, 71, 74, 122, 190, 248, 254, 255,
    270, 271, 323.
Leverett, Governor John, letters of, 98, 110.
Levies and rates assessed, 28, 45, 51, 64,
    79, 81, 122, 128, 140, 151, 162, 185, 207.
Levingston, John, 229.
Lexington Alarm, 268,
Library Committee, 3, 4.
Licensed traders, 263, 327.
    innkeepers, 327, *et seq.*
Lilley, Jonathan, 243.
Lime and Limestone, 57.
Lincoln, *Lincorne*, William, 89, 316, 317,
    323.
Linton, *Lenton*, Richard, 20, 30, 32, 35, 37,
    40, 41, 70, 248, 249, 250, 251, 252, 261,
    265, 275, 306, 322.
Littlejohn, Thomas, 242.
Locke, Samuel, 289.
Log house, last in Lancaster, 58.
Loker, Mary, 279, 321.
Long Hill, 71, 83.
Lots, casting, 42, 71, 186, 246.
Lotteries for Sudbury Bridge, 14.
Louisburg, expedition against of 1745, 237.
Love, Reverend William De Loss, Jr., 344.
Lovewell, *Lovell*, Captain, 227, 229, 230,
    240, 241, 242, 331.
Lovewell's War, 215.
Lunenburg, *see Turkey Hills*, 224, 336.
Lunn, *Lund*, Thomas, 130, 216.
Lusher, Major [*Eleazar*], 38, 87.
Luxford, Reuben, 321.

MAC LOUD, *Maclode*, *Mukload*, *Muke
    Load*, *Mukeloade*, *Mucklode*,
    John, 104, 270, 324.
    Mordecai, 31, 54, 71, 78, 99, 122,
    178, 248, 255, 267, 270, 317,
    321, 323.
McNeil, William H., 4.
Magistrates, nomination of, 48.
Makamachekamuck's, *Mahamachekam-
aks*, *Mahaneknits* hill, 97, 271, 303.
Maliompe, Sagamore of Quabaug, 117.
Malone, Walter, 243.
Manning, Benjamin, 243.
Mansfield, John, 31.
Map of Lancaster, 1653-1883, 8.

Map showing home lots on the Neek 1653, 244, 247.
showing home lots west of rivers 1653, 244, 247.
Maquas, 97, 130, 146, 155, 166, 179.
Marble, Mary, 321.
Marlborough, *Marlbrow, Marlburrow, Marlburry*, &c., 71, 74, 98, 100, 101, 103, 119, 120, 124, 146, 155, 165, 269, 270, 281, 282, 285, 287, 293, 304, 305, 310, 311, 325, 326, 329.
Marriages of Lancaster, early, 320, *et seq.*
Marshall, John, diary of, quoted, 132, 149.
Marvin, Reverend Abijah Perkins, 344.
Mascononoco, *Massaconomet*, 10, 11.
Massachusetts Historical Society, 149, 327.
State Library, 327.
Massacre of 1675, 99, 270, 306, 323.
1676, 102, 284, 324.
1697, 132, 283, 325.
Joslin family, 130, 325.
Massapoag Hill and Pond, *Masapauge, Mashapoag, Mashapoge*, 8, 174, 194, 219.
Mason, Captain John, 87.
Mather's, Reverend Cotton, Magnalia, quoted, 133, 340.
Mattamuck, Sachem of Quabaug, 115.
Matthew, Sagamore of Nashaway, 39, 309.
Maynard, *Mainer*, John, 268, 320.
Joseph, 243.
Maze, Henry, 321.
Meadows, 29, 39, 41, 44, 69, 70, 83, 246.
Meadow, Bare Hill, 71, 177, 191, 203, 211.
Birch, 274.
Bridge, 121, 274.
Broad, 188, 199.
Brook, 71, 97, 271, 307.
Cranberry, 294.
Cumbery, 184.
Frog-holes, 82, 291.
Great-pond, 71, 78, 307.
Hog Swamp, 304, 305.
Hosokie, *hasokie, hassocky*, 253, 254, 255.
Plumtrees, 54, 62, 70, 80, 97, 182, 183, 184, 197, 209, 271, 303.
Pollopod, 190.
Prescott's, 182, 183.
Quasaponikin, 42, 61, 197.
Rocky Hill, 220.
Rosemary, 294.
Round, 201, 293.
South, 295.
Spectacle, 304.
Three Fountains, 294.
Tobacco-pipe, 294.
Mears, Robert, 244.
Medfield, 100.
Meeting-houses, 27, 29, 50, 123, 299, 340, 341, 342, 343, 344, 345.
twice burnt by Indians, 146, 147, 151, 153, 156, 159, 160, 162, 340, 341.
rebuilding, 123, 156–165.
Meeting of the rivers, 67, 273, 278, 300.
Mellen, Reverend John, 342.
Honorable Prentiss, 337.

Meminimisset, *Menemesse* [*New Braintree*], 101.
Merrimack River, 16, 224, 225, 236, 238, 240, 241.
Mile, the, 8, *map*.
Military Journals, 215, *et seq.*
Mill, Samuel Bennett's, 307.
Jonas Prescott's, 97, 297.
John Prescott's corn, 31, 106, 121, 144, 161, 177.
John Prescott's saw, 56, 72, 121.
Thomas Sawyer's, 155, 290, 295.
Joseph Whitcomb's, 199, 200, 201.
Miller's River, 238.
Milton, 253, 257, 285, 304, 321, 326.
Ministerial lands, 27, 45, 156, 182, 184.
Minister's house, 27, 55, 163, 197.
maintenance, 27, 28, 44, 55, 64, 122, 137, 140.
Ministers of Lancaster, list of, 340.
Minott, Captain James, 138, 156, 160, 162.
Mohawk, *Mohaug, Mohege, Mohauck*, 100, 225, 226, 227, 235, 240, 241.
Monadnock, *Wanadnock, Menadnick, Wenadnuck*, 219, 234, 235, 238.
Monipnet Brook, 219.
Monoco, Sagamore of Nipnets, 98, 100, 107, 112, 117, 306, 324.
Monoosuc Hills, *Manosok, Monosuck, Monosek, Menousnuck*, 174, 193, 194, 219.
Moore, *Moor, More*, Jacob, 237.
John, Sen., 24, 30, 94, 108, 120, 122, 127, 128, 129, 266, 326, 333.
John, Jr., Ensign, 24, 30, 34, 35, 39, 40, 41, 52, 60, 64, 71, 76, 88, 125, 128, 134, 139, 173, 177, 248, 249, 250, 256, 262, 273, 281, 282, 286, 287, 288, 289, 293, 305, 306, 314, 315, 316, 320, 323, 326, 333.
John, 3d, 143, 145, 211, 249, 289, 305, 306, 315, 321.
Jonathan, 143, 145, 171, 177, 187, 198, 208, 211, 249, 289, 305, 306, 316.
Joseph, 289, 305, 306, 315.
Samuel, 229.
Moose, black, 233.
Mordacoy, 189.
Morton's "New England's Memorial," 103.
"New English Canaan," 46.
Mosley, Captain Samuel, letter of, 98.
Mosman, Samuel, 224, 232.
Moss, *Morse*, John, ransomed, 114.
Mountain, Kearsage, *Cusagee*, 238.
Monadnock, 219, 234, 235, 238.
Wachusett, 10, 11, 85, 112, 130, 138, 217, 219, 220, 234, 346.
Watatic, 219.
Mulipus, *Mulipurs*, River, 219.
Murder of Indian women and children, 117.
Murrill, Stephen, 229.
Muster Rolls, 215, 220, 221, 229, 242, 243.

NASHAWAY, *Nashawog, Nashawake, Nassua, Nashuah*, 9, 10, 16, 17, 22, 25, 86, 98, 103, 104, 111, 139, 256, 263, 275,

INDEX. 357

281, 307, 340.
Nashaway Indians, 16, 17, 38, 91, 97, 102, 263.
   proprietors, 10, 13, 15, 245, 279.
   River, 9, 22, 25, 64, 80, 139, 144, 193, 219, 220, 273, 274, 278, 279, 283, 290, 291, 292, 296, 304.
   Sagamores, 11, 16, 39, 102, 107, 111, 112, 115, 116, 117, 138, 139, 309.
   wading-place, 8, 25, 59, 67, 273.
Nashacowam *Nashoonon, Showanon, Sholan*, 10, 11, 38, 139.
Nashobah [*Littleton*], 112.
Naticook, *Neticoock*, 239.
Natick Indians, 85, 100, 102.
Naukeag Pond. *Nockeeg*, 237.
Neal's, Daniel, "Present State of N. E." quoted, 246.
Neck, the, 29, 33, 79, 144, 145, 161, 180, 183, 185, map, 244, 249, 250, 252, 254, 255, 264, 265, 275.
Neck Bridge, 183.
Neglect of public worship, 91, 94, 129.
Nepanet, *Nepponet, Nepenomp*, alias Tom Dublet, 109, 111, 113.
Nesonkeeg Brook, 233.
New Braintree, 101.
New Boston, 345.
Newbury, 57.
New England Historic Genealogical Society, 91, 119, 276, 327.
   Historical and Genealogical Register, 230, 312.
"New England Canaan," quoted, 46.
"New England Prospect," quoted, 21.
"New England's Memorial," quoted, 103.
New Grant, 8, 138, 174, 177, 179, 192, 194.
Newby, *Nube*, George, 128, 300, 302, 303.
Newhall, Michael, 335.
New Jerusalem Church, 345.
Newton, 165.
Newton, Anthony, 30.
   Reverend D. Augustine, 344.
   Joseph, 167.
"News from New England," quoted, 104.
News Letter, Boston, quoted, 146, 149, 165.
Nichewaug, [*Petersham*], 229, 331.
Nichols, *Nicholds*, Benjamin, 216, 221.
———. 269.
Nicholson, Captain Francis, 125.
Night Pasture, 20, 85, 97, 183, 236, 262, 272, 299, 331.
Nipnets or Nipmucks, 98, 102.
Nonaicoiacus, *Nonacoyecos*, [*Ayer*] 94, 272, 276.
Norcross, Reverend Nathaniel, 11, 12, 13, 340.
Northfield, 224, 232.
North Hampton, 146.
Nourse, Henry Stedman, 1, 3, 4, 336.
   Stedman, 296.
Nowell, Increase, 38.
   Reverend Samuel, 106.
Noyes, *Noyce*, Ensign Thomas, Survey by,

8, 64, 65, 74, 139.
Nutfield, 242.
Nutting, John, 244.
   Nathaniel, 244.

OAKES, Reverend Edward, 123, 340.
   Oath of fidelity, 22, 26.
Old Book, of records, 5, 31, 37, 248, 250, 273, 288, 338.
Old burying field, 55, 183, 204, 273, 278, 279.
Old Common, 145, 212, 294' 298, 341.
Old Common burial ground, 164, 341.
Old Queen, 112.
Old Rock, 278.
One-eyed John, alias Monoco, 98, 100, 107, 112, 117, 324.
Orchards, 55, 85, 260, 305, 331.
Orders of Selectmen, 40, 50, 52, 64, 69.
Orthodox Congregational Church, 343.
Osgood, Benjamin, 216, 221.
   David, 216, 220, 221, 243, 338.
   Hooker, 175, 185, 186, 191, 195, 199, 201, 203, 205, 261, 300, 319, 329, 331.
   Hooker, Jr., 188, 319.
   Jonathan, 243.
   Joseph, 339.
Ossipee, *Ossipy*, 240.
Oyster River, 233.
Oyster shells, 57.

PACKARD, Reverend Asa, 343.
   Reverend Charles, 343.
   Reverend Hezekiah, 343.
Page, Joseph, 243.
   Onesiphorus, petition of, 115.
Paige, Reverend Lucius R., 343.
Pakashoag, Sachem, *Pakashokag*, 115, 116.
Palmer, Reverend James S., 342.
Park, the, 218, 294.
Parker, Benjamin, 229.
   Edmund, 30, 32, 37, 39, 40, 41, 71, 91, 122, 248, 255, 256, 257, 301, 314, 322, 326.
   Elizabeth, bastard of, 91.
   George A., 295, 336.
   Harold, 2.
   Herbert, 4.
   Isaac, 243.
   Captain James, 96, 97, 116, 130.
   Joshua, 234, 237.
   Phineas, 216, 221, 243.
Parks, Jonathan, 229.
   Deacon William, 93.
Pasturage, Common, 21, 50, 53, 83, 171.
Pasture, the night, 20, 85, 97, 183, 236, 262, 272, 299.
Patterson, Reverend Richard J., 344.
Pautucket, [*Lowell*,] 16.
Peage, or Wampum, 11, 263.
Pearly, Jacob, 229.
   Jeremiah, 229.
Peewunsenn Pond, 238.
Pelham, *Pellam*, Captain William, 15.
Pemigewasset River, *Pemichewashet,Pemisiwassett, Pimiwachet*, etc., 231, 234, 235,

238, 240, 241.
Penecook River, *Penecuck, Penicooke, Penicook*, 8, 33, 45, 60, 144, 199, 249, 250, 251, 252, 253, 254, 255, 256, 260, 262, 266, 275, 280, 283, 293, 294, 295, 299.
Penecook wading-place, 20, 60, 97, 249, 331.
Pennacook, [*Concord, N. H.*,] *Penekoock, Pennecook, Pennicook*, 33, 231, 233, 238, 239.
Penequid intervals, 219.
Penhallow's, Samuel, Indian Wars, quoted, 146.
Pequid, [*New London*,] 69, 264.
Perry, Seth, 112.
Petapawag, [*Groton,*] 263.
Petersham, 229.
Petitions of Nashaway Company, 11, 12, 15, 21, 23.
Petitions, of the town of Lancaster, 37, 49, 59, 79, 90, 94, 95, 107, 119, 120, 123, 125, 131, 136, 138, 140, 151, 152, 155, 157, 158, 161, 163, 171, 172, 175, 193.
Petitions of sundry persons, 47, 48, 63, 73, 86, 90, 115, 118, 127, 136, 142, 147, 148, 153, 166, 168, 225, 227, 309.
Pettee, Reverend Joseph, 345.
Phelps, Edward, 180, 259, 319.
    Joshua, 243.
    Robert, 229.
Philip, 107, 112, 116.
Philip's War, 98, *et seq.*
Phillips, Seargeant, [*John,*] 17, 18, 19, 128.
Phips, Sir William, his Canada Expedition, 127.
Pierce, John, 31.
Pierpont, *Perpont*, Mr. [*Ebenezer or Jonathan?*] 175.
Pierson, Jonathan, 243.
Pigwacket, 226, 227, 230, 238, 241.
Pike, John, his journal quoted, 146, 148.
Pine Hill, *Pin*, 180, 190, 205, 206, 258.
Pine trees, 56, 176.
Pisquataqua River, 233.
Pittime, Andrew, 118.
Planters of Lancaster, first, 30, 39.
Platts, Mary, 278, 313.
Plumtrees, 54, 62, 70, 80, 97, 182, 183, 184, 197, 209, 256, 260, 271, 283, 303.
Pollard, Christopher A., 346.
    John, 229.
    Oliver, 229.
Polley, Ebenezer, 243.
Pomhom, *Pumham*, 10, 112.
Pompoweagon, 276.
Ponikin, [*see Quasaponikin,*] 184.
Ponds.—Bare Hill, 8.
    Cateconimaug, 219.
    Chesquonopog, 70.
    Clamshell, 298.
    Cumbery, 184.
    Cusumpe, 230, 236, 240, 241,
    Great. [*Bare Hill,*] 73, 78.
    Massapoag, *Masapauge, Mashapoag, Mashapoge,* 8, 174, 194, 219.

Ponds.—Naukeag, *Nockeeg*, 237.
    Peewunsenn, 238.
    Saco, 242.
    Uncachewalunk, *Unchecowalounk, Unkachewalunck, Kachewalunck,* 8, 174, 193, 219.
    Wachusett, 220.
    Wanominock, *Wanomihouck*, 219.
    Washacum, *Washacom, Washacome, Washacombe, Whashacom,* 8, 61, 74, 79, 82, 83, 91, 180, 186, 204, 218, 219, 276.
    West, 211.
    White's, 184, 220.
    Winnipiseogee, *Winipisocket, Winneepseockey, Winepiseocket*, 130, 131, 138.
Pope, Beatrix, 144, 321.
    John, 127, 294, 321.
    Reverend Rufus S., 342.
Population of Lancaster in 1715, 176.
Postmasters, list of, 345.
Potato, wild, [*Apios tuberosa?*] 33.
Potter, Sarah, 321.
Pound, 50, 137.
Power, Daniel, 243.
Powowwing, *pauwauing*, 17.
Pratt, Edward, 243.
Praying Indians, 98, 99, 100, 110, 113.
Precinct, second, church in, 342.
Prentice, *Prentes*, Reverend John, 5, 24, 164, 169, 173, 176, 182, 184, 185, 187, 202, 208, 228, 278, 289, 300, 305, 332, 342.
    Doctor Stanton, 182.
    Captain Thomas, 120, 125, 165.
Prescott, Benjamin, 217.
    Ebenezer, 144, 318, 332.
    John, 10, 12, 13, 14, 15, 17, 18, 19, 22, 24, 25, 30, 32, 33, 34, 39, 40, 41, 46, 47, 48, 49, 50, 61, 65, 67, 71, 72, 73, 75, 76, 77, 79, 91, 94, 97, 108, 119, 120, 121, 246, 248, 250, 251, 264, 272, 273, 275, 276, 277, 278, 279, 280, 281, 283, 284, 287, 288, 289, 290, 293, 294, 295, 297, 298, 306, 308, 311, 313, 325, 329.
    John, Jr., 24, 120, 121, 144, 156, 162, 168, 173, 277, 279, 317, 318, 321.
    John, 3d, 144, 156, 182, 196, 202, 208, 317.
    Jonas, 97, 192, 276, 279, 313, 321.
    Jonathan, 24, 94, 108, 113, 120, 127, 138, 174, 192, 193, 277, 278, 279, 299, 300, 313, 317, 321, 323.
    Doctor Jonathan, 136, 167.
    Samuel, 138, 141, 144, 145, 148, 150, 182, 278, 341.
Prescott's Mills, 31, 56, 106, 274.
Presentments by grand jury, 48, 68, 74, 86, 94, 117, 128, 137, 172, 175, 181.
Prices of Commodities, 49, 55, 154.
Priest, Gabriel, 210.
    Daniel, 182, 209, 210.
    John, 143, 145, 153, 173, 206, 248,

INDEX.   359

302, 326.
Priest, John, Jr., 143, 189, 302.
Priest and Houghton's lime kiln, 57.
Prince Library, 114.
Printing press, first in N. E., 308.
Proprietors, Clerks of, 43, 77, 176.
          Covenant of, 27.
          Estates of, 39, 248.
          Homes of, maps, 244.
          Petitions of, 13, 15, 22, 37, 49.
          Records of, 5, 176, 245.
Prudential managers, 22, 25.
Public houses, 327, *et seq.*
Puckataugh, Peter, 139.
Pulpit, building of, 164.
Pummannommon, 276.
Purchase of Nashaway, 9.
        of additional grant, 138, 179.
Putnam, Captain William, 335, 336.

QUABOAG, *Quabogud, Quabacoke, Quoahbauge, Quapaug,* [*Brookfield*], 11, 16, 98, 103, 117.
Quanapaug, *Quannapohit, Quenepenett,* 91, 100, 139, 275.
Quanohit, Sagamore, alias James Wiser, 111.
Quanipun, Sagamore, 116.
Quarlls, Joanna, 285, 320.
Quasaponikin, *Ponikin, Quascacanaquen, Quosopanagon, Quasaponacin, Quassaponikin, Quasaponacan, Quosaponikin, Quasoponican,* 42, 61, 78, 79, 179, 184, 196, 197, 218, 249, 252, 254, 255, 257, 258, 259, 260, 265, 267, 270.
Queen Anne's War, 140, *et seq.*
Qurrin, William, 243.
Quiticus Hills, 219.

RAND, Christopher A., 346.
      Nathaniel, 345, 346.
Ransom of captives, 109, *et seq.*
Rates, 28, 45, 51, 64, 79, 81, 122, 128, 140, 151, 162, 185, 207.
Rattlesnakes, 233.
Rattlesnake Hill, 301.
Rayner, *Raner, Reynor,* Samuel, 17, 18, 19, 273.
Raynham, 49.
Reading, 221, 342.
Records of Births, 5, 312, *et seq.*
          Church, 5.
          Deaths, 5, 322.
          Estrays, 6.
          Lands, 43, 51, 52, 245.
          Marriages, 5, 320, *et seq.*
          Proprietors, 5, 245.
          Roads, 6, 53, 60.
          Town-meetings, 5, 41, 48, 55, 56, 69, 74, 78, 176 to 211.
Red Spring, 176, 177, 179, 199.
Redstone Hill, 219.
Reed, *Read,* Reverend James, 345.
                    Joseph, 229, 334, 338.
Rendezvous tree, *Randevou,* 190, 191.
Renie, Henry, 322.

Representatives of Lancaster, list of, 332, *et seq.*
Resettlement, petition for, 1679, 119.
Revolution of 1688, the town's action in, 126.
Rice, Edmund, 45.
    John A., 278.
    Joseph, 293.
    Merrick, 338.
    Captain Peter, 192.
    Richard, 243.
Richardson, Jonathan, 243.
          William, 334, 338, 339.
Rigby, John, 31, 44, 52, 54, 72, 108, 248, 262, 280, 291, 295, 296, 315, 320.
Rigby Brook, 196.
Rivers.—Androscoggin, *Amrescoggin,* 226.
    Connecticut, 227, 232, 236.
    Contocook, *Contockock,* 231, 235, 238.
    Kennebeck, 226.
    Lancaster, 174, 194.
    Merrimack, *Merimak, Meremack, Marrimack,* 16, 46, 224, 225, 231, 236, 238, 240, 241.
    Miller's, 238.
    Mulpus, *Mullipur's,* 219.
    Nashaway, *Nashuway,* 22, 25, 33, 61, 79, 144, 193, 219, 220, 273, 274, 278, 279, 283, 290, 291, 292, 296, 301.
    North, 9, 33, 34, 174, 193, 195, 199, 200, 219, 220, 250, 257, 259, 260, 262, 265, 267, 268, 269, 270, 273, 281, 284, 286, 287, 288, 291, 296, 297, 299, 300, 304.
    Ossipee, *Ossippy,* 240.
    Oyster, 233.
    Pemigewasset, *Pemichewashet, Pimiwachet, Pemisiwassett,* &c., 231, 234, 235, 238, 240, 241.
    Penecook, *Penecuck, Penicook, Pennicook, Penicooke, Pennecook,* 9, 33, 45, 60, 144, 199, 231, 233, 238, 239, 249, 250, 251, 252, 253, 254, 255, 256, 258, 260, 262, 266, 275, 280, 283, 293, 294, 295, 299.
    Piscataquog, 233.
    Saco, *Sawco,* 230, 236, 241, 242.
    Sowhegan, *Sowhaig,* 219, 240.
    Squanicook, 219.
    Still, 54, 61, 62, 70, 97, 141, 236, 251, 271, 272, 273, 274, 280, 296, 301.
    Stillwater, 218.
    Ware, 234, 237.
Roads, earliest, 45, 60, 64, 77, 96.
Robbins, *Robin,* Daniel, 339.
        Eleazar, 243.
Robertson, Doctor David Steuart, 145.
Robinson, Elder Dores Alonzo, 345.
        Reverend John, 137, 340.
        Nathaniel, 122, 288.
        Nehemiah, 229.
Rogers, *Rodgers,* Jeremiah, 30, 72, 78, 86, 122, 207, 248, 257, 258, 259, 270,

293, 314, 315, 316, 317, 321, 322, 324, 325.
Rogers, Samuel, 200, 202.
Rollstone, *Rolestone*, Hill, 219, 220.
Roofs, forms of early, 58.
Roper, Ephraim, 105, 133, 135, 136, 282, 317, 318, 321, 324, 326.
    John, 31, 39, 40, 45, 60, 71, 77, 79, 80, 106, 108, 135, 177, 248, 280, 281, 282, 288, 291, 309, 310, 311, 325, 331.
Roper's Brook, 61, 273, 278, 282, 288, 296.
Ross, Thomas, 141, 144, 146, 152, 156, 243, 286.
Rowlandson, *Rolenson, Rowlinson, Roulison*, Bridget, 62, 284, 300, 320.
    Reverend Joseph, 20, 24, 31, 40, 41, 44, 46, 50, 51, 55, 60, 62, 64, 71, 102, 104, 106, 109, 111, 114, 115, 119, 132, 134, 248, 254, 262, 263, 274, 296, 299, 300, 301, 303, 314, 315, 316, 320, 322, 324, 325, 340.
    Joseph, Jr., 105, 115, 299, 300, 301, 314.
    Mrs. Mary, Narrative of, 98, 102.
    Thomas, Sen., 24, 48, 62, 274, 300, 322, 340.
    Thomas, 3d, 104.
Rowley, 290.
Roxbury, 21, 92, 165, 254, 256.
Rugg, Benjamin, 243.
    Daniel, 141, 144, 187, 196, 206, 283, 332.
    Hannah, 133, 136, 283, 315, 326.
    John, 24, 31, 39, 40, 41, 48, 64, 72, 82, 120, 122, 196, 247, 248, 262, 274, 279, 280, 281, 282, 283, 291, 314, 315, 316, 317, 320, 322, 325, 326.
    John, Jr., 144, 171, 283, 315.
    Joseph, 133, 283, 316, 326.
    Samuel, 180, 211, 325.
Rum, 106, 329, 330.
Rutland, 217, 218, 219, 220, 234, 235, 237, 238.
Rutter (*John?*), 303.
Rye-field, Prescott's, 60, 182, 273, 278, 288, 289.

SABBATH ordinances, neglect of, 91, 94, 96, 129.
Sabbath scene in 1706, 164.
Saco, *Sawco*, River, 230, 236, 241, 24-.
Sacononoc, 10.
Saint Francis, 227, 234.
Sagamore, election of, 38.
Salary of minister, 28, 55, 64, 185.
    of representative, 207, 333.
    of schoolmaster, 185, 202, 207.
Salem, 253, 259, 323, 341.
Salmon Falls, 242.
Salisbury, 62, 115.
Sam, alias Shoshanim, Sagamore, 39, 102, 107, 111, 112, 115, 116, 117, 324.

Sanders, Reverend Daniel C., 341.
Sanderson, Robert, 252.
Satell, David, 216,
Sawyer, *Sayer, Sauier*, Amos, 202.
    Bezaliel, 156, 187, 202, 206.
    Caleb, 143, 173, 182, 183, 189, 209, 210, 248, 290, 306, 314.
    Elias, 155, 184, 188, 190, 195, 203.
    Ephraim, 106, 290, 313.
    Ezra, 220, 221, 229, 242.
    Ezra, 2d, 336.
    Henry, 242.
    James, 321,
    John, 191, 229, 315, 319.
    Jonathan, 187, 203.
    Joseph, 143, 177, 178, 180, 201, 204, 211.
    Joshua, 321.
    Nathaniel, 141, 144, 145, 154, 156, 168, 179, 188, 195, 196, 201, 204, 316, 328.
    Samuel, 216, 221, 229, 242.
    Thomas, 22, 25, 31, 34, 39, 40, 41, 43, 44, 48, 50, 52, 61, 64, 71, 79, 108, 120, 122, 138, 144, 248, 273, 274, 279, 289, 290, 291, 292, 297, 306, 313, 314, 320, 323, 326.
    Thomas, Jr., 108, 120, 122, 138, 144, 145, 152, 155, 173, 182, 186, 211, 290, 295, 313, 317, 321, 323, 334.
    William, 143, 173, 177, 178, 202, 205, 332.
Scalps, bounty upon, 106, 229.
Scar Bridge, 177, 180.
Scate, *Skait, Skeath*, John, 133, 135, 261, 286, 326.
Schools, 172, 175.
School-house Hill, 341.
Schoolmasters, 172, 175, 185, 202, 207,
Scituate, 266.
Scouts, Journals of, 215, *et seq.*
Scripter, Samuel, 216, 221.
Sears, *Sers*, Anna, 292.
    John, 292.
    Reverend Edmund Hamilton, 342.
Selectmen, 50, 69, 74, 77, 128, 158, 171, 172, 175, 181, 187, 198, 202, 208, 328.
Senators, list of, 336.
Servant, bought, 267.
Seventh Day Adventists Church, 290, 291, 345.
Sewall, Samuel, Diary of, 109, 117, 126, 132, 155.
Shattuck Manuscripts, 91, 119, 276.
Shattuck, James, 216, 221.
    Samuel, 229.
Shaw, John, 20.
Sheaf, William, 260, 306.
Shepard, Daniel, 243.
    John, 243.
    Reverend Thomas, 73.
Shepley, John, 243.
    Jonathan, 216, 221, 243.
Sherborn, 130, 253, 326.
Sheriffs, 337.
Sherman, John, 177.

Sholan, *Showanon, Shaumanw,* 11, 16, 38, 66, 139, 322.
Shoshanim, alias Sam, 39, 102, 107, 111, 112, 115, 116, 117.
Shrewsbury, *Shrubury,* 219, 342.
Shrewsbury Leg, map, 8.
Signatures of early settlers, 24.
Silvanus, negro, 93.
Silver, Reverend Abiel, 345.
Sill, *Scyll,* Captain Joseph, 106.
Simon Boshakum, alias Pottoquam, 116.
Simon Pipo's planting-field, 145.
Simson, Thomas, 231.
Singletary, *Singleterry,* Richard, 166.
Skeath, John, see *Scate.*
Skidmore, *Scidmore,* Thomas, 13, 15.
Slave, 267.
Sleeping Rock, 267.
Smadley, John, 45.
Smith, Moses, 336, 338.
    James, 143.
    John, 30, 34, 39, 40, 41, 71, 146, 248, 261, 269, 284, 285, 286, 287, 314, 323.
    Richard, 18, 19, 20, 24, 32, 37, 39, 40, 41, 60, 246, 248, 261, 262, 263, 283, 284, 285, 286, 296, 299, 314, 320, 322.
Snow, James, 144, 173, 184, 202, 203.
    James, Jr., 144.
Snowshoes, 101, 142.
Soldiers, lists of, 127, 215, 216, 220, 221, 229.
Sollendine, John, 130.
Sowhegan, *Sowhaig,* Indians, 16.
    River, 219, 240.
Spalding, *Spalden,* John, 146, 148.
    William, 229.
Spectacle meadow, 304.
Sprague, Honorable John, 335, 336, 337.
Spring, Cold, 145, 301, 304.
    Red, 176, 177, 179, 199, 297.
Spung or Spong, 54, 262.
Sqnanicook River, 219.
Squaws and sannups, 240.
Squaw Sachem, [*Weetamoo,*] 11.
Stated Common, 178, 179, 180, 181, 187, 281, 283, 287, 292, 297.
Stearns, Eli, 335.
Stedman, William, 335, 337.
Steevens, Cyprian, 24, 84, 86, 101, 108, 121, 127, 128, 141, 144, 156, 162, 168, 177, 211, 243, 261, 272, 312, 317, 318, 321, 338.
    Simon, 84, 141, 144, 152, 156, 168, 173, 180, 215, 251, 261, 272, 299, 318.
Stephens, John, 216, 229.
Sterling, 91, 166, 245, 260, 276, 286, 298, 336, 342.
Stevens, Reverend Benjamin, 341.
    Captain, [*Phineas,*] 217.
    Elizabeth, 267.
    Samuel, 166.
    Reverend Timothy, 134.
    William, 242.
Stickney, Samuel, 229.

Still River, 54, 61, 62, 70, 86, 97, 141, 236, 251, 253, 271, 272, 273, 274, 280, 296, 301, 330.
Stillwater River, 218.
Stockade, Watertown to Wamesit, 106.
Stocks, 50, 137.
Stoddard, Anthony, 73.
Stone, Joseph, 202.
    Deacon, [*Daniel,*] 120.
Stoughton, Governor William, 133.
Stow, 128.
Stow, Samuel, 185, 243.
Stratton, H. B., 285, 331.
Street, the so-called, 33, 61, 196, 273, 280, 281, 282, 283, 284, 286, 288, 289, 291, 294, 295.
Strong drink, sale of, 85, 263, 327, *et seq.*
Stuart, John, 338.
Sudbury, *Sudbery, Sudburye,* 13, 14, 22, 23, 26, 47, 63, 65, 100, 107, 119, 120, 224, 258, 268, 279, 281, 284, 285, 286, 287, 288, 289, 321.
Sudbury River and Marsh, 13, 14.
Sumner, Deacon Roger, 24, 31, 39, 40, 72, 74, 75, 96, 97, 107, 248, 257, 259, 269, 304, 315, 316, 317, 320, 322, 326.
    Samuel, 128, 257.
Suncook, 233, 239.
Survey of additional grant, 174, 192.
    of original grant, 65.
Surveyor for proprietors, 70, 178, 179.
Sutton, Richard, 31.
Swamp, Hemp, 297.
    Hog, 196, 198, 204, 205, 304, 305.
    Horse, 294.
    Swan, 45, 46, 60, 97, 188, 189, 198, 249, 260.
    Walnut, 61, 187, 188, 189, 196, 206, 287, 297, 300, 302.
Swagon, 118.
Swans in Merrimack River, 46.
Swift, Thomas, 122, 285.
Symmes, Caleb T., 261, 272.
Symonds, Henry, 9, 34, 321.
Symonds and King trucking house, 9, 34, 83, 246, 261, 275, 277, 329.

TAHANTO, *Dahannata,* George, 138, 173, 179, 193.
Tailer, Colonel William, 128, 153, 192.
Tar and Turpentine, 176.
Tarbol, Samuel, 229.
Tatatiquinea, Peter, 111.
Taylor, Frank D., 146, 285, 331.
    John, 231.
Taxation without representation, 23.
Taxes abated, 56, 120, 151.
Teachers, 172, 175, 185, 202, 207.
Temple, Abigail, 321.
    Isaac, 253.
    Jonathan, 243.
Thatching tools, 57.
Thayer, Eugene V. R., 182.
    Nathaniel, 4.
    Reverend Nathaniel, D. D., 342.
Thompson, Doctor J. L. S., 249, 336, 339.

Thurston, Captain John, 335.
   John Gates, 335, 336, 339.
   John, Jr., 336.
   Samuel, 334.
   Silas, 336.
   Wilder S., 346.
Timber Plain, 258.
Tinker, *Tincker,* John, 20, 24, 25, 31, 37, 40, 50, 52, 59, 60, 64, 68, 246, 248, 261, 262, 263, 264, 272, 274, 280, 298, 299, 320, 322, 337, 338.
Tobacco, 106, 111, 265.
Todd, Reverend John E., 343.
Tom Dublet, alias Nepanet, 110, 111, 113.
Toombs, William, 277.
Torrey, Ebenezer, 338.
Towers, John, 31.
Town Clerks, list of, 338, 339.
Town brand marks, 16, 80.
Town meetings, attendance at required, 80.
   records of, 5, 41, 55, 56, 69, 74, 78, 176 to 211.
   warning, 56.
Town officers elected, 77, 185, 187, 202, 208, 212.
Townsend, Hezekiah, 191, 195, 206, 211.
Township, grant of, 21, 25.
   full liberty of a, 37, 49, 78, 90.
Training field, 186, 187.
Trainings, 56, 74, 87, 88.
Trucking house of Symonds and King, 9, 34, 83, 246, 261.
Trull, Samuel, 229.
Tucker, *Tooker,* Arthur, 128.
   Thomas, 197, 209, 210, 211, 298.
Tuells, *Tuel, Twoells,* Barnard, 209, 243.
Turner, Stevens H., 346.
   Captain William, 135.
Turpentine, 176.
Turkey Hills, [*Lunenburg,*] 194, 217, 218, 219, 222, 223, 224, 236, 244.
Twitchell, *Tuchel,* Benjamin, 30.
Tyng, Edward, 91.
   Colonel Eleazar, 136, 138, 142, 162, 168, 215, 222, 223, 231, 235.
   Jonathan, 156.
   Captain William, 146, 147, 148, 154, 168.

UNITARIAN Church, 340, 341, 342.
   Universalist church, 342.
Uncachewalunk Pond, *Unchecowalounk, Unkachewalunck, Kachewalunck,* 8, 174, 193, 219.
Uppanippaquum, 116.
Usher, John, 216.
Uskattuhgun, alias Sam, 111, 324.

VALUE of estates of first settlers, 39.
   lands, 189.
   Schoolmaster's services, 203, 207.
   a bought servant, 267.
   sundries, 49, 51, 118, 134, 142, 154, 167, 168, 185, 189, 330.

Varnum, John, 229.
Veiwing highways, bounds and fences, 54, 81.
Virgin, Ebenezer, 221.
Volunteers, 107, 225, 226, 229.
Vose, Jane, 321.
   Samuel J. S., 261, 331.
Voters, qualifications for, 52.

WABAN, 115.
   Wachusett, *Warehasset, Watchusett, Wachusets, Wochoosett,* 10, 11, 85, 112, 130, 138, 217, 219, 220, 234, 332, 346.
Wading places, 8, 20, 59, 60, 67, 97, 249, 273, 331.
Wadsworth, Captain Samuel, 101, 103.
Wales, Joseph, 338, 339, 345.
   Nathaniel, 303, 304.
Walker, Benjamin, 229.
   Isaac, 10, 13, 15, 16.
   Isabel, 323.
   Seth, 200.
Walnut Swamp, 61, 187, 188, 189, 196, 206, 207, 287, 297, 300, 302.
Wamesit, [*Tewksbury, now Lowell,*] 106.
Wampom, or peage, 11, 110, 263.
Wanomenock Pond, 219.
War, Queen Anne's, 140.
   Lovewell's, 215.
   Philip's, 98.
   King William's, 125.
Ward, Henry, 31.
   Nahum, 176, 177, 304.
   Nathaniel, his "New England's Prospect," 21.
   Reverend Richard, 345.
   Samuel, 167, 335.
   Captain Samuel, 338, 339.
   Deacon William, 120, 192.
Ware, Mrs. Mary G., 134.
Ware River, 234, 237.
Warner, Lieutenant Eleazar, 239, 240, 242, 243.
   John, 143, 189, 209, 210, 249, 302, 303.
   Samuel, 179, 187, 203, 204, 207, 210, 302.
Warning out of town, 89, 181, 209.
Washacum, *Washacombe, Whashacom, Weshecum, Washacom, Weshakum, Washakim, Waschacomb,* 61, 74, 79, 82, 83, 91, 115, 180, 186, 195, 204, 218, 275, 276, 308.
Washburn, John M., 336.
Wassamagoin, *Wassamequin,* 10, 11.
Wataquadock, *Wataquadocke, Wataquatock, Wataquodoke, Wadaquadock,* 42, 45, 60, 71, 132, 141, 145, 157, 188, 195, 270, 289, 290, 301, 304, 305, 306.
Watatick, 219.
Watch house, 149.
Waters, Adam, 260, 261, 286, 313, 323.
   Joseph, 122, 128, 143, 252, 260, 261, 307, 313, 318.
   Lawrence, 18, 19, 20, 24, 29, 30, 32, 37, 39, 40, 41, 52, 60, 72, 74,

76, 85, 118, 122, 135, 246, 248, 252, 260, 261, 262, 273, 275, 283, 293, 313, 314, 322, 325, 331.
Waters, Samuel, 261, 321.
    Stephen, 122, 135, 260, 261, 286.
Watertown, 10, 11, 21, 31, 35, 86, 106, 109, 134, 251, 256, 260, 275, 278, 279, 281, 295, 298, 321, 322, 326, 340.
Watkins, Andrew, 244.
Weights and Measures, 68, 74, 137.
Wedge, Thomas, 316.
Wells, *Wels*, 242.
    Richard, 62, 115.
Wenham, 254.
Wentworth, Colonel [*John*], 226.
West, Mary, 209.
West Towne, 23.
Wethersfield, 119, 266, 301, 325, 340.
Whaley, Lieutenant George, 17, 18, 19.
Wheeler, Abraham, 132, 133, 318.
    Ephraim, 216, 220, 221, 243.
    George, 45.
    Isaac, 319.
    Joseph, 99, 323.
    Josiah, 143, 173, 189, 191, 195, 196, 198, 204, 304.
    Richard, 71, 80, 82, 106, 157, 248, 279, 292, 293, 315, 316, 317, 322.
    Samuel, 127, 128, 293, 325.
    Sergeant, Thomas, 15.
    Zebediah, 307, 315.
Wheelock, John, 242.
    Joseph, 141, 144, 160, 161, 189, 210, 216, 220, 221, 229, 319, 332.
    Josiah, 205, 249.
    Timothy, 127.
Whipping post, 129.
Whip sufferage, plantation, 65.
Whitcomb, *Whetcombe, Whetcom*, Colonel Asa, 334, 336.
    David, 143, 180, 188, 196, 197, 200, 201, 202, 207, 266, 293, 321, 328, 329, 331.
    Widow, Hannah, 130, 266.
    Hezekiah, 143, 187, 201, 205, 207, 266, 293, 318.
    Job, 64, 108, 265, 266, 317, 321.
    Colonel and General John, 338.
    John, Senior, 24, 30, 37, 39, 40, 41, 63, 71, 248, 250, 252, 264, 265, 266, 322, 323.
    John, Jr., 30, 39, 40, 41, 71, 108, 121, 188, 231, 248, 264, 265, 266, 267, 317, 321, 325.
    Jonathan, 89, 94, 108, 121, 141, 144, 152, 156, 265, 266, 316, 317, 319, 320, 325.
    Joseph, Doctor, 229, 231, 242.
    Josiah, 124, 137, 143, 158, 160, 161, 171, 173, 265, 266, 315, 316, 317, 318, 319, 320, 323, 334.
    Garrison, 145.
White's Pond, 184, 220.
White, Emory H., 259.
    Eunice, 227.

White, Captain John, 166, 176, 187, 188, 190, 198, 208, 222, 225, 226, 227, 228, 229, 230, 232, 254, 319, 328, 329, 331.
    John, Senior, 30, 32, 36, 39, 40, 41, 44, 54, 56, 61, 72, 76, 191, 195, 248, 253, 254, 293, 300, 322.
    Jonathan, 166, 228.
    Josiah, 24, 97, 120, 122, 128, 141, 145, 156, 162, 166, 168, 177, 184, 187, 191, 195, 196, 197, 198, 199, 200, 202, 206, 208, 210, 228, 254, 255, 256, 266, 318, 319.
    Josiah, Jr., 228, 334.
Whiting, Alice, (*Cook*), 24, 126, 134, 138.
    James, 30.
    Reverend John, 126, 132, 134, 138, 326, 340.
    General John, 335, 337.
    Timothy, 126.
    Timothy, Jr., 337, 338, 345.
    Solon, 335, 339.
Whitman, Davis, 335, 336.
    Reverend Samuel, 137, 341.
Whitney, Anna H., 4.
    Jonathan, 204, 209, 210.
    Reverend Peter, history of, quoted, 43, 155, 224.
Whittborn, William, 325.
Whittemore, Benjamin, S. T. D., 343.
Wickapeket, *Wakapaket, Wacapacit, Wakapacet, Wacapacet, Wecapickit, Wickepocket, Wecapeket*, 189, 190, 195, 196, 203, 204, 205, 206, 218, 220, 286.
Wickapimsee, 218.
Wild-cat, 124.
Wilder, *Wyelder, Willder*, Aaron, 346.
    Caleb, 6, 67, 214, 247, 339.
    Carter, 346.
    Charles Lewis, 20, 299.
    David, 334, 338.
    Ebenezer, 177, 178, 188, 190, 191, 197, 199, 200, 205, 206, 208, 209, 210, 211, 298, 332, 334.
    Captain Ephraim, 141, 144, 146, 152, 154, 156, 162, 166, 172, 178, 180, 186, 187, 189, 191, 197, 198, 199, 200, 202, 223, 277, 318, 334, 336, 337.
    Colonel James, 178, 180, 183, 184, 186, 187, 189, 195, 197, 198, 199, 202, 203, 204, 205, 206, 209, 210, 296, 318, 328, 332, 338.
    Deacon Joel, 335, 336.
    Joel, 2d, 282.
    Joel, Jr., 2d, 336.
    John, 108, 144, 158, 160, 161, 170, 179, 183, 184, 190, 191, 204, 205, 215, 244, 298, 317, 318, 319, 321.
    John, Jr., 244.
    Jonathan, 139, 152, 156, 165, 166, 318, 319.
    Jonathan, Jr., 335.
    Judge Joseph, Senior, 6, 142, 154, 171, 172, 176, 178, 179, 180, 184, 186, 187, 188, 190, 191, 197, 199, 200, 202, 205, 206, 208, 212, 213,

Wilder, Judge and Colonel Joseph, Jr., 318, 328, 332, 334, 337, 338, 339, 171, 214, 334, 337, 338, 339.
Doctor Josiah, 319, 338, 339.
Luke, 339.
Lieutenant Nathaniel, 108, 117, 124, 128, 136, 139, 141, 144, 146, 152, 156, 261, 277, 281, 282, 298, 318, 319, 321, 325, 328, 329.
Nathaniel, Jr., 202, 203, 204, 281, 282, 318, 319.
Lieutenant and Colonel Oliver, 187, 196, 203, 204, 206, 224, 242, 261, 281, 319, 329, 331, 338.
Samuel, 338.
Solon, 341, 346.
Thomas, 24, 31, 69, 72, 73, 75, 77, 79, 82, 88, 108, 247, 248, 260, 271, 280, 281, 296, 297, 298.
Thomas, Jr., 120, 121, 125, 127, 144, 145, 153, 158, 160, 161, 164, 170, 171, 172, 173, 197, 206, 209, 212, 256, 298, 318, 319, 320, 332, 338.
William G., 346.
Wilds, *Wiles*, Joseph, 205.
Richard, 205, 215, 243, 244, 332.
Willard, Aaron, 190, 221, 243.
Colonel Abijah, 237, 337, 338, 339.
Abel, 338, 339.
Benjamin, 127, 128, 142, 307, 338.
Henry, 197, 199, 200, 202, 229, 236, 243, 272, 307, 319, 321, 330.
Hezekiah, 143, 173, 200, 319.
John, 143, 191, 200, 202, 209, 249, 272, 306, 307, 321.
Jonathan, 200, 243, 272, 316, 319.
Joseph, Esquire, 43, 66, 67, 126, 137, 138, 145, 150, 164, 212, 335, 338.
Joseph, 200, 272, 314, 319.
Captain Josiah, 196, 200, 202, 209, 222, 224, 243, 244, 272, 319.
Joshua, 338.
Levi, 237, 338, 339.
Moses, 220.
Paul, 338.
Captain Samuel, 171, 187, 199, 200, 201, 203, 204, 205, 226, 234 to 240, 241, 142, 243, 244, 250, 272, 299, 303, 319, 329, 331, 332, 334, 337, 338, 339.
Samuel, Jr., 338.
Major Simon, 15, 24, 33, 45, 46, 47, 50, 52, 60, 64, 65, 75, 77, 78, 84, 85, 86, 89, 90, 92, 98, 108, 109, 122, 134, 247, 261, 263, 264, 270, 271, 272, 283, 296, 299, 303, 314, 315, 316, 320, 322, 324, 329, 331, 337.
Willard, Simon, Jr., 143, 145, 272, 276.
William, 338.
Williams, Jason, 221.
John, 222.
Thomas, 128.
Wilson, Benjamin, 202, 305, 332.
Jeremiah, 144, 171, 173, 188, 199, 249, 304, 305.
Reverend John, 73.
Joseph, 229, 242.
Nathaniel, 260, 305, 321.
Windows in early houses, 58.
Windsor, Ct., 262.
Winnepiseogee, *Winipisocket, Winnepeseockey, Winepiseocket*, 130, 131, 138.
Winslow, Edward, "Glorious Progress of the Gospel," 16.
Winter Harbor, 230, 242.
Winter Plain, 271.
Winthrop, Governor John, "History of N. E. quoted," 10, 11, 12, 14.
Wiser, James, alias Quanapaug, 91, 100, 139, 275.
Witchcraft, 307, 308.
Witherby, Josiah, 244.
Woburn, *Houbourne*, 123, 192, 221, 249, 257, 285, 287, 292, 301, 302, 321.
Wolf pen, 21.
Wolves, 21, 124, 128, 302.
Won, an Indian Soldier, 243.
Wonchesix, 121.
Wonsquon, *Womsquam*, John, 124, 139.
Woodrop, *Wooddroffe*, Reverend William 123, 340.
Woods, Cornet, (*Henry*), 120.
Isaac, 216, 221, 243.
Joseph, 243.
Matthew F., 339.
Woonksechocksett, *Wonksacoxet, Chocksett, Oxsechoxets, Ocsechoxit*, 195, 219, 220, 260, 341, 342.
Worcester, *Wossester*, 219.
Writing School, 172, 175.
Wright, Ebenezer, 229.
Isaac, 322.
John, 221, 329.
Joseph, 229.
Captain Samuel, 177, 215, 234.
Wyman, Captain Benjamin, 335, 338, 339.
Benjamin F., 202.
Captain Seth, 225, 226, 232, 233.

www.ingramcontent.com/pod-product-compliance
Lightning Source LLC
Chambersburg PA
CBHW071951220426
43662CB00009B/1092